CONTENTS

Published by Diamond Publications Ltd
PO Box 59, Bideford, Devon EX39 4YN.
Tel: 01271 860183 Fax: 01271 860064
Email: info@gethooked.co.uk
www.gethooked.co.uk

Editor: Graham Sleeman 01566 785754
Distribution: 01271 860183
Advertising: Mandi and Jane 01271 860183

Cover Picture: Henry Gilbey

Get Hooked is printed on environmentally friendly paper

ISBN 978-0-9549175-2-4

Welcome...

To the 15th annual edition of the Get Hooked Guide to Angling in South West England published in partnership with the Environment Agency.

You now have access to the most complete and up to date information available for over 800 fishing venues - game, coarse and sea - throughout the south west. This information covers species, weights, prices, clubs, charters and more, all comprehensively updated for this year. To get the most from your copy please take a minute to read the 'how to use your guide' instructions on page 18 - it's very easy!

The Environment Agency section (starting opposite) contains up to date information on national and regional byelaws and important information for all south west river systems, as well as dates and detail for events promoting the sport throughout the year.

After 15 years we are pretty sure we know of all the fisheries in the area. However If you know of any fisheries or clubs and charters that have escaped our attention please let us know. You can email us (info@gethooked.co.uk), phone (01271 860183) or use the form on the website at www.gethooked.co.uk. Please take the time to do this as an entry in this guide and on the web site costs absolutely nothing and we are very keen to maintain the quality of the information we provide.

Articles this year include, among others, fishing for trout on tiny streams, using your freshwater tackle for sea fishing and fishing with light tackle.

When you set out for the riverbank, lakeside or coast to enjoy a day's fishing, you may be unaware of the many organisations that work tirelessly behind the scenes to promote and preserve the quality of our rivers, streams, stillwaters and shores and therefore the quality of the fishing you enjoy so much.

Many of these organisations are represented within our pages and all of them need your support to continue their essential work. Please take the time to read their articles, visit their websites and, if possible, make a contribution to their efforts. You, the angler, will benefit and so will generations to come.

Our sport is still growing in strength. More participants, more promotional events, cleaner rivers, more lakes, more awareness of the benefits of angling - socially and economically. It is a fact that fishing is good for you! and there is nowhere, possibly on the planet, that offers the diversity and quality of fishing we do here in the Westcountry.

Why not make this the year you introduce a friend/child/grandchild to the sport? Make sure they catch a fish and neither of you will ever forget the experience.

Have your best season ever, and always....

enjoy your fishing

Graham Sleeman - Editor
editor@gethooked.co.uk

Please note..

All of the information on fisheries, clubs and charters in this guide is published in a fully searchable format on our web site at

www.gethooked.co.uk

The web site includes additional information and advertisements that do not appear in the guide, as well as an archive of editorials from previous editions.

We are the Environment Agency. It's our job to look after your environment and make it a better place for you, and for future generations. Your environment is the air you breathe, the water you drink and the ground you walk on. Working with business, Government and society as a whole, we are making the environment cleaner and healthier.

We tackle flood and pollution incidents, reduce industry's impact on the environment, clean up rivers, coastal waters, and contaminated land and improve wildlife habitats.

Visit our website at
www.environment-agency.gov.uk
to find out more about our work and your local environment.

There are extensive fisheries pages on our website, which include interesting news stories about our work.

In the South West, fisheries play a very important role. Fish are one of the best indicators of the state of rivers and lakes. Healthy and abundant freshwater fish stocks will demonstrate our success.

Our work helps fisheries in many ways. Some good examples are pollution-prevention, dealing with low river flows and habitat improvements.

In addition, fisheries staff carry out a number of vital tasks.

- We issue licences and make byelaws to control the pressure on fisheries;
- Enforce fishery laws to prevent damage to fish and stocks;
- Ensure the health and abundance of fish stocks through regular fisheries surveys;
- Rescue fish when pollution incidents occur and minimise damage to fish stocks;
- Carry out habitat improvements;
- Construct and maintain fish passes;
- Monitor fish stocks i.e. catch returns, juvenile surveys and fish counters;
- Carry out fisheries research to allow future improvements and developments;
- Stock fish to restore and improve fisheries.

Fisheries contacts:

Cornwall:

Environment Agency
Sir John Moore House
Victoria Square
BODMIN PL31 1EB
Tel: 01208 265012
Fax: 01208 78321

Devon:

Environment Agency
Exminster House
Miller Way
EXMINSTER EX6 8AS
Tel: 01392 316032
Fax: 01392 316016

Wessex (North):

Environment Agency
Rivers House
East Quay
BRIDGWATER TA6 4YS
Tel: 01278 484540
Fax: 01278 452985

Wessex (South):

Environment Agency
Rivers House
Sunrise Business Park
Higher Shaftesbury Road
BLANDFORD DT11 8ST
Tel: 01258 483324
Fax: 01258 455998

The strategic environment planning staff, based at our regional Exeter office, co-ordinate our regional policies and forward planning issues, telephone 01392 352439.

The South West Regional Fisheries, Ecology and Recreation Advisory Committee (RFERAC) advises us on fisheries issues. The committee sits three times a year with their meetings open to the public and media.

National rod licences

Before you fish for salmon, sea trout, trout, freshwater fish or eels in any* water in England and Wales, you need to have both a current Environment Agency rod fishing licence and permission to fish from the owner of the fishery.

**Except in waters where a general licence is in force - please check with the owner of the fishery in advance.*

If you fish for salmon, sea trout, trout, freshwater fish or eels in an estuary or in the sea, up to six miles from shore, you will require a licence. In most cases in tidal waters, a rod licence is not required to fish for freshwater eels, although there are exceptions. Before fishing for eels in tidal waters, please check with your local area Environment Agency office.

The Environment Agency has a national rod fishing licence. This means that fishing in all regions, including Wales, is covered by one licence. It does not cover you to fish in Scotland.

Licences are available for coarse fish and non-migratory trout or for all-inclusive fishing, including the above species in addition to salmon and sea trout.

The licence structure is aimed at raising approximately £22 million for essential fisheries work.

Coarse fish and non-migratory trout

The price of the full annual licence (2008/2009) for coarse fish and non-migratory trout is £25 (£16.75 concessions [anyone aged 65 years and over, if you have a Blue Badge parking concession or are in receipt of Disability Living Allowance]).

A short-term coarse fish and non-migratory trout licence covers a period of eight consecutive days, which gives anglers the benefit of being able to fish over two weekends. This costs £9 (no concessions). A one-day licence, aimed at beginners and casual anglers, costs £3.50 (no concessions).

Junior licence - NEW £5 SALMON LICENCE!!!

Children under 12 years of age do not require a licence. A full annual junior licence is available for salmon, sea trout, coarse fish and non-migratory trout priced £5. Junior licences are available to anyone less than 17 years old.

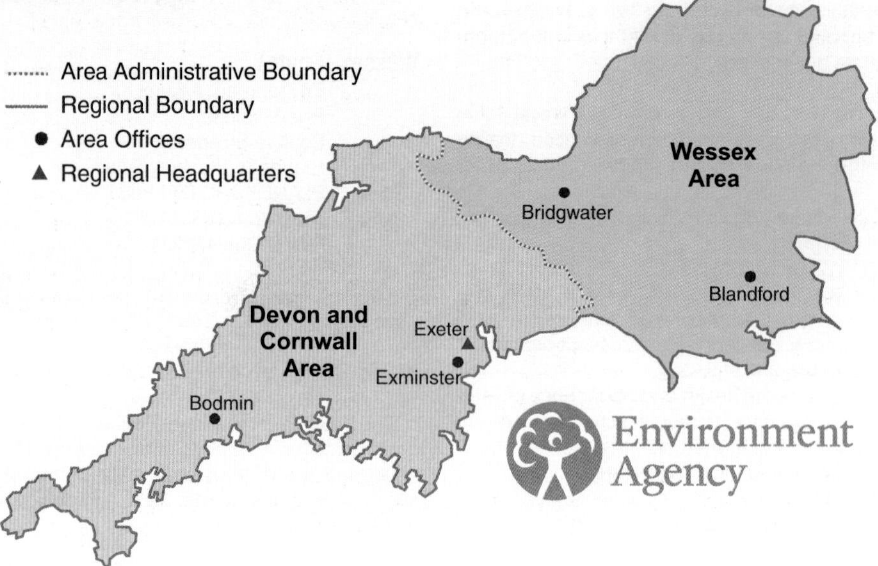

Salmon and sea trout

The price of the full annual licence (2008/2009) for salmon and sea trout (also including coarse fish, eels and non-migratory trout) is £68 (concessionary £45, junior licence ONLY £5 – take your kids salmon fishing all season for only FIVE POUNDS each!).

An 8-day licence costs £22.00 and a 1-day licence is £7.50. There are no concessions on the 8-day or 1-day licence.

Licences are available from every Post Office in England and Wales or from a range of local distributors. A list of these local distributors is available from Environment Agency offices. If necessary, you may obtain your licence by post. A form to do this is available from Environment Agency offices.

Alternatively a 'telesales' service operates from 8am to 8pm, 7 days a week, except bank holidays, for full, junior and concessionary licences. The number to ring is 0870 166 2662.

It is also now possible to obtain full licences, 8-and 1-day and the new full junior licence - through the Environment Agency's 'on-line licensing system'. Details are available on the fisheries web site:

www.environment-agency.gov.uk/fish

Payment by credit/debit card for 'telesales' and 'online': the licence will be immediately valid as the purchaser will be provided with a reference number to quote if challenged when fishing. Proof of identity will also be needed until the full licence has been received.

The 2008/2009 licences will be valid until 31 March 2009. Licences are issued on a 12-month basis and are subject to price reviews.

The licence has the following benefits:

* You can use a rod and line anywhere in England and Wales.
* You can use up to two rods per licence, subject to the national byelaws included in this guide and subject to any local rules.
* Your rod licence will help the Environment Agency continue to improve the vital work it carries out, including:

  • Management of fish stocks.
  • Improvements in fisheries and the fish's environment.
  • Protection of stocks through enforcement activities, including anti-poaching patrols.
  • Rescue of fish which would otherwise be lost through drought, pollution or other causes.
  • Surveys, essential for picking up changes and problems.
  • Advice on fishing and management issues.
  • Fish rearing and stocking of rivers.

Please note that:

1. The licence gives you the right to use a fishing rod and line but does not give you the right to fish. You should always check that you have the permission of the owner or tenant of the fishing rights before starting to fish.

2. Your licence is valuable - if it should be lost, a duplicate can be issued from PO Box 432, National Rod Licence Administration, Environment Agency, Richard Fairclough House, Knutsford Road, Warrington, WA4 1HH. A charge of £5 will be made.

Please make a note of the Licence Stamp Number before going fishing.

3. The licence is yours alone; it cannot be used by anyone else. Please make sure that you sign the licence before you go fishing.

4. Your licence must be produced on demand to an enforcement officer of the Environment Agency who produces his or her warrant, a police officer or to any other licence holder who produces his or her licence. Failure to do so is an offence and may make you liable to prosecution (maximum fine £2,500).

5. The licence is only valid if the correct name, address and date of birth of the holder, and the date and time of issue are shown without amendments, a stamp of the correct duty is attached and the licence is signed by the holder and the issuing agent.

6. A national rod licence is not required where a General Licence is in force. Please check with the owner in advance.

7. The catch return form attached to the salmon and sea trout licence is very important.

This information is required by law and you should send in the return form, even if you recorded a 'nil' catch. Please fill in and return the form in an envelope when your licence expires, using the FREEPOST address.

8. Details of local rod fishing byelaws and angling information can be obtained from Environment Agency offices. Fishery byelaws may vary between different Environment Agency regions - if in doubt, check first before going fishing.

Details of the main byelaws applying to the Environment Agency in the South West can be found on our website
www.environment-agency.gov.uk

Rod fishing seasons

The 'Open Seasons', i.e. the periods when it is permitted to fish, are set out in the table opposite.

There is no statutory close season for coarse fish and eels in stillwaters, but some clubs and fishery owners may impose their own close seasons.

There may also be a close season in place because of the status afforded to the area as a site of scientific interest. If in doubt check with your local office.

National byelaws to protect salmon stocks

Here is a summary of the byelaws:

Mandatory catch and release of all salmon for all rivers before 16 June.

Fly and spinner only (where not already limited by existing byelaws) before June 16 for salmon fishing.

These measures replace some of the existing measures already in place.

Catch and release of salmon is mandatory to 16 June, removing the earlier bag limit of two salmon before 1 June on the Taw and Torridge. It also supersedes any early season voluntary bag limits.

Anglers are still encouraged to fish catch and release after 16 June and especially to return any large red fish late in the season which may be 'springers'. The 70 cm limit

FISHERY DISTRICT	MAJOR RIVERS WITHIN DISTRICT	ROD & LINE OPEN SEASON (dates inclusive)	
SALMON		**Starts**	**Ends**
Avon (Devon)	Avon (Devon)	15 Apr	30 Nov
	Erme	15 Mar	31 Oct
Axe (Devon)	Axe, Otter, Sid	15 Mar	31 Oct
	Lim	1 Mar	30 Sept
Camel	Camel	1 Apr	15 Dec
Dart	Dart	1 Feb	30 Sept
Exe	Exe	14 Feb	30 Sept
Fowey	Fowey, Looe, Seaton	1 Apr	15 Dec
Tamar & Plym	Tamar, Tavy, Lynher,	1 Mar	14 Oct
	Plym, Yealm	1 Apr	15 Dec
Taw & Torridge	Taw, Torridge	1 Mar	30 Sept
	Lyn	1 Feb	31 Oct
Teign	Teign	1 Feb	30 Sept
Frome (Dorset) & Piddle		1 Mar	31 Aug
	All other rivers in Wessex Area	1 Feb	31 Aug
MIGRATORY TROUT			
Avon (Devon)	Avon (Devon)	15 Apr	30 Sept
	Erme	15 Mar	30 Sept
Axe (Devon)	Axe, Otter, Sid	15 Apr	31 Oct
	Lim	16 Apr	31 Oct
Camel	Camel, Gannel, Menalhyl Valency	1 Apr	30 Sept
Dart	Dart	15 Mar	30 Sept
Exe	Exe	15 Mar	30 Sept
Fowey	Fowey, Looe, Seaton, Tresillian	1 Apr	30 Sept
Tamar & Plym	Tamar, Lynher, Plym, Tavy, Yealm	3 Mar	30 Sept
Taw & Torridge	Taw, Torridge, Lyn	15 Mar	30 Sept
Teign	Teign	15 Mar	30 Sept
	All rivers in Wessex Area	15 Apr	31 Oct
BROWN TROUT			
	Camel	1 Apr	30 Sept
	Other rivers in Devon & Cornwall Area	15 Mar	30 Sept
	All rivers in Wessex Area	1 Apr	15 Oct
	All other waters in Devon & Cornwall Area	15 Mar	12 Oct
	All other waters in Wessex Area	17 Mar	14 Oct
RAINBOW TROUT			
	Camel & Fowey	1 Apr	30 Sept
	Other rivers in Devon & Cornwall Area	15 Mar	30 Sept
	All rivers in Wessex Area	1 Apr	15 Oct
	Reservoirs, Lakes & Ponds	★ No statutory close season	
GRAYLING, COARSE FISH & EELS			
	Rivers, Streams and Drains including the Glastonbury Canal	16 Jun	14 Mar
	Enclosed waters - Ponds, Lakes & Reservoirs All other Canals	★ No statutory close season	

in August/September on the Taw and Torridge still applies.

Permitted baits are restricted to artificial fly and artificial lure until 16 June. Exceptions where other restrictions remain include the Taw and Torridge (fly only from April 1) and North and South Wessex (fly only before 15 May).

These national byelaws are designed as a baseline and are considered to be the lowest common denominator across the country addressing the national problem of a decline in early-run large salmon.

Measures to address other local stock problems will continue to follow a river-by-river approach based on the programme of individual salmon action plans being managed by the Environment Agency with local fisheries interests.

Mandatory bag limits

Wessex (North)

The bag limits set out in the table below are imposed by the byelaws, however, some riparian owners or angling associations obtain dispensation to increase their bag limits. Anglers should familiarise themselves with bag limits before fishing.

Once a bag limit has been taken, the angler may continue fishing for the same species, provided that any fish caught are returned without injury. Freshwater fish other than grayling, pike and eels may not be permanently removed from the water.

Taw and Torridge

The original size limit and bag limit byelaws, introduced following a public inquiry in 1997, expired in September 2001. The Department for Environment, Food and Rural Affairs (Defra) has renewed these byelaws which remain in place during 2008.

NOTE: Since 1 April 1999, with the introduction of national salmon byelaws, the bag limits apply after 16 June.

Catch and release

With stocks of salmon under increasing pressure, we will seek to do everything possible to protect the species for the future.

Catch and release is now becoming an established management technique for increasing spawning escapement, particularly where stocks are low. Salmon anglers are encouraged to consider this approach as a means of safeguarding salmon stocks in our rivers.

When you are carrying out catch and release, the following guidelines may be useful to give the fish the best chance of surviving after you have returned it to the river:

Hooks - single hooks inflict less damage than doubles or trebles. Barbless hooks are best. Flatten the barbs on your hooks with pliers. If worm-fishing, consider using circle hooks.

Playing fish - fish are best landed before complete exhaustion (of the fish!) and therefore all elements of tackle should be strong enough to allow them to be played firmly.

Landing fish - Fish should be netted and unhooked in the water, if possible. Use knotless nets - not a tailer or gaff.

Handling and unhooking - Make every effort to keep the fish in the water. Wet your hands. Carefully support the fish if you really must take it out of the water. Do not hold the fish up by the tail, this may cause kidney damage. Remove the hook gently - if necessary, cut the line if deeply hooked. Take extra care with spring fish, as they are more susceptible to damage and fungal infection.

MANDATORY BAG LIMITS

RIVER OR AREA	SPECIES	PERIOD		
		24 HOURS	7 DAYS	SEASON
Wessex (North)	Non-migratory Trout	2	N/A	N/A
	Grayling	2	N/A	N/A
Taw	Salmon	2	3	10
	Migratory Trout	5	15	40
Torridge	Salmon	2	2	7
	Migratory Trout	2	5	20

If a fish is to be returned, do not under any circumstances keep it out of the water for more than 30 seconds. Changes in the fish's body affect survival within one minute.

Reviving the fish - Support an exhausted fish underwater in an upright position facing the current. Estimate weight and length in the water. Avoid weighing. Handle the fish as little as possible. Be patient and give it time to recover and swim away on its own.

Only three out of our 20 salmon rivers (Fowey, Camel and Devon Avon), are predicted to be 'not at risk' of failing to meet their management objectives for salmon in 2011. Wherever possible, PLEASE consider returning salmon to the water alive so that they can go on to spawn.

Voluntary bag limits

See section on national byelaws to protect salmon stocks (page 6).

Spring salmon - In addition to the national byelaws, the Environment Agency is encouraging salmon anglers to return any larger salmon, particularly red ones caught later in the season, as these are likely to be multi-sea-winter fish and valuable to the spawning stock.

On many rivers a variety of voluntary measures have been adopted to protect fish stocks. All anglers should familiarise themselves with these rules before they fish.

Tesco swap a salmon scheme

An arrangement, originally negotiated with Tesco for the Hampshire Avon, by Wessex Salmon Rivers Trust, entitles an angler catching and returning a salmon after 16 June to a voucher to be exchanged for a farmed salmon. This scheme now applies to other rivers as follows: Frome, Piddle, Dart, Teign, Camel, Fowey, Tavy, Lynher, Plym, Otter and Fal. Contact your local fisheries office (see page 3) for further details.

PERMITTED BAITS

FISHERY DISTRICT	SPECIES	BAITS (REAL OR IMITATION)
South West Region	Salmon	Artificial fly and artificial lure ONLY before 16 June
Avon (Devon)	Salmon & Trout ★★	No worm or maggot.
Axe (Devon)	Salmon & Trout	No shrimp, prawn, worm or maggot. Fly only after 31 July below Axbridge, Colyford.
Dart	Salmon	No worm or maggot. No shrimp or prawn except below Staverton Bridge. No spinning above Holne Bridge.
	Trout	Fly only.
Exe	Salmon & Trout	No worm or maggot.
Barnstaple Yeo (tidal)	All species (inc. sea fish)	No fishing
Taw & Torridge (except Lyn)	Salmon & Trout	No shrimp, prawn, worm or maggot. No spinning after 31 March. ★★★
Lyn	Trout	No worm or maggot before 1 June.
Teign	Salmon	Artificial fly and artificial lure ONLY after 31 August
	Trout	No worm or maggot before 1 June.
Camel & Fowey	Salmon	No byelaw restrictions on bait after 16 June
	Trout	No byelaw restrictions on bait
Tamar	Salmon & Migratory Trout	No worm, maggot, shrimp or prawn after 31 August.
Wessex Area	Salmon & Migratory Trout	Artificial fly only before 15 May.
Wessex Area	All species in rivers, drains and canals	No maggot (or pupae), processed product, cereal or other vegetable matter during the coarse fish close season. ★

Wild Trout Trust

Anglers are asked to return all brown trout caught on the East Dart above Postbridge, on the Cherry Brook and the Blackbrook; while on the West Dart between Blackbrook and Swincombe they are to return fish between 10" and 16" long, as part of a research project.

Landing nets, keepnets and keepsacks

A national byelaw makes it illegal to use landing nets with knotted meshes or meshes of metallic material.

Similarly, keepnets should not be constructed of such materials or have holes in the mesh larger

SIZE LIMITS

AREA, DISTRICT OR CATCHMENT	MIGRATORY TROUT	NON-MIGRATORY TROUT	GRAYLING
Camel, Fowey, Tamar and Plym	18 centimetres	18 centimetres	N/A
Avon (Devon), Axe (Devon), Dart, Exe, Taw & Torridge, Teign	25 centimetres	20 centimetres	N/A
River Lim	N/A	22 centimetres	N/A
Wessex (North) (except By Brook)	35 centimetres	25 centimetres	25 centimetres
By Brook & tributaries	35 centimetres	20 centimetres	25 centimetres
Wessex (South)	35 centimetres	25 centimetres	N/A

than 25mm internal circumference; or be less than 2.0 metres in length. Supporting rings or frames should not be greater than 40cm apart (excluding the distance from the top frame to the first supporting ring or frame) or less than 120cm in circumference.

Keepsacks should be constructed of a soft, dark coloured, non-abrasive, water permeable fabric and should not have dimensions less than 120cm by 90cm if rectangular, or 150cm by 30cm by 40cm if used with a frame or designed with the intention that a frame be used. It is an offence to retain more than one fish in a single keepsack at any time.

The retention of salmonids (adults or juveniles) in keepnets is illegal except when specially approved by the Environment Agency for collecting broodstock.

National byelaws

A number of national byelaws are now in place. These replace or modify regional byelaws that existed before.

A summary of the national byelaws is given below.

Phase I

1. The annual close season for fishing for rainbow trout by rod and line in all reservoirs, lakes and ponds has been dispensed with.
2. A close season for brown trout is to be retained on all waters.
3. Use of the gaff is prohibited at all times when fishing for salmon, trout and freshwater fish or freshwater eels.
4. The number of rods that may be used at any time is as follows:
a. One rod when fishing for salmonids in rivers, streams, drains and canals.
b. Two rods when fishing for salmonids in reservoirs, lakes and ponds (subject to local rules).
c. Up to four rods when fishing for coarse fish and eels (subject to local rules). When fishing with multiple rods and lines, rods shall not be left unattended and shall be placed such that the distance between the butts of the end rods does not exceed three metres.
5. Catch returns for salmon and migratory trout should be submitted no later than 1 January in the following year.
6. See separate section on landing nets, keepnets and keepsacks.

Phase II

1. Crayfish of any species whether alive or dead, or parts thereof may not be used as bait for salmon, trout, freshwater fish or eels.
2. Livebait may only be retained and used at the water they were taken from.
3. All salmon, migratory trout or trout, hooked other than in the mouth or throat, shall be returned immediately to any river, stream, drain or canal.
4. The byelaw limiting the length of a rod to not less than 1.5 metres (that may be used in the Wessex Area) has been revoked.
5. A rod and line with its bait or hook in the water must not be left unattended or left so that the licence holder is unable at any time to take or exercise sufficient control over the rod and line.

Coarse fish close season on canals

There is no close season for coarse fish on

canals within the region, with the exception of the Glastonbury Canal which is an open system with the South Drain.

Fish with adipose fins removed

As indicated on your rod licence, you may catch a fish from which the adipose fin has been completely removed. (These fish may carry a micro tag implanted within their nose - invisible to you.) If this occurs, you should follow the licence instructions.

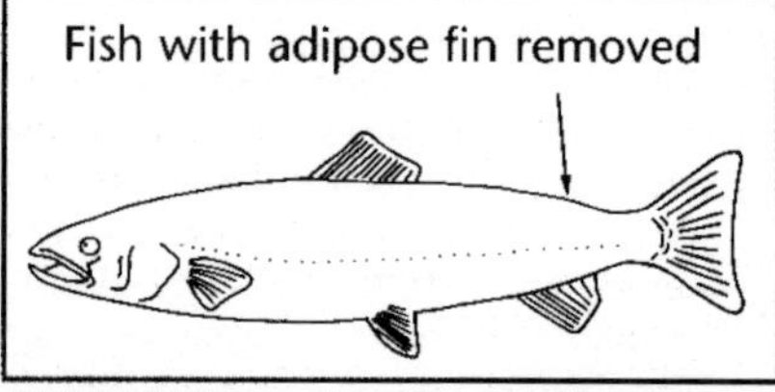

Before 16 June, any salmon caught without an adipose fin should be returned to the water and reported to your local fisheries office.

* Tell us your name, address and telephone number.
* Record details of your catch (where, when, size and species of fish).
* If the fish is caught after 16 June, keep the fish (or just the head) frozen if necessary and we will contact you to make arrangements for it to be inspected.

We will pay you a reward of £5 if it carries a micro tag and, of course, you keep the fish.

Details should be sent to the appropriate area fisheries office.

Purchase and release of salmon from licensed nets

For several years the Mudeford netsmen at Christchurch Harbour have voluntarily signed up to catch and release of salmon. Catch and

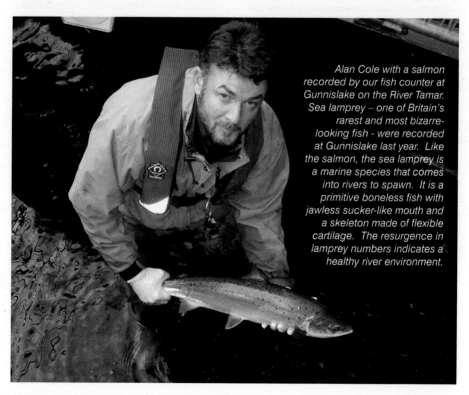

Alan Cole with a salmon recorded by our fish counter at Gunnislake on the River Tamar. Sea lamprey – one of Britain's rarest and most bizarre-looking fish - were recorded at Gunnislake last year. Like the salmon, the sea lamprey is a marine species that comes into rivers to spawn. It is a primitive boneless fish with jawless sucker-like mouth and a skeleton made of flexible cartilage. The resurgence in lamprey numbers indicates a healthy river environment.

release of salmon is also voluntarily practised by the rod anglers and the two together are an important component of work to protect and improve salmon stocks.

Similar schemes to reduce the numbers of salmon caught by legal netting also operate on the rivers Tamar, Tavy, Lynher, Fowey, Camel, Taw/Torridge, Dart and Teign, funded by fishery owners and a variety of other sponsors.

Stocking fish - buyer beware

Before introducing (stocking) any fish (or fish spawn) into inland waters, you must obtain written consent of the Environment Agency. Failure to meet this obligation is a criminal offence and could lead to prosecution, with a fine of up to £2,500. In addition, the stocking of non-native species such as Wels Catfish or Grass Carp requires Defra approval under the Import of Live Fish Act - Prohibition of Keeping or Release of Live Fish Order 1998.

Mandatory health checks will be required where fish are to be moved into rivers, streams, drains or canals, or where the risk to other fisheries is high. Health checks will not normally be required in waters where the risk of fish escape is minimal (e.g. enclosed waters). However, there may be occasions where the Environment Agency will still insist on a health examination.

Regardless of the Environment Agency's requirement for health checks, it should be stressed that establishing the health of fish before any stocking is essential.

Stop the spread of crayfish plague

Crayfish plague now has an extensive hold in the south of the country although it is also spreading northwards. In the whole of the south west, native crayfish are now only known to occur in the catchments of the Bristol Avon, the Piddle and Allen in Dorset, the Fonthill Brook in Wiltshire and the Creedy in Devon. Meanwhile, signal crayfish are widespread on many other rivers in the south west region.

The plague can be accidentally spread on damp equipment such as fishing tackle, farm machinery etc.

Do not move between river catchments without either disinfecting or drying completely any equipment that has been in contact with river or lake water.

Look out! - Look up!

Advice on safe fishing near overhead electric power lines

Several people have died and others have been seriously injured whilst using fishing rods and poles near overhead electric power lines. The following advice is designed to prevent these events recurring:

i Because rods and poles conduct electricity, they are particularly dangerous when used near overhead electric power lines. Remember that electricity can jump gaps and a rod does not even have to touch an electric line to cause a lethal current to flow.

ii Many overhead electric power lines are supported by wood poles which can be and are mistaken for telegraph poles. These overhead lines may carry electricity up to 132,000 volts, and have been involved in many of the accidents that have occurred.

iii The height of high voltage overhead electric power lines can be as low as 5.2 metres and they are therefore within easy reach of a rod or pole. Remember that overhead lines may not be readily visible from the ground. They may be concealed by hedges or by a dark background. Make sure you 'Look Out' and 'Look Up' to check for overhead lines before you tackle up and begin fishing.

iv In general, the minimum safe fishing distance from an overhead electric power line is 30 metres from the overhead line (measured along the ground).

v When pegging out for matches or competitions, organisers and competitors should, in general, ensure that no peg is nearer to an overhead electric power line than 30 metres (measured along the ground).

vi For further advice on safe fishing at specific locations, contact your local Electricity Company.

vii Finally, remember that it is dangerous for any object to get too close to overhead electric power lines, particularly if the object is an electrical conductor, e.g. lead cored fishing line, damp fishing line, rod or pole.

Have a go at fishing in 2008...

Devon

More than 1000 people of all ages – including a large number of ladies – enjoyed a taste of fishing in Devon last season thanks to the Environment Agency's free coaching sessions. The coarse angling days were particularly popular with families enjoying a free fun day, but the game angling days were also well attended.

Plenty was caught at Town Parks, Paignton, Devon.

Coarse fishing taster days

13 July	Grand Western Canal, Tiverton
19 July	Kia Ora Ponds, Cullompton (Start of national fishing week)
2 August	Rackerhayes, Newton Abbot
August (TBC)	Filham Lake, Ivybridge

Fly fishing instruction days

We are holding a series of six free taster days for beginners to learn to fly fish at Kennick Reservoir, near Christow between May and September: 31 May, 13 June, 5 July, 8 August, 30 August, 12 September (all dates provisional at time of printing, please phone to confirm).

In partnership with South West Lakes Trust and John Dawson Fly Fishing we are holding low cost, full day instruction courses at Wimbleball Reservoir. The days include instruction on casting, fly tying and an opportunity to catch a fish and run from 9am to 5pm. Contact local coach John Dawson 01398 331498 for details or visit www.johndawson.co.uk

6 April	Bank fishing	10 May	Boat fishing
18 May	Bank fishing	22 June	Boat fishing
6 July	Bank fishing	7 September	Bank fishing
21 September	Boat fishing		

For further information about any of the Devon events contact Diane Holland 01392 316032, diane.holland@environment-agency.gov.uk

Cornwall

A great series of events in Cornwall last year introduced more than 500 youngsters to angling. Another busy programme is being planned this year.

In 2007 we worked with schools, youth clubs and youth inclusion programmes to introduce young people from Plymouth, Kerrier, St Just and elsewhere to angling.

Junior fishing

Trout fishing introduction (ages 10-16)

27 May	Siblyback Lake, near Liskeard
28 May	Tavistock Trout Fishery, Tavistock
30 May	Stithians Lake, near Redruth
29 October	Treemeadow Trout Fishery, near Hayle

Coarse fishing (suitable for younger children)

26 May	Milemead Fishery, Tavistock
13 August	Bake Lakes, near Saltash
27 August	Milemead Fishery, Tavistock

Trout and coarse fishing (juniors)

29 May	Bake Lakes, near Saltash

Adult days (over 16s)

Trout fishing introduction

26 April	Siblyback Lake, near Liskeard
3 May	Stithians Lake, near Redruth
18 October	Siblyback Lake, near Liskeard
25 October	Stithians Lake, near Redruth

Coarse fishing

28 June	Bake Lakes, near Saltash

For further information on events in Cornwall call 01208 265012 or visit our website www.environment-agency.gov.uk

A first catch for one youngster, at Porth Reservoir, Cornwall

Wessex

There's a host of free events across the Wessex Area.

Come and try fishing at a national fishing venue in Somerset. The Division One National Angling Championships are being held on the Huntspill River on 6 September. We are inviting budding anglers to fish the same stretch of river on 7 September.

As owners of the river the Environment Agency hosts the championships with the National Federation of Anglers, and the Bridgwater Angling Association who lease the water. For more information contact Iain Turner on 01278 484848.

Sally Mitchell, who organised last year's impressive programme of events in Cornwall, gives a hand to her daughter Amber, and friend Wenna Parsons, at Milemead Fishery, Tavistock.

Wessex dates

26 May	Sherborne Game Fayre, Dorset
22 June	Eastville Park, Bristol
28/29 June	Angling Coaching and Freshwater Fayre, Moors Valley Country Park near Ringwood, New Forest
3 August	Apex Park, Highbridge
9/10 August	Bowood House, near Chippenham. Wiltshire
16 August	River Avon, Chippenham
14 Sept	Apex Park, Highbridge
27/28 Sept	Ringwood Angling Club, New Forest

We'll be offering free flyfishing tuition at the Flax Bourton game fayre, north Somerset on 28 June. All instruction - with qualified coach Mike Gleave - and fishing gear is provided.

New to the angling diary this year is our Angling Coaching and Freshwater Fayre at the Moors Valley Country Park, near Ringwood in June. You can try your hand at coarse fishing, fly casting and beach casting. There's lots for the children - trails, foodchain jigsaws and much more.

Also at Moors Valley Country Park, throughout the school summer holidays we are holding sessions aimed at 6-8s, 8-11s and over 11s.

People in Poole now have a new fishing lake stocked with mainly carp and rudd at Alderney recreation ground. We've helped create it with local councils, wildlife organisations and water companies as part of the Bourne Stream Project. We also plan to hold events at the lake this summer.

To check our Wessex events visit our website: **www.environment-agency.gov.uk** or contact:

Weston-super-Mare and Yeovil areas
Iain Turner on 01278 484848, iain.turner@environment-agency.gov.uk
Chippenham area
Andy Don 01278 484676, andy.don@environment-agency.gov.uk
Bristol area
Dave Lloyd 01278 484848, dave.lloyd@environment-agency.gov.uk
Dorset and Wiltshire
Allan Frake 01258 483328, allan.frake@environment-agency.gov.uk

The national BBC prime-time TV programme The One Show featured the success of our webcam at Oath Lock in Somerset in monitoring eel migration.

A company making inserts for the show filmed presenter Ellie Harrison, a trained ecologist and natural history expert, with technical specialist Pete Sibley.

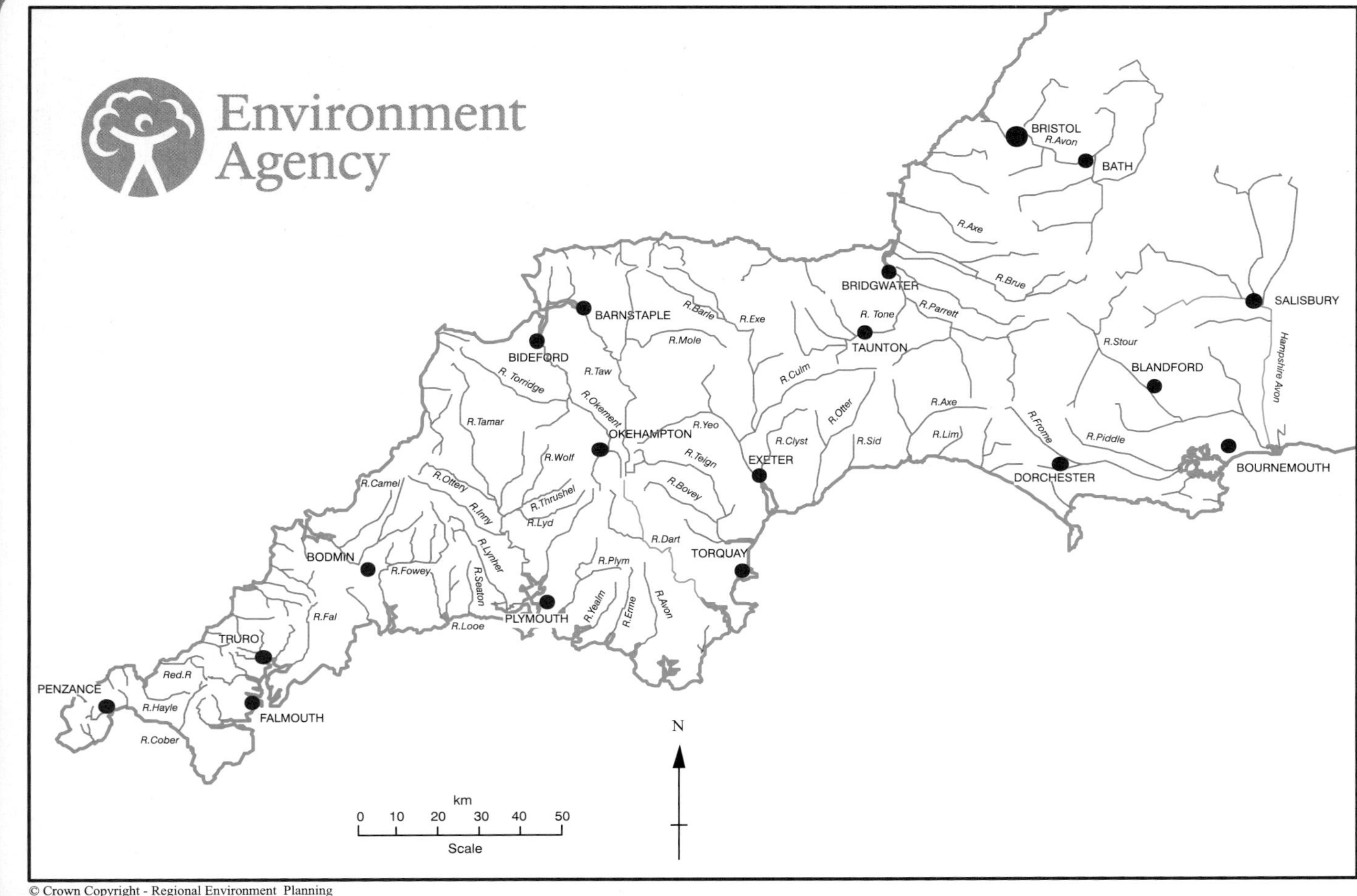

THE GET HOOKED GUIDE

A Fresh Approach

Wayne Thomas

As an all-round angler I frequently use tackle designed primarily for freshwater angling in salt water. My approach to fishing is to use tackle appropriate to the species I seek and in many cases that can mean getting more enjoyment from the fish hooked and an even greater success rate. After all tackle designed for freshwater angling is often designed for fish that are on average bigger than those hooked from Britain's coastal waters. In general the only reason sea anglers use heavy tackle is to combat the harsh environment. Strong tides may require heavy leads to anchor the weight to the seabed. Rock and weed may make strong tackle essential to extract fish from their safe haven. So if we give it some thought we can use our freshwater tackle for a vast range of venues and target a large variety of species.

Light float fishing

Mention the use of freshwater tackle on the coast and many will automatically think of grey mullet. These hard fighting fish are prolific all around our coastline during spring, summer and autumn. They can be caught using light float tackle or quiver-tip tactics. A twelve-foot float rod in conjunction with 6lb line, a chubber or Avon style float, size 8 to 10 hook and a pinch of bread flake will bring success. Harbours, rocks and piers are ideal venues where the application of ground-bait will entice not just mullet but garfish, pollock, mackerel, and even black bream. In addition to float-fishing a cage feeder packed with breadcrumb with a two hook paternoster baited with bread flake will provide excellent sport. A quivertip rod designed for barbel is ideal.

Free lining for bass

After dark an exciting method to try is free lining for bass using a 2lb test curve carp rod and 15lb line. Harbours, beaches and some rock marks can give anglers the opportunity to catch large bass.

Choose a calm night, a flooding tide is generally more productive though this will depend on the venue. A large mackerel bait is my favourite, either a head and guts or a whole side mounted on a size 6/0 hook. I always use a hook length of 30 to 50lb as a precaution against sharp rocks, or the teeth of an unexpected conger.

At many venues a pair of waders are a distinct advantage. Under the cover of darkness large bass will ghost around harbours and beaches in search of prey or discarded food. There is no need to cast far, do not shine a light on the water, as this will spook the fish. Lob the bait out into the flooding tide, it is surprising just how close in bass will venture. Try to keep in contact with the bait at all times, I hold a loop of line in my left hand and feel for bites. On the first indication of a take I pay out a bit of slack, as the line tightens and the fish moves purposefully away raise the rod to set the hook. If the area is snaggy you will need to put plenty of pressure on the fish to prevent it breaking free in rocks or amongst ropes or structures in the harbour. This can be very exciting fishing, the electrifying pull of a fish taking the bait and a short tense battle on a straining line with a rod bent double to the pull of a powerful bass.

Getting light on the boat

A pike spinning rod, carp rod or salmon spinning rod is ideal for spinning for bass from a boat using plugs or spinners. Another fun tactic is to use a light paternoster set up to target flatfish, triggerfish, whiting, pollock and a multitude of other species. I spent a day on a boat last autumn when two of us landed a total of ten species using mackerel strip fished on a two- hook paternoster. Braided line will give greater sensitivity and enable lighter weights to be used to hold bottom.

Estuary Fishing

Many of the South West's estuaries provide great autumn sport with the humble flounder. A light carp rod and fixed spool reel loaded with 10 to 15lb line is ideally suited to casting out a two or three hook rig baited with ragworm or peeler crab. Put the rod in a rest and await the rattle on the rod tip that signifies the arrival of a flounder, this is laid back fishing, give the fish time to devour the bait and then reel it in. On this light gear they give a surprisingly spirited tussle. From time to time the rod will surge over in a more spectacular fashion as a bass picks up the bait.

Fly Fishing

Bass are the top sporting sea fish to target with the fly rod and can give some spectacular sport. A rod capable of casting a weight forward 9 line is ideal. A leader of 8lb to 10lb fluorocarbon is suitable. A streamer style fly is used to imitate a sand eel, whitebait or prawn. Shallow water at the mouth of an estuary is excellant territory, as the tide floods in over the warm rock and sand wade out up to your knees and cast the lure into likely spots. A pair of good quality polarised sunglasses are an essential piece of kit to spot the bass that will move into water that barely covers their backs. It can prove extremely exciting casting at fish as they hunt the margins. On a hot summers day this fishing has elements that make it comparable to fly-fishing for bonefish in tropical waters.

From The rocks

A wide variety of species can be targeted from rock marks. During the summer months a strip of mackerel suspended beneath a sliding pike float will tempt mackerel, pollock garfish and bass.

If the seabed is not too rough carp rods can be used in conjunction with a large fixed spool reel to target species such as smoothound. These members of the shark family will take small crab baits fished on size 1 to 4 hooks as used for carp angling. Take care to engage the bait-runner facility, as these fish tend to take off at a rate of knots and will take a rod from a rest and out to sea in seconds.

Plugs and spinners

A spinning rod that is used for pike or salmon is perfect for casting lures for bass, Pollock and mackerel. The use of braided line will help to set the hook and feel the takes.

Gear for the roving angler

I have given a brief summary of areas where tackle designed primarily for freshwater angling can be used. I often smile to myself when I see rods labelled for carp, pike, salmon or bass such rods are often remarkably similar. They can often cast a weight of between 2oz and 4oz, handle lines of 10lb to 15lb b.s and have a test curve of between 2lb and 3lb. There are now a number of excellent telescopic rods available that meet this criteria and matched with fixed spool reel loaded with 15lb b.s line they will provide the roving angler with sport virtually anywhere in the world whether the water be salt or fresh.

I hope that I have given a little inspiration to cast a line into new waters. I believe the barriers are coming down between the disciplines with anglers horizons starting to widen as they realise there is not a gulf between freshwater and salt, just a wide variety of different species to seek in refreshingly different surroundings.

How to use your Guide

The guide is divided into the following colour coded County sections.

Cornwall
Devon
Dorset
Hampshire
Somerset
Wiltshire/Gloucestershire

Purely for ease of use Bristol has been incorporated into Somerset.

Please Note. *The guide covers the Environment Agency South West Region as depicted by the map on page 4. This area includes only part of Hampshire and a very small area of Gloucestershire.*

Within each county section the directory categories are:

River Fishing
Stillwater Coarse
Stillwater Trout
Sea Fishing
Where to Stay

There is a **Tuition Feature** on pages 178 - 180 providing details covering Game, Coarse and Sea angling across the region. There is also a **Trade Supplies and Services** section featuring advertisers providing services to fisheries throughout the area.

All directory entries **highlighted in blue** indicate an advertiser. The advert may contain additional information about the facilities on offer. If the advertisement is not adjacent to the directory entry it may be found by looking in the advertisers index at the back of the guide. Advertisers offering fishing are also located on maps (with road directions) at the beginning of each county section. There is a rivers map on page 15 which can be used in conjunction with the location maps at the beginning of each county section. The contents page gives a clear indication of where the sections appear.

Where clubs and organisations have fishing on rivers and stillwaters they will be listed or cross referenced under both sections. Fisheries offering both game and coarse fishing will be cross referenced, or have separate entries, under the relevant sections. Where advertisers offer both coarse and game fishing their advert will appear in the most relevant section and they will be indexed under all relevant sections. We have also asked fisheries to provide information on disabled facilities and this is denoted by a ♿ symbol after the fishery name. Please note you should contact the fishery direct to establish exactly what facilities they offer.

Tackle shops are located within the above sections. If you are, say, looking for tackle shops in Bristol then look within the Somerset section and under Stillwater Coarse - Bristol, Stillwater Trout - Bristol, Sea Fishing - Bristol or River Fishing - Bristol Avon.

The **Advertisers Index** at the back of the guide lists all advertisers, cross referenced under all relevant headings.

Please note..

All of the information on fisheries, clubs and charters in this guide is published in a fully searchable format on our web site at

www.gethooked.co.uk

The web site includes additional information that does not appear in this guide.

The opinions expressed within the editorials in this guide are those of the contributors and not necessarily that of the publishers. Whilst every effort has been made to ensure that the information in this publication is correct at the time of going to press, the publishers cannot accept responsibility for any errors or omissions which may have occurred. Remember fisheries change hands and rules change.
Always phone if in doubt.

CORNWALL

RIVER FISHING

STILLWATER COARSE

STILLWATER TROUT

SEA FISHING

WHERE TO STAY

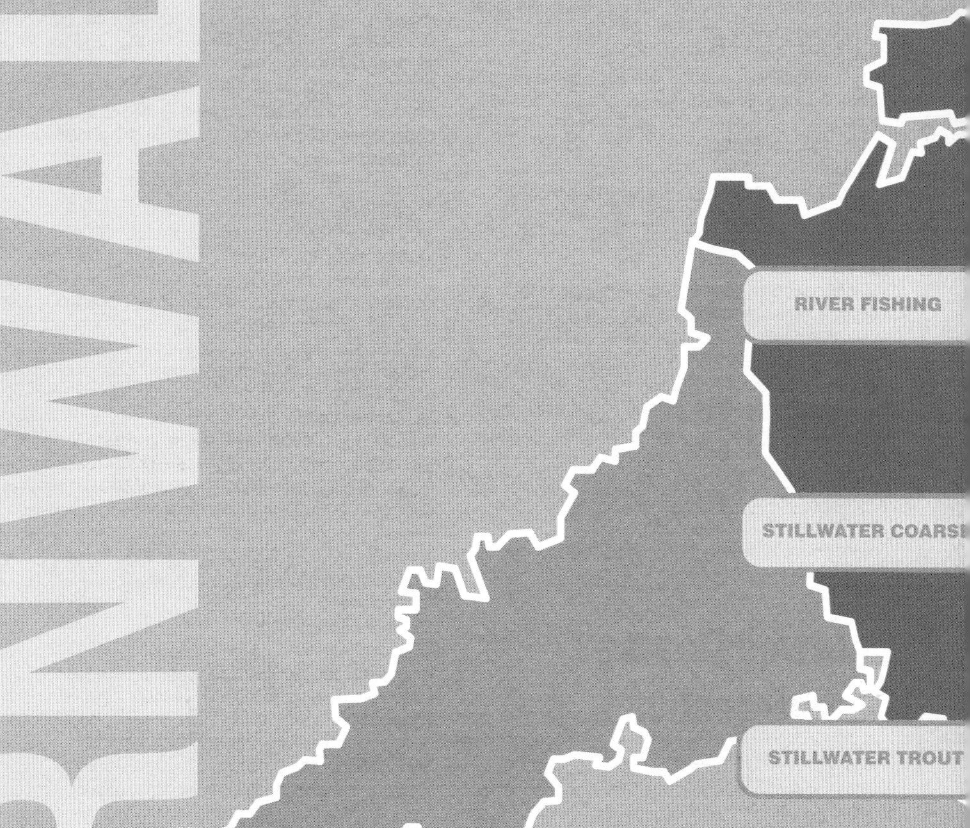

Cornwall Game Road Directions

1. Angling 2000 (Game & Coarse)
41 beats on the Tamar, Taw, Torridge, Fal, Tresillian & Camel catchments plus 2 lakes. Tel: 0870 77 40704.

2. Bake Lakes (Game & Coarse)
A38 to Trerulefoot. At roundabout (half way between Plymouth & Liskeard) take minor road to Bake. Turn right at T junction, then take first left. Fishery is 200 yards on right. Tel: 01752 849027 or 07798 583836.

3. Colliford
Signed from the A30 near Bolventor. Tel: 01579 346522.

4. Crowdy
Signed from the A39 near Camelford. Tel: 01579 346522.

5. Drift Reservoir
Take A30 towards Lands End. In Drift village, turn right signposted "Sancreed". Reservoir car park is approx. 0.25 mile along this lane. Ticket sales enquiries please Tel: 01736 363021 before travelling.

6. Siblyback
Signed from Jamaica Inn off A30 and A38 at Dobwalls. Tel: 01579 346522.

7. Stithians
Signed from Redruth town centre, on Helston Road and from Rame on the A394. Tel: 01209 860301.

8. Tree Meadow Trout Fishery
Off B3302 Hayle to Helston. Tel: 01736 850899 mobile 07971 107156.

Cornwall Coarse Road Directions

9. Adamsfield Fishery
A30 from Exeter - A395 to North Cornwall/Camelford. Turn right at Hallworthy. Drive through Warbstow then Canworthy Water, turn right for Tresmeer then first left to Tremaine. The fishery is 500 yards on the right. Please Tel: 01566 781243.

10. Argal
Signed from Mabe Burnthouse on the A394/A39. Tel: 01209 860301.

11. Badham Farm Holidays
A30 Liskeard turn off - Follow signs for St. Keyne. At St. Keyne take left hand turn just before church signed St Keyne Well & Badham. A38 at Dobwalls. Turn for Duloe & St. Keyne, then from St. Keyne as A30 route. Tel: 01579 343572.

12. BK Fisheries
Follow A30 to Hayle on to St Ives/Hayle roundabout, exit A30 to Penzance. Take St Erth turning after 100yds. Follow to St Erth over River Hayle bridge turn sharp right. Continue 200 yards. Fishery is on the right. Tel: 01736 365638.

13. Borlasevath Fishing Lakes
From Bodmin on A30 to Gossmore Bridge. Turn right on B3274 signposted Padstow. Continue 3.5 miles, turn right at Tremayne Farm by stone barn. You will find Borlasevath Manor Farm 1.25 miles on your left. Tel: 01637 880826 mobile: 07973 767147.

14. Boscathnoe
Off A30, turn to Heamoor, turn left past the school to Boscathnoe. Tel: 01209 860301.

15. Bush Lakes
Over Tamar Bridge, at Saltash roundabout turn right (A388). Continue 3 miles to Hatt, turn left onto Pillaton road. Bush is signposted after 1 mile on the left. Tel: 01759 351102.

16. Bussow
Off B3311 at Penbeagle. Tel: 01209 860301.

17. Crafthole
Tel: 01579 346522.

18. Glenleigh Farm Fishery
From St. Austell take A390 towards Truro, after approx. 3 miles second hand car garage on left, turn left to Sticker, follow road to top of hill, immediately before bus shelter turn left, past mobile homes park, over bypass, around corner, gate on left marked Glenleigh Farm Fishery car park. Please shut gate. Tel: 01726 73154.

19. Gwinear Pools
From M5 after Exeter take A30 signposted to Bodmin. Continue past Bodmin heading for Truro. At Carling Cross roundabout go straight on, after 1.5 miles turn right onto B3285 signposted Goonhaven/ Perranporth. After 0.5 mile turn right signposted to Rejerrah (Scotland Road) after 1.5 mile turn right onto A3075 signposted Newquay. Continue 0.5 mile and Gwinear Pools is situated on the left just after Cubert turning. Tel: 01637 830165 for directions.

20. Middle Boswin Farm
Take Scorrier exit off the A30, follow signs to Helston (B3297) through Redruth. Take B3297 for approx. 5 miles passing Four Lanes, Nine Maidens, Burras and Farms Common. Turn Left at sign to Porkellis, follow for less than a mile. Turn left after White Bridge Weare 0.5 mile on left.Tel: 01209 860420.

21. Millbrook Fishery
Approach Millbrook on B3247, follow brown tourist signs from Tregantle Fort. Tel: 01752 823210.

22. Perran Springs Holiday Park
Travelling westwards through Cornwall by-pass the village of Indian Queens,remaining on the A30. Continue straight over roundabout by wind farm,signed 'Redruth A30' and 'Perranporth B3285'. After 1.5 miles turn right at the Boxheater junction onto the B3285 signed 'Perranporth' and Goonhavern. Continue along the B3285 for 1.5 miles, following the brown tourism signs marked ' Perran Springs'. The easily accessible park entrance will then be clearly seen on the right hand side. Please Tel: 01872 540568 for directions.

23. Porth
Signed off the A3059. Tel: 01637 877959.

24. Retallack Waters
Just off the A39 between Newquay and Wadebridge at Winnards Perch, signposted 'American Theme Park'. Tel: 01637 881160.

25. St Tinney Farm Holidays

Take A39 signposted Wadebridge, drive through the village of Wainhouse Corner on the A39. 11 miles from Bude, after a short stretch of uphill dual carriageway, when you reach the brow of the hill you will see a sign for Otterham village. Turn left, then follow the road to your right, then take the first turning on your right, following the road around through Churchtown farm, following the brown signs to St. Tinney Farm. Tel: 01840 261274 for directions.

26. Trevella Park

Proceed on the A30 as far as Indian Queens, turn right on to A392, follow signs to Newquay until you come to Quintrell Downs roundabout. Take signposted Crantock road which brings you to the Trevemper Bridge roundabout, turn left on to A3075, the Redruth road for 200 yards and you will see Crantock signposted. If you are in Newquay, take the A3075 to Redruth for 1.5 miles until you see Crantock signposted. If you are approaching from the west you will see Crantock signposted from A3075. Follow this road for 1 mile to T junction sign to Newquay where you turn right and then into Trevella Park entrance. Tel: 01637 830308.

27. Upper Tamar

Signed off the A39 at Kilkhampton and B3072 at Holsworthy. Tel: 01288 321262.

28. White Acres Country Park

Follow the M4/M5 to Exeter, then the A30 past Okehampton and Bodmin. From the A30 turn onto the A392 to Newquay, travel over 1st roundabout. You will see entrance to White Acres shortly after the roundabout on the right hand side. Tel: 01726 862113.

29. Wooda Farm Park

From the A39 take the road signposted Poughill, Stampford Hill, continue for 1 mile, through crossroad. Wooda Farm Park is 200yds on the right. Tel: 01288 352069.

Devon - page 53

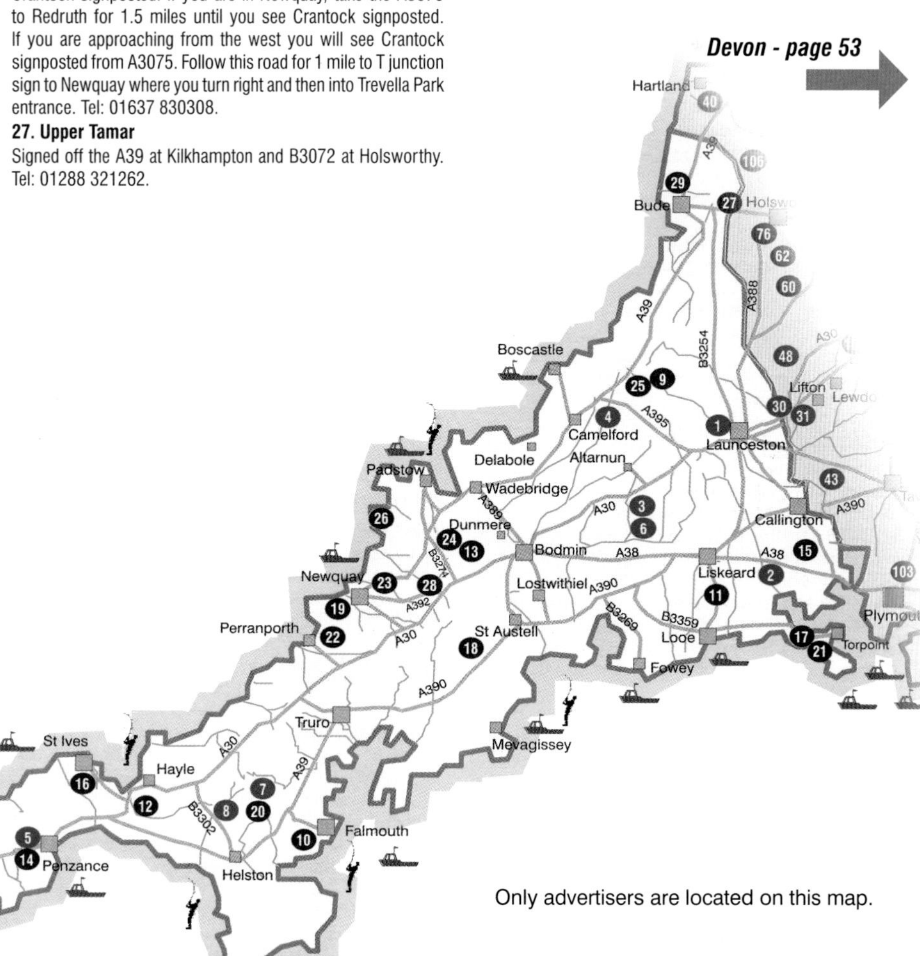

Only advertisers are located on this map.

Cornwall River Fishing

CAMEL

The Camel rises on the north west edge of Bodmin Moor and flows past Camelford to its estuary at Wadebridge. The run of Salmon tends to be late with some of the best fishing in November and December. Sea Trout in summer. Brown Trout in upper reaches and tributaries.

Angling 2000 (Camel)
Contact: Westcountry Rivers Trust, 10 Exeter Street, Launceston, *Tel:* 0870 774 0704, *Water:* 1250m of single bank on the Camel. 1400m of single left hand bank on the De Lank and 1500m of single right hand bank on the Allen. *Species:* Salmon, Brown Trout & Sea Trout on Camel. Brown Trout - De Lank. Brown Trout & Sea Trout - Allen. *Permits:* From the above. *Charges:* From £5 per day. *Season:* Camel - 1 May to 31 August. De Lank - 1 April to 30 September. Allen - 1 May to 30 September. *Methods:* Please contact Angling 2000 for individual beat methods.

Bodmin Anglers Association (Camel)
Contact: Ivan Lyne, Ivy Cottage, Dunmere, Bodmin, *Tel:* 01208 72306, *Water:* 12 Miles on River Camel, 0.25 miles on River Fowey. *Species:* Salmon, Sea Trout. *Permits:* Mr D. Odgers "Gwendreath", Dunmere, Bodmin, Cornwall PL31 2RD. Rogers Tackle Shop, above Stan May's Store, Higher Bore Street, Bodmin. *Charges:* From £15 per day and £40 per week. *Season:* 1st May to 30th November juniors half price membership details available from the secretary. *Methods:* Fly, bait or spinner restrictions apply on certain beats at certain times of year.

Butterwell
Contact: Tyson Jackson, Butterwell, Nr Nanstallon, Bodmin, *Tel:* 01208 831515, *Water:* 1.5 miles River Camel, mainly double bank. *Species:* Sea Trout (to 10lb 8oz) & Salmon (to 18lb). 5 year average 50 Salmon and 200 Sea Trout. *Permits:* On site. *Charges:* £20/day, maximum 5 rods/day. Priority given to residents staying at owners self catering cottage. *Season:* 1st May - 30th August, night fly fishing only for Sea Trout. 1st September - 15th December for Salmon. *Methods:* Any method for Salmon after 1st September.

River Camel Fisheries Association
Contact: John Evans (Sec), Butterwell, Nr Nanstallon, Bodmin, *Tel:* 01208 831515, *Water:* The association represents all major riparian owners and fishing clubs on the River Camel and agrees fish limits, conservation policy and enhancement projects in co-operation with the Environment Agency.

Tresarett Fishery
Contact: Mr Pope, Tresarret Manor Farm, Blisland, Bodmin, *Tel:* 01208 850338, *Water:* 0.75 miles on the Camel. *Species:* Salmon, Sea Trout and Brown Trout. *Permits:* You must have a valid EA licence. *Charges:* From £10-£20 depending on time of year. *Season:* May 1 to August 31 for Brown and Sea Trout. Until December 15 for Salmon. *Methods:* Fly only to June 1. All legal methods after.

Wadebridge & Dist. Angling Association
Contact: Jon Evans, Polgeel, Polbrock, Washaway, *Tel:* 01208 812447, *Mobile:* 07732 921015, *Water:* 10 miles River Camel, 1 mile River Allen. *Species:* Salmon to 20lb, Sea Trout to 6lb in 2007. *Permits:* Day / Week permits, Best Friends, The Platt, Wadebridge: 01208 816113. Rogers Tackle Shop, Stan Mays Store, Higher Bore Street, Bodmin: 01208 78006. *Charges:* May to September - Day £15 / Week £60. October to November - Day £25 / Week £100. *Season:* Visitor permits limited to three per day in October and November. *Methods:* No maggots permitted. Fly and spinning, natural baits on some beats. Circle hooks only when worming for Salmon. Please use barbless circle hooks.

FAL

The Fal rises on the Goss Moor and flows down to join with the Truro and Tresillian Rivers entering the Carrick Roads estuary. Salmon have been making a few rare appearances back to the River due to an improvement in water quality, but the Fal is predominately a Brown Trout river with some Sea Trout present.

Angling 2000 (Fal & Tresillian)
Contact: Westcountry Rivers Trust, 10 Exeter Street, Launceston, *Tel:* 0870 774 0704, *Water:* 1000m mixed double/single on Fal. 2000m of single bank on the Tresillian. *Species:* Sea Trout, Brown Trout and occasional Salmon. *Permits:* From the above. *Charges:* From £5 per day. *Season:* 1st April - 30th September. *Methods:* Please contact Angling 2000 for individual beat methods.

FOWEY

Rises near the highest point of Bodmin Moor from which it flows south, then turns to the west, and finally south again through Lostwithiel to its long estuary. A late Salmon river. Also good Sea Trout fishing and some Trout fishing.

Bodmin Anglers Association (Fowey)
Contact: Ivan Lyne, Ivy Cottage, Dunmere, Bodmin, *Tel:* 01208 72306, *Water:* See also entry under Camel. 0.25 miles River Fowey.

Fowey River Association
Contact: Jon Evans (sec.), Polgeel, Polbrock, Washaway, Bodmin, *Tel:* 01208 812447, *Mobile:* 07732 921015, *Water:* An association of representatives of angling clubs and riparian owners on the Fowey whose aim is to secure and maintain the well being of the river and its ecology. It exists largely as a pressure group and negotiating body on behalf of its members. *Permits:* No fishing permits sold through the Association. For membership details please contact the secretary at the above address. *Methods:* E.A. Byelaws apply. Catch restrictions: Salmon 1/day, 2/week, 5/season; Sea Trout 4/day, all Sea Trout to be returned in September.

Lanhydrock Angling Association
Contact: Brian Muelaner, The National Trust, Regional Office, Lanhydrock, Bodmin, *Tel:* 01208 265211 or 01208 265235, *Water:* 2 miles on River Fowey. *Species:* Sea Trout, Salmon.

Permits: Available from the above telephone number. *Charges:* £15 Daily, £30 Weekly (maximum 6 tickets daily). *Season:* 1st April - 30th September, Sea Trout 31st August. *Methods:* Artificial bait only.

Liskeard & District Angling Club (Fowey)

Contact: Bill Eliot (Hon Sec), 64 Portbyhan Road, West Looe, Looe, *Tel:* 01503 264173, *Water:* 23 miles of Rivers: Fowey, Lynher, Inny, Seaton and West Looe; Map of waters provided with ticket. *Species:* Salmon to 20lb (typically 5-12lb) & Sea Trout to 10lb (typically 2-4lb) *Permits:* Visitor tickets (available until 30 November for winter Salmon) and membership application forms from: Tremar Tropicals Shop, Liskeard. Lashbrooks Tackle Shop, Bodmin. East Looe Chandlers, The Quay, East Looe. Fishing Mayhem, Higher Lux Street, Liskeard. Osborne and Cragg, The Barbican, Plymouth. *Charges:* Adult: £20/day, £55/week, Membership £75 (OAP £70). Joining fee £15. Membership limited to 250 adults. *Season:* River Fowey 1st April - 15th December; Sea Trout season closes end September. *Methods:* Spinning, fly fishing or bait. Artificials only on one beat. No groundbait, no maggots.

Newbridge Angling Association

Contact: Mrs Ruth Murphy, Trebyan Forge, Lanhydrock, Bodmin, *Tel:* 01208 75244, *Water:* One mile single bank on River Fowey. *Species:* Trout, Sea Trout & Salmon. *Permits:* Members only - no day tickets. For membership details please contact Mrs Ruth Murphy.

Rivermead Farm

Contact: Julie Simpson, Rivermead Farm, Twowatersfoot, Liskeard, *Tel:* 01208 821464, *Mobile:* 07959 924838, *Water:* Half a mile on River Fowey. *Species:* Salmon 12lb. Sea Trout 8lb. Brown Trout 1.5lb *Permits:* Only from Rivermead Farm - pre-booking required. *Charges:* April - May £10 per day. June - October £15 per day. November - December £20 per day. *Season:* April 1 to December 15. *Methods:* Fly. lure, worm.

LERRYN

Largest tributary of the Fowey.

Angling 2000 (Lerryn)

Contact: Westcountry Rivers Trust, 10 Exeter Street, Launceston, *Tel:* 0870 774 0704, *Water:* 1200m of single bank. Flexible day permits for Trout, Sea Trout and occasional Salmon. *Species:* Sea Trout, Trout, Mullet and Salmon. *Permits:* From the above. *Charges:* £5 per day. *Season:* Salmon - 1st April to 15th December. Trout/Sea Trout 1st April to 30th September. *Methods:* Any method. No more than 1 Salmon, 2 Trout or 2 Sea Trout to be retained per day.

LYNHER

Rises on Bodmin Moor and joins the Tamar estuary opposite Plymouth. Brown Trout and runs of Salmon and Sea Trout.

Angling 2000 (Lynher)

Contact: Westcountry Rivers Trust, 10 Exeter Street, Launceston, *Tel:* 0870 774 0704, *Water:* 650m of left hand bank and 1500m of right hand bank on the Lynher. *Species:* Trout, Salmon and Sea Trout. *Permits:* From the above. *Charges:* £7.50 to £10 per day. *Season:* Trout 16 March to 30 September. Salmon March 1 to October 14. Please contact Angling 2000 for individual beat

seasons. *Methods:* Please contact Angling 2000 for individual beat methods.

Liskeard & District Angling Club (Lynher)

Contact: Bill Eliot, 64 Portbyhan Rd, West Looe, Looe, *Tel:* 01503 264173, *Water:* 23 miles of Rivers: Fowey, Lynher, Inny, Seaton and West Looe; Map of waters provided with ticket. *Species:* Salmon to 16lb & Sea Trout to 6lb (some very big ones April/ May). *Permits:* Visitor tickets and membership application forms from: Tremar Tropicals Shop, Liskeard. Lashbrooks Tackle Shop, Bodmin. East Looe Chandlers, The Quay, East Looe. Fishing Mayhem, Higher Lux Street, Liskeard. Osborne and Cragg, The Barbican, Plymouth. *Charges:* Adult: £20/day, £55/week, Membership £75 (OAP £70). Joining fee £15. Membership limited to 250 adults. *Season:* River Lynher & Inny; 1st March - 14th October; Sea Trout season closes end September. *Methods:* Spinning, fly fishing or bait. No groundbait, no maggots.

River Lynher Fisheries Association

Contact: Arthur White (hon.secretary), River Lynher Fisheries Association, 14 Wadham Road, Liskeard, *Tel:* 01579 345428, *Water:* Consultative body for the River Lynher. Membership comprises riparian owners, angling clubs, lessees of fishing rights, individual anglers and others interested in the Lynher valley environment. *Species:* Salmon, Sea Trout, Trout. *Permits:* Not applicable. *Charges:* £5 annual membership. Riparian owners £20

MENALHYL

Small stream starting near St. Columb Major and entering the sea north of Newquay. Brown Trout fishing.

St. Mawgan Angling Association

Contact: Mr. P. Parkinson, 17 Challis Avenue, St. Mawgan, Newquay, *Tel:* 01637 860720, *Water:* Stretch around Mawgan Porth. *Species:* Trout, Brown Trout. *Charges:* Limited day tickets from The Merrymoor, Mawgan Porth. Club membership restricted to those in parish of St. Mawgan. *Season:* April 1st - end September. *Methods:* See details on site.

SEATON

Small river to the east of Looe with good Sea Trout but very few Brown Trout.

Liskeard & District Angling Club (Seaton & West Looe)

Contact: Bill Eliot (Hon Sec), 64 Portbyhan Road, West Looe, *Tel:* 01503 264173, *Water:* Seaton River, West Looe River; Map of waters provided with ticket. *Species:* Good small waters for Sea Trout (typically 2 to 4lbs). *Permits:* Visitor tickets and membership application forms from: Tremar Tropicals Shop, Liskeard. Lashbrooks Tackle Shop, Bodmin. East Looe Chandlers, The Quay, East Looe. Fishing Mayhem, Higher Lux Street, Liskeard. Osborne and Cragg, The Barbican, Plymouth. *Charges:* Adult: £20/day, £55/week, Membership £75 (OAP £70). Joining fee £15. Membership limited to 250 adults. *Season:* As for River Fowey 1st April - 15th December; Sea Trout season closes end September. *Methods:* Spinning, fly fishing or bait. No groundbait, no maggots.

TAMAR

The Tamar rises near the north coast, and for most of its course forms the boundary between Devon and Cornwall. It is always a lowland stream flowing through farmland and this fact is reflected in the size of its Trout which have a larger average size than those in the acid moorland streams. Around Launceston, the Tamar is joined by five tributaries - Ottery, Carey, Wolf, Thrushel and Lyd - which offer good Trout fishing, as does the Inny which enters a few miles downstream. There is a good run of Salmon and Sea Trout, the latter being particularly numerous on the Lyd. There are also Grayling in places.

Angling 2000 (Tamar)
Contact: Westcountry Rivers Trust, 10 Exeter Street, Launceston, *Tel:* 0870 774 0704, *Water:* 14 beats on the Tamar, Inny, Lyd, Ottery, Carey and Kensey. Flexible permits fishing for Trout, Salmon, Sea Trout and Grayling. *Species:* Salmon, Roach, Dace, Sea Trout, Trout and Grayling. *Permits:* From the above. *Charges:* £5 to £10 per day depending on beat. *Season:* Trout - 15th March to 30th September. Salmon - 1st March to 14th October. Grayling - 16th June to 15th November. Please contact Angling 2000 for individual beat seasons. *Methods:* Please contact Angling 2000 for individual beat methods.

Arundell Arms
Contact: Mrs Anne Voss-Bark, The Arundell Arms, Lifton, Devon. *Tel:* 01566 784666, *Water:* 20 miles of private fishing on Rivers Tamar, Lyd, Carey, Thrushel, Wolf and Ottery. Also 3 acre private lake stocked with Rainbow and Brown Trout. *Species:* Rivers: Salmon, Sea Trout and Brown Trout. Lake: Rainbow & Brown Trout. *Permits:* Arundell Arms. *Charges:* Trout £25. Salmon & Sea Trout from £25. Lake £31. *Season:* Salmon March 1st to October 14th. Trout and Sea Trout March 15th to September 30th. Lake open all year. *Methods:* Fly and spinner for Salmon (1 in 3 fish after June 16 then catch and release). Fly only for Trout and Sea Trout.

Bude Angling Association
Contact: Mr L. Bannister, 2 Creathorn Road, Bude, *Tel:* 01288 353986, *Water:* 3 miles on the upper reaches of the River Tamar. *Species:* Brown Trout (wild) and occasional Grayling. *Permits:* Day tickets from Waterfront Tackle on the canal wharf. *Charges:* £5 day, week tickets available £15. *Season:* March 15th - Sept 30th. *Methods:* Fly only.

Dutson Tamar Fishery
Contact: Mr Broad, Lower Dutson Farm, Launceston, *Tel:* 01566 773147, *Mobile:* 01566 776456, *Water:* Half a mile on the River Tamar at Launceston. *Species:* Brown Trout, Salmon and occasional Sea Trout, Grayling. *Permits:* Homeleigh Angling and Garden Centre, Dutson, Launceston. Tel: 01566 773147. *Charges:* £5 per day. Charges may change in 2008. *Season:* 1st March - 14th October, Salmon as current EA Byelaws. *Methods:* See current EA Byelaws.

Launceston Anglers Association
Contact: Colin Hookway, 7 Grenville Park, Yelverton, *Tel:* 01822 855053, *Water:* 6 miles on River Tamar and Carey, 7 miles River Inny. *Species:* Brown Trout, Sea Trout, Salmon, Grayling. *Permits:* Launceston Sports, 1 Market Street, Launceston, PL15 8EP, Tel: 01566 774127. Lewannick Post Office, Lewannick, PL15 7QD. Tel: 01566 782269 (open 6 and a half days a week). *Charges:* Salmon & Sea Trout; Day £15, Week £40. Brown Trout: Day £7.50, Week £25, Juniors £2 a day. Day tickets valid for 24 hours from time of purchase. Annual membership from £60. *Season:* From 1st March to 14th October. Winter Grayling on some beats. *Methods:* Brown Trout - fly only, Salmon & Sea Trout - any method subject to byelaws. Grayling - fly only.

Stillwater Coarse

BODMIN

East Rose Farm
Contact: Matthew Morris, East Rose Farm, St. Breward, Bodmin Moor, *Tel:* 01208 850674, *Water:* Complex of five lakes with 22 permanent pegs. 3 acres of water. *Species:* Top Lake: Tench to 7lb. Deep Pool: Carp to 22lb. Island Lake and Eery Pool: Mixed fishing, Roach, Rudd, Bream, Crucians. *Permits:* Day tickets available from Farmhouse at East Rose. *Charges:* £6 Adults, £4 under 16, disabled and O.A.P's. *Season:* No closed season, no night fishing. *Methods:* No keepnets. Barbless hooks only. An EA rod licence is required.

Lakeview Coarse Fishery
Old Coach Road, Lanivet, Bodmin, *Tel:* 01208 831808 extn 4, *Water:* Two lakes, 3.5 acres in total. *Species:* 12 in total inc. Carp to double figures, Tench to 4lb, Bream to 5lb, Roach to 5lb 3oz & Rudd. *Permits:* Permits from main reception. *Charges:* £10 a day adult/children. O.A.P./concessions £6. Children must be accommpanied by fishing adult. *Season:* Open all year 9am - 5pm. Closed Christmas Day. *Methods:* No boilies or nuts. No night fishing or keepnets. 6lb minimum line weight.

Lostwithiel Hotel Golf & Country Club
Contact: David Picton, Lower Polscoe, Lostwithiel, Nr Bodmin, *Tel:* 01208 873550, *Water:* 2.5 acre lake. *Species:* Common, Mirror and Crucian Carp. Roach, Eels 2 to 5lb. Also some unidentified large fish at 15lb plus! *Charges:* Day ticket £9. Free fishing for residents in low season. *Methods:* Barbless or micro barb hooks only. No keepnets. All fish to be returned.

Prince Park Lake
Contact: John Brown, Prince Park Farm, St Wenn, Nr Bodmin, *Tel:* 01726 890095, *Water:* Half acre pond. *Species:* Crucian Carp to over 3lb, Common to 9lb, Tench, Roach, Bream to 4lb and Golden Rudd. *Permits:* Please telephone before travelling. *Charges:* £5 Adults, £4 Juniors/OAP. *Season:* Open all year, dawn to dusk. *Methods:* Nets must be dipped, barbless hooks only, no boilies.

Remember a ♿ means the fishery has disabled facilities - contact them direct for further details

BUDE

Bude Canal Angling Association

Contact: Mr Dick Turner, 2 Pathfields, Bude, *Tel:* 01288 353162, *Water:* Bude Canal (1.25 miles). *Species:* Mirror, Common, Crucian Carp, Bream, Tench, Roach, Rudd, Perch, Eels, Gudgeon, Dace. *Permits:* On the bank. *Charges:* Seniors day £4, Seniors week £18, Juniors & O.A.Ps day £2, Juniors & O.A.Ps week £10. *Season:* Closed season April 1st to May 31st inc. *Methods:* Micro barb or barbless hooks only, Strictly one rod only. No camping or any equipment deemed to be associated with camping. Unhooking mats advised.

Hele Barton Coarse Fishery

Contact: Jonathan Chapman, Hele Barton, Week St. Mary, Bude, *Tel:* 01288 341622, *Water:* 1.5 Acre Lake. Well Stocked with Carp (common, mirror, leather and ghost) and Tench. There are lots of carp in the 1lb to 8lb category and a decent number of bigger carp up to 15lbs and growing fast! *Species:* Carp to 15lb. Tench to 5.5lb. *Permits:* Pay at Self Service Kiosk in car park. *Charges:* All day ticket (dawn to dusk): £5 one rod, £6 two. Concessions - Under 16's, OAPs etc. £3.50 one rod, £4.50 two rods. Evening Fishing (4pm to dusk) £2.50. Night Fishing by arrangement. *Season:* Open all year. *Methods:* BARBLESS HOOKS ONLY (Micro barb hooks and flattened barbed hooks are still barbed hooks). No fixed rigs/leads (which could tether fish). No keepnets or carp sacks. No particle baits (nuts and pulses) except sweetcorn. No fires. No radios. Under 14's to be accompanied by an adult at all times. Anglers must have a suitable landing net and disgorger.

Houndapitt Farm

Contact: Mr Heard, Houndapitt Farm, Sandymouth, Bude, *Tel:* 01288 355455, *Mobile:* 07815 835375, *Water:* Small pond. *Species:* Golden Tench, Rudd, various Carp. *Charges:* £3 per day. *Methods:* Barbless hooks.

South West Lakes Angling Association

Contact: Roy Retallick, 21 Alstone Road, Tiverton, Devon. *Tel:* 01884 256721, *Water:* All 14 South West Lakes Trust fisheries plus 1 exclusive member only water at Lower Tamar. *Species:* All coarse fish - Carp 35lb, Pike 20lb plus, Bream 8lb plus, Tench 7lb plus, Roach 2lb, Perch 3lb 7oz, Eel 4lb. *Permits:* Please contact Roy Retallick. *Charges:* £10 per year membership, £7.50 junior, OAP and disabled. Entitles 10% discount on day and season tickets to fish any South West Lakes Trust coarse waters. *Season:* Open all year. *Methods:* As South West Lakes Trust rules displayed on site.

A South West Lakes Trust Reservoir

Upper Tamar Lake

Contact: South West Lakes Trust Fishery Assistant, *Tel:* 01288 321262, *Water:* Reservoir 81 acres. *Species:* Carp to 28lb, 50lb plus bags of Bream, 30lb plus bags of Rudd. Regular competitions. *Permits:* Self service on site *Charges:* Full day £5.25, concession £4.25, 24 hour £9.50, Season tickets available from Summerlands Tackle (01237 471291) - additional fisheries £25 each. *Season:* Open all year 24 hours a day.

CALLINGTON

Angling 2000 (Polhilsa)

Contact: Westcountry Rivers Trust, 10 Exeter Street, Launceston, *Tel:* 0870 774 0704, *Water:* 2 acre lake. *Species:* Carp, Rudd and Eels. *Permits:* From the above. *Charges:* £5. *Season:* Open all year. *Methods:* No Carp in keep nets, barbless hooks only.

DELABOLE

Ferndale

Contact: Steve Davey, Rockhead, Delabole, *Tel:* 01840 212091, *Mobile:* 07817 520417, *Water:* Three half acre lakes set in a sheltered valley 3 miles off the North Cornwall coast. *Species:* Roach to 1.5lb, Rudd to 1.5lb, Bream to 5lb and Carp to 21lb, Tench to 2lb & Crucian Carp 1.5lb. *Charges:* Adults £4 per day. OAP's and juniors £3 per day. After 5pm £3. Extra rod £1 per day. *Season:* Open all year. Times as specified at lakes *Methods:* Barbless hooks and no keepnets

FALMOUTH

Argal

Contact: South West Lakes Trust Fishery Assistant, *Tel:* 01209 860301, *Water:* Reservoir 65 acres. *Species:* Carp to 30lb +, Pike to over 30lb (no live baiting), Bream, Tench & Eels. *Permits:* Self service on site. *Charges:* Full day £5.25, concession £4.25, 24 hour £9.50. Season tickets available from Stithians Centre and Summerlands Tackle (01237 471291) - additional fisheries £25 each. *Season:* Open all year 24 hours a day.

HAYLE

Billy Knott Fisheries (BK Fisheries)

Contact: Billy Knott, Green Lane, St Erth, Nr Hayle, *Tel:* 01736 365638, *Mobile:* 07919 130244, *Water:* 3 acre lake (Bill's Pool). 2 acre lake (Billy's Pool). *Species:* Bill's Pool - Big Carp to mid 20's, Bream to 12lb, Roach, Rudd, Perch, Tench and Crucian Carp. Billy's Pool - Large head of Carp to 18lb, Bream to 5lb, Roach, Rudd and Perch. *Permits:* On the bank. *Charges:* £6 per day. £4.50 juniors. Evening permit (after 5pm) £4.50. £3.50 juniors. Night permits available on request. Coaching available from qualified NFA Sport England coach. *Season:* Jan to Dec. *Methods:* Pole, waggler, feeder, bomb. No barbed hooks. No keepnets (except in matches). No nuts, beans or meat baits. Disabled platforms and Disabled toilets.

Marazion Angling Club

Contact: Mr Barry Little, 32 Trehayes Meadow, St Erth, Hayle, *Tel:* 01736 756767, *Water:* St. Erth Fishery (3 acres), Wheal Grey (4 acres), Sharkey's Pit (60 Pegs). *Species:* Carp, Bream, Tench, Roach, Rudd, Perch, Golden Orfe, Golden Rudd, Gudgeon, Trout, Flounders & Eels; Wheal Grey reputed to hold Cornwall's biggest Carp (30lb plus). *Permits:* Available in local shops: Newtown Angling Centre, Praa Sands. West Cornwall Angling, Penzance. County Angler, Camborne. Post Office, St. Erth. Atlantic Tackle, Helston. Hayle Bait and Tackle, Pratts' Market, Hayle. plus many more outlets (Please phone for more details). *Charges:* Membership fees: Full Senior £55, Ladies £40, Juniors (up to 16) £18.50, OAP & Disabled £40, Out of county £40. Family (2 adults & 2 children) £85. Ticket prices: Day £5 - Ladies, Seniors, (OAP, Disabled, Juniors £3.50). Night permit £75 - Wheal Gray only. *Season:* Open all year dawn till dusk, night fishing by appointment only, matches held regularly throughout the year. *Methods:* Barbless hooks, full rules & byelaws displayed at lake side (best baits: maggot, worm, pellet, sweetcorn, meat, boilies).

HELSTON

Middle Boswin Farm

Contact: Jonno, Middle Boswin Farm, Porkellis, Helston, *Tel:* 01209 860420, *Water:* 1 x Pleasure lake, 1 x Carp lake. *Species:* Roach 2lb, Rudd 1.5lb, Bream 4lb, Tench 3lb, Perch 2lb, Hybrid (Roach/Bream) 2.5lb plus single figure Mirror and Common Carp. Carp lake - Carp to 26lb. *Permits:* Day tickets available at farm. *Charges:* Adult £5, concessions/junior £4, Carp lake £6. *Season:* Winter; Dawn to Dusk, Summer 7am - 9 pm. (Night fishing only if pre-booked). *Methods:* Barbless hooks only, no fixed legers, no cereal groundbait, cat food, hemp or nuts, no Trout pellets. No keepnets (except Matches) or Carp sacks.

LAUNCESTON

Adamsfield Fishery ♿

Contact: Mr Roger Pooley, Adamsfield Farm, Canworthy Water, Launceston, *Tel:* 01566 781243, *Water:* 2 acre and 1.25 acre lakes. *Species:* Carp to 26lb, Tench to 6lb, Roach to 3lb, Perch to 4lb, Bream, Orfe to 1lb, Chub to 3lb. *Charges:* £5 - 2 Rods, £4 Children/OAP's. *Season:* Open all year. *Methods:* No keepnets, ground bait in feeders only, barbless hooks, no boilies

Dutson Water ♿

Contact: Mr Broad, Lower Dutson Farm, Launceston, *Tel:* 01566 773147, *Mobile:* 01566 776456, *Water:* 0.75 acre lake. *Species:* Carp 19lb, Tench to 6lb 2oz, Bream to 5lb 2oz, Rudd, Perch to 3lb 4oz etc. *Permits:* Available at farm and Homeleigh Garden and Angling Centre, Dutson. Tel: 01566 773147. *Charges:* Day ticket £5. Charges may change in 2008. *Season:* Open all year. *Methods:* No Groundbait, Barbless hooks only.

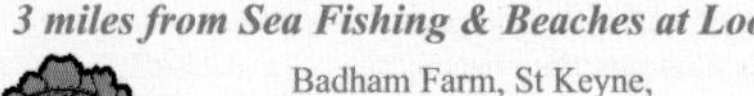

Hidden Valley Coarse Fishing Lakes

Contact: Mr P. Jones, Tredidon, Nr Kennards House, Launceston, *Tel:* 01566 86463, *Water:* 2 acre & 0.75 acre lake. Both in secluded valleys, tree lined. *Species:* Carp to 25lbs, Tench to 5lbs, Roach and Bream. *Permits:* Day tickets from Hidden Valley reception. *Charges:* Adults £6 for 2 rods, OAP's £5, Children £5 for 2 rods, extra rod £1. *Season:* Open all year, dawn till dusk. *Methods:* Only barbless hooks allowed, keep nets allowed for fish under 2lb.

St. Leonards Coarse Fishing Lake

Contact: Andy Reeve, St. Leonards Equitation Centre, Polson, Launceston, *Tel:* 01566 775543, *Mobile:* 07860 431225, *Water:* 0.75 acre lake. *Species:* Tench, Crucian, Leather, Mirror and Common Carp. *Permits:* From house. *Charges:* £4 per rod per day. *Season:* Open all year. *Methods:* Barbless hooks only.

LISKEARD

Badham Farm

Contact: Mr Jan Sroczynski, Badham Farm, St Keyne, Liskeard, *Tel:* 01579 343572, *Water:* 0.75 acre lake. *Species:* Carp 15lb, Roach 2.5lb, Tench 3lb and Rudd 2lb. *Permits:* On site. *Charges:* £5 per rod per day. *Season:* Open all year dawn to dusk. *Methods:* Barbless hooks only, no boilies, no keepnets, landing nets to be used at all times, no groundbait.

NEWQUAY

Goonhavern Fishery

Contact: S. Arthur, Oak Ridge Farm, Bodmin Road, Goonhavern, *Tel:* 01872 575052, *Water:* 2 acres. *Species:* Carp, Tench, Rudd, Roach, Perch. *Permits:* On the bank. *Charges:* £5 Adults. £4 children and OAP's. *Season:* Open all year. *Methods:* Barbless hooks, no Carp keepnets.

Gwinear Pools ♿

Contact: Charlie and Rhona Nichol, Gwinear Farm, Cubert, Newquay, *Tel:* 01637 830165, *Mobile:* 07802 400050, *Water:* 3 acre specimen lake, Carp to 30lb. 60 peg match lake, 5 hour match record 294lbs. Matches on Sundays and Tuesdays. *Species:* Carp, Roach, Bream, Perch, Rudd. *Charges:* Day tickets from self service kiosk: £6 adult. £4 OAP's & Juniors. *Season:* No close season. *Methods:* Barbless hooks, no keepnets, no meat products.

Legonna Farm Fishery

Contact: Mr Trebilcock, Legonna Farm, Lane, Newquay, *Tel:* 01637 872272, *Mobile:* 07833 596120, *Water:* 1 acre lake. *Species:* Tench, Roach, Rudd, Perch, Carp to 20lbs. *Permits:* Permits/Day tickets available from local Post Office. *Charges:* Adult £5 (2 rods), Junior/OAPs (2 rods) £3. Prices may change in 2008. Children under 14 to be accompanied by an adult. *Season:* No close season. *Methods:* Barbless hooks, no nuts of any type, no litter, no large fish in keepnets.

Mawgan Porth Pools & Lakes ♿

Contact: Jeff & Janet Reynolds, Retorrick Mill, Mawgan Porth, Newquay, *Tel:* 01637 860770, *Water:* 2 lakes - 1.5 acre 47 peg lake, plus specimen pool with 10 pegs. *Species:* Carp, Tench, Bream Grass Carp, Gold and Blue Orfe. *Permits:* On site. Disabled toilet on site, all paths and pegs disabled angler friendly. *Charges:* £6 (one rod). *Season:* Open all year, 7.30am to dusk or nights. *Methods:* Nets must be dipped, no tiger nuts. 2 kilo groundbait max. Full list of rules at fishery. No keepnets except for competitions.

Oakside Fishery & Fish Farm

Contact: Brian & Sandra Hiscock, 89 Pydar Close, Newquay, *Tel:* 01637 871275, *Water:* 3 acre lake. *Species:* Carp to 27lb, Tench 10lb, Rudd, Bream 8lb, Perch, Roach 2lb, Crucians 2lb. *Permits:* Pay kiosk, checked by bailiff. *Charges:* Adult £5 (Two rods), Junior, O.A.P's, Disabled £4 (Two Rods). *Season:* All year round. *Methods:* Barbless hooks, no tiger nuts or peanuts and no Carp in keepnets.

Penvose Farm Holidays

Contact: Jonathan Bennett, St. Mawgan, Nr. Newquay, *Tel:* 01637 860277/860432, *Mobile:* 07811 531881, *Water:* 5 acres of water set in a beautiful valley. *Species:* Carp (Common 15 - 16lb, Mirror 16-19lb, Ghost 19.5 - 22lb), Tench (Green 3 - 4lb, Golden 1lb) Bream 2lb, Crucians 1.5lb, Rudd 1.5lb, Roach 1lb. *Permits:* Post Offices nearby. *Charges:* Adults £5. under 14 £4. Prices may change during 2008. *Season:* No closed season, fishing dawn till dusk. *Methods:* Anglers must hold a valid licence. All nets to be dipped in solution tanks, no keepnets except for matches, landing nets must be used. Ground bait up to 2kg maximum. Barbless hooks only.

Porth ♿

Contact: South West Lakes Trust Fishery Assistant, *Tel:* 01209 860301, *Water:* Reservoir 40 acres. *Species:* Carp, Bream (best 9lb 12oz), Roach, Rudd, Pike (to 26lb - no livebaiting). Mixed bags of 130lb have been caught. *Permits:* Self service on site. *Charges:* Full day £5.25, concession £4.25, 24 hour

STILLWATER COARSE

Nice Common from a Cornish stillwater

£9.50. Season tickets available from Summerlands Tackle (01237 471291) - additional fisheries £25 each. *Season:* Open all year 24 hours a day.

The Barn Fisheries

Contact: Kevin Harmer, *Mobile:* 07779 285550, *Water:* No day tickets, but limited syndicate vacancies at £250 per annum. New 16 peg match lake now opened, £5 per day ticket. *Species:* Mirror and Common Carp to 27lb, 3 acre lake stocked with 65 fish. *Permits:* 20 purpose built swims, totally private. *Season:* Open all year.

Trebellan Park & Fisheries

Contact: Mr Eastlake, Cubert, Nr. Newquay, *Tel:* 01637 830522, *Water:* 3 lakes ranging from 1 to 2.5 acres. *Species:* Carp 26lbs, Roach 3-4lbs, Rudd 3-4lbs, Tench 3-4lbs. *Permits:* Permits paid for on the bank. Bailiff collects. *Charges:* Day tickets - £4 for 1 rod, £6 for 2 rods. Season ticket (12 months) £60. *Season:* Lakes open all year. No night fishing. *Methods:* No keepnets, barbless hooks only, no ground baiting, no high protein baits, no night fishing, no cat or dog meat.

White Acres Country Park ♿

Contact: Tackle Shop, White Acres Country Park, Newquay, *Tel:* 01726 862526, *Mobile:* 01726 862519, *Water:* 15 lakes totalling approx. 36 acres. *Species:* Wide range of almost all species (no Pike or Zander). *Permits:* Available from Fishing Lodge. Residents fish all year and non-residents can fish Friday and Saturday. *Charges:* Please call for info. £10 Adult, £5 Junior. *Season:* Fishery open all year round. *Methods:* 'The Method' is banned, barbless hooks only, some keepnet restrictions, no peas, nuts, or beans. No Catmeat or Trout Pellet. No bloodworm or joker.

PADSTOW

Borlasevath

Contact: Robert Hurford, Borlasevath Manor Farm, St. Wenn, Bodmin, *Tel:* 01637 880826, *Mobile:* 07973 767147, *Water:* 10 acres of water (5 lakes). *Species:* Carp, Bream, Tench, Rudd. *Methods:* Barbless hooks. All children under 14 years to be accompanied by an adult. No keepnets.

PENZANCE

Boscathnoe

Contact: South West Lakes Trust Fishery Assistant, *Tel:* 01209 860301, *Water:* Reservoir 4 acres. *Species:* Common and Mirror Carp into 20lb range. Crucian Carp, Bream, Roach, Rudd and Tench stocked. *Permits:* Newtown Angling (01736 763721), Heamoor Post Office (01736 363083), Ayr Newsagents, St. Ives (01736 791800) *Charges:* Full day £5.25, concession £4.25, 24 hour £9.50. Season tickets available from Stithians Centre and Summerlands Tackle (01237 471291) - additional fisheries £25 each. *Season:* Open all year 24 hours a day. *Methods:* No child under 14 years may fish unless accompanied by an adult over 18 years. No child under 16 may fish overnight unless accompanied by an adult over 18 years, and then only with permission of parent or legal guardian (letter to this effect must be produced).

Choone Farm Fishery

Contact: Mr E.V. Care, Downs Barn, St. Buryan, Penzance, *Tel:* 01736 810658, *Water:* 2 lakes. *Species:* Carp, Tench, Perch, Rudd. *Charges:* 1 rod - £5 per person, 2 rods - £5. *Season:* Please telephone before travelling. *Methods:* Barbless hooks only, no Carp in keepnets, no ground bait.

Tindeen Fishery ♿

Contact: J. Laity, Bostrase, Millpool, Goldsithney, Penzance, *Tel:* 01736 763486, *Water:* Two lakes approx. 1 acre each. *Species:* Carp, Roach, Rudd, Gudgeon, Perch to 5lb, Tench, Carp to 30lbs. *Permits:* From above address. *Charges:* Adults £4, Juniors (under 12) £2.50, Extra rod £1. *Season:* All year, night fishing by arrangement. *Methods:* Barbless hooks to be used.

SALTASH

Bake Fishing Lakes (Coarse)

Contact: Tony Lister, Bake, Trerule Foot, Saltash, *Tel:* 01752 849027, *Mobile:* 07798 585836, *Water:* 9 lakes totalling over 15 acres, Coarse and Trout. *Species:* Mirror 28lb, Common over 30lb, Ghost 24lb, Crucian Carp, Tench 7lb, Bream 8lb 4oz, Roach, Rudd. *Permits:* At Bake Lakes. *Charges:* £8 per day Specimen Lake. £6.50 per day small fish lakes. 2 rods per person, reduced

rates for pensioners and juniors subject to change. *Season:* 7am to dusk. Earlier by appointment, open all year. *Methods:* Barbless hooks. No nuts. No keepnets for specimen fish. Landing mats. All nets to be dipped before fishing.

Bush Lakes ♿

Contact: J Renfree, Bush Farm, Saltash, *Tel:* 01579351102, *Water:* 3 Lakes from half to one acre. *Species:* Carp to 30lb plus, Tench to 3.5lb, Rudd to 1.5lb, Roach to 1.5lb, Bream, Perch to 4.5lb. *Charges:* Day ticket £7-2 rods / £10-3 rods. *Season:* Open all year. *Methods:* Barbless hooks, landing mat, no nets for big Carp. No keepnets.

Club Brunel ♿

Contact: Vincent Riley, 81 Brentford Avenue, Whitleigh, Plymouth, Devon. *Mobile:* 07791 798361, *Water:* One acre coarse lake abundantly stocked. Small, friendly club welcoming new members. *Species:* Carp to 19lb. Bream, Roach, Rudd, Crucians, Goldfish, Tench. *Permits:* Membership only. No day tickets. Please contact the above. *Charges:* £25 per year plus one off stocking fee of £25 in the first year. Reductions for juniors and concessions. *Season:* Open all year. *Methods:* Barbless hooks only. No litter. Disabled friendly pegs. Phone for more info.

Trewandra Lake

Contact: Mr & Mrs S.F. Delbridge, Trewandra Cottage, Saltash, *Tel:* 01752 851258, *Mobile:* 07833 666899, *Water:* One acre lake. *Species:* Carp to 19lb. Tench to 6lbs. Roach to 2.5lbs and Bream to 3lb. *Permits:* Local Post Office. *Charges:* £5 day, children £3. Evening Ticket £3, £2 children. Children under 13 years must be supervised by an adult at all times. *Season:* Open all year (dawn to dusk only). Toilet available 1st April - end of September. *Methods:* No dogs allowed, barbless hooks, no keepnets for Carp, no tiger nuts and no peanuts.

ST AUSTELL

Court Farm Holidays

Contact: Simon / Bill Truscott, Court Farm Holidays, St Stephen, St Austell, *Tel:* 01726 823684, *Mobile:* 07971 971673, *Water:* Natural Spring fed 0.75 acre lake. *Species:* Roach, Rudd and Tench. Grass, Common and Mirror Carp. *Permits:* You must have a valid EA Rod Licence. *Charges:* Day tickets £5. *Season:* Open all year. *Methods:* Barbless hooks only. No keepnets. No boilies.

Glenleigh Farm Fishery ♿

Contact: Mr & Mrs A Tregunna, Glenleigh Farm, Sticker, St Austell, *Tel:* 01726 73154, *Mobile:* 07816 953362, *Water:* One acre lake. Access to enable parking adjacent to lake, allowing easy access for disabled persons and fully disabled friendly fishing platforms. *Species:* Carp (Common, Ghost, Mirror, Leather), Tench, Rudd, Roach, Eels, Gudgeon, Perch. *Permits:* Tickets from lakeside, permits from Sticker post office. *Charges:* £5 day, £4 child / OAP. £3 evening, £2 child /OAP. 12 month membership available. *Season:* Open all year dawn to dusk. *Methods:* Barbless hooks. No nuts, peas or beans. Max 2 rods per person. Mats to be used. No groundbait. No keepnets. No artificial baits.

Roche (St Austell) Angling Club

Contact: Mr Ian Holland (Membership Secretary), Sparry Farm, Sparry Bottom, Carharrack, Redruth, *Tel:* 01209 822631, *Water:* 6 freshwater lakes in St Austell area. *Species:* Roach, Perch, Rudd, Tench, Eels, Carp, Pike & Bream. *Permits:* Fishing restricted to Members and their guests only. Membership applications available from membership secretary direct. Day tickets from local tackle shops. *Charges:* Full Annual membership £85, concessionary £35 plus initial joining fee. Membership to Game and Sea sections only at reduced rates. *Season:* Open all year. *Methods:* As specified in club byelaws.

ST COLUMB MAJOR

Meadowside Fishery

Contact: Mick Brown, Meadowside Farm, Winnards Perch, St. Columb, *Tel:* 01637 880544, *Mobile:* 07800 740561, *Water:* 2 lakes mixed coarse fishery. *Species:* Carp 24lb, Roach 2lb, Perch 3lb, Rudd 1lb, Tench 5lb, Bream 6lb. *Permits:* Personal licence required. *Charges:* £6 up to 2 rods. Concessions £5 up to 2 rods. Children £4.50 - 1 rod. *Season:* No close season, 7.30am to dusk daily all year round. *Methods:* Barbless hooks, no keepnets, unhooking mats preferred.

Retallack Waters ♿

Contact: Retallack Waters, Winnards Perch, St Columb Major, *Tel:* 01637 881160, *Mobile:* 01637 880057, *Water:* 6.5 acre main lake, separate match canal. *Species:* Common, Mirror and Ghost Carp, Pike, Bream, Tench, Perch, Roach and Rudd. *Permits:* Night fishing only available to season ticket holders. Please enquire for details. *Charges:* Canal: £6 adults, £5 children/OAPs. Main specimen lake: £7 adult, £6 children/OAP's. Prices may change in 2008. *Season:* Open all year. *Methods:* Barbless hooks only. Unhooking mats and specimen landing net required on specimen lake. Dogs allowed by prior arrangement, please phone first.

ST IVES

Amalwhidden Farm Coarse Fishery

Contact: Neil Hodder, Towednack, St. Ives, *Tel:* 01736 796961, *Water:* 3 ponds & 1 acre lake. *Species:* Mirror Carp 18lb, Common Carp 24lb, Ghost Carp 12lb, Tench 4lb, Perch 3.5lb, Bream, Rudd, Roach and Gudgeon. *Charges:* Day tickets £5. *Season:* No closed season. *Methods:* No Carp sacks, barbless hooks only, no night fishing.

Bussow

Contact: South West Lakes Trust Fishery Assistant, *Tel:* 01209 860301, *Water:* Reservoir 7 acres. *Species:* Rudd to 1.5lb. Roach, Bream and Carp. *Permits:* Ayr Newsagents, St. Ives (01736 791800), Newtown Angling Centre (01736 763721). *Charges:* Full day £5.25, concession £4.25, 24 hour £9.50. Season tickets available from Stithians Centre and Summerlands Tackle (01237 471291) - additional fisheries £25 each. *Season:* Open all year 24 hours a day.

Nance Lakes

Contact: Mr or Mrs Ellis, Nance Lakes, Trevarrack, Lelant, St Ives, *Tel:* 01736 740348, *Water:* Three lakes, various sizes. *Species:* Carp, Roach, Bream and Tench. *Charges:* £5 per day. Evening tickets - £3 after 5pm. *Season:* Open all year 8am to 5pm. *Methods:* Barbless hooks, no keepnets unless competition.

St. Ives Freshwater Angling Society

Contact: Jim Elgar, 52 Trelawney Avenue, St. Ives, *Tel:* 01736 796696, *Water:* 1.5 acre spring-fed lake with depths from 6 to 24 feet, situated in farmland 5 miles from St.Ives. *Species:* Bream, Carp, Tench, Roach, Rudd, Perch, Gudgeon, and Eels. *Permits:* 1) Mr. K. Roberts, Woonsmith Farm, Nancledra, Nr. Penzance. 2) Newtown Angling Centre, Newtown, Germoe, Penzance. Location maps available with permits. *Charges:* Adults: Day £5, Weekly £15. Juniors (under 16): Day £3, Weekly £9. *Season:* Open all year. No night Fishing. *Methods:* Barbless hooks only. No fish over 3 lb to be retained in a keepnet. All nets to be dipped in disinfectant tank before use. Good baits are maggots, casters, sweetcorn and Trout pellets. Floating crust for Carp in summer.

TORPOINT

Crafthole

Contact: South West Lakes Trust, *Tel:* 01579 346522, *Water:* Reservoir 2 acres. *Species:* Quality Carp to 30lb and Tench. *Permits:* Limited season ticket only, day and night. Available from Summerlands Tackle (01237 471291). *Charges:* Season Day £190, Concession £170. Family £285 (Husband, wife and up to 2 children under 16). Additional Fisheries £25 each. *Season:* Open all year, 1 hour before sunrise to one hour after sunset (day tickets).

Millbrook

Contact: Mark or Rebecca Blake, Tregonhawke Farm, Millbrook, Torpoint, *Tel:* 01752 823210, *Water:* 1 acre water in sheltered, wooded valley. 150 year old reservoir. *Species:* Perch, Tench, Ghost Carp, Crucians, Common Carp, Mirror Carp, Roach, Rudd, Bream. *Charges:* £6 per day, £12 night fishing ticket. Annual permits £120. *Season:* Dawn until dusk, no closed season. *Methods:* Barbless hooks only. Keepnets are permitted, landing nets and disgorgers to be used.

South East Cornwall Taught Angling Society

Contact: Tony Savage, 79 Peacock Avenue, Torpoint, *Tel:* 01752 812637, *Water:* The aim of SECTAS is not only to promote angling as a pastime amongst the youth of South East Cornwall, but also to promote social inclusion. SECTAS offers youngsters a way to meet new people, make new friends and become part of a group of like minded people. SECTAS is a not for profit group and funds are put back into the group to improve it, it's resources and to increase membership. *Charges:* There is a joining fee of £10 to show commitment and thereafter a £5 per year membership fee. The club caters for all aged 8 upwards.

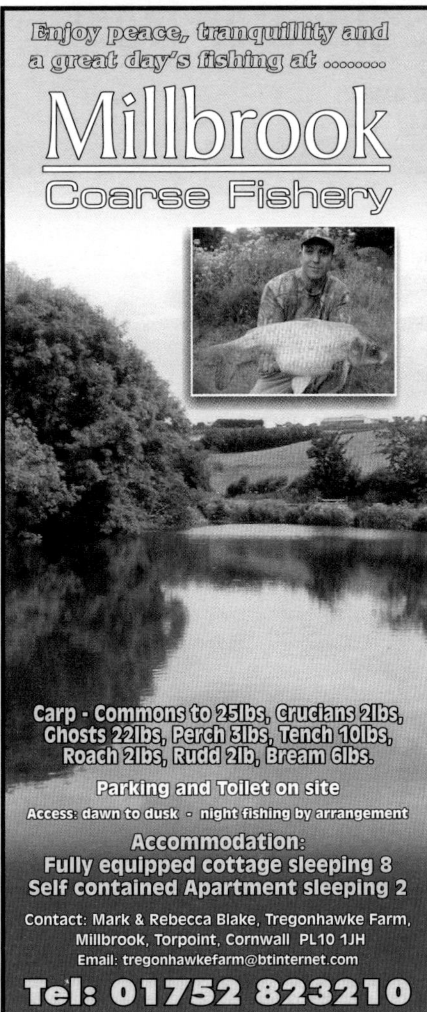

TRURO

Mellonwatts Mill Coarse Fishery

Pensagillas Farm, Grampound, Truro, *Tel:* 01872 530808, *Mobile:* 07967827340, *Water:* 2 acre lake. *Species:* Carp to 25lb, Common & Mirror, Roach, Tench, Golden Rudd. *Charges:* Day ticket £5, Evening £3. *Season:* Open all year. Night fishing by arrangement only.

Nanteague Farm Fishing

Contact: Viv George, Marazanvose, Zelah, Truro, *Tel:* 01872 540351, *Water:* 1.5 acre lake *Species:* Carp to 25lb, Roach, Rudd, Bream and Perch. *Permits:* Limited season tickets by prior arrangement. Please telephone/e-mail. No day tickets.

Threemilestone Angling Club (Coarse Lakes)

Contact: Mrs T. Bailey, 9 Sampson Way, Threemilestone, Truro, *Tel:* 01872 272578, *Mobile:* 07734 445133, *Water:* Langarth Pools (2 Pools). *Species:* Carp, Tench, Roach, Rudd, Bream, Perch, Goldfish. *Permits:* At lakeside. *Charges:* Seniors £5, Juniors £3. *Season:* All season, no night fishing. *Methods:* Barbless hooks only, no Peanuts etc.

Tory Farm Angling

Contact: David Worlledge, Tory Farm, Ponsanooth, Truro, *Tel:* 01209 861272, *Mobile:* 07971 859570, *Water:* 2.5 acre lake. *Species:* Mirror, Common, Wild and Ghost Carp to 20lb. Crucian to 2.5lb. Tench to 5.5lb. Rudd to 2.25lb. *Charges:* Please telephone for details. Annual membership £100. No day tickets unless by previous arrangement. *Season:* Open all year. *Methods:* Barbless hooks only, no keepnets, unhooking mats to be used. No nut baits. Hemp-specialist prepared only.

Stillwater Trout

BODMIN

Colliford Lake

Contact: South West Lakes Trust, *Tel:* 01579 346522, *Water:* Reservoir 911 acres. *Species:* Brown Trout. *Permits:* Jamaica Inn 01566 86250 *Charges:* Full day £11.50, Concession £9.50. Season tickets available from Summerlands Tackle (01237 471291). *Season:* Opens 15 March - 12th October. *Methods:* Catch & release option (Barbless hooks only). Fly fishing only.

Temple Trout Fishery ♿

Contact: Mr Julian Jones, Temple Trout Fishery, Temple Road, Temple, Bodmin, *Tel:* 01208 821730, *Mobile:* 07787 704966, *Water:* 2.7 acre lake. Plus 4.5 acre 'any method' lake. *Species:* Rainbows (18lb 9oz) & Brown Trout (16lb 6oz). *Permits:* Available at fishery Tel: 01208 821730. *Charges:* 2008 Club membership £8, entitles members to 10% discount on tickets, to fish club events and to purchase a season ticket at £131.25 for 25 Trout. Full day £25, 5 fish. 3/4 day £22, 4 fish. Half day £17.50, 3 fish. Evening £13, 2 fish. Child under 16 & disabled £13, 2 fish all day, extra fish £7. To fish the 'any method' lake is half the above prices. *Season:* Open all year round from 9 a.m to dusk, in winter open 4 days a week Wednesday, Thursday, Saturday and Sundays or by appointment. *Methods:* Fly fishing on 2.7 acre lake. Any legal method may be used on 4.5 acre lake. A sporting ticket is available on 4.5 acre lake.

BUDE

Angling 2000 (Woolstone)

Contact: Westcountry Rivers Trust, 10 Exeter Street, Launceston, *Tel:* 0870 774 0704, *Water:* 1.25 acre lake and 500m on the River Neet. *Species:* Brown Trout. *Permits:* From the above. *Charges:* £7.50 per day. *Season:* 15 March to 30 September. *Methods:* Please contact Angling 2000 for individual fishery methods.

CAMELFORD

Crowdy

Contact: South West Lakes Trust, *Tel:* 01579 346522, *Water:* Reservoir 115 acres. *Species:* Wild Brown Trout. *Charges:* Free to holders of a valid Environment Agency Licence. *Season:* 15th March - 12th October. *Methods:* Angling by spinning, fly or bait.

HAYLE

Tree Meadow Trout Fishery

Contact: John Hodge, Tree Meadow, Deveral Road, Fraddam, Hayle, *Tel:* 01736 850899, *Mobile:* 07971 107156, *Water:* Two lakes. 4 acres in total. Sedge lake to 14lb, Willow lake to 25lb plus. *Species:* Rainbow and Brown Trout. Also Blue, Brook and Tiger Trout. *Permits:* At Lodge Shop. *Charges:* Contact for details. *Season:* Open all year 9am to 1 hour after dusk. *Methods:* Catch and release after fish limit. Max hook size 10.

Remember a ♿ means the fishery has disabled facilities - contact them direct for further details

LAUNCESTON

Rose Park Fishery

Contact: Rose Park Fishery, Trezibbett, Altarnun, Launceston, *Tel:* 01566 86278, *Water:* Two lakes. 2 acre and half acre. *Species:* Rainbow 13lb, Wild Browns 2.5lb. Stocked Brown Trout 9lb 5oz. *Permits:* From the fishery. *Charges:* Rainbows £1.75 per lb, Browns £2.25 per lb (will increase in 2008). Fishing charge £5.00. *Season:* Open all year from 8am till Dusk. *Methods:* Fly fishing. No catch and release.

LISKEARD

Siblyback

Contact: South West Lakes Trust, Angling and Watersports Centre, *Tel:* 01579 346522, *Water:* Reservoir 140 acres. *Species:* Premier rainbow fishery, boats available booked in advance via the centre. Rod average 2006: 3.43 fish per rod per day. *Permits:* Angling and Watersports Centre. *Charges:* Charges: Full day £19.50, Concession £16, Evening £16, boats £12 per day. Season permits also available from Summerlands Tackle (01237 471291). *Season:* 21st March - 31st October. *Methods:* Catch and release available (barbless hooks must be used), fly fishing only.

www.gethooked.co.uk
Check out our Web Site!
Get HOOKED!
ON THE WEB

Nice 15lb 6oz Rainbow for Jim Husband of St Austell at Temple Trout.

PENZANCE

Drift Reservoir

Contact: David Williams, Drift, Penzance, *Tel:* 01736 786613, *Water:* 65 acre reservoir. *Species:* Brown and Rainbow Trout. *Permits:* Self Service at reservoir. West Cornwall Angling, Penzance. Newton Angling, Germoe and Chyandour. *Charges:* £9 half day. £12 full day. £35 per week. Float Tubing Season ticket available to full season ticket holders only. Additional charge £25. Season £130. Prices may change in 2008. *Season:* 1 April to mid November. *Methods:* Fly fishing only.

REDRUTH

Cast Fly Fishing Club

Contact: Graham Baker, Parc Nor Farm, Goonvrea, St Agnes, *Tel:* 01872 552918, *Mobile:* 07891 772579, *Water:* Membership of 80, fishing Stithians and other waters. Monthly competitions. Juniors and ladies welcome. Tuition can be arranged. Club boat available at £2 per day. *Species:* Rainbows and Browns. Browns are wild fish, some Blues are occasionally stocked. *Charges:* £10 p/a Adult. Juniors first year free. *Season:* Please telephone Graham for info pack.

Stithians

Contact: South West Lakes Trust, Angling & Watersports Centre, Redruth, *Tel:* 01209 860301, *Water:* Reservoir 274 acres. *Species:* Intermediate Rainbow & Brown Trout Fishery to 6lb, boats available booked in advance via the centre. *Permits:* Angling & Watersports Centre. *Charges:* Full day £14, Concession £12.50, Evening, £12.50, boats £12 per day. Season permits also available from Stithians Centre and Summerlands Tackle (01237 471291). *Season:* 15 March - 31 October. *Methods:* Fly fishing only. Catch and release available - barbless hooks must be used.

SALTASH

Bake Fishing Lakes (Trout)

Contact: Tony Lister, Bake, Trerule Foot, Saltash, *Tel:* 01752 849027, *Mobile:* 07798 585836, *Water:* 9 lakes totalling over 15 acres, Coarse and Trout. Troutmaster Water. *Species:* Rainbow 16lb 7oz, Brown Trout 10lb. *Permits:* At Bake lakes. *Charges:* Sporting ticket £11 per day. Catch only £6.50 plus £5.50 - 1 fish, £14 - 2 fish, £18.50 - 3 fish, £23 - 4 fish, £26 - 5 fish. *Season:* 7am to dusk, earlier by appointment. *Methods:* Catch and release on 1 lake. Barbless or debarbed hooks when releasing.

ST AUSTELL

Innis Fly Fishery ♿

Contact: Mrs Pam Winch, Innis Fly Fishery & Innis Inn, Innis Moor, Penwithick, St. Austell, *Tel:* 01726 851162, *Water:* 15 acres (3 lakes), stream fed enclosed water. *Species:* Rainbow Trout. *Permits:* As above. *Charges:* Full day £22 (5 Fish), half day £12 (2 Fish), Catch and release £12.50, Parent and child £22 (5 fish) shared bag. *Season:* All year, 8am to dusk. *Methods:* Barbless hooks when catch & release, no static fishing.

Sea Fishing

BOSCASTLE

Boscastle Peganina

Contact: Ken Cave, *Tel:* 01288 353565, *Permits:* Book at The Rock Shop in Boscastle.

CAMBORNE

Choughs S.A.C.

Contact: Sue, *Tel:* 01209 712361, *Water:* Club fishing around the coast of Cornwall, membership open to all, meetings every 4th Sunday at the Choughs Inn, Camborne at 6pm. Regular matches every other weekend. Ladies, junior and boat section. Please contact Sue for more details.

CORNWALL REGION

Camborne Angling Association

Contact: Mr Ralph Elcox (Hon Sec), Wayside, Menagissey, Mount Hawke, Truro, *Tel:* 01209 890225, *Mobile:* 07814 989707, *Water:* Sea Fishing Association. Shore and boat. Affiliated to the Cornish Federation of Sea Anglers and the Bass Anglers Sporting Society. *Species:* All sea fish apart from protected species. Minimum weight for all species. *Permits:* None required, other than possible harbour/pier charges. *Charges:* Family membership - £11, Couple - £9, Senior £8 and £3 Junior. *Season:* None *Methods:* Two rods, three hooks maximum on club competitions. When fishing independantly of club competition an angler may use three rods and three hooks at any one time. No netting.

Cornish Federation of Sea Anglers

Contact: Mr Ralph Elcox (Hon Sec), Wayside, Menagissey, Mount Hawke, Truro, *Tel:* 01209 890225, *Mobile:* 07814 989707, *Water:* Sea Fishing Federation. Shore and boat. Affiliated to The Conger Club of Great Britain, The Bass Anglers Sporting Society and The European Federation of Sea Anglers. *Species:* All sea fish apart from protected species. Minimum weight for all species. *Permits:* None required, other than possible harbour/pier charges. *Charges:* C.F.S.A. affiliation £34 per annum per club. Personal members £7.50. Family membership (ie husband, wife and children under 16) £10. Optional third party insurance an extra £35 per club per annum. *Season:* None *Methods:* Two rods three hooks maximum on CFSA and affiliated club competitons. When fishing independantly of CFSA and affiliated club competion and angler may use three rods and three hooks at any one time. No netting.

FALMOUTH

Falmouth Duchy A.C.

Contact: Mrs L Crichton, 15 Trewarton Road, Penryn, *Tel:* 01326 372832, *Mobile:* 07837 309135, *Water:* Shore fishing. *Season:* April - September.

Leo I

Contact: Ken Dodgson, 10 Stratton Terrace, Falmouth, *Tel:* 01326 312409, *Mobile:* 07854 695281, *Water:* Normally up to 20 miles to sea from Falmouth. Longer trips by arrangement. *Species:* Conger Eel - 80lb 8oz (C.F.S.A. record). Ling 44lb 8oz (C.F.S.A. record). Coalfish to 27lb. Pollack to 25lb. Cod to 38lb. Whiting to 4lb 4oz. Plus all other usual species. Including Blue

Dogfish at sunset.
Pic. Wayne Thomas

Shark (released alive) up to 184lbs. *Charges:* Individuals with own tackle £40 per day. Individuals with tackle supplied £45 per day. Full boat charter from £200. Please ring for details. *Season:* Fishing all year round. *Methods:* Wreck, Reef and Shark. Anchored and drifting. Keep your catch, but release when possible and not required.

Mawnan Angling Club

Contact: Steve Rees & Steve Carey, 48 The Beacon, Falmouth, *Tel:* 01392 212890, *Mobile:* 01326 377029, *Water:* Sea fishing club with boat and shore sections. *Species:* Sea fish. *Charges:* £15 family, £10 senior, £3 junior. Club meet on 1st Wednesday of month at Watersports Centre, Falmouth. New members welcome. Enquiries to Tackle Box, Falmouth or Telephone Steve on number above.

Patrice II

Contact: Michael Tuffery, *Tel:* 01326 313265, *Mobile:* 07979 335181.

St Mawes S.A.C.

Contact: Mr P.A. Miller, 18 Percuil View, St Mawes, Truro, *Tel:* 01326 270953, *Water:* Shore angling, wreck trips. *Season:* Boat - from May onwards.

HAYLE

Carnhell Green S.A.C.

Contact: Mrs J Williams, 55 Cathebron Road, Carnhell Green, Cambourne, *Tel:* 01209 831720, *Water:* Wreck, reef and rock fishing. *Species:* Pollack, Mullet, Conger, Mackerel, Bass, Flounder, Wrasse, Three Bearded Rockling, Shore Rockling, Plaice. *Charges:* £6 Seniors / OAP's. £3 Junior/ladies. £10 Family (2 Adults / 1 Child). *Season:* All year - annual open competition Sept 2008.

San Pablo III

Contact: Dougie Wright, *Tel:* 01209 716970, *Mobile:* 07974 409567, *Water:* Alternative mobile - 07816 450388 *Species:* Blue Shark 120lb, Tope 90lb, Ling 27lb, Porbeagle 300lb, Pollack, Conger, Black Bream, Red Gurnard.

HELSTON

Helston & District Sea Angling Club

Atlantic Tackle, 36 Wendron Street, Helston, *Tel:* 01326 561640, *Charges:* 10% discount for club members in shops. *Season:* All year.

ISLES OF SCILLY

Faldore, Firethorn & Cyclone

Contact: David Stedeford, *Tel:* 01720 422886.

LISKEARD

Liskeard & District Sea Angling Club

Contact: Mr White, 14 Wadham Road, Liskeard, *Tel:* 01579 345428, *Water:* Mixture of sea fishing with club based in Liskeard. *Charges:* Annual subscription £10. *Season:* Shore fishing - all year. Boat - April to October (Newquay, Cornwall).

LOOE

Force Ten

Contact: Peter Davis, *Tel:* 01503 262316, *Mobile:* 07989 395360, *Water:* Offshore 105 licenced for 11. Deep sea and shark fishing all year round.

Looe Angling Club

Contact: Billy Martin, Quay Street, East Looe, *Tel:* 01503 263337, *Water:* Clubhouse with club prices on all drinks. Open all day everyday. Membership full, but holiday membership available. Please contact clubhouse.

Mystique

Contact: David Bond, 11 Springfield Road, East Looe, *Tel:* 01503 264530, *Mobile:* 07900 472252.

Shark Angling Club of Great Britain

Contact: Linda Reynolds, Middletons Corner, The Quay, East Looe, *Tel:* 01503 262642, *Water:* Established 50 years. Boat booking agent for 8 boats in Looe for Shark, Reef fishing and Mackerel trips. Club open to new members - required to catch a qualifying length shark prior to joining. For more details please contact above.

MEVAGISSEY

Mevagissey S.A.C.

Contact: Mike Barker, 30 Lavorrick Orchard, Mevagissey, *Tel:* 01726 843357, *Mobile:* 07748042088, *Water:* Wreck fishing, charter boat, lock and dingy, shore fishing. *Species:* All species on NFSA weight list. *Permits:* N/A. *Charges:* Seniors £10 per year, O.A.P.s 75p per year, Juniors £1 per year. *Season:* All year. *Methods:* Fish under NFSA rules - 2 rods, 3 hooks maximum

Venus

Contact: Mevagissey Shark & Angling Centre, Mevagissey, *Tel:* 01726 843430.

NEWQUAY

Newquay Rowing Club Sea Anglers

Contact: Wayne Row, Newquay, *Mobile:* 07974 021796, *Water:* Wreck, shore, reef and Shark. *Charges:* Annual club membership £5. *Season:* Shore fishing all year. Seasonal boat fishing.

Treninnick Tavern Angling Club

Contact: NFSA Head Office: 01364 644643.

PADSTOW

Blue Fox

Contact: Phil Britts, Padstow, *Tel:* 01841 533293, *Mobile:* 07977 563807, *Water:* All day charter fishing trips. *Charges:* Book at Padstow Angling Centre.

Emma Kate II (Lockin 33)

Contact: John Wicks, *Tel:* 01841 533319, *Mobile:* 07970 595244, *Water:* All day trips, 4 hour trips and Mackerel trips.

Grenville Sea Angling Club

Contact: John Keast, 23 Halimont Road, St.Dennis, St.Austell, *Tel:* 01841 533592, *Water:* Meetings 1st Wednesday of each month, at St Dennis football club, St Dennis, St Austell at 8pm. New members welcome (Adult & Junior). *Species:* Sea angling from rocks or boat, covering cornish coast. *Permits:* Please telephone John for further information, or come to one of our meetings.

Padstow Angling Centre

Contact: Ed Schliffke, The Drang, Strand House, *Tel:* 01841 532762, *Water:* Shore fishing trips.

PENZANCE

Goldsithney S.A.C.

Contact: NFSA Head Office: 01364 644643.

M.B.A.S.

Contact: Mr G Wallen, 6 Alexandra Gardens, Penzance, *Tel:* 01736 351414, *Water:* Shore/boat fishing - wreck/reef.

Mounts Bay Angling Society

Contact: David Cains, Shangri-La, 9A Arundel Park, Connor Downs, Hayle, *Tel:* 01736 752037, *Mobile:* 07919 253065, *Water:* Regular monthly meetings open to all in area, regular matches fishing on Cornish waters. *Charges:* Seniors £15 per year, Juniors £6.50 per year, Family membership £25 (2 adults & 2 children). Senior NFSA members £12.

Southwest Angling
Contact: Danny Mayers, 15b Gwavas Rd, Newlyn, Penzance, *Tel:* 01736 364889, *Mobile:* 07816 345471, *Water:* Guided shore fishing in south west Cornwall. *Charges:* £5 per person, per hour. All tackle & bait is supplied. *Methods:* To teach tourists the art of sea fishing for sport & pleasure, and to keep safety in mind at all times.

Westward Casting Association
Contact: NFSA Head Office: 01364 644643.

PORTHLEVEN

The Starfish & The Danda
Contact: Porthleven Angling Centre, 8 Celtic House, Harbour Head, Porthleven, *Tel:* 01326 561885, *Water:* Wreck Fishing.

REDRUTH

Redruth Sea Angling Association
Contact: Brian Collick, *Tel:* 01209 217617, *Water:* Founded in 1962 by a group of anglers who regularly fished Porthowan beach which is not far from Redruth. HQ is the Redruth Albany Rugby Football Club at the bottom of Station Hill, Redruth. Meetings are held at 8pm on the first Monday of each month or the first Monday following a Bank Holiday. The club runs it's own competitions, social events, and takes part in team inter club competition. *Permits:* Meetings 1st Monday or each Monday 8pm. *Charges:* Subscriptions £10 for Seniors over 16 years and £3 for under 16 years.

ST AUSTELL

E.C.C. Ports S.A.C.
Contact: NFSA Head Office: 01364 644643.

Roche Angling Club
Contact: Ian Holland, Sparry Farm, Sparry Bottom, Carharrack, Redruth, *Tel:* 01209 822631, *Water:* South coast sea fishing. *Charges:* Membership £11. *Season:* Fishing all year round.

ST IVES

Dolly Pentreath & The James Stevens (No.10)
Contact: Mike Laity, *Tel:* 01736 797269, *Mobile:* 07821 774178, *Season:* Easter - October.

St. Ives S.A.C.
Contact: NFSA Head Office: 01364 644643.

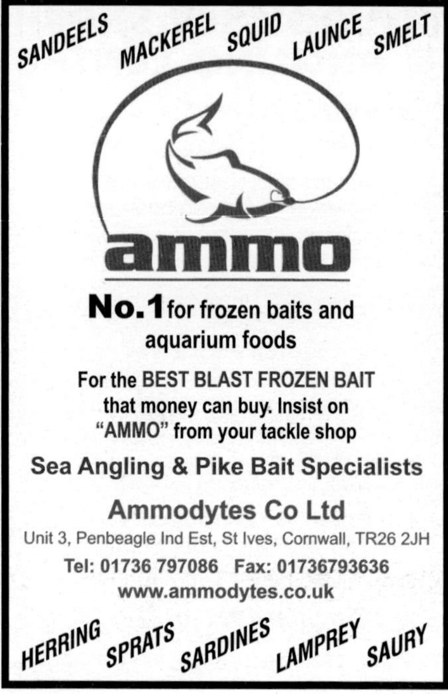

TINTAGEL

Tintagel Sea Angling Club
Contact: Nigel Rundle, Polkerr House, Tintagel, *Tel:* 01840 770382, *Water:* North Cornish coast. *Species:* Bass, Bull Huss, Brill, Cod, Conger, Dab, Dogfish, Flounder, Garfish, Gurnard, Mackerel, Mullet, Plaice, Pollack, Pouting, Ray, Rockling, Scad, Turbot, Weaver, Whiting, Wrasse. *Charges:* Club membership - senior £7.50. Junior £3. Prices may change in 2008. *Season:* Fishing all year round.

TORPOINT

Pot Black Sea Angling Club
Contact: Mr Joseph Hobbs, Secretary, 76 Grenfell Avenue, Torpoint, *Tel:* 01752 816104, *Mobile:* 07878 923343, *Charges:* Senior memberships for 2008 are £12, Junior memberships for 2008 are £5, discounts for family membership of 2 or more adults with 1 or more children. *Season:* Year runs from January 1st to December 31st, membership available from club secretary Joe Hobbs, cheques payable to Pot Black SAC.

Raleigh S.A.C.
Contact: Mr S Marriott, 40 York Road, Torpoint, *Tel:* 01752 814582, *Water:* Established 25 years. New members welcome, youngsters encouraged. Fun club, with two competitions per month. Fishing from Saltash to Looe (shore and boat). *Permits:* Now afiliated with Cornish Federation of Sea Anglers.

TRURO

Threemilestone Angling Club (Sea Fishing)
Contact: NFSA Head Office: 01364 644643.

Where to Stay in Cornwall

Josh with a whip caught Mirror Carp caught at Anglers El Dorado

WHERE TO STAY

White Acres

Near Newquay

Cornish holiday park set in 184 acres

13 Fishing Lakes – covering more than 36 acres offering the best variety of coarse fishing in the country

Two Specimen Lakes – 1-2.2 acres
- Carp to 29lb / Catfish to 59lb

11 Pleasure Lakes – 1-5 acres
- Carp to 19lb, Tench to 6lb, Bream, Roach, Perch, Rudd

- Luxury lodge and caravan accommodation
- Live evening entertainment
- Expert fishing advice
- Indoor swimming pool
- Bars, restaurants and more!

0871 641 0286 Call us now to book or request a brochure

or visit **www.news-reel.com**

CARP OVER 20 lbs

Three Privately-Owned Coarse Fishing Lakes On-Site Tackle Shop
Spacious Level Pitches Hook-ups Eurotents Caravan Holiday Homes

Perran Springs holiday park

Award Winning Park

The friendly quiet family park, set in over twenty acres, with panoramic countryside views, licensed shop, launderette + children's play areas. Superb fishing for the experienced angler and fun for families. A variety of fish inc. carp (common, mirror, leather, crucian and ghost), bream, perch, tench, rudd + roach.

Nr. Perranporth + Newquay

Fishing for Residents Only

We are a No Dog Park

tel 01872 540 568 or

www.fishing-shop.co.uk for tackle

visit **www.perransprings.co.uk** for fishing details, 'big catch' photos and an online brochure

WHERE TO STAY

David Reeves returns a Carp at Whiteacres. Pic ©Brian Gay. www.angling-images.com

WHERE TO STAY

Trout on Tiny Streams

Mike Weaver

Size is not everything in fishing and that applies as much to the rivers that we fish as the fish that we catch. I enjoy casting a fly across a big and famous trout stream as much as anyone but, let's face it, big rivers can often be moody and finding the trout when nothing is showing at the surface can be really frustrating. Small streams, however, are quick to reveal their secrets and even when nothing is rising it is easy to pick out the spots that are likely to hold some good trout.

A couple of years ago I was far from home and having a great time on some of the world-famous trout streams of Yellowstone National Park yet when I took a day off from the serious stuff and headed for the high mountains to fish some tiny streams, there was no sense of loss. Indeed, as I waded up tiny Dead Indian Creek at nearly 10,000 feet, picking off rainbows, cutthroats and the occasional brook trout less than half the size of the trout that I had been catching a day earlier, I realised that I was enjoying myself just as much. And with not another angler to be seen, I was certainly not missing the crowds on the more famous rivers.

Closer to home, I recall days on the Kennet and other noted chalk streams when the main river has been decidedly dour, yet the tiny carriers created in the past to irrigate the meadows, have been alive with rising trout.

It is in the south west of England, however, where the opportunities for fishing tiny trout streams, so many of which you could almost jump across, seem almost endless – whether in meadow country or high on the moors. I experienced a vivid example of just how good the tiniest stream can be during a day with the fly rod on the edge of Exmoor. I was fishing the Bray on day when a morning's hard fishing had produced only a few trout when I decided to try the bottom half mile of Hole Water, a tiny tributary that was included in the beat. In the clear sparkling water the trout were there for all to see and after a careful approach I dropped a buoyant Elk Hair Caddis onto a small pool where several trout could be seen holding in the current. The first cast had hardly touched down before there was a slashing rise and I was into a fish. It proved to be about eight inches and was quickly followed by a better fish of 10 inches from the head of the pool. Those Hole Water trout were really on the feed and every pool produced a fish or two, in sharp contrast with my lack of success on the main river.

Far to the west in Cornwall I recall a day on the Angling 2000 beat on the River Allen at Lemail Mill. Much of this beat is heavily overgrown and the jungle tactics required will test any angler, so deep wading with a short rod is the only way to success. Fortunately trout in such inaccessible places are usually unsophisticated and those River Allen browns came readily to just about any dry fly that I threw at them.

The Arundell Arms has around 20 miles of fishing on the Tamar and its tributaries, but one of my favourite beats is on the tiny River Lew, just above its confluence with the Lyd. This meandering brook is absolutely packed with browns up to around 12 inches and, although it can fish well at any time, is always worth a try when the mayflies bring the bigger fish to the surface.

The Creedy and the Yeo at Crediton, where the Crediton Fly Fishing Club has around five miles of water, offer small stream fishing at its most productive. And the lengthy Angling 2000 beat on the Little Dart at Essebeare near Witheridge has always delivered the goods for me, including a wonderful July afternoon when the blue-winged olives never stopped hatching and the trout came steadily to the fly for several hours. Another Angling 2000 beat on the Ottery at Wiggaton near Canworthy Water is a wonderful place to be when the black gnats are swarming in late spring. The list of tiny streams that have given me countless enchanting days is almost endless and every season I find more to explore.

So, what is the technique that will bring you success with trout on these miniature rivers? First of all, the rod needs to be short – about 7 ft is ideal and certainly no more than 7 ft 6 in. When I started fishing that meant one of the hideous little "brook rods" with their sloppy action totally unsuited to fishing in confined spaces. Fortunately, carbon now means that even the lightest little rod has the crisp action necessary for casting a tight loop under the overhanging tree. An AFTM 4 line is about right, with a shortish leader – I use a 5-ft braided butt attached to about 5 ft of nylon tapered to a 6X tippet, or lighter in very low clear water.

When a specific insect is on the water it makes sense to match it but standard dry patterns like Adams, Klinkhamer, Elk Hair Caddis or Black Gnat will usually bring the trout to the surface, with a small beadhead nymph for those occasions when nothing is showing. To get the best of both worlds, many anglers now turn to the New Zealand dropper. Tie on something like a heavily dressed 16 or 14 Klinkhamer, attach 24 to 30 inches of fine nylon to the bend of the hook, with a 16 or 14 goldhead Hare's Ear or Pheasant Tail at the other end. The nymph goes in search of any trout that are lying deep, while the dry fly acts as an indicator while attracting any fish that are looking towards the surface. The results can be spectacular.

Finally get yourself a good pair of body waders – preferably breathable for warm summer days. Small overgrown streams just cannot be fished from the bank and many are surprisingly deep – far too deep for thigh waders. Slip into the river and wade carefully upstream under the canopy of branches and you will enjoy a world of peace and, if all goes well, some great fishing.

South West Lakes Trust

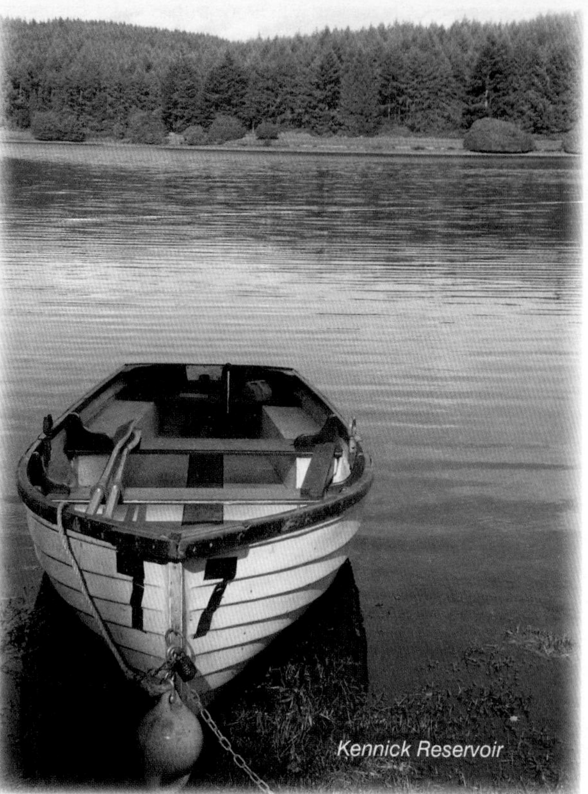
Kennick Reservoir

South West Lakes Trust manages over 26 lakes as fisheries in the South West of England. The Trust was formed to provide, promote and enhance sustainable recreation, access and nature conservation at these lakes.

2008 Season:

We intend to follow on the success of training and family days into 2008 and have a number of events and introductory days planned. Juniors will be further encouraged to fish for both coarse fish and trout with the parent / child ticket again being available allowing youngsters to fish for free (sharing parent bag limit). Please note that children under 14 years should be accompanied by an adult (over 18) at all times

Beginners' Days:

These will again be held in conjunction with local qualified professional instructors and the Environment Agency. They will include National Fishing Week family events at Siblyback and Stithians, as well as Beginners' Days, Junior Days, Ladies Days, and Family Days at Kennick, Siblyback, Wimbleball, and Stithians (contact the Trust's Head Office for more details - 01566 771930 – or see the website).

These events have been very successful over the past few seasons, with many novices taking up the sport (including a new Ladies' Club at Kennick). All equipment is provided, and with a team of professional instructors on hand, the days prove to be very popular, so prior booking is essential. In addition, individual tuition can be arranged with local qualified instructors.

Wheelyboats

Through its partnership with the Wheelyboat Trust, South West Lakes Trust is able to provide wheelyboats suitable for wheelchair access at Roadford, Wimbleball, Siblyback, and Kennick. These must be booked through the sites at least 48 hours in advance. There is also a Wheelyboat at Wistlandpound, which is operated by the Calvert Trust.

Competitions:

Once again the Trust will be holding its annual game fishery competitions : The Peninsula Classic bank competition at Kennick in June, supported by Wellard and Scott; The Snowbee Team bank competition at Siblyback in July; and the Wimbleball 2000 boat pairs competition in September, supported by Orvis. See the website or fisheries for details and booking information(www.swlakestrust.org.uk). The Trust organised two popular carp weekend competitions in 2007, and we intend to build on this success with further competitions in 2008.

Porth and Upper Tamar are both popular coarse fishing venues which may be booked in advance through the Trust's headquarters. Details of competitions at these sites and other Trust waters in the region may be found on the Fishing Diary page on the Trust's website. Fishing news items and catch reports may also be found on the Fishing News page on the website.

Season Permits:

Following the success of the new season ticket arrangements last year, season tickets for 2008 will be sold locally through the Trust's Angling and Watersports Centres, or through Summerlands Tackle in Westward Ho!, either in person or over the telephone (01237 471291).

'Angling 2000' tokens (available through the West Country Rivers Trust and other outlets) may now be used as part payment for fishing on the Trust's trout fisheries. This is a new joint promotional venture for 2008. This payment option may be used at self-service lodges and at ticket agents.

If you would like to receive copies of the Trust's Fisheries Newsletter, please telephone 01566 771930, or e-mail info@swlakestrust.org.uk to be included on the mailing list.

The Trust remains committed to angling and customer care, and welcomes all comments to help us provide what the angler really wants.

For further information, including instruction and competition information, please contact:

Chris Hall, Head of Fisheries
on 01566 771930 or 01647 277587
Or E-mail: chall@swlakestrust.org.uk
Or visit our website: www.swlakestrust.org.uk

Common Carp from Upper Tamar

Three superb caster caught Roach
Pic - ©Brian Gay. www.angling-images.com

Vranch House School
Fly Fishing Charity Challenge 2008
for children with cerebral palsy & all children with physical difficulties

Pairs of anglers are invited to enter the 17th Fly Fishing Charity Challenge to raise funds for children with cerebral palsy & other physical difficulties at Vranch House School & Centre, Exeter.

Heats and semi finals will take place from April to September at Bellbrook Valley, Kennick, Roadford, Stithians, Tavistock, Temple and Tree Meadow. The semi-finals are at Bellbrook, Stithians & Tavistock and and the finals are both at Temple.

The prize bag is £3,000. Prizes including lines, leaders, day tickets, hooks and fly tying materials. Entry is free provided the minimum sponsorship of £20 per person is raised. (Tavistock is £100 minimum)

Anglers who wish to enter please contact the fisheries or Sue Gould, Marketing Manager of Vranch House: Tel Exeter 01392 873543

Provisional Heat Dates:

Stithians	Redruth 01209 821431	Sun 30th March
Kennick Reservoir	Bovey Tracey 01626 206027	Sun 27th April
Bellbrook Valley	Tiverton 01398 351292	Sat 11th May
Temple	Bodmin 01208 821730	Sun 22nd June
Tree Meadow	Hayle 01736 850899	Sun 7th July
Tavistock Trout	Tavistock 01822 615441	Sun 7th Sept
Roadford Lake	Okehampton 01392 873543	Sun TBA

South West Rivers Association in 2008

Roger Furniss - Secretary

SWRA is the voice of riparian owners and game angling in the South West. It is the umbrella of the individual river associations in the South West and a powerful lobbying body regularly consulted by the Environment Agency and Government. Its Council of representatives from every river is supported by a Secretary, Roger Furniss, a former Fisheries Officer and Environmental Protection Manager whose whole career has been in the South West.

As with many aspects of modern life, angling and our freedom to enjoy it are affected by an ever-growing bureaucracy. Our rivers are also subject to pressure from abstraction, pollution and public access By enabling individual rivers to work together to speak with one voice SWRA continues to influence the political and environmental agenda in a number of key areas. Just some of the issues we are engaged in are:-

- **Salmon Stock Assessment** - to manage salmon stocks effectively it is essential to know more about their status, ie adult runs, juvenile production, vulnerable life stages. SWRA is working hard to influence the Environment Agency to adopt the best possible methods to ensure the long-term improvement of our sport.

- **Salmon Stocking Policy** - there are some situations where stocks are so threatened that artificial stocking is necessary to kick start recovery or overcome specific local problems. SWRA actively supports voluntary efforts by individual rivers to carry out scientifically based stocking and to ensure that Agency policies are not too restrictive.

- **National Salmon Strategy** - the Environment Agency is producing a new strategy to replace the1996 version. We are determined that the new strategy aims at abundant stocks rather than the old strategy's targets of only enough to ensure a self-sustaining population. We successfully lobbied for sea trout to be given as much prominence as salmon - for many anglers in the South West they are the major quarry

- **Canoeing** - the British Canoe Union is campaigning for a change in the law to allow unrestricted access to all rivers. Our position is the same as current Government policy, ie voluntary, negotiated access agreements are the way forward. Any change in the law would severely affect angling and riparian property rights.

- **The Threat of Abstraction** - SWRA continues to be very active in protecting our rivers and their fish stocks from over-abstraction. This watchdog role is vital against a background of ever growing demand for water and changing flow patterns as a result of climate change.

- **European Water Framework Directive** - this directive, which requires all rivers to achieve 'Good Ecological Status' by 2015, presents a major opportunity for fisheries interests to make an input into water abstraction, habitat protection and pollution prevention policy. Our Secretary sits on a Panel guiding implementation of the Directive in the South West

If you would like to know more about the work of South West Rivers Association by joining the mailing list for its Newsletter, or wish to become an individual member, please contact the Secretary, Roger Furniss at email@furniss2733.fsnet.co.uk

THE GET HOOKED GUIDE

The Westcountry Rivers Trust

The Westcountry Rivers Trust is an environmental charity, established in 1995 to secure the preservation, protection, development and improvement of the rivers and streams in the Westcountry, and advance the education of the public in the management of water.

The Trust has been instrumental in applying a whole catchment approach to tackling diffuse water quality problems and conserving freshwater habitats in the Westcountry. Previous catchment based projects include the Tamar 2000 SUPPORT Project, Westcountry Rivers Project and more recently the Cornwall Rivers Project.

To date these projects have involved working closely with over 2000 farmers and landowners across nearly 20 Westcountry catchments and have delivered many social, economic and environmental outputs including: over 250 miles of river restored; 16 wetlands restored; 350+ sites of accelerated erosion controlled and 35 demonstration sites developed and operational. These projects have also brought over 95,000ha of land under revised environmentally sensitive management and delivered an average direct economic benefit of approximately £2500 /farm/ year for farmers in receipt of an advisory visit.

Angling 2000 - providing access to wild fishing

As a response to the Trust working with farmers across the Westcountry a considerable undeveloped fishing resource was discovered on some farms. It was apparent that developing this resource would help the Trust's aims of protecting and enhancing the rivers and streams of the Westcountry by adding an economic incentive to improve management.

However, the challenge facing the Trust was to devise a scheme that would be easy to set up and administer, simple for riparian owners to join and would offer anglers of all ages uncomplicated access to reasonably priced fishing.

Following an initial scoping study, the Trust launched an angling marketing and development scheme, called Angling 2000. The scheme is operated on a flexible day token basis meaning that, instead of having to buy a separate ticket for each fishery, anglers can buy a book of tokens which gives them access to any of the participating fisheries when they want and without the need to contact anyone beforehand. Anglers simply buy the tokens, decide which of the fisheries they want to go to, and hey presto – get fishing!

The Trust manages the marketing and advertising of the fisheries and publishes a yearly angling brochure which details the fisheries and everything anglers need to get fishing. The website, www.angling2000.org.uk, hosts details of the fisheries, how and where to buy tokens and various other useful information.

THE GET HOOKED GUIDE

The Token System - a sheer delight for the 'roving' angler...

The scheme has been a massive success and it continues to grow every year with more and more anglers using and enjoying it. Indeed, feedback from anglers on the token system is always very positive and, with increasing pressures on our leisure time, Angling 2000 offers the flexibility to choose when and where to go.

Angling tokens cost £2.50 each and can only be used once. Tokens come in three parts - the first part is posted in a marked letterbox located close to the fishery, at the start of the day's fishing. The second part is a catch return to be posted in the same letterbox at the end of the day's fishing and the final part is the angler's record. The fisheries are rated according to their quality, 'fishability' and species of fish and cost from 2 tokens to 5 tokens a day (£5 to £12.50) making it extremely good value fishing!

Tokens can be bought online form our website at www.angling2000.org.uk, by mail or in person from the Trust Office in Launceston (9am – 5pm) or from a number of registered outlets in Devon and Cornwall. The tokens are supplied as books of either 5 or 10 (£12.50 or £25) and are available for use over a calendar year.

The innovative concept and success of Angling 2000 has been recognised by other Rivers Trusts with the Wye and Usk Foundation (South Wales), the Eden Rivers Trust (Cumbria) and the Tyne Rivers Trust (Northumberland) subsequently developing their own schemes. Angling tokens are interchangeable between regions and this means anglers can now access many miles of wild fishing across the UK using a single token (make sure to pack a book of tokens when next going on holiday).

Sustainable angling development...

One of the most frequently asked questions by those new to the scheme is whether it is sustainable? And the answer is absolutely yes! Year on year we are pleased to see how anglers are aware of the need to protect fish stocks and are actively practicing catch and release (on average 95% of fish are returned which is a tremendous effort). The real beauty of the scheme is that profits go straight back to the fishery owner and the owner, in turn, looks after the river which is the net beneficiary.

Fishing this season...

The streams, rivers and pools of Devon and Cornwall offer a massive variety of fantastic fishing: the rushing moorland spate streams that clear quickly after rain, the languid peaceful lowland streams with their exceptional dry fly fishing for trout, the short streams of Cornwall with their heavy runs of peal and last but not least the secluded, previously forgotten farm lakes with their carp and tench.

For the 2008 season, the scheme has grown to 41 fisheries covering over 50kms of streams and rivers from Truro to Tiverton and we hope this will provide a wealth of watery delights for the game and coarse angler to explore. WRT are also delighted to announce we have teamed up with the South West Lakes Trust and now tokens can be redeemed against a day's fishing at the following trout fisheries; Kennick, Wimbleball, Siblyback, Stithians, Wistlandpound, Roadford, Colliford and Fernworthy. Whether you enjoy bank or boat fishing, are a novice or seasoned angler, prefer stocked or wild fisheries, these lakes provide fantastic sport in some of the regions most beautiful surroundings.

The Trust works hard on many fronts to achieve its vision of having living, working landscapes that deliver employment, food and amenity without impacting on rivers and biodiversity and without the need for heavy regulation and supervision. The Trust can, however, only operate with the help of its supporters and the Trust's work is only relevant if it represents the needs and aspirations of its supporters. With this in mind we will be communicating with you as regularly as we can about our work and if you would like to receive our e-newsletter please email: newsletter@wrt.org.uk. We hope that in turn you will guide us to address your concerns and that you will direct others with similar concerns to our door so that they can become supporters and help the Trust in pursuit of its vision.

Please visit our website for news and information:
www.wrt.org.uk

Contact details for the Trust:
Dr Dylan Bright CBiol MIBiol - Director
Westcountry Rivers Trust
10, Exeter Street
Launceston
Cornwall PL15 9EQ
Tel: + 44 (0) 870 774 06 91
dylan@wrt.org.uk

Contact details for Angling 2000:
www.angling2000.org.uk
Toby Russell CEnv MIFM
Westcountry Rivers Trust
10, Exeter Street
Launceston
Cornwall PL15 9EQ
Tel: + 44 (0) 870 774 06 96
toby@wrt.org.uk

DEVON

DEVON

Devon Game Road Directions

30. Angling 2000 (Game & Coarse)
41 beats on the Tamar, Taw, Torridge, Fal, Tresillian & Camel catchments plus 2 lakes. Tel: 0870 77 40704.

31. Arundell Arms Hotel
Leave the A30 Dual Carriageway east of Launceston and follow signs for Lifton. The Arundell Arms is in the centre of the Village. Tel: 01566 784666.

32. Avon Dam
Walk the lane from Shipley Bridge Car Park.
Tel: 01822 855700.

33. Bellbrook Valley Trout Fishery
From Tiverton roundabout on A361 head towards Barnstaple. Take 3rd right (6 miles) signposted Bellbrook & Spurway. Continue down lane for 2 miles then sharp right signed "To the fishery" then 200yds on the right. From Oakford leave uphill, bear left at Pinkworthy Post (signposted Rackenford). Follow lane down hill, cross stream then fork left. Fishery 200yds on right. Tel: 01398 351292.

34. Blakewell Fishery
Take A39 from Barnstaple towards Lynton. 1.5 miles from Barnstaple turn left on to B3230 and follow signs to the fishery. Tel: 01271 344533.

35. Buckfastleigh River Fishing
Tel: 01566 771930.

36. Burrator
Turn south off B3212 at Dousland by the Burrator Inn.
Tel: 01579 384649.

37. Clinton Arms
Take the Bideford to Torrington road (A386) and approx. 5.5 miles from Bideford there is a sign to Tarka Trail. Turn left and park outside the Puffing Billy. (Car park is council owned and free). Fishing is to the right, (with Puffing Billy behind you.) Maps available at the Clinton Arms. Tel: 01805 623279.

38. Environment Agency Fisheries
Watersmeet & Glenthorne Fisheries. Directions are supplied with permits.

39. Fernworthy
Signed from Chagford. Tel: 01647 277587.

40. Fosfelle Country Manor
(Game & Coarse) Please Tel: 01237 441273 for directions.

41. Half Moon Hotel
Sheepwash lies 1 mile North of Highampton (A3072) between Hatherleigh & Holsworthy. Tel: 01409 231376.

42. Highampton Trout & Coarse Lakes (Coarse & Game)
We are approx. 1.5 miles south of the village of Highampton heading for Northlew. Tel: 01409 231216.

Remember a ♿ means the fishery has disabled facilities - contact them direct for further details

43. Hotel Endsleigh
From the M5 turn off at junction 31 and follow the A30 to the second Launceston turn off (towards Callington) A388 turn at the B3362 towards Tavistock. Drive through the village of Milton Abbot, turn right for Endsleigh then right again at the lodge at the top of driveway of hotel. Tel: 01822 870000 for directions.

44. Kennick
East off the A382 at the Slade Cross. Tel: 01647 277587.

45. Meldon
Signed from the A30 at the juction west of Okehampton. Tel: 01409 211507.

46. Newhouse Fishery
From Totnes take A381 south towards Kingsbridge. After 5 miles turn right to Moreleigh on the B3207. After 2 miles turn right down the lane signposted Newhouse Farm Fishery. Tel: 01548 821426.

47. Old Mill House
Please Tel: 01598 763514.

48. Roadford
Signed of the A30 at Stowford Cross. Tel: 01409 211514.

49. Robert Jones Fly Fishing
Please Tel: 070 20 90 20 90.

50. Southwood Fishery
Please Tel: 01271 343608 or 07767 492800 for directions.

51. The Devil's Stone Inn
From Okehampton, turn opposite the White Hart and follow the A386 towards Hatherleigh. At the roundabout outside Hatherleigh take the Holsworthy road and follow this to the village of Highampton. Just beyond Highampton turn right and follow signs to Shebbear. We are the only pub in the village. Tel: 01409 281210.

52. The Sea Trout Inn
Please Tel: 01803 762274 for directions.

53. The Stag Hunters Hotel
From Bridgwater take A39 to Minehead and Porlock. Approx. 8 miles past Porlock turn left off A39 signposted Brendon.Tel: 01598 741222.

54. Upper Yealm Fishery
Please contact Snowbee. Tel: 01752 334933.

55. Venford
Between Holne and Hexworthy. Tel: 01566 771930.

56. Wistlandpound
Signed off the A39 at Blackmoor Gate. Tel: 01598 763719.

Devon Coarse Road Directions

57. Anglers Paradise

From M5 take A30 to Okehampton. Through Okehampton, up hill, turn right to Bude / Holsworthy, straight on to Halwill junction, turn right at mini roundabout, half mile right turn to Anglers Paradise (sign up in hedge). Tel: 01409 221559.

58. Bakers Farm

Please Tel: 01805 623260 for directions.

59. Bickerton Farm Fishery

Please Tel: 01548 511220 for road directions.

60. Braddon Cottages

From M5 take A30 Dual Carriageway, exit at J31 signposted Okehampton/Bodmin, to Stowford interchange (34 miles). Turn right to Roadford Lake. Cross dam, after 4 miles turn left at T junction (Ivyhouse Cross) then right (Reservoir Cross). Over stone bridge at Ashmill, bearing right up steep hill signposted Holsworthy. After 2 miles turn right into concrete road signposted Braddon and East Venn. Bear left at fork. Continue past Braddon Cottage, crossing the cattle grid marked Braddon. Go to the Byre for your key. Tel: 01409 211350.

61. Bussells Farm

From the M5 leave the motorway at junction 27 for Tiverton following the A361. At Tiverton take the A396 signposted to Bickleigh. Go through Bickleigh and on to Stoke Canon. Go left at the church signposted to Huxham. When you reach the Barton Cross restaurant take the next left turn (50 yds) signposted to Columbjohn. Follow this narrow road for 0.25 mile and Bussells will be found on your left. Tel: 01392 841238.

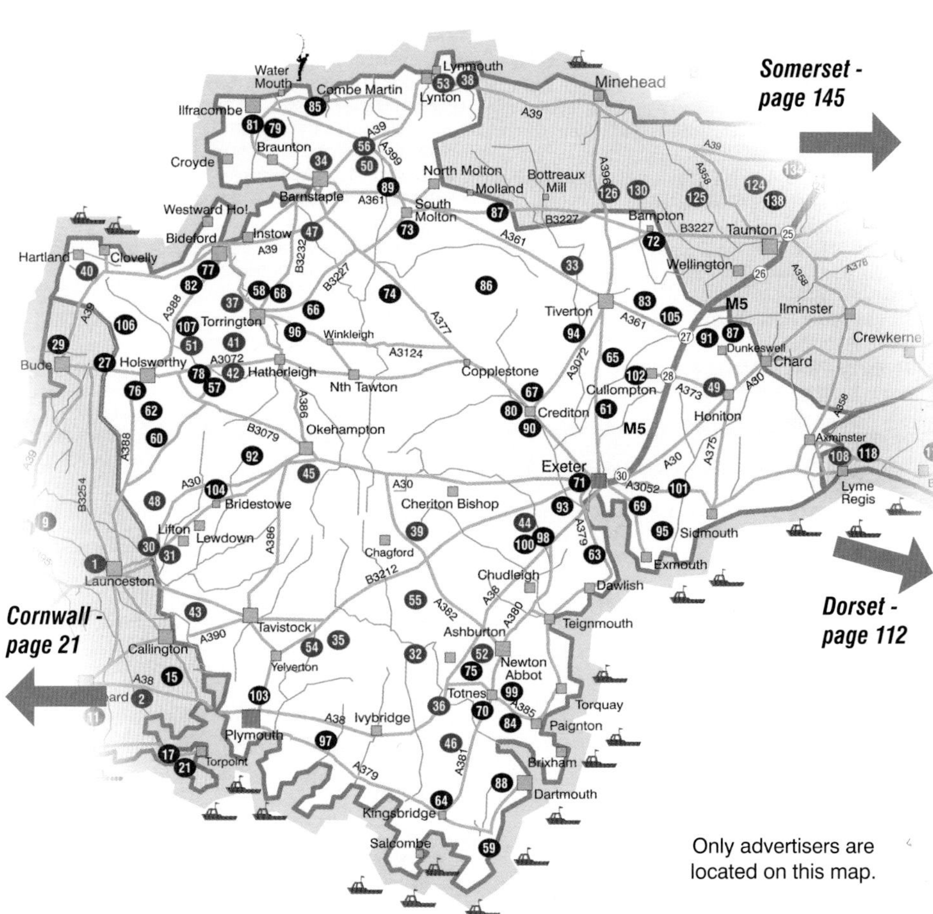

62. Clawford Vineyard

Take A388 from Holsworthy to Launceston. Turn left at crossroads in Clawton. After 2.5 miles turn left at T junction. Clawford is a further 0.6 miles on left. Tel: 01409 254177 or 07786 332332.

63. Cofton Country Holidays

From Junction 30, M5 Exeter, take A379 signed Dawlish. Park is on the left 0.5 mile after small harbour village of Cockwood. Tel: 0800 085 8649 or 01626 89011.

64. Coombe Water Fisheries

0.5 mile from Kingsbridge on the B3210 road to Loddiswell. Tel: 01548 852038 or 07971 077980 for directions.

65. Coombelands Coarse Fishery

Only 15 minutes from M5 junction 28 Cullompton, 2.5 miles from town centre; turn right by HSBC bank (signed Tiverton). 0.5 mile turn left onto the Knowle road, next left, then right. Higher Coombelands is the last property on the left before Bunniford Cross; or 1 mile from Butterleigh on the Bradninch road; 3.5 miles from Tiverton and Silverton. Tel: 01884 32320.

66. Cranford Inn & Holiday Cottages

Please Tel: 01805 624697 for directions.

67. Creedy Lakes

Travelling south down the M5 exit at junction 27. From Tiverton take the A3072 Exeter/Crediton road. At Bickleigh bear right towards Crediton. At Crediton town sign turn right. Follow blue and white fishery signs. Tel: 01363 772684.

68. Darracott

Approximately 2 miles north of Great Torrington. Details available from Ticket Agents. Tel: 01288 321262.

69. Darts Farm

Leave M5 at junction 30. Follow signs to Exmouth (A376). After 2 miles follow brown tourist signs to Darts Farm Shopping Village. Tel: 01392 878209.

70. East Moore Farm Fishery

Please Tel: 078558 92879.

71. Exeter & District Angling Association

Please Tel: 01392 677744. Mobile: 07970 483913 or enquire in local Tackle Shops.

72. Four Ponds

From Bampton take B3227 towards Taunton, after 1.8 miles you will enter village of Shillingford, take last lane on left, Bowdens lane, pass childrens park and lower Bowdens Farm on right, pass Four Ponds bungalow on right and fishing car park is on left, next to stables. Please Tel: 01398 331169 for directions.

73. Furzebray Carp Lakes

Furzebray Lakes are located in South Molton, North Devon,which is about 30 minutes from the M5 motorway via the A361 North Devon Link Road. Once in South Molton, take the B3226 travel South West. Then take the second left opposite Horse Pond Meadow Ind Est, signposted Kings Nympton & George Nympton, travel 500yds, the lakes are on right by the last bungalow. Go down the lane and follow the signs for Lakes and car parking. Please Tel: 07792 510305 for directions.

74. Golland Farm

Please Tel: 01769 520550.

75. Hatchland Fisheries (Coarse & Game)

Between Exeter & Plymouth. A38 turn off at 'Marley Head' junction (South Brent) A385, South Brent to Dartington Road about 500 yards on that road on right. Tel: 01364 73500 for directions.

76. Higher Shorston Coarse Fishing Lakes

After leaving Holsworthy take the A388 for Launceston. After 3/4 mile at Whimble Cross turn left into Staddon Road. Fishing is 500 yards on the left. Please Tel: 01409 253657.

77. Jennetts

Signed off A386 near Bideford. Tel: 01288 321262.

78. Kingslake Fishing Holidays

From Exeter at end of M5 take A30 to Okehampton, in the centre of Okehampton at the lights, turn right onto A386 to Hatherleigh. At Hatherleigh (7 miles) take left onto A3072 Holsworthy/Bude. Travel 7 miles then turn left at sign 'Chilla 2 miles' Kingslake is 0.75 mile along this road on left. Tel: 01409 231401.

79. Lower Aylescott

From J27 M5 follow A361 for Barnstaple, shortly after South Molton take A399 to Ilfracombe. After Blackmoor Gate look for the A3123 where A399 heads to Ilfracombe. Turn left onto A3123, through Berry Down Cross and on towards Mullacott Cross. After A3123 crosses B3230 look out for left turn to West Down. On arriving in village centre take left hand road at crossroads, past church, down hill to Aylescott. Continue to a sharp right hand bend heading down to Lower Aylescott. Fishery entrance is clearly signed on the left. Tel: 01271 864054.

80. Lower Hollacombe Fishery

Please Tel: 01363 84331 for directions.

81. Lower Slade

From Ilfracombe drive through Slade village. Slade Reservoir 0.5 mile on the left. Tel: 01288 321262.

82. Melbury

Between Prowlers Piece and Parkham. Tel: 01288 321262.

83. Minnows Touring Caravan Park

From the North or South exit M5 at junction 27 onto A361 signposted Tiverton. After about 600 yards take first exit signposted Sampford Peverell. Turn right at roundabout, cross bridge over A361. Straight across at next roundabout signposted Holcombe Rogus. Site is on left. From N. Devon on the A361 go to end of A361 to junction 27 of the M5. Go all the way round and return back onto the A361. Then follow the above directions. Tel: 01884 821770.

84. New Barn Angling Centre

From Paignton bypass traffic lights, take the A385 to Totnes/ Plymouth. Turn left after 2 miles into farm track signposted New Barn Angling Centre. From Totnes take the A385 to Paignton, turn right 200 yards past the Texaco garage into farm track signposted New Barn Angling Centre.Tel: 01803 553602.

85. Newberry Valley

On A399 western edge of Combe Martin, heading from the seaside end of village towards Ilfracome. Tel: 01271 882334.

Remember a ♿ means the fishery has disabled facilities - contact them direct for further details

86. Newhouse Farm Cottages
Exit M5 at J27. Take A361 North Devon Link Road towards Tiverton/Barnstaple. Leave A361 Dual Carriageway turning left at roundabout following signs to Witheridge and B3137. At second roundabout turn right (Kennedy Way) passing Morrison's on your left (straight across that roundabout). Turn right at next roundabout. Look for sign B3137 Witheridge Road, second turning left. Continue through Witheridge, turn right after church, down hill, cross river. Newhouse Farm second entrance on left. Tel: 01884 860266.

87. Oaktree Carp Farm & Fishery
From Barnstaple take the A361 to Newtown. Left onto B3227 Bampton Road for 2.5 miles and left at fishery signpost. Down hill and entrance signposted on right. From M5 junction 27 take A361 to Newtown, then as above. Tel: 01398 341568.

88. Old Mill
Tel: 01647 277587.

89. Riverton House & Lakes
From M5 junction 27 take the A361 to Barnstaple. After 25 miles you will come to only the third roundabout since leaving the Motorway. It has The Northgate Inn next to it. Keep on the A361 for 2 more miles then, turn first right to West Buckland. First junction (250 metres) turn left, signposted to Riverton. Tel: 01271 830009.

90. Salmonhutch Fishery
A377 to Crediton, turn left after Shell Garage, follow road signed Tedburn St Mary for 1.5 miles, right at junction marked Uton, follow fishery signs. Tel: 01363 772749.

91. South Farm Holiday Cottages & Fishery
Between the villages of Blackborough & Sheldon. Tel: 01823 681078.

92. South Reed Farm Holidays
Please Tel: 01837 871258 for directions.

93. South View Farm Fishery
From Bristol follow M5 onto A38. After 1.5 miles turn off into Kennford. Continue through village following Dunchideock signs until Shillingford signs are seen. Follow Shillingford signs. Entrance to fishery on left at sharp bend before village. From Plymouth turn left off A38 following Dunchideock until sign for Clapham is seen on right heading down the hill. At Clapham follow signs for Shillingford. From Exeter follow signs to Alphington then Shillingford St. George. Fishery on right after village. Tel: 01392 833694.

94. South West Lakes Angling Association
Please Tel: 01884 256721.

95. Squabmoor
Off B3179 between Knowle and Woodbury. Tel: 01566 771930.

96. Stafford Moor Country Park
Clearly signposted on the A3124, 3 miles North of Winkleigh, 9 miles South of Torrington. Tel: 01805 804360.

97. Sunridge Fishery
Travelling west on A38, just after South Brent take slip road for Ugborough & Ermington, turn left, travel 2 miles to crossroads, turn right onto B3210, continue 3 miles to T junction, turn right onto A379 towards Plymouth, continue 2 miles to second crossroads (just before garage) and turn right. Travel 1 mile and you will find Sunridge Nurseries on left. Lodge and lake situated within grounds. Tel: 01752 880438.

98. Tottiford
East off the A382 at Slade Cross. Tel: 01647 277587.

99. Town Parks Coarse Fishing Centre
From Paignton take A385 towards Totnes. Look for signs to Town Parks, approx. 2.5 miles on the right. Tel: 01803 523133.

100. Trenchford
East off the A382 at Slades Cross. Tel: 01647 277587.

101. Upham Farm Carp Ponds
From J30 on M5, take A3052 signposted Sidmouth. After approx. 4 miles, after passing White Horse Inn on right, sign to fishery will be seen on left. Turn left and after 700 yds fishery will be found on left hand side. Tel: 01395 232247.

102. Upton Lakes Fishing Holidays
From Junction 28 of the M5 head towards Cullompton, then turn left towards Broadclyst, follow the main street, through the town and take left turning (Meadow lane) signposted Sports centre. Next T junction turn right and cross over the motorway bridge. Take next left signposted Upton Lakes, take first left along lane. Tel: 07830 199690.

103. Warleigh Barton Fishery
Please Tel: 07811 339569 for directions.

104. Week Farm
From Exeter bypass Okehampton, leave A30 dual carriageway at Sourton junction. At end of sliproad cross A386 at staggered crossroad (signposted Bridestowe). Week signpost on right after 1.5 miles (bottom of hill left 0.5 mile). Or, from Bridestowe village turn right towards Okehampton, pass garage on left & take next left, Week is 0.75 mile. Tel: 01837 861221.

105. West Pitt Farm Fishery
Junction 27 off M5, take Barnstaple signed dual way, almost immediately exit signed to Sampford Peverell. Right at mini roundabout, straight over second roundabout. Turn left signed to Whitnage, next right, then at Pitt Crossroads turn left. Fishery is a few 100 yds on left. Tel: 01884 820296.

106. Wooda Lakes Holiday Homes
From M5 turn onto A30 towards Okehampton. After about 25 miles take turning for Holsworthy. On reaching Holsworthy turn right at Bude Road Garage signposted Chilsworthy. Follow road for about 4 miles then turn left at Youlden Moor crossroads. After 1.5 miles Wooda Lakes will be straight in front of you. Tel: 01409 241934.

107. Woodacott Holiday Park
Proceed north off the A3072 at Anvil Corner, turn right at Blagdon Moor Cross or proceed south off the A388 at Holsworthy Beacon, turn left at Blagdon Moor Cross. After approx. 1.5 miles turn sharp left at Woodacott Cross, Woodacott Arms immediately right. Tel: 01409 261162.

www.gethooked.co.uk
Check out our Web Site!
Get HOOKED!
ON THE WEB

Devon River Fishing

AVON

South Devon stream not to be confused with Hampshire Avon or Bristol Avon. Rises on Dartmoor and enters the sea at Bigbury. Expect to catch Brown Trout, Sea Trout and Salmon.

Avon Fishing Association
Contact: Mr M Pickup, Grey Wethers, Vineyard, Dartington, Totnes, *Tel:* 01803 867460, *Water:* River Avon *Species:* Salmon 11lb, Sea Trout 7lb 12oz and Brown Trout to 13 inches. *Permits:* Weekly, fortnightly and monthly tickets from Loddiswell Post Offices. *Charges:* £57 weekly, £73 fortnightly, £90 monthly. *Season:* Brown Trout 15th March to 30th September. Salmon and Sea Trout 15th April to 30th September. *Methods:* Fly only.

Newhouse Fishery (River Avon)
Contact: Paul Cook & Kirsty Cook, Newhouse Farm, Moreleigh, Totnes, *Tel:* 01548 821332, *Mobile:* 07803 128777, *Water:* 0.25 mile on the River Avon (also see entry under Stillwater Trout, Totnes, Devon). *Species:* Brown Trout, Sea Trout and Salmon. *Permits:* On site. *Charges:* Various tickets available. *Season:* As current E.A. Byelaws. *Methods:* As current E.A. Byelaws.

AXE AND TRIBUTARIES

This quiet meandering stream rises in the hills of west Dorset, runs along the boundary with Somerset before flowing past Axminster to the sea at Seaton. The Axe is a fertile river with good Trout fishing and a run of Salmon and Sea Trout. The two main tributaries, the Coly and Yarty, are also Trout streams and the Yarty has a good run of Sea Trout.

Axmouth Fishing
Contact: Chris Chappell, Seaton Tackle Shop, The Harbour, Axmouth, *Tel:* 01297 625511, *Mobile:* 07930 398313, *Water:* Axmouth from lower end pool below Coly-Axe confluence to Axmouth Bridge. *Species:* Mullet, Bass, Sea Trout. *Permits:* Seaton Tackle Shop. *Charges:* Day ticket £5 adult, £2.50 child. Week ticket £25 adult, £12.50 child. *Methods:* Fishing from east bank of estuary only.

Stillwaters (River Axe)
Contact: Michael Ford, Lower Moorhayne Farm, Yarcombe, Honiton, *Tel:* 01404 861284, *Water:* One Sea Trout rod on River Axe. Approx. one mile including sea pool. Also 1 acre lake, see entry under Stillwater Trout, Honiton.

Willows
Contact: Mark & Aneita Regan, Weycroft Mill, Axminster, *Tel:* 01297 34565, *Mobile:* 07912 567209, *Water:* 100 yards on the River Axe (max 2 people per day). *Species:* Sea Trout and Salmon. *Permits:* Only from above address. *Charges:* £15 per day per person. *Season:* 15 March to 31 October. *Methods:* Fly and spinner.

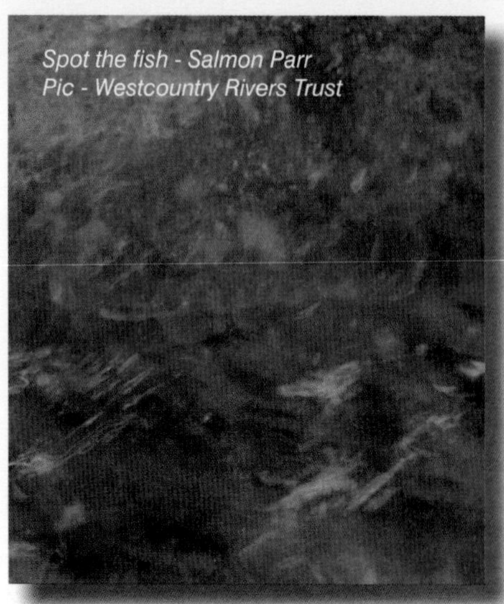

Spot the fish - Salmon Parr
Pic - Westcountry Rivers Trust

BRAY

One of the larger tributaries of the river Taw rising on Exmoor, the Bray offers good wild Trout fishing along with Salmon and Sea Trout fishing.

Little Bray House
Contact: Mr and Mrs C. Hartnoll, Little Bray House, Brayford, Barnstaple, *Tel:* 01598 710295, *Water:* One mile on the River Bray. *Species:* Small Brown Trout. *Permits:* From South Molton Tourist Information. *Charges:* £3 per day. *Methods:* Fly only.

CLAW

This is a small tributary of the Upper Tamar River and has good Brown Trout fishing.

Tetcott Angling Club (Claw)
Contact: Mrs Nicola Mitchell, 2 Harkaway Cottage, Tetcott, Holsworthy, *Tel:* 01409 271381, *Mobile:* 07787 335566, *Water:* Approx. half a mile of the River Claw. *Species:* Brown Trout. *Permits:* No day tickets - private club. *Season:* 16th March to 30th September. Daylight hours only. *Methods:* Artificial lures, fly, spinning, worm.

COLY

A tributary of the river Axe, the Coly offers good Brown Trout and Sea Trout fishing set in the unspoilt rolling countryside of East Devon.

Higher Cownhayne Farm
Contact: Graham Pady, Higher Cownhayne Farm, Cownhayne Lane, Colyton, *Tel:* 01297 553040, *Water:* Fishing on River Coly. *Species:* Brown & Sea Trout. *Charges:* On application. *Methods:* Fly fishing, no netting.

CULM

The Culm is a tributary of the river Exe and issues from the Blackdown Hills. In its upper reaches it is a typical dry fly Trout stream, with good hatches of fly and free-rising fish. From Cullompton until it joins the Exe, the Culm becomes a coarse fishery, with the Dace in particular of good average size.

Angling 2000 (Culm)
Contact: Westcountry Rivers Trust, 10 Exeter Street, Launceston, Cornwall. *Tel:* 0870 774 0704, *Water:* 1900m double bank. *Species:* Trout, Chub, Dace, Roach and Pike. *Permits:* From the above. *Charges:* £5 to £7.50 per day. *Season:* Trout - 1st April to 30th September. Coarse - 16th June to 31st December. *Methods:* No dogs. Any method. No more than two Trout to be retained per day. All Salmon to be returned.

DART AND TRIBUTARIES

Deep in the heart of lonely Dartmoor rise the East and West Dart. Between their separate sources and Dartmeet, where they join, these two streams and their tributaries are mainly owned by the Duchy of Cornwall and provide many miles of Salmon, Sea Trout and Trout fishing for visitors. The scenery is on the grand scale and the sense of freedom enjoyed when you can fish away over miles and miles of river is seldom realised on this crowded island. This is a moorland fishery - swift flowing, boulder strewn, usually crystal clear.
Below Dartmeet the river rushes through a spectacular wooded valley before breaking out of the moor near Buckfastleigh and flowing on to its estuary at Totnes. Although there are Brown Trout throughout the river, these middle and lower reaches are primarily Salmon and Sea Trout waters.

Buckfastleigh
Contact: South West Lakes Trust, Lidn Park, Quarry Crescent, Pennygillam, Launceston, Cornwall. *Tel:* 01566 771930, *Water:* 0.25 miles on River Dart. Austins Bridge to Nursery Pool. *Species:* Salmon & Sea Trout. *Permits:* Summerlands Tackle (01237 471291). *Charges:* Season - £90.

Dart Angling Association
Contact: Philip Prowse, 2 School Cottages, Stoke-in-Teignhead, Newton Abbot, *Tel:* 01626 872434, *Water:* 9 miles on River Dart. (3.9 miles of main river open to visitors plus the tidal Totnes weir pool). *Species:* Salmon, Sea Trout, Brown Trout. *Permits:* All permits - Sea Trout Inn, Staverton Tel: 01803 762274. *Charges:* Membership details from secretary. Totnes weir pool £25 per day (only 1 day Salmon, 1 night Sea Trout ticket available). Buckfast (Austin's Bridge) - Littlehempston (left bank) only 2 per day (unless resident at the Sea Trout Inn). *Season:* Salmon 1st February - 30th September. Sea/Brown Trout 15th March - 30th September. *Methods:* Fly (some stretches fly only), spinning, prawn (below Staverton) see club regulations i.e. conservation measures in force.

Duchy Of Cornwall
Contact: Duchy Of Cornwall Office, Duchy Hotel, Princetown, Yelverton, *Tel:* 01822 890205, *Water:* East & West Dart Rivers and its tributaries down to Dartmeet. *Species:* Salmon and Trout. *Permits:* Buckfast Post Office, Buckfast Road, Buckfast. Holne Chase Hotel, Ashburton. Two Bridges Hotel, Two Bridges, Princetown, Yelverton. The Post Office, Postbridge, Yelverton. Princetown Post Office, Princetown, Yelverton. Prince Hall Hotel, Two Bridges, Princetown, Yelverton. The Arundell Arms, Lifton. James Bowden & Sons, The Square, Chagford. Badger's Holt Ltd., Dartmeet, Princetown. Exeter Angling Centre, Smythen Street, Exeter. The Forest Inn Hexworthy, Princetown, Yelverton. Peter Collings, Huccaby's News, 33 Fore St., Buckfastleigh. *Charges:* Salmon Season: £145, Week £80, Day £25. Trout Season: £65, Week £20, Day £7. *Season:* Salmon: 1st February to 30th September. Trout: 15th March to 30th September. *Methods:* Fly only. Additional information on permit.

Hatchlands Trout Farm
Contact: Malcolm Davies, Greyshoot Lane, Rattery, South Brent, *Tel:* 01364 73500, *Water:* 600 yards, both banks of the River Harbourne (tributary of the Dart). *Species:* Brown Trout. *Permits:* EA Licence required. *Charges:* On application. *Season:* See current E.A. Byelaws. *Methods:* Barbless hooks only.

Prince Hall Hotel
Contact: Ci & Chris Daly, Nr. Two Bridges, Dartmoor, *Tel:* 01822 890403, *Water:* Access to all Duchy water. *Species:* Wild Brown Trout 1.5lb, Sea Trout 6lb, Salmon 11lb. *Permits:* EA Licences available locally. *Charges:* Brown Trout Duchy day ticket £7. Brown Trout week Duchy £20. Salmon/Sea Trout day ticket Duchy £25. Salmon/Sea Trout week, Duchy £80. Prices may change in 2008. *Season:* March - September for Salmon and Sea Trout. March - October for Brown Trout. *Methods:* Fly only.

The Forest Inn
Contact: James Glenister, Hexworthy, Dartmoor, *Tel:* 01364 631211, *Water:* East and West Dart. *Species:* Sea Trout, Brown Trout, Salmon. *Permits:* Day, Week, Season. *Charges:* Not yet known. *Season:* 30th March - 30th September *Methods:* Fly only.

Two Bridges Hotel
Contact: Two Bridges Hotel, Two Bridges, Dartmoor, *Tel:* 01822 890581, *Water:* Stretch of 600yds double bank fishing. *Species:* Trout & Salmon. *Permits:* At hotel reception. *Charges:* See Duchy permit. *Season:* E.A. Byelaws apply.

DEER

This is a small tributary of the Upper Tamar River and has good Brown Trout fishing.

Tetcott Angling Club (Deer)
Contact: Mrs Nicola Mitchell, 2 Harkaway Cottage, Tetcott, Holsworthy, *Tel:* 01409 271381, *Mobile:* 07787 335566, *Water:* Approx. one mile of the River Deer. *Species:* Brown Trout. *Permits:* No day tickets - private club. *Season:* 16th March to 30th September. Daylight hours only. *Methods:* Artificial lures, fly, spinning, worm.

EAST LYN

see Lyn description

Southernwood Farm
Contact: C.M. Boyd, Brendon, Lynton, *Tel:* 01598 741174, *Mobile:* 07961 461340, *Water:* Half a mile on the East Lyn. *Species:* 14lb Salmon in 2004. (not fished 2005). 8lb Salmon, 3lb Sea Trout and 2.5lb Sea Trout all caught on 1 rod in 3 days in 2006. 18lb Salmon landed in 2007. *Permits:* Relevant EA rod licence required. *Charges:* £15 per day. £35 per week (5 days) *Season:* March 1 to end September. *Methods:* Worming allowed. Barbless hooks. Fly fishing.

ERME

A small Devon stream rising on Dartmoor and flowing south through Ivybridge to the sea. The Erme is probably best known for its Sea Trout, but there is also a run of Salmon and Brown Trout are present throughout its length.

EXE AND TRIBUTARIES

The Exe rises high on Exmoor and flows through open moorland until it plunges into a steep wooded valley near Winsford. By the time Tiverton is reached the valley has widened and from here to the sea the Exe meanders through a broad pastoral vale until it flows into the estuary near Exeter and finally into the sea between Exmouth and Dawlish Warren. It is the longest river in the south west. Throughout most of its length the Exe is a good Trout stream, the fast flowing, rocky upper reaches abounding in fish of modest average size, which increases as the river becomes larger and slower in its middle and lower reaches, where fish approaching a pound feature regularly in the daily catch. The Exe has a good run of Salmon and can produce big catches when the grilse arrive in summer. In the deep slow waters around Exeter there is a variety of coarse fish, as there is in the Exeter Ship Canal which parallels the river from Exeter to the estuary at Topsham. The Exe only has a small run of Sea Trout, but Grayling are plentiful in the middle and lower reaches. The two main tributaries - the Barle and the Culm - could not be more different in character. The Barle is a swift upland stream which rises high on Exmoor not far from the source of the Exe, and runs a parallel course, first through open moor and then through a picturesque wooded valley, before joining the parent river near Dulverton. It has good Trout fishing throughout and Salmon fishing on the lower reaches.
The Culm issues from the Blackdown Hills and in its upper reaches is a typical dry fly Trout stream, with good hatches of fly and free-rising fish. From Cullompton until it joins the Exe, the Culm becomes a coarse fishery, with the Dace in particular of good average size.

Bridge House Hotel
Contact: Brian Smith, Bridge House Hotel, Bampton, *Tel:* 01398 331298, *Water:* 1 Mile on River Exe. 0.75 mile on Little Exe. 0.5 mile on Batherm. *Species:* Salmon, Trout and Grayling; (2006 Season: 12.5lb Salmon, 3.75lb Brown Trout 1.5lb Grayling). *Permits:* As above. *Charges:* Salmon from £25 per day, Trout £15 per day. *Season:* March 15th - Sept 30th. *Methods:* Fly, occasional spinner. Barbless until 16th June (Salmon). No Keepnets. Brown Trout catch and release under 1lb or 10 inches Barbless.

Exe Duck's Marsh (River Exe)
Contact: Exeter City Council, River & Canal Manager, Civic Centre, Exeter, *Tel:* 01392 274306, *Water:* River Exe, left bank 1 mile downstream Salmonpool weir. *Species:* Salmon (Trout). *Permits:* River & Canal Office, Canal Basin, Haven Rd, Exeter. Angling Centre, Smythen Street, Exeter. Civic Centre, Paris Street, Exeter. *Charges:* Day tickets only at £7. *Season:* 14th February - 30th September; no night fishing. *Methods:* Permit restrictions & E.A. byelaw controls; only artificial fly & lures and all fish returned before June 16th.

Exeter & District Angling Association (River Creedy)
Contact: Terry Reed (Hon. Sec.), PO Box 194, Exeter, *Mobile:* 07970 483913, *Water:* Cowley Bridge; just a short walk from the Exe. *Species:* Roach, Dace, Gudgeon, Carp, Pike. *Permits:* Exeter Angling Centre, Smythen Street (Off Market Street, Exeter). Bridge Cafe, Bridge Road, Exeter. Exmouth Tackle & Sport, The Strand, Exmouth. Tackle Trader, Wharf Road, Newton Abbot. Exe Valley Angling, West Exe South, Tiverton. Saunders Pet Supplies, Fore Street, Cullompton. Tiverton Parkway Station (Cafe), Sampford Peverell. *Charges:* £34 Adults, £4 for Juniors (annual). £5 day. *Season:* Close season March 14th - June 16th. Details in association handbook or from agents. *Methods:* Stick/waggler with maggot, light groundbaiting. Details in association handbook.

Exeter & District Angling Association (River Culm)
Contact: Terry Reed (Hon. Sec.), PO Box 194, Exeter, *Mobile:* 07970 483913, *Water:* Paddleford Pool, Killerton and Beare Gate; Smaller faster flowing river. *Species:* Superb catches of Chub, Roach and Dace possible throughout. An excellent, yet relatively easy Pike water. Barbel now showing throughout. *Permits:* Exeter Angling Centre, Smythen Street (Off Market Street, Exeter). Bridge Cafe, Bridge Road, Exeter. Exmouth Tackle & Sport, The Strand, Exmouth. Tackle Trader, Wharf Road, Newton Abbot. Exe Valley Angling, West Exe South, Tiverton. Saunders Pet Supplies, Fore Street, Cullompton. Tiverton Parkway Station (Cafe), Sampford Peverell. *Charges:* £34 Adults, £4 for Juniors (annual). £5 day. *Season:* Close Season March 14th - June 16th. Details in association handbook or from agents. *Methods:* Different restrictions on each water. Details in association handbook.

Exeter & District Angling Association (River Exe)
Contact: Terry Reed (Hon. Sec.), PO Box 194, Exeter, *Mobile:* 07970 483913, *Water:* Tidal stretch of Exe at Countess Wear; big catches of Mullet, Dace and Bream upstream. Non tidal stretch at Weirfield; big bags of Bream and Carp from 15 to 20lb. Shillhay runs nearly through the City centre; can produce big bags of Bream and Roach. Exwick is a faster flowing section adjacent to St David's railway section; good nets of quality Roach and Dace, fishes well in the autumn. Cowley Bridge is a relatively under fished stretch; good nets of Roach and Dace along the whole length. Oakhay Barton; fewer fish but good size and high quality fish. *Species:* Roach, Dace, Bream, Chub, Perch, Carp, Mullet. *Permits:* Exeter Angling Centre, Smythen Street (Off Market Street, Exeter). Bridge Cafe, Bridge Road, Exeter. Exmouth Tackle & Sport, The Strand, Exmouth. Tackle Trader, Wharf Road, Newton Abbot. Exe Valley Angling, West Exe South, Tiverton. Saunders Pet Supplies, Fore Street, Cullompton. Tiverton Parkway Station (Cafe), Sampford Peverell. *Charges:* £34 Adults, £4 for Juniors (annual). £5 day. *Season:* Close Season March 14th - June 16th. Details in association handbook or from agents. *Methods:* Feeder or waggler/stick float, over heavy groundbaiting. Details in association handbook.

Hatswell - Tiverton
Contact: Clive Edwards, West Tosberry Farm, Hartland, Bideford, *Tel:* 01237 441476, *Water:* Half mile of River Exe. *Species:* Salmon, Brown Trout and Grayling. *Season:* Occasional day tickets available (No Sundays). *Methods:* Fly and barbless hooks.

River Exe (Exeter)
Contact: Exeter City Council, River & Canal Manager, Civic Centre, Exeter, *Tel:* 01392 274306, *Water:* River Exe, 13 beats between Head Weir & Countess Wear. *Species:* Salmon (Trout). *Permits:* Annual, available by post with payment and photograph to Exeter City Council, Civic Centre, Exeter. EX1 1RQ. *Charges:* £65.30, limited annual permits. *Season:* 14th Febuary - 30th September. *Methods:* Permit restrictions and E.A. Byelaws apply. Only artificial fly & lures. All fish returned before June 16th.

Robert Jones Fly Fishing (Exe)
Contact: Valley Barn, Hawkerland, Colaton Raleigh, Sidmouth, *Tel:* 07020 902090, *Mobile:* 07970 797770, *Water:* River Exe. Private and Hotel water. *Species:* Brown Trout and Salmon. *Permits:* Day permits. E.A. Beginners Licence agent. *Charges:* On application *Season:* 15th March - 30th September. *Methods:* Fly and spinner.

Tiverton & District Angling Club (River Culm)
Contact: Exe Valley Angling, 19 Westexe South, Tiverton, *Tel:* 01884 242275, *Water:* 0.75 miles River Culm at Stoke Cannon. Various stretches on several rivers in Somerset. See also entry under Stillwater Coarse, Tiverton. *Species:* Roach, Dace, Chub, Perch, Pike and Eels. Salmon and Trout in season. *Permits:* Please ring Exe Valley for details. Also available from: Exeter Angling Centre, Enterprise Angling Taunton, Topp Tackle Taunton & Minnows Caravan Park - beside Grand Western Canal. *Charges:* Senior: Day £5, Annual £25. Conc: Junior & OAP Day £3, Annual £12. *Season:* Coarse: closed 15th March to 16th June. Trout: open from 15th March to 30th September. Salmon: open 14th February to 30th September. *Methods:* Canal Methods: Any. Restrictions: Fish from permanent pegs, no night fishing, no cars on bank, no digging of banks or excessive clearance of vegatation. Lakeside Methods: Any. Restrictions: No night fishing, no boilies, Trout pellets or nuts, one rod only, fishing from permanent pegs, no dogs, nets to be dipped. Ring Exe Valley Angling for full details.

Tiverton Fly Fishing Association
Contact: Exe Valley Angling, 19 Westexe South, Tiverton, *Tel:* 01884 242275, *Water:* 3.5 Miles on River Exe. *Species:* Trout & Grayling. *Permits:* Exe Valley Angling: 01884 242275. Fishing available to members and guests. Members must be in EX16 postcode area. *Charges:* Senior £20, Conc. £5, Guests £5, OAP £5. *Season:* 15th March - 30th September. *Methods:* Fly only.

LYN

Chalk Water, Weir Water, Oare Water, Badgeworthy Water - these are the streams that tumble down from the romantic Doone Country of Exmoor and join to form the East Lyn, which cascades through the spectacular wooded ravine of the National Trust's Watersmeet Estate. The main river has good runs of Salmon and Sea Trout, and wild Brown Trout teem on the Lyn and the tributary streams.

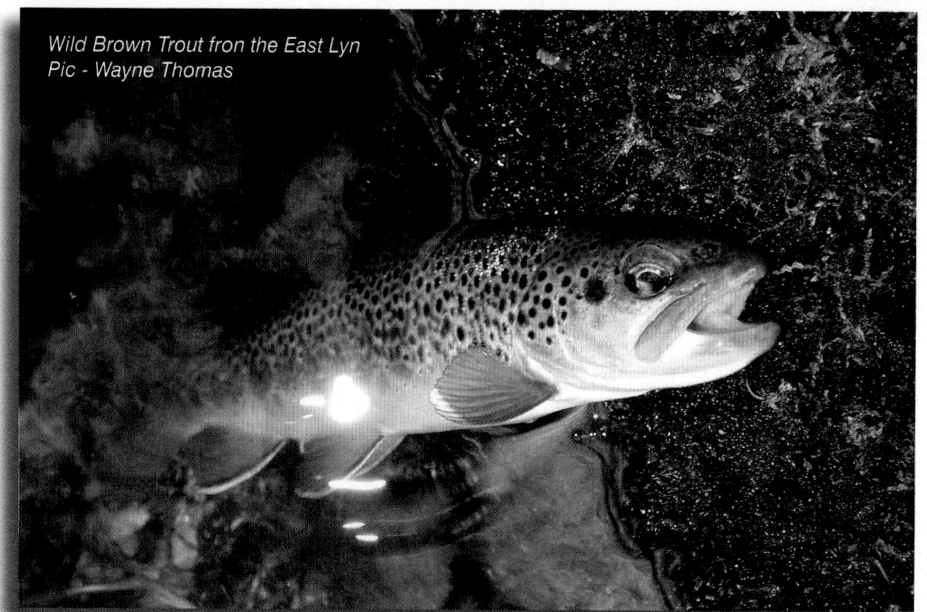
Wild Brown Trout from the East Lyn
Pic - Wayne Thomas

Cloud Farm Fishing
Contact: Colin and Jill Harman, Cloud Farm, Oare, Lynton, *Tel:* 01598 741234, *Mobile:* 07836 333548, *Water:* Badgeworthy Water, tributary of the Lyn - 0.75 miles single bank fishing. *Species:* Salmon and Brown Trout. *Charges:* From £5 per day.

Environment Agency - Watersmeet and Glenthorne
Tel: 08708 506506, *Water:* The fishery is in two parts: The Watersmeet Fishery, leased by the Agency from the National Trust - Tors Road, Lynmouth to Woodside Bridge, right bank only; Woodside Bridge to Watersmeet both banks; upstream of Watersmeet right bank only to Rockford. The Glenthorne Fishery - right bank only upstream of Rockford to 300 yards downstream of Brendon Road Bridge. Half a mile of Trout fishing is available on the Hoaroak Water between Hillsford Bridge and Watersmeet; this is specifically for children, who only require a Trout rod licence when fishing this particular stretch if they are aged 12 years or over. WARNING: Anglers are advised that parts of the river are exceptionally steep and rocky and can be dangerous. River Lyn information line - 01392 316221. *Species:* Salmon, Sea Trout, Brown Trout. *Permits:* Brendon House Hotel, Brendon. Tourist Information Centre, Town Hall, Lynton; Variety Sports, 23 Broad Street, Ilfracombe; Taunton Angling Centre, 63 Station Road, Taunton. Porlock Visitor Centre, West End, High Street, Porlock. Rockford Inn, Brendon, Lynton, N.Devon. The National Trust, Watersmeet House, Lynmouth. Environment Agency, Exminster House, Miller Way, Exminster. *Charges:* Salmon & Sea Trout, season withdrawn for conservation reasons, week £35, day £13.50, evening (8 pm to 2 am) £4; Brown Trout, season £27.50, week £10, day £3. Bag Limits: 2 Salmon, 4 Sea Trout, 8 Brown Trout per day. 2 Salmon week, 6 Salmon per season. *Season:* Salmon 1st March - 30th September; Sea Trout & Trout 15th March - 30th September. Fishing permitted 8 am to sunset, except from 1st June - 30th September when fishing by traditional fly fishing methods is permitted until 2 am between Tors Road & Rockford. *Methods:* Brown Trout, fly only. Salmon, no shrimp or prawn. Artificial fly or lure only before 16th June. Catch and release of all Salmon prior to 16th June. No weight may be used whilst fly fishing. The weight used for worm fishing and spinning must be lead free and not weigh more than 0.5 ounce and must be attached at least 18 inches from the hook.

West Lyn Farmhouse
Contact: Paul Spratley, West Lyn Farmhouse, Barbrook, Lynton, *Tel:* 01598 753618, *Water:* One mile of single bank on the East Lyn, Watersmeet to Ash Bridge. *Species:* Salmon, Sea Trout and Brown Trout. *Permits:* Only from the owners at West Lyn Farmhouse. *Charges:* £10 per day before 1 June. £15 per day after. Maximum of two rods. *Season:* Salmon - 1 March to 31 Oct. Sea Trout and Brown Trout - 15 March to 30 Sept. *Methods:* Spinner, fly and worm. Worming only permitted between 16 June and 30 Sept. Only two fish to be retained per day.

OTTER

The Otter springs to life in the Blackdown Hills and flows through a broad fertile valley to join the sea near the little resort of Budleigh Salterton. This is primarily a Brown Trout stream noted for its dry fly fishing for Trout of good average weight. There is also an improving run of Sea Trout.

Clinton Devon Estates
Contact: John Wilding, Rolle Estate, East Budleigh, Budleigh Salterton, *Tel:* 01395 443881, *Water:* 0.75 mile single bank fishing on the River Otter near Budleigh Salterton. Fishery starts at White Bridge (first road bridge over river) and ends at Clamour Bridge (first footbridge over river). *Species:* Brown Trout. *Charges:* Free to EA rod licence holders. *Season:* 1st April to 30th September.

Deer Park Hotel
Contact: Reception, Deer Park Hotel, Weston, Nr Honiton, *Tel:* 01404 41266, *Water:* Approx. 6 miles on River Otter. *Species:* Brown Trout, Salmon, Sea Trout and. *Permits:* From reception desk at hotel. Day tickets from Otter Sporting Services 07980 783072. *Charges:* £20 per rod per day, £15 evening ticket. Season permits available, but limited. £400 a season or £200 half rod. *Season:* 15th March - 30th September Salmon / Brown Trout. Salmon - 15th March - 31st October, Sea Trout 15th April - 31st October. *Methods:* Dry & Wet Fly only.

River Otter Association
Contact: Alan Knights (Secretary), Cottarson Farm, Awliscombe, Honiton, *Tel:* 01404 42318, *Water:* Comprises riparian owners, anglers and conservationists concerned with the preservation of the total ecology of the River Otter. *Species:* Brown Trout, Sea Trout and occasional Salmon.

Robert Jones Fly Fishing (Otter)
Contact: Valley Barn, Hawkerland, Colaton Raleigh, Sidmouth, *Tel:* 07020 902090, *Mobile:* 07970 797770, *Water:* River Otter. Private and Hotel water. *Species:* Brown Trout and Sea Trout. *Permits:* Day permits. E.A. Beginners Licence agent. *Charges:* On application *Season:* 15th March - 30th September. *Methods:* Fly only.

PLYM

A short stream rising on Dartmoor and running into Plymouth Sound. Trout fishing on the Plym and its tributary the Meavy, some good Sea Trout fishing on the lower reaches and a late run of Salmon.

Plymouth & Dist Freshwater Angling Assoc. (Plym)
Contact: David L. Bickell, 2 Boundary Road, Dousland, Yelverton, *Tel:* 01822 854241, *Water:* 1 mile on River Plym, 1.5 miles on River Tavy. *Species:* Salmon, Sea Trout, Brown Trout. *Permits:* Tavistock Country Pursuits, Russel St, Tavistock. The Fisherman, 2 King St, Tavistock. Yelverton Garage, The Parade, Yelverton. *Charges:* £10 a day up to 30th September. £25 a day from 1st October to 30th November for fishing the water on the River Plym. To join the association, contact secretary. Annual subscription is about £105. *Season:* Plym: April - 15th December; Tavy: March - 14th October. *Methods:* Artificial baits only.

Plymouth Command Angling Association (River)
Contact: Mr Vic Barnett Hon.Sec., 5 Weir Close, Mainstone, Plymouth, *Tel:* 01752 708206, *Mobile:* 07710 552910, *Water:* Fishing rights on the Plym, Tavy and Walkham plus a small private pond near Ivybridge. Access to rivers for serving members only. *Species:* Salmon, Sea Trout and Trout. *Permits:* Membership is open to all serving members of HM Forces. Associate membership is also open to ex-serving members of HM Forces, no matter when the time was served. *Charges:* Costs for full membership or associate membership are available on application or enquiry at the above contact. *Season:* Plym, Tavy and Walkham as per Environment Agency Byelaws.

Tavy, Walkham & Plym Fishing Club (Plym)
Contact: Roger Round, 7 Buena Vista Close, Glenholt, Plymouth, *Tel:* 01752 701945, *Water:* River Plym. Also water on Tavy and Walkham. See entry under Tavy. *Species:* Salmon, Sea Trout and Brown Trout. *Permits:* From: Osborne & Cragg, Barbican, Plymouth. Moorland Garage, Yelverton. The Fisherman, 2 Kings Street, Tavistock. *Charges:* Season Tickets for Salmon, Sea Trout and Brown Trout. Day Tickets available. Sea Trout and Salmon - Season £130, Weekly £50, Day £20. Brown Trout - Season £50, Monthly £22, Weekly £15. Reduced prices for under 18 yrs. *Season:* As E.A. byelaws. No day tickets after 30 September. *Methods:* No worm, prawn or shrimp fishing. Complete rules are issued with permit. Full returns must be made to the club secretary as a condition of purchase.

TAMAR

The Tamar rises near the north coast, and for most of its course forms the boundary between Devon and Cornwall. It is always a lowland stream flowing through farmland and this fact is reflected in the size of its Trout which have a larger average size than the acid moorland streams. Around Launceston, the Tamar is joined by five tributaries - Ottery, Carey, Wolf, Thrushel and Lyd - which offer good Trout fishing, as does the Inny which enters a few miles downstream. There is a good run of Salmon and Sea Trout, the latter being particularly numerous on the Lyd. There are also Grayling in places.

Angling 2000 (Tamar)
Contact: Westcountry Rivers Trust, 10 Exeter Street, Launceston, Cornwall. *Tel:* 0870 774 0704, *Water:* 16 beats on the Tamar, Inny, Lyd, Ottery, Carey and Kensey. Flexible permits fishing for Trout, Salmon, Sea Trout and Grayling. *Species:* Salmon, Roach, Dace, Sea Trout, Trout and Grayling. *Permits:* From the above. *Charges:* £5 to £10 per day depending on beat. *Season:* Trout - 15th March to 30th September. Salmon - 1st March to 14th October. Grayling - 16th June to 15th November. Please contact Angling 2000 for individual beat seasons. *Methods:* Please contact Angling 2000 for individual beat methods.

Arundell Arms
Contact: Mrs Anne Voss-Bark, The Arundell Arms, Lifton, *Tel:* 01566 784666, *Water:* 20 miles of private fishing on Rivers Tamar, Lyd, Carey, Thrushel, Wolf and Ottery. Also 3 acre private lake stocked with Rainbow and Brown Trout. *Species:* Rivers: Salmon, Sea Trout and Brown Trout. Lake: Rainbow & Brown Trout. *Permits:* Arundell Arms. *Charges:* Trout £25. Salmon & Sea Trout from £25. Lake £31. *Season:* Salmon March 1st to October 14th. Trout and Sea Trout March 15th to September 30th. Lake open all year. *Methods:* Fly and spinner for Salmon (1 in 3 fish after June 16 then catch and release). Fly only for Trout and Sea Trout.

Endsleigh Fishing Club
Contact: Mrs Julia Medd, Abbey Cottage, Pyrford Road, Working, Surrey. *Tel:* 01932 342584, *Mobile:* 01932 342584, *Water:* 12 miles double bank River Tamar. *Species:* Salmon maximum 23lb & Sea Trout maximum 9lb. *Charges:* To end of April £30. May

A fly caught Grayling is gently returned. Pic - Westcountry Rivers Trust

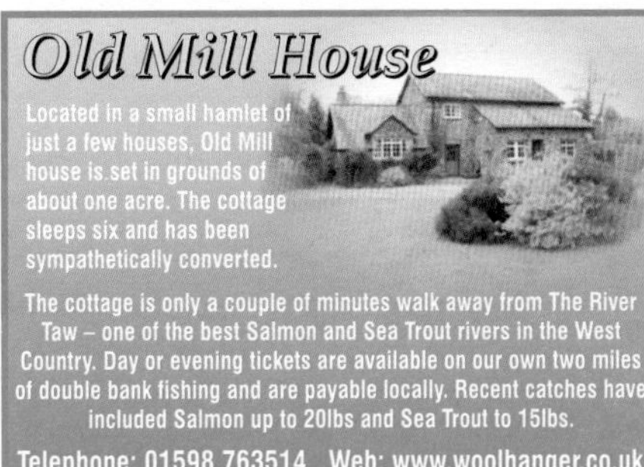

1st - June 15th £40. June 16th - Aug 31st £50. Sept 1st - Oct 14th £60. Sea Trout £15 from 5 pm. Trout £20 p/day (last minute bookings only). *Season:* March 1st - October 14th incl. *Methods:* Fly. Spinning only under certain conditions.

Hotel Endsleigh

Milton Abbot, Nr Tavistock, *Tel:* 01822 870000, *Water:* Eight miles on the Tamar. *Species:* Salmon and Sea Trout *Permits:* E.A. national rod licence required. *Charges:* From £24 to £48. *Season:* March 1 to October 14 subject to availability. *Methods:* Fly only.

TAVY

A Salmon and Sea Trout river which rises high on Dartmoor and flows through Tavistock to its junction with the Tamar estuary north of Plymouth. There is moorland Brown Trout on the upper reaches and on the Walkham, its main tributary.

Plymouth & Dist Freshwater Angling Assoc. (Tavy)

Contact: David L. Bickell, 2 Boundary Road, Dousland, Yelverton, *Tel:* 01822 854241, *Water:* River Tavy above Tavistock. *Species:* Salmon, Sea Trout and Brown Trout. *Permits:* Tavistock Country Pursuits, Russel St, Tavistock. The Fisherman, 2 King St, Tavistock. Yelverton Garage, The Parade, Yelverton. *Charges:* Tavy fishing is available to members of the association and day ticket holders. Contact the secretary for membership details. See entry under River Plym. *Season:* 1st March to 14th October. *Methods:* Artificial baits only.

Tavy, Walkham & Plym Fishing Club (Tavy)

Contact: Roger Round, 7 Buena Vista Close, Glenholt, Plymouth, *Tel:* 01752 701945, *Water:* Rivers Tavy, Walkham, Plym, Meavy. *Species:* Brown Trout, Salmon, Sea Trout. *Permits:* Only through Osborne & Cragg, Barbican, Plymouth. Moorland Garage, Yelverton. The Fisherman, 2 Kings Street, Tavistock. *Charges:* Season Tickets for Salmon, Sea Trout and Brown Trout. Day Tickets available. Sea Trout and Salmon - Season £130, Weekly £50, Day £20. Brown Trout - Season £50, Monthly £22, Weekly £15. Reduced prices for under 18 yrs. *Season:* See Environment Agency season dates. Please note, no day tickets after 30th September. *Methods:* No worm, prawn, shrimp on club permit waters. Please note club rules on back of permit including the dates by which accurate returns must be made as a condition of taking a permit.

TAW AND TRIBUTARIES

The Taw is a noted Salmon and Sea Trout river that rises high on Dartmoor and then flows through the rolling farmland of North Devon to its estuary at Barnstaple. Its main tributary, the Mole, also has good Salmon and Sea Trout fishing, and the Moles own tributary, the Bray, is a good little Trout stream.

Angling 2000 (Taw)

Contact: Westcountry Rivers Trust, 10 Exeter Street, Launceston, Cornwall. *Tel:* 0870 774 0704, *Water:* Four beats on the Little Dart. *Species:* Trout, Salmon and Sea Trout. *Permits:* From the above. *Charges:* £5 to £10 per day. *Season:* Brown and Sea Trout - 15 March to 30 September. Salmon 1 March to 30 September. *Methods:* Please contact Angling 2000 for individual beat methods.

Barnstaple & District Angling Association (River)

Contact: S.R. Tomms (Secretary), Barnstaple & District Angling Association, Upcott Farm, Brayford, *Tel:* 01598 710857, *Water:* Approx. 3 miles on the River Taw. See also under Stillwater Coarse, Barnstaple. *Species:* Salmon, Sea Trout, Brown Trout, Rainbows. *Permits:* No day tickets. Fishing by membership only. Details from the Secretary above or Kingfisher Tackle Shop, Barnstaple Tel. 01271 344919. *Charges:* Membership £30, Juniors £10. *Season:* Current EA byelaws apply. *Methods:* Current EA byelaws apply.

Crediton Fly Fishing Club (Taw)

Tel: 01363 773557, *Water:* See entry under Yeo. 1.5 miles River Taw. *Species:* Brown Trout. *Permits:* 01363 773557, or Crediton T.I.C. *Charges:* 1 Day £15, Weekly (5 days) £30, Season £86, Juniors £10. Over 65 £62. Cadet member (under 18 in full time education) £20. Two day weekend (Sat-Sun) £30. Joining fee £25. *Season:* EA Seasons. *Methods:* Fly only.

Fox & Hounds Hotel

Contact: Fox & Hounds Hotel, Eggesford, Chulmleigh, *Tel:* 01769 580345, *Water:* Fishing on River Taw *Species:* Prime Salmon, Sea Trout & Brown Trout. *Permits:* Fox & Hounds *Charges:* Prime Salmon, Sea Trout and Brown Trout fishing £20 a day or £10 for half day. Season ticket 1 day per week £350. Evening fishing 6pm-6am. *Season:* 1st March - 30th September. *Methods:* Spinning March only. Rest of season fly only.

Highbullen Hotel
Contact: Chris Taylor, Chittlehamholt, Umberleigh, *Tel:* 01769 540561, *Water:* 0.75 miles on Mole plus access to additional beats on Mole, Taw and the Bray. *Species:* Salmon 24.5lb (2000), Sea Trout 12lb (1998) & Brown Trout 2lb (2002). *Permits:* From Highbullen Hotel. *Charges:* Prices on application. *Season:* Salmon 1st March - 30th September, Brown and Sea Trout 15th March - 30th September. *Methods:* Spinner March. Fly March - September. Local byelaw, August and September all Salmon over 70cm have to be returned.

Rising Sun Inn
Contact: Mark Izzard, Rising Sun Inn, Umberleigh, Nr Barnstaple, *Tel:* 01769 560447, *Mobile:* 07711 218949, *Water:* Day tickets available. Approx. 6 miles of Taw fishing. *Species:* Sea Trout 11.5lb, Brown Trout, Salmon 23lb. *Permits:* Post Office, Umberleigh for licence. *Charges:* £35 for 24 hours, 6am to 6am. *Season:* Salmon 1st March - 30th Sept, Sea/Brown Trout 15th March - 30th Sept. *Methods:* As per E.A. rules.

Taw Fishing Club
Contact: Mr E.A.P. Jourdan, Moorside, South Zeal, Okehampton, *Tel:* 01837 840488, *Water:* 3.25 miles on River Taw between Brushford and Hawkridge bridges. *Species:* Brown Trout, Sea Trout and Salmon. *Permits:* Fishing by membership of club only. *Charges:* £60 season. *Season:* 15th March to 30th September. *Methods:* Fly only, barbless encouraged.

Tremayne Water
Contact: J.G. Smith, *Tel:* 01363 84804, *Water:* 1.5 miles single & double bank fishing on the upper Taw and Little Dart. *Species:* Salmon, Sea Trout. *Charges:* Limited season rods only. *Season:* E.A. Byelaws apply. *Methods:* E.A. Byelaws apply.

TEIGN

The Teign has two sources, high up on Dartmoor, which form the North and South Teign but the two branches quickly leave the moor to join west of Chagford while still very small streams. Between Chagford and Steps Bridge the river runs through a dramatic wooded gorge which is at its most spectacular at Fingle Bridge, a popular beauty spot. All along the Teign the Spring fisherman is greeted by myriads of daffodils, which are at their most numerous around Clifford Bridge. The upper Teign offers good fishing for wild Trout and Sea Trout, with Salmon fishing in suitable conditions from April to the end of the season. Much of the upper river is controlled by the Upper Teign Fishing Association. From just south of the Moretonhampstead to the estuary at Newton Abbot. the Teign is mostly controlled by the Lower Teign Fishing Association.
This water has plenty of Brown Trout but is essentially a Sea Trout and Salmon fishery.

Lower Teign Fishing Association
Contact: Mr R Waters (Secretary), 121 Topsham Road, Exeter, *Tel:* 01392 251928, *Water:* 14 miles River Teign. *Species:* Salmon, Sea Trout. *Permits:* 3 Beats with 3 tickets on each (beat 3 only available between 1st May and 31st August). One junior ticket per beat per day available. *Charges:* £20 per day (24 hour period - night Sea Trout fishing). Available from Tackle Trader, Newton Abbot. 01626 331613. 24hr bag limit (4 Sea Trout). From 1st February 2008 Salmon catch and release only (returned to river unharmed). *Season:* 1st Febuary - 30th September - Salmon. 15th March - 30th September - Sea Trout. *Methods:* Spinning, fly (fly only at night), no worming or maggots. No natural bait to be used from September.

Mill End Hotel
Sandy Park, Chagford, *Tel:* 01647 432282, *Water:* 3 miles plus access to a further 8 miles. *Species:* Brown Trout, Salmon and Sea Trout. *Permits:* At Hotel. *Charges:* £10 per day. Prices may change in 2008.

Robert Jones Fly Fishing (Teign)
Contact: Valley Barn, Hawkerland, Colaton Raleigh, Sidmouth, *Tel:* 07020 902090, *Mobile:* 07970 797770, *Water:* River Teign. Private and Hotel water. *Species:* Brown Trout, Sea Trout and Salmon. *Permits:* Day permits. E.A. Beginners Licence agent. *Charges:* On application *Season:* 15th March - 30th September. *Methods:* Fly and spinner.

Teign Fisheries Association
Contact: Pat Howgill, Sunbeam, Hind Street, Bovey Tracey, Newton Abbot, *Tel:* 01626 322331, *Water:* Riparian Owners Association representing interest of owners of fishing waters on River Teign. *Species:* Salmon to 18lb, Sea Trout to 11lb and Brown Trout to 3lb. *Permits:* No day tickets available through the Association. Lower Teign Fishing Association tickets available from Tackle Trader, Newton Abbot. Upper Teign Fishing Association tickets available from Chagford Inn or Fingle Bridge Inn. Local Association rules apply. Details at time of purchase or by enquiry. *Charges:* Not Known *Season:* 1 Feb - 30 Sep

Methods: Salmon caught before 16 June to be returned. Limit of one Salmon a season a rod.

Upper Teign Fishing Association

Contact: Richard Penrose, 12 Bretteville Close, Chagford, *Tel:* 01647 433559, *Water:* Approx. 8 miles on upper Teign. *Species:* Brown Trout to 1lb 4oz, Sea Trout to 8lb & Salmon to 18lb. *Permits:* From: Fingle Bridge Inn, Drewsteignton (01647 281287). Drewsteignton Post Office. Bowdens, Chagford. CP Angling, 3 The Arcade, Okehampton, Dundford Post Office, Exeter Angling Centre (01392 436404). Orvis, Exeter (01392 272599). Post Office & General Stores, Cheriton Bishop. All anglers must be in possession of a current Environment Agency licence. *Charges:* 2007 prices (prices may change in 2008) - Ordinary Member - Annual Subscription £173 - full season for Salmon, Sea Trout & Brown Trout. Trout Member - Annual subscription £67 - full season for Brown Trout. Temporary Members' Tickets - Salmon & Sea Trout £20 per day (6 ticket limit per day from Anglers Rest plus 4 ticket limit - Salmon and Sea Trout from Drewsteignton Post Office). Chagford weir pool Sea Trout tickets £15 (4 per day from Bowdens, Chagford). Brown Trout tickets: week £40 adult, £10 juvenile, day £10 adult, £5 juvenile. All enquiries to hon sec. Richard Penrose. *Season:* Brown Trout: March 15th - September 30th. Sea Trout: March 15th - September 30th. Salmon: February 1st - September 30th. *Methods:* No bait fishing for Salmon in September. One Salmon only to be killed per angler per season on the whole river (no matter how many permits are purchased).

TORRIDGE

Throughout its length the Torridge flows through the rolling farmland of North Devon. It rises close to the coast near the Cornish border and swings in a great arc before flowing into the estuary that it shares with the Taw. The middle and lower reaches are best known for their Salmon and Sea Trout, but can offer surprisingly good Trout fishing.

The upper reaches and its tributaries, the Waldon and Lew, offer plenty of opportunities for Brown Trout fishing.

Angling 2000 (Torridge)

Contact: Westcountry Rivers Trust, 10 Exeter Street, Launceston, Cornwall. *Tel:* 0870 774 0704, *Water:* Six beats on the Torridge. Flexible day permits. *Species:* Trout, Salmon and Sea Trout. *Permits:* From the above. *Charges:* £5 to £10 per day. *Season:* 1st March to 30th September. Please contact Angling 2000 for individual beat seasons. *Methods:* Please contact Angling 2000 for individual beat methods.

Clinton Arms

Contact: Peter Robertson, Clinton Arms, Frithelstock, Torrington, *Tel:* 01805 623279, *Water:* Approx. 1.5 mile of double bank on River Torridge (left hand bank only last 200yds). *Species:* Brown Trout, Sea Trout to 9.5lb, Salmon. *Permits:* The Clinton Arms on 01805 623279. *Charges:* £20/day/rod. *Season:* March to September. *Methods:* Fly fishing only.

Gortleigh Fishing

Gortleigh Farm, Sheepwash, Beaworthy, *Tel:* 01409 231291, *Mobile:* 07968 020254, *Water:* 1.5 miles double bank fishing.

Species: Brown Trout, Sea Trout and occasional Salmon. *Permits:* From Farmhouse by prior arrangement - please phone first. You can fish this beat with Angling 2000 tokens. *Season:* E.A. Byelaws apply. *Methods:* No dogs.

Half Moon Inn

Contact: Half Moon Inn, Sheepwash, Beaworthy, *Tel:* 01409 231376, *Water:* 10 miles River Torridge. *Species:* River: Sea, Brown & Wild Brown Trout, Salmon. *Permits:* Day tickets for residents & non-residents. *Charges:* Non-residents - Sea Trout & Salmon: £27, Brown Trout: 3 - fish £18. *Season:* Mid March - 30th September. *Methods:* Dry & Wet Fly only, Spinning in March.

Little Warham Fishery

Contact: Thesera Norton-Smith, Little Warham House, Beaford, Winkleigh, *Tel:* 01805 603317, *Water:* Nearly 2 miles of River Torridge. *Species:* Salmon, Sea Trout, Brown Trout. *Permits:* As above. *Charges:* £25/day/rod, all species. *Season:* March 1st - September 30th. *Methods:* Fly only.

Mill Leat (River Fishing)

Contact: Mr Birkett, Thornbury, Holsworthy, *Tel:* 01409 261426, *Water:* Half mile of single bank on the Waldon (tributary of the Torridge). *Species:* Brown Trout & Coarse fish. *Charges:* £6 to fish the river. *Season:* E.A. Byelaws apply. *Methods:* E.A. Byelaws apply.

Parsonage Farm

Contact: Mr and Mrs Ward, Parsonage Farm, Iddesleigh, *Tel:* 01837 810318, *Water:* 400 metres on the River Torridge. *Species:* Wild Brown Trout, Sea Trout and Salmon. *Permits:* From Stafford Moor Fishery. *Charges:* £10 per rod per day. *Season:* Mid March to end September

The Devil's Stone Inn
Contact: Steve Hurst, The Devil's Stone Inn, Shebbear, Beaworthy, *Tel:* 01409 281210, *Water:* Access to 8 miles on the Torridge. *Species:* Salmon, Sea Trout and Brown Trout. *Permits:* From the Devil's Stone Inn. *Charges:* Night fishing available. *Season:* 1 March to 30 September. *Methods:* Fly and Coarse.

Torridge Fishery Association
Contact: Charles Inniss, Beeches, East Street, Sheepwash, Beaworthy, *Tel:* 01409 231237, *Water:* An association of riparian owners and Torridge fishermen, whose aim is to secure and maintain the well being of the river and its ecology. Several day permits available, please phone for details. *Species:* Salmon to 15lb. Sea Trout to 8lb. Brown Trout to 1lb. *Permits:* Half Moon Inn, Sheepwash, Beaworthy, Devon 01409 231376. Mrs T Norton-Smith, Little Warham, Beaford, Winkleigh, Devon 01805 603317. *Charges:* Salmon and Sea Trout from £15 to £25 daily. Brown Trout from £7 to £15 daily. *Season:* March 1st to September 30th. *Methods:* Fly Only.

YEALM

The Yealm, (which is pronouced "Yam"), rises in the south of Dartmoor National Park, and runs into the picturesque Yealm Estuary. Brown Trout and Sea Trout fishing on the main River - a small late run of Salmon.

Upper Yealm Fishery
Contact: Snowbee U.K. Ltd., Drakes Court, Langage Business Park, Plymouth, *Tel:* 01752 334933, *Water:* 1 mile both banks River Yealm. *Species:* Sea Trout, Brown Trout, Salmon. *Permits:* Snowbee U.K. Ltd. *Charges:* Full season £100 unlimited visits to the fishery. Daily rate £10 (or purchase 10 tickets at half the daily rate) All bookings to be made through the office at Snowbee (UK) Ltd. (To preserve the tranquility of the fishery and to avoid over-crowding - no more than 2 anglers on one beat at any one time). *Season:* Brown Trout & Sea Trout 15th March - 30th Sept, Salmon 1st April - 15th December. *Methods:* Fly fishing & spinning.

YEO

A tributary of the River Creedy which drains into the main Exe from the West close to Crediton. The Yeo has a good wild Brown Trout population.

Crediton Fly Fishing Club (Yeo)
Contact: David Pope, 21 Creedy Road, Crediton, *Tel:* 01363 773557, *Water:* 9 miles Rivers Yeo, Creedy and Culm. 1.5 miles River Taw. *Species:* Brown Trout. *Permits:* 01363 773557, or Crediton T.I.C. *Charges:* 1 Day £15, Weekly (5 days) £30, Season £86, Juniors £10. Over 65 £62. Cadet member (under 18 in full time education) £20. Two day weekend (Sat-Sun) £30. Joining fee £25. *Season:* Environment Agency Season. *Methods:* Fly only.

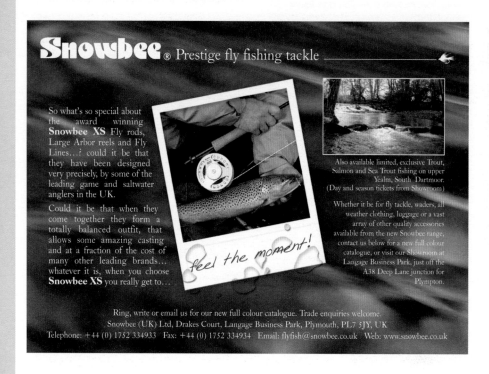

Stillwater Coarse

AXMINSTER

Summerleaze Pond

Contact: Summerleaze Farm, Kilmington, Axminster, *Tel:* 01297 32390, *Water:* 1 coarse fishing lake. *Species:* Carp, Roach, Perch. Best Carp 20lbs. *Charges:* On site, £4 adults, £2 children under 16. *Season:* Open all year, dawn to dusk. *Methods:* Please ask at fishery.

BAMPTON

Four Ponds Fishery ♿

Contact: Phil & Geraldine Newton, Bowdens Lane, Shillingford, Nr Bampton, *Tel:* 01398 331169, *Mobile:* 07864 697721, *Water:* 1.25 acre and 0.75 acre coarse lakes. 3 acre specimen Carp lake. *Species:* Carp 28.5lb, Tench 8lb, Perch 5lb (not verified), Roach 3lb, Koi 13lb, Bream 9lb, Rudd and Golden Rudd to 1lb. (verified) true Crucians to 3lb. *Charges:* Day tickets available on bankside or in tackle shop. Coarse day tickets £7 for 2 rods and £8 for 3 rods. Night ticket £8 for 2 rods, £9 for 3 rods. Specimen lake (6 swims) has to be booked, Price for 3 rods: day ticket £10, Night £12, 24hrs £20, 48hrs £38. *Season:* All year round. *Methods:* Coarse:- Strictly barbless hooks only, minimum 30" landing nets, no nut type baits to be used, no dogs. No Carp over 3lb in keepnets. Specimen lake:- minimum 36" landing net, mats & klin-ik must be used at all times. No sacking of fish, photos in kneeling position only, no nut baits.

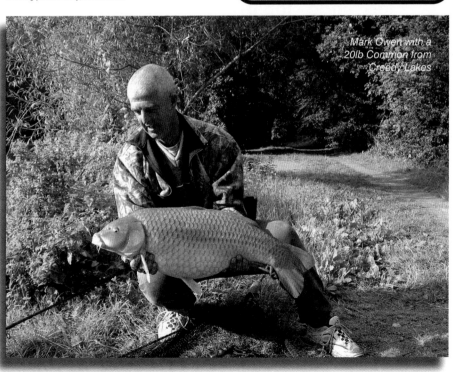

Mark Owen with a 20lb Common from Creedy Lakes

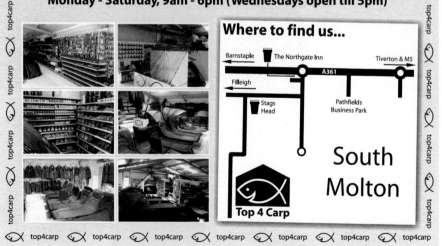

BARNSTAPLE

Barnstaple & District A. A. (Coarse Ponds)

Contact: S.R. Tomms (Secretary), Barnstaple & District Angling Association, Upcott Farm, Brayford, *Tel:* 01598 710857, *Water:* 4 mixed coarse fishing ponds in the Barnstaple area ranging from 0.5 acres to 2 acres. *Species:* Roach, Rudd, Carp, Perch, Bream, Tench and Eels. *Permits:* Members only. Details from the secretary or Kingfisher Tackle Shop, Barnstaple Tel. 01271 344919. *Charges:* £30 per year adult. Children (18 and under) £10 per year. *Season:* All year, dawn to dusk. *Methods:* Full rules in the membership book. Barbless hooks only.

Riverton House & Lakes ♿

Contact: Geoff and Sharon Dodd, Riverton House & Lakes, Swimbridge, Barnstaple, *Tel:* 01271 830009, *Mobile:* 07711 842810, *Water:* 3.5 acre specimen lake, plus half acre junior pond and 2.5 acre lake match/pleasure lake. *Species:* Carp to 25lb, Bream 5lb, Tench 8lb, Roach over 1lb, Perch 3lb, Rudd 3lb & Eels 6lb. *Charges:* Adult day £6, Junior £4, Match bookings £5 (min 10 pegs). Specials: 'Dads and Lads' (one adult & one junior) £8. Night fishing by appointment. *Season:* Open all year. *Methods:* Barbless hooks, care and consideration. No keepnets on specimen lake or junior lake.

BEAWORTHY

Anglers Eldorado

Contact: Zyg, The Gables, Winsford, Halwill,, Beaworthy, *Tel:* 01409 221559, *Water:* Four lakes from 1 acre to 4 acres. *Species:* Carp to 25lb, Grass Carp to 18lb, Wels Catfish to 20lb, Golden Tench to 5lb, Golden Orfe to 6lb, Blue orfe to 5lb, Golden Rudd to 2lb, Koi to 10lb. *Permits:* Also from Halwill Newsagents. *Charges:* £5 per day per rod, £4 Juniors & O.A.Ps. £3 excess if found fishing without a permit. *Season:* All year, 8am-9pm or dusk (Which ever is earlier). *Methods:* Barbless hooks, No keepnets or sacks. Landing nets must be used.

Anglers Shangrila

Contact: Mr Zyg Gregorek, The Gables, Winsford, Halwill, Beaworthy, *Tel:* 01409 221559, *Water:* Three match only lakes, 240 pegs. *Species:* Carp, Golden Tench, Golden Orfe. Top weights of 100lbs possible. *Permits:* From Zyg only. *Charges:* You can book the whole lake, charges depending on how many people. Minimum up to £50 for 10 anglers, then £5 per angler after that. *Methods:* Barbless hooks.

Fatboys (Specimen) Carp Lake

Contact: Mr Zyg Gregorek, Anglers Nirvana, The Gables, Winsford, Halwill, *Tel:* 01409 221559, *Water:* 2 acres. *Species:* Carp to over 25lbs. *Permits:* Only at Anglers Paradise. Pre booking advisable. *Charges:* £10 per day (2 rods) £10 per night. *Season:* All year. 8am to 9pm or dusk (which ever is earlier). *Methods:* Barbless hooks, no keepnets, no braided main line, minimum 8lb line, no particle baits except sweetcorn and hemp. Anglers Paradise rules and regulations apply. Minimum landing net size of 30".

Kraking Karp (Specimen) Carp Lake

Contact: Mr Zyg Gregorek, Anglers Nirvana, The Gables, Winsford, Halwill, *Tel:* 01409 221559, *Water:* 2 acres. *Species:* Carp to over 25lbs. *Permits:* Only at Anglers Paradise. Pre booking advisable. *Charges:* £10 per day (2 rods) £10 per night. *Season:* All year. 8am to 9pm or dusk (which ever is earlier). *Methods:* Barbless hooks, no keepnets, no braided main line, minimum 8lb line, no particle baits except sweetcorn and hemp. Anglers Paradise rules and regulations apply. Minimum landing net size of 30".

Silver Fish Lake

Contact: Mr Zyg Gregorek, Anglers Nirvana, The Gables, Winsford, Halwill, *Tel:* 01409 221559, *Water:* 2 acres. *Species:* Green Tench, Bream, Gudgeon, Perch, Rudd, Orfe, Barbel, Chub and Crucian. *Permits:* Only at Anglers Paradise. Pre booking advisable. *Charges:* £10 per day (2 rods) £10 per night. *Season:* All year. 8am to 9pm or dusk (which ever is earlier). *Methods:* Barbless hooks, no keepnets, no braided main line, minimum 8lb line, no particle baits except sweetcorn and hemp. Anglers Paradise rules and regulations apply. Minimum landing net size of 30".

Specimen Catfish Lake

Contact: Mr Zyg Gregorek, Anglers Nirvana, The Gables, Winsford, Halwill, *Tel:* 01409 221559, *Water:* 2 acres. *Species:* Dozen Wels Catfish average size 35lbs. *Permits:* Only at Anglers Paradise. Pre booking advisable. *Charges:* £10 per day (2 rods) £10 per night. *Season:* All year. 8am to 9pm or dusk (which ever is earlier). *Methods:* Barbless hooks, no keepnets, no braided main line, minimum 8lb line, deadbaits permissable provided they are bought at Anglers Paradise tackle shop. Anglers Paradise rules and regulations apply. Minimum landing net size of 30".

BIDEFORD

Bideford & District Angling Club (Coarse + Game) ♿

Contact: Mr Graham Mountjoy, Honestone Street, Bideford, *Tel:* 01237 472916, *Water:* Bideford based club with coarse, game, boat & sea sections;over 600 members fishing throughout South West. Please phone for further details. New Coarse Lake: Tarka Swims (previously Anniversary Waters) 1.75 acres at Gammaton Road, East Bideford. Competitions 2nd Sunday each

STILLWATER COARSE

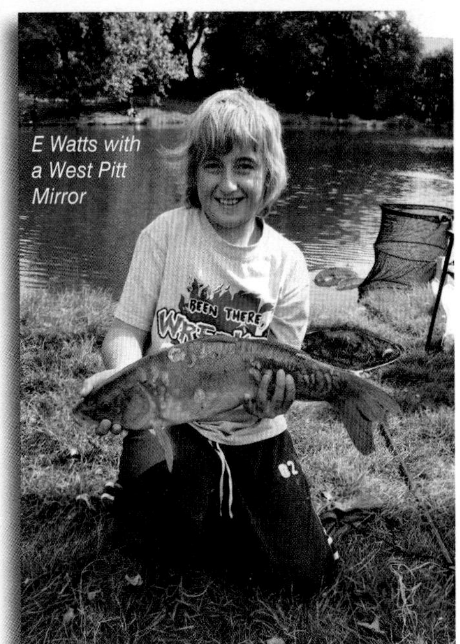
E Watts with a West Pitt Mirror

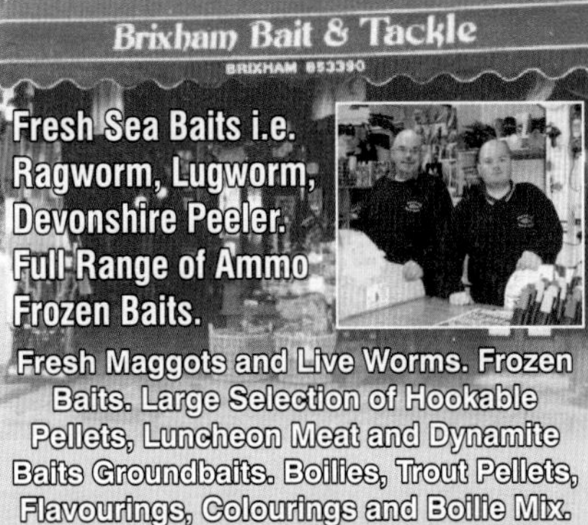

month, game competitions last Sunday each month. *Permits:* Membership form from club, open 7pm-11pm. *Charges:* Members £7, associate membership £3, OAP £2, juniors £1. *Season:* Open all year. *Methods:* Coarse lakes barbless hooks.

Fosfelle Country House Hotel (Coarse)
Hartland, Bideford, *Tel:* 01237 441273, *Water:* Approx. half acre pond. *Species:* Carp, Tench, Roach, Rudd. *Charges:* £7 per day. *Season:* Open all year. *Methods:* Displayed on site.

Jennetts
Contact: South West Lakes Trust Fishery Assistant, *Tel:* 01288 321262, *Water:* Reservoir 8 acres. *Species:* Commons to 22lb, Mirrors to 23lb. *Permits:* Summerlands Tackle (01237 471291), Bideford TIC (01237 477676), or Kingfisher (01271 344919). *Charges:* Full day £5.25, Concession £4.25. *Season:* Open all year strictly 6.30am - 10pm. *Methods:* Quality bags of smaller Carp, Roach and Tench to pole and float.

Little Weach Fishery
1 Weach Cottage, Westleigh, Bideford, *Tel:* 01237 479303, *Water:* 2 lakes totalling approx. 1 acre. *Species:* Crucian, Common, Mirror and Koi Carp to 16lb, Tench 7lb, Roach 1.5lb, Rudd, Bream, Goldfish 1lb. *Charges:* £5 per day, £2.50 Children. Under 12's must be accompanied by an adult. *Season:* Open all year dawn to dusk. *Methods:* No keepnets or boilies.

Melbury
Contact: South West Lakes Trust Fishery Assistant, *Tel:* 01288 321262, *Water:* Reservoir 12 acres. *Species:* Best Mirror 27.5lb, Tench, Bream, Roach. Perch, Rudd & Eels. *Permits:* From Summerlands (01237 471291) and Bideford TIC (01237 477676). *Charges:* Full day £5.25, concession £4.25. Season tickets available from Summerlands Tackle (01237 471291) - additional fisheries £25 each. *Season:* Open all year from 6.30am to 10pm. *Methods:* Good mixed bags of Roach, Rudd and quality Bream to pole, float and feeder. Also Perch and Carp.

Tarka Swims ♿
Contact: Mr Graham Mountjoy, Bideford & District Angling Club, Honestone Street, Bideford, *Tel:* 01237 472916, *Water:* Two acre lake at Gammaton. *Species:* Carp to 15lb, Tench, Roach, Rudd and Bream to 2lb. *Charges:* Day tickets available soon, limited to 4 per day. Lake membership available one payment £20 joining fee (life membership) then £5 per year. *Season:* Open all year. *Methods:* Disabled toilets on site plus access to 26 pegs.

Torridge Angling Club
Contact: A.J. Kelly (secretary), 42 King Alfred Crescent, Northam, *Tel:* 01237 476665, *Mobile:* 07779 193085, *Water:* Coarse match fishing at local waters. Quarterly meetings. New members welcome. Please contact the secretary. *Charges:* £5 per year. Concessions for juniors. New members welcome.

Valley View Lakes and Lodges (Coarse)
Contact: Matt Pearce and Brett Bassett, Buckland Brewer, Nr Bideford, *Tel:* 01237 459049/459053, *Mobile:* 07919 102287, *Water:* 1 acre lake. *Species:* Carp to 20lbs and Tench. *Charges:* £5 day ticket. *Season:* All year. *Methods:* Barbless hooks, no keepnets and no nuts.

BOVEY TRACEY

Bradley Pond
Contact: Newton Abbot Fishing Association., PO Box 1, Bovey Tracey, Newton Abbot, *Tel:* 01626 834032, *Water:* See entry under Newton Abbot Fishing Association. Full members only. 4 acre former clay pit. *Species:* Popular match and Carp venue with Roach to 2lb, Perch to 3lb 9oz, Tench, Skimmers, Carp to 28lb and large Trout.

BRAUNTON

Little Comfort Farm

Little Comfort Farm, Braunton, *Tel:* 01271 812414, *Water:* 1.5 acre lake. *Species:* Carp - 17lbs, Rudd, Roach, Bream. *Permits:* From office or lakeside. *Charges:* £6 all day, 2 rods £5 half day, 2 rods £3 evening, 2 rods concessions £1 off all prices for OAPs and under 14. *Season:* Open from dawn to dusk, closed January and February to day tickets. *Methods:* Barbless hooks, no keepnets.

BUCKFASTLEIGH

Nurston Farm Fishery

Contact: Mabin Family, Nurston Farm, Dean Prior, Buckfastleigh, *Tel:* 01364 642285, *Water:* 2.5 acre lake. *Species:* Roach to 3lb, Tench to 5lb, Rudd to 1lb, Bream to 6lb, Carp (different species) to 30lb. *Charges:* Dawn till dusk £5 / u14s £3 / 4pm till dusk £3. *Methods:* Barbless hooks, no keepnets, no boilies / match bookings.

CHUDLEIGH

Trenchford

Contact: South West Lakes Trust Fishery Assistant, *Tel:* 01647 277587, *Water:* Reservoir 33 acres. *Species:* Pike up to 30lb. *Permits:* From Kennick self-service hut. *Charges:* Full day £5.25, concession £4.25. Season tickets available from Summerlands Tackle (01237 471291) - additional fisheries £25 each. Boats available booked 48 hours in advance £12 per day. *Season:* Open all year 24 hours a day. *Methods:* Spinners, plug, fly, dead sea fish (no livebaiting).

COMBE MARTIN

Newberry Valley Coarse Fishing

Contact: Newberry Valley, Woodlands, Combe Martin, *Tel:* 01271 882334, *Water:* 2 acre lake. *Species:* Carp to 18lb & Green Tench to 8lb, Roach, Rudd & Perch. *Permits:* From above address. EA rod licence required. Available from local Post Office or by 'Telesales' service on 0870 1662662. *Charges:* £6/day, max 2 rods; evening permit £4. *Season:* Open 23rd March till end October 8am - 8pm, or dusk if earlier. *Methods:* Barbless hooks only, No ground bait or keepnets. Children under 16 must be accompanied by an adult over 18 years. No dogs.

CREDITON

Creedy Lakes ♿

Contact: Sandra Turner, Longbarn, Crediton, *Tel:* 01363 772684, *Water:* 4.5 acre & 1.75 acre spring fed lakes. *Species:* Common to 31lb 3oz, Mirror to 29lb 14oz. Koi Carp plus Tench. *Permits:* Self service on site, in car park. *Charges:* Day ticket £7 (up to 2 rods). £10 (3 rods), Evening ticket £3.50 (up to 2 rods). £5 (3 rods). *Season:* March through to end December. *Methods:* Barbless Hooks, minimum line 8lbs, no keepnets, no hemp, seed or nut baits. No poles or beachcasters. Unhooking mats and 'Klinik' antiseptic compulsory. No night fishing. No unaccompanied children under 16.

Lower Hollacombe Fishery

Contact: Mr. C. Guppy, Lower Hollacombe, Crediton, *Tel:* 01363 84331, *Water:* Approximately 1 acre. *Species:* Common Carp, Koi Carp, Rudd, Tench, Mirror Carp, Crucian Carp, Roach, Perch. *Permits:* At bank side. *Charges:* £6 per day. £4 per day under 16. £4 per evening. Under 16 must be accompanied by adult. *Season:* All year round. *Methods:* Barbless hooks, no boilies or nut baits.

Salmonhutch Coarse Fishery ♿

Contact: Mr & Mrs Mortimer, Uton, Crediton, *Tel:* 01363 772749, *Water:* Three 1 acre spring fed lakes. *Species:* Mirror Carp over 29lb and Common Carp to 24lbs. Rudd, Tench and Perch. *Permits:* The Post Office (fishing licence), Market Street, Crediton. Daily tickets to fish collected on site. *Charges:* Day fishing 7am to 10pm, from £5 for Adults. Night fishing 9pm to 7am, from £5 (prior booking required) Evening fishing from £3. *Season:* All Year. *Methods:* Barbless hooks, no long shank bent hooks, no permanently fixed lead rigs. Minimum 8lb line for Carp, 4lb for general fishing. No Carp in keepnets. Full rules from the fishery.

Shobrooke Lake

Contact: Clare Shelley, Shobrooke Park, Crediton, *Tel:* 01363 775153, *Water:* 9 acre lake in superb parkland setting. *Species:* Tench, Carp, Mirror, Rudd, Perch, Roach. *Permits:* Not from above address - Ladd's Sport Shop, Exeter Rd, Crediton 01363 772666 or Crediton Tourist Information Centre, Town Hall, High Street, Crediton 01363 772006. *Charges:* Adult: £10/day, £20/ week, £130/year. Under 16, Student & Pensioner: £5/day, £10/ week, £65/year. *Methods:* Fishing by rod or line from bank only, no night fishing, no keepnets.

CULLOMPTON

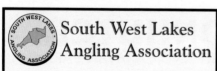

Coombelands Coarse Fishery ♿

Contact: Mr & Mrs Berry, Higher Coombelands, Bunneford Cross, Knowle, Cullompton, *Tel:* 01884 32320, *Water:* 3 Lakes totalling approx. 3 acres *Species:* Mixed coarse fishing ponds with Carp in excess of 20lb. *Permits:* Higher Coombelands. *Charges:* From £7 per day or £15 for 24 hours. evening and season tickets available. Night fishing £8. *Season:* Open all year. *Methods:* Barbless hooks only, no keep nets, no boilies, night fishing with prior permission only, no dogs.

Exeter & District A.A. (Kia Ora)

Contact: Terry Reed (Hon. Sec.), PO Box 194, Exeter, *Mobile:* 07970 483913, *Water:* A recently built Association water and now the clubs premier water offering big nets of Carp, Tench, Bream, Crucian, Roach. Pleasure Fishing often produces 25lb fish. *Species:* Heavily stocked with mixed species coarse fish. *Permits:* Exeter Angling Centre, Smythen Street (Off Market Street, Exeter). Bridge Cafe, Bridge Road, Exeter. Exmouth Tackle & Sport, The Strand, Exmouth. Tackle Trader, Wharf Road, Newton Abbot. Exe Valley Angling, West Exe South, Tiverton. Saunders Pet Supplies, Fore Street, Cullompton. Tiverton Parkway Station (Cafe), Sampford Peverell. *Charges:* £34 Adults, £4 for Juniors (annual). £5 day. *Season:* No Close Season. Details in association handbook or from agents. *Methods:* Different restrictions on each water. Details in association handbook.

Goodiford Mill Fishery (Coarse Lakes) ♿

Contact: David & Anne Wheeler, Goodiford Mill, Kentisbeare, Cullompton, *Tel:* 01884 266233, *Water:* 4.5 acre Coarse lake with over 100 doubles & twenties to 32lbs. *Species:* Carp: Common, Mirror, Crucian, Leather and Ghost. Tench, Roach and Bream. *Permits:* At Lodge. *Charges:* £6 day ticket (1 rod). £5 concession/Children under 14 must be accompanied by an adult (1 rod). Extra rod £1 each. *Season:* All year. 6am - Dusk *Methods:* Full rules on application, no keepnets, barbless hooks, nets must be dipped.

Goodiford Mill Fishery (Specimen Carp) ♿

Contact: David & Anne Wheeler, Goodiford Mill, Kentisbeare, Cullompton, *Tel:* 01884 266233, *Water:* 4 acre Coarse lake. *Species:* Ghost, Mirror and Common Carp. *Permits:* At Lodge. Rod Licence required. *Charges:* £10 for 2 rods. No concessions. Under 16 years must be accompanied. *Season:* Open all year. 6am - dusk. *Methods:* Full rules on application, barbless hooks only, nets must be dipped.

Knapp Farm Lakes ♿

Contact: Mr B. Pretty, Knapp Farm Lakes, Clayhidon, Cullompton, *Tel:* 01823 680471, *Water:* Three lakes covering approx. 3 acres. *Species:* Common and Ghost Carp to 12lb. Roach, Rudd and Tench to 3lb. *Permits:* Pay on site. Self service or pay Warden. *Charges:* £4 per day - all ages. *Season:* Open all year. *Methods:* No boilies. No keepnets for fish over 3lb. Barbless hooks only. Under 16s must be accompanied by an adult.

Millhayes Fishery

Contact: Mr Tony Howe, Millhayes, Kentisbeare, Cullompton, *Tel:* 01884 266412, *Water:* 2 acre spring fed lake, 0.5 acre Crucian and Bream lake. *Species:* Carp 31lb, Tench 5lb, Roach, Rudd to 2lb. *Charges:* £5 Adults, £3 Under 16, £4 Evenings. *Season:* 1st March - 31st December. *Methods:* Barbless hooks only, no night fishing, no Carp over 1lb in nets, nets to be dipped, no dogs. Absolutely no fish to be removed from site.

Newcourt Ponds
Contact: Andy Hitt, Newcourt Barton, Langford, Cullompton, *Tel:* 01884 277326, *Water:* Four lakes totalling 1.5 acres. *Species:* Carp, Tench, Bream, Golden Orfe, Rudd, Golden Tench. *Permits:* Collected on bank. *Charges:* Adults £4 two rods. Under 14 £3 one rod. Extra rods £1. *Season:* Open all year dawn to dusk. No night fishing. *Methods:* No Boilies. Barbless Hooks. No Carp over 2lb in nets. No dogs.

Padbrook Park
Contact: Garry Scargill, Padbrook Park, Cullompton, *Tel:* 01884 836100, *Water:* 3 acre lake. *Species:* Many Carp up to 20lb. *Charges:* £5 Day. *Season:* Open all year.

Pound Farm ♿
Contact: Mrs A.M.Davey, Butterleigh, Cullompton, *Tel:* 01884 855208, *Water:* Small spring fed pond. *Species:* Mirror, Common Carp, Roach, Tench, Perch, Rudd. *Charges:* £4 per rod per day. Children under ten £1.50. Under 16 £3. *Season:* All year. *Methods:* Barbless hooks only. No Boilies.No keepnets.

DARTMOUTH

Old Mill
Contact: South West Lakes Trust Fishery Assistant, *Tel:* 01647 277587, *Water:* Reservoir 4 acres. *Species:* Carp to over 20lb, Roach to 2lb. Tench and Bream. *Permits:* Limited season ticket only, day & night; *Charges:* Full £190, concession £170, family £285 from Summerlands Tackle (01237 471291). Additional fisheries £25 each. *Season:* Open all year 24 hours a day. *Methods:* Dam Wall, Stumpy area, surface fishing produces good sport in summer. Late season Dam Wall to centre.

DAWLISH

Ashcombe Fishery
Contact: Ashcombe Adventure Centre Ltd., Ashcombe, Dawlish, *Tel:* 01626 866766, *Water:* 3 Lakes approx. 3 acres. Just off B3192 *Species:* Carp 18lb, Tench 4lb, Roach 2lb. *Permits:* Day tickets/permits available from reception (fishing inspector). EA licence required. *Charges:* Adults £4.50, Juniors / OAP's £3.50. *Season:* Open all Year 09.00 - 17.00 Monday to Saturday, except 24/25/26 December and 1st January. Closed Sunday 13.00. *Methods:* Barbless Hooks, No large Carp to be kept in keepnets, No boilies.

EXETER

Broadclyst Pond
Contact: Jarvis Hayes / Mr T Hammet, Broadclyst, Exeter, *Tel:* 01392 461268, *Water:* One half acre lake. *Species:* Carp to 20lb plus.Tench 3.5lb, Perch 1.5lb, Rudd 12oz. *Permits:* On site - contact for details. *Charges:* £5 per day. *Season:* Open all year. No night fishing. *Methods:* No keepnets, barbless hooks only.

Bussells Farm
Contact: Lucy or Andy Hines, Bussells Farm, Huxham, Exeter, *Tel:* 01392 841238, *Mobile:* 07802 435934, *Water:* Three lakes covering 2.5 acres. *Species:* Carp to 25lb, Bream to 7lb, Tench, Roach, Eels, Pike. *Charges:* £5 per day, £3 after 2pm. *Season:* Open all year. *Methods:* Barbless hooks only. No night fishing. No boilies.

Darts Farm Fishing Lakes
Darts Farm, Clyst St George, Topsham, Nr Exeter, *Tel:* 01392 878209, *Water:* 2 acres lakes. *Species:* Carp max 27lb, Bream max 8-10lb, Roach. *Permits:* Available from Darts farm shop.

E.A. licence required. *Charges:* Max two rods. Adult £8 per day. O.A.P and under 16 - £5. *Season:* All year round; Night Fishing by arrangement. *Methods:* Barbless hooks, disinfectant tanks for dipping tackle, no Carp in keep nets.

Exeter & District A.A. (Feneck Ponds) ♿
Contact: Terry Reed (Hon. Sec.), PO Box 194, Exeter, *Mobile:* 07970 483913, *Water:* Two very prolific ponds. Small but set in a beautiful, quiet environment, solitude fishing at its best. *Species:* Tench, Carp, Crucians, Roach and Rudd. *Permits:* Exeter Angling Centre, Smythen Street (Off Market Street, Exeter). Bridge Cafe, Bridge Road, Exeter. Exmouth Tackle & Sport, The Strand, Exmouth. Tackle Trader, Wharf Road, Newton Abbot. Exe Valley Angling, West Exe South, Tiverton. Saunders Pet Supplies, Fore Street, Cullompton. Tiverton Parkway Station (Cafe), Sampford Peverell. *Charges:* £34 Adults, £4 for Juniors (annual). £5 day.

Season: Different on each water. Details in association handbook or from agents. *Methods:* Different restrictions on each water. Details in association handbook.

Exeter & District A.A. (Sampford Peverall Ponds) ♿

Contact: Terry Reed (Hon. Sec.), PO Box 194, Exeter, *Mobile:* 07970 483913, *Water:* Two small ponds adjacent to railway line, relatively easy fishing. *Species:* All coarse fish present with Carp to 20lb. *Permits:* Exeter Angling Centre, Smythen Street (Off Market Street, Exeter). Bridge Cafe, Bridge Road, Exeter. Exmouth Tackle & Sport, The Strand, Exmouth. Tackle Trader, Wharf Road, Newton Abbot. Exe Valley Angling, West Exe South, Tiverton. Saunders Pet Supplies, Fore Street, Cullompton. Tiverton Parkway Station (Cafe), Sampford Peverell. *Charges:* £34 Adults, £4 for Juniors (annual). £5 day. *Season:* No close season. Details in association handbook or from agents. *Methods:* Different restrictions on each water. Details in association handbook.

Exeter & District Angling Association (Exeter Canal)

Contact: Terry Reed (Hon. Sec.), PO Box 194, Exeter, *Tel:* 01392 677744, *Mobile:* 07970 483913, *Water:* This very old waterway is approximately 12ft deep, throughout its six mile length. *Species:* Carp to 40lb, Tench, Chub, Roach and specimen Pike to 30lb. *Permits:* Exeter Angling Centre, Smythen Street (Off Market Street, Exeter). Bridge Cafe, Bridge Road, Exeter. Exmouth Tackle & Sport, The Strand, Exmouth. Tackle Trader, Wharf Road, Newton Abbot. Exe Valley Angling, West Exe South, Tiverton. Saunders Pet Supplies, Fore Street, Cullompton. Tiverton Parkway Station (Cafe), Sampford Peverell. *Charges:* £34 Adults, £4 for Juniors (annual). £5 day. *Season:* No close season on canal. Details in association handbook or from agents. *Methods:* Different restrictions on each water. Details in association handbook.

Exeter Ship Canal

Contact: Exeter City Council, River & Canal Manager, Civic Centre, Exeter, *Tel:* 01392 274306, *Water:* 5.25 miles of canal, both banks; upper 2 miles free permits. *Species:* Roach, Bream, Tench, Carp, Pike & Eels. *Permits:* Free permits from - River & Canal Office, Canal Basin, Haven Rd, Exeter and Exeter City Council, Civic Centre, Phase II Reception, Paris Street. Angling Association permit from tackle shops. *Charges:* Free permits with proof of identity and E.A. licence. Lower level 3.25 miles on Exeter & District A.A. permit. *Season:* Open all year. *Methods:* No live or dead bait coarse fish.

Hogsbrook Lakes

Contact: Desmond & Maureen Pearson, Russett Cottage, Greendale Barton, Woodbury Salterton, Exeter, *Tel:* 01395 233340, *Water:* One 1.5 acre and one 2 acre lake. *Species:* Bream, Tench, Roach, Rudd, Golden Rudd, Carp. *Charges:* Private club Membership £275 per year, max 100 members. Prices may change in 2008. *Season:* Open all year. *Methods:* Members rules: Barbless hooks, keepnets by arrangement, no Carp in nets or sacks, all Carp anglers must have unhooking mats. No alcohol. Take all rubbish home. Night fishing by prior arrangement for members only.

Home Farm Fishery ♿

Contact: Mr F Williams, Red Cedars, Mamhead, Kenton, Exeter, *Tel:* 01626 866259, *Mobile:* 07779 811386, *Water:* 1 lake approx. one acre. *Species:* Carp 20lb plus, Roach to 2lb, Tench to 4lb, Rudd to 12oz, Koi. *Permits:* From the cabin by the lake. *Charges:* 1 rod - £6, 2 rods - £6.50, weekly ticket £28 max two rods, concessions for children. Night fishing by arrangement. *Season:* Open all year. *Methods:* No groundbaiting with boilies, no tiger nuts.

Luccombes Coarse Fishery

Contact: Mr Julian Harrod, Luccombes Fishery, Towsington Lane, Exminster, Exeter, *Tel:* 01392 832858, *Mobile:* 07748 568316, *Water:* 5.25 acres of mature ponds with lillies, rushes and fishing platforms. *Species:* Common and Mirror Carp to 18lb. Koi and Ghost to 8.5lb. Perch 4lb, Bream 2.5lb, Tench 2lb, Roach and Rudd. *Permits:* On site. *Charges:* Adult day £6 two rods. Under 16 (must be accompanied by an adult) £4.50. Evening after 4pm £4. Season tickets: £120 12 months, £70 6 months. *Season:* Open all year from 6.30am to 30 mins before dark. *Methods:* Nets to be dipped. Barbless hooks only. No keepnets, no boilies, no nuts, no fixed feeders. Please use unhooking mats and handle all fish with care.

South View Farm

Contact: Wilf and Dorothy Turner, Shillingford St George, Exeter, *Tel:* 01392 832278, *Mobile:* 07976048165, *Water:* 3 lakes totalling 3 acres. *Species:* Mirror, Common up to 28lb & Ghost Carp 19lb, Roach 2.5lb, Rudd 2.5lb, Perch 4lb, Bream, Green & Gold Tench to 3.5lb. *Permits:* Tickets on the bank. *Charges:* £6 for two rods, £5 Juniors (under 16, must be accompanied). Evening ticket after 5pm £4 adult, £3 junior. Weekly ticket £30 Adult, £25 Junior. *Season:* Open all year dawn to dusk. *Methods:* Barbless hooks, no boilies or keepnets, nets must be dipped, unhooking mats essential. Boilies only allowed as hookbait.

Upham Farm Ponds

Contact: S.J.Willcocks, Upham Farm, Farringdon, Exeter, *Tel:* 01395 232247, *Mobile:* 07971 827552, *Water:* 6 well stocked ponds. *Species:* Carp 27lb 4oz, Tench 8lb 8oz and Bream. *Permits:* Day tickets on bank. *Charges:* £6/day (concessions for O.A.P's, Junior). *Methods:* Barbless hooks, no keepnets, no groundbait.

EXMOUTH

Squabmoor

Contact: South West Lakes Trust Fishery Assistant, *Tel:* 01647 277587, *Water:* Reservoir 4 acres. *Species:* Good head of Carp to 25lb. Roach to 3lb 2oz, Tench. *Permits:* Exmouth Tackle (01395 274918), Exeter Angling Centre (01392 436404), and Budleigh News (01395 443272). *Charges:* Full day £5.25, concession £4.25, 24 hour £9.50. Season tickets available from Summerlands Tackle (01237 471291) - additional fisheries £25 each. *Season:* Open all year 24 hours a day.

HATHERLEIGH

Highampton Lakes (Coarse Lake)

Contact: Greenacre Farm, Highampton, Beaworthy, *Tel:* 01409 231216, *Water:* Two acre Coarse Lake. Also 2 Trout lakes. Re stocking for spring 2008. *Species:* Carp to 20lb plus Tench, Roach, Rudd, Bream and Crucian Carp. *Permits:* Day tickets available from lakes car park. Available for competitions by prior arrangement. *Charges:* Coarse fishing £6. *Season:* Open all Year. *Methods:* Barbless hooks only.

Legge Farm Coarse Fishery ♿

Contact: Des Hudd, Church Road, Highampton, Beaworthy, *Tel:* 01409 231464, *Water:* 1.25 acre lake & four other ponds. *Species:* Carp (common to 20lb plus), Tench, Perch to 4.3lb, Roach, Rudd, Crucians, Grass Carp, Bream. *Charges:* After 4pm adults £3.50, Adults £5 a day, O.A.P's, £3.50, Children £3. Prices may vary for 2008. *Season:* All year 7am - Dusk. *Methods:* Barbless hooks. No radios or plastic bait, no boilies. Children must be accompanied by adults.

HOLSWORTHY

Clawford Vineyard ♿

Clawford Vineyard, Clawton, *Tel:* 01409 254177, *Mobile:* 07786 332332, *Water:* 16 lakes totalling over 45 acres of water. *Species:* Common, Mirror, Crucian, Ghost & Grass Carp, Tench, Roach, Rudd, Orfe, Barbel, Golden Tench, Blue Tench, Golden/Pink Orfe, Green Rudd, Gold Carp, Goldfish, Catfish, Ide, Chub, Gudgeon. *Charges:* On application. *Season:* Open all year. *Methods:* No live or deadbait. No particles or nuts except hemp or sweetcorn. Barbless hooks only. No Carp whatsoever in keepnets. Full rules at the fishery.

Higher Shorston Coarse Fishing Lakes ♿

Contact: Mr R Fursdon & Mrs L. Fursdon, Staddon Road, Holsworthy, *Tel:* 01409 253657, *Water:* Two Coarse Lakes, each lake in excess of one acre. *Species:* Common Carp, Mirror Carp, Roach and Rudd. Carp to over 10lb. *Charges:* Day Tickets Self Service £6. *Season:* Open all year Dawn until Dusk. *Methods:* Barbless hooks, no keep nets, no rigs or fixed leads, no beans or nuts. Other particles to be properly prepared. Unhooking mats to be used for Carp.

Mill Farm Fishery

Bradworthy, *Tel:* 01409 241047, *Water:* One large lake. *Species:* Carp, Ghost Carp, Tench, Perch and Bream. *Charges:* £6 per day. From farmhouse. *Season:* Open all year, dawn till dusk. *Methods:* Please read full rules on side of lodge before fishing.

Woodacott Arms

Contact: Stewart Le Comber, Woodacott Cross, Thornbury, Holsworthy, *Tel:* 01409 261162, *Water:* Two lakes, 1.25 acre and 1 acre. *Species:* Carp 30lb, Tench 7lb, Bream 5lb, Rudd 2lb, Roach 2lb. *Charges:* Adults: Day Tickets 2 Rods £6, Juniors: 2

Rods £3. *Methods:* Barbless hooks, no keepnets, no boilies or peanuts, no surface fishing.

HONITON

Fishponds House

Contact: Mr Michael Harley, Fishponds House, Dunkeswell, Honiton, *Tel:* 01404 891358, *Water:* 2 Lakes each over 1 acre. *Species:* Carp to 20lb, Rudd, Roach and Tench. *Charges:* £6.00 per day, Children under 11yrs £3.00 per day. *Season:* Open all year dawn to dusk. *Methods:* Barbless hooks, no boilies, no keepnets.

Hartsmoor Fisheries

Contact: John Griss, Bolham Water, Clayhidon, Cullompton, *Tel:* 01823 680460, *Water:* Two day ticket lakes - 2 acres and 1.25 acres, One syndicate lake - 3.5 acres, plus new 5 acre lake opened Jan 2008. *Species:* Roach and Rudd to 2lb, Tench 6lb, Bream 7lb, Perch 3lb, Crucians 3.5lb (not hybrids!), Chub 5lb, Carp 26.5lb (syndicate 35lb) Gudgeon 4oz. *Permits:* Day tickets on the bank, Syndicate - get your name on the waiting list. *Charges:* £6 per day. £6 per night by arrangement. *Season:* Day tickets dawn to dusk all year round. *Methods:* Barbless hooks. No nuts of any kind. No Carp over 2lb in keepnets. Loose feed and groundbait is permitted.

Hollies Fishery ♿

Contact: Fiona Downer, Sheldon, Honiton, *Tel:* 01404 841428 or 0845 2267714, *Water:* Spring fed lake. *Species:* Carp and mixed coarse fish. *Charges:* £5 per day. £3.50 per half day (4 hours). *Season:* Open all year, dawn to dusk. Night fishing by prior arrangement.

Milton Farm Ponds

Contact: Brian Cook, Milton Farm, Payhembury, Honiton, *Tel:* 01404 850236, *Mobile:* 07977 940443, *Water:* 5 lakes approx. 2 acres. *Species:* Carp to 27lb, Tench 8lb, Roach 2lb, Bream, Rudd. *Permits:* Collected on bank. *Charges:* £5 per person per day - no charge for extra rods, £3.50 children 14 or under. Evening ticket £3.50 adults £2 children. Night fishing by arrangement. *Season:* Open all year round. *Methods:* No groundbaiting with boilies.

ILFRACOMBE

Lower Aylescott

Contact: Paul Henstridge, Lower Aylescott, West Down, Ilfracombe, *Tel:* 01271 864054, *Mobile:* 07766 102535, *Water:* Half acre lake. *Species:* (Common, Leather, Mirror, double figures), Crucian, Roach, Rudd, Bream, Golden Tench, (Ghost Koi double figures). *Charges:* £5 per person per day. *Season:* Open all year. *Methods:* No keepnets, barbless hooks only.

Lower Slade

Contact: South West Lakes Trust Fishery Assistant, *Tel:* 01288 321262, *Water:* Reservoir 6 acres. *Species:* Mirror & Common Carp to 20lb plus. Bream to 5lb. Perch to 2lb 4oz, Roach, Rudd, Gudgeon and Pike (no livebaiting). *Permits:* From: Variety Sports (01271 862039), Kingfisher (01271 344919), Summerlands (01237 471291) and North Devon Angling Centre (01271 889123). *Charges:* Full day £5.25, concession £4.25, 24 hour £9.50. Season tickets available from Summerlands Tackle (01237 471291) - additional fisheries £25 each. *Season:* Open all year, 24 hours a day.

Mill Park Coarse Fishing Lake

Contact: Jo and Andy Hill, Mill Park, Mill Lane, Berrynarbor, Ilfracombe, *Tel:* 01271 882647, *Water:* 1.5 acre lake between Ilfracombe and Combe Martin. *Species:* Bream, Carp, Roach, Tench, Golden Orfe, Golden Tench, Chub. *Permits:* From reception on site or from Berrynarbor Post Office and Ilfracombe Post Office. *Charges:* Adult £6, Junior £3.50. All juniors (under 16) must be accompanied by adult. Evening ticket available - 4pm to 9pm or dusk. Prices may change in 2008. *Season:* Open March to October, 8am to 9pm. *Methods:* Barbless hooks only, dip all nets, no night fishing.

KINGSBRIDGE

Bickerton Farm Fishery

Contact: Mr Graham Tolchard, Bickerton Farm, Hallsands, Kingsbridge, *Tel:* 01548 511220, *Water:* 0.3 acre and 0.75 acre ponds. *Species:* Carp 15lb, Roach, Rudd, Perch, Tench, Bream. *Charges:* £4 Under 14's, £5 per rod Adults. *Methods:* Barbless hooks, No keepnets unless fishing match. No night fishing.

Coombe Water Fisheries ♿

Contact: J.W. Robinson, Coombe Farm, Kingsbridge, *Tel:* 01548 852038, *Mobile:* 07971077980, *Water:* 3 Lakes. *Species:* Carp to 25lb, Bream to 4lb, Roach to 2.5lb. *Permits:* No E.A. licence required. Lakes are covered by general E.A. licence. *Charges:* £6 day ticket, £3 Under 16. 1/2 day ticket £4. *Season:* All year dawn to dusk. Night fishing by arrangement only. *Methods:* Barbless hooks, no ground bait, no Carp over 1lb in keepnets.

Slapton Ley National Nature Reserve

Contact: Nick Binnie, Slapton Ley Field Centre, Slapton, Kingsbridge, *Tel:* 01548 580685, *Water:* Please note all fishing suspended to 2010.

LEWDOWN

Alder Lake

Contact: Mr Bob Westlake, Alder, Lewdown, Okehampton, *Tel:* 01566 783444, *Water:* 4 acre Lake. *Species:* Perch, Carp to 25lb, Bream to 8.25lb, Specimen Roach and Tench. Plus natural stock of Trout. *Charges:* £5 per rod per day. *Season:* No closed season. *Methods:* No restrictions. Night fishing allowed.

Plymouth Command Angling Association (Stowford Grange)

Contact: Mr Vic Barnett, 5 Weir Close, Mainstone, Plymouth, *Tel:* 01752 708206, *Mobile:* 0771 0552 910, *Water:* Three Lakes. 2.5, 1.5 and 0.75 acres. Plus some river fishing on the Thrushel. *Species:* Carp, Bream, large Perch, Golden and Green Tench, Roach. *Permits:* Bookings from the above ONLY. Valid EA licence required. *Charges:* On application. *Season:* No close season. *Methods:* Deep water methods.

NEWTON ABBOT

Exeter & District A.A. (Abrook Pond)

Contact: Terry Reed (Hon. Sec.), PO Box 194, Exeter, *Mobile:* 07970 483913, *Water:* Good looking pond with rustic bridges and plenty of lily pads. Relatively easy fishing for the pleasure or specimen Carp angler. *Species:* Tench, Beam, Roach and Carp to mid twenties. *Permits:* Exeter Angling Centre, Smythen Street (Off Market Street, Exeter). Bridge Cafe, Bridge Road, Exeter. Exmouth Tackle & Sport, The Strand, Exmouth. Tackle Trader, Wharf Road, Newton Abbot. Exe Valley Angling, West Exe South, Tiverton. Saunders Pet Supplies, Fore Street, Cullompton. Tiverton Parkway Station (Cafe), Sampford Peverell. *Charges:* £34 Adults, £4 for Juniors (annual). £5 day. *Season:* Close season March 14th - June 16th. Details in association handbook or from agents. *Methods:* Different restrictions on each water. Details in association handbook.

Learn To Fish In Newton Abbot

Contact: Paul Power, 103 Broadlands Ave., Newton Abbot, *Tel:* 01626 205941, *Mobile:* 07814 060147, *Water:* Open to all who would like to learn to fish in Newton Abbot area. NFA & NFSA qualified Coach, coarse and sea angling covered. Tuition free of charge. *Species:* Carp - 33lb, Tench - 11lb, Bream - 9.5lb, Perch - 5lb, Roach - 2.5lb, Rudd - 2lb and Pike - 20lb. *Permits:* Tackle Trader, Newton Abbot - 01626 331613. Torbay Angling - 01803 552496. Quay Stores, Torquay. Take the Bait, Teignmouth. Oakford Service Station, Kingsteignton. *Charges:* Dawn - Dusk £6, 24hr ticket £10 *Methods:* Barbless hooks. No nut baits, club rules apply.

Newton Abbot Fishing Association (Coarse Ponds)

Contact: Adam Bojar (Hon. Secretary), PO Box 1, Bovey Tracey, Newton Abbot, *Tel:* 01626 834032, *Water:* 17 coarse ponds in the Newton Abbot Area. Also member of S.L.A.C. (Somerset Levels Association of Clubs) with stretches of the Parret, Brue and Isle. *Species:* Carp to 36lb, Tench to12lb, Bream to 8lb, Roach to 2lb, Perch to 5lb, Rudd to 1.5lb. *Permits:* From Tackle Trader, Newton Abbot. Oakford Filling Station, Kingsteignton. Torbay Angling, Paignton and Exeter Angling, Exeter. *Charges:* Day Tickets: £6 senior, £2 junior, 24 hour ticket £10. Associate licence £50 senior (1 year fishing majority of waters). Full member £75 adult. £15 junior, £30 OAP/conc. (must live within 20 miles of Newton Abbot). Association key for gates £2. *Season:* Ponds and lakes are open 24 hours a day, 365 days a year. Rivers are controlled by the national close season for coarse fish; Rocombe Ponds and Wapperwell Ponds open from dawn to dusk. *Methods:* Barbless or crushed barbs. 2 rods 1st April to 30th September. 3 rods 1st October to 31st March. No lead shot. No nut baits. No fires. No dogs. No keepnets at Rocombe.

Preston Ponds

Contact: Newton Abbot Fishing Association, *Tel:* 01626 834032, *Water:* See entry under Newton Abbot Fishing Association. Three ponds at Kingsteignton. Key Transport: Popular match water (full members only). Eddison Pond: small water. Sawmills: about 3 acres coloured by run off from local clay works but don't be put off! *Species:* Key Transport: Skimmers, Bream, big Roach, Rudd, Perch, Tench and Crucians to over a pound. Eddison Pond: Most species with Tench, Crucians and mid-double Carp. Sawmills: Skimmers, Bream, Perch, Tench Carp and Roach to over 1lb with odd Perch to 3lb, Carp to 20lb a rumours of a single large Catfish!. New Cross: Some good Roach, Perch, the odd Tench.

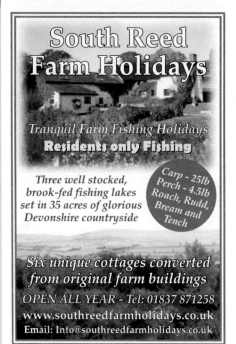

Joseph Seery with his first ever Carp from Stafford Moor

Rackerhayes Complex

Contact: Newton Abbot Fishing Association, *Tel:* 01626 834032, *Water:* See entry under Newton Abbot Fishing Association. 6 waters just outside Newton Abbot. Island Pond 5 acres (full members only), First Pond 2 acres, Dores Pond 9 acres, Linhay Pond 3 acres, Weedy Pond (just under 1 acre) and Wheel Pond (juniors have preference). *Species:* Island Pond: most species, numerous Carp over 30lb.Tench over 10lb. Good sized Roach, Rudd, Pike, Bream and Eels. First Pond: Good head of Carp to 28lb, Tench, Roach, Bream etc. and a large number of Jack Pike. Wheel Pond: Carp to 14lb, Roach, Rudd, Perch, Golden Orfe, Tench and occasional small Pike. Linhay Pond: Most coarse species with some excellent Bream. Dores Pond: Very large head of Carp to 30lb, superb Tench averaging 6lb and up to 11lb 15oz. Weedy Pond: most coarse fish including good Tench and some large Carp. *Permits:* See main entry.

Spring Ponds ♿

Contact: Newton Abbot Fishing Association, *Tel:* 01626 834032, *Water:* See entry under Newton Abbot Fishing Association. Three small farm ponds. Disabled toilets on site. *Species:* Middle pond has been heavily re-stocked. Top and bottom ponds well stocked with Carp averaging 2lb. Odd Carp to low double plus Tench, Roach and Bream. Almost guaranteed action.

Wapperwell Pond

Contact: Newton Abbot Fishing Association, Adam Bojar (Hon. Secretary), PO Box 1, Bovey Tracey, Newton Abbot, *Tel:* 01626 834032, *Water:* A small secluded pool, good for evening or morning sessions. Now open to juniors if accompanied by over 21 year old. *Species:* Crucians 1lb and Tench 2 to 3lb.

West Golds

Contact: Newton Abbot Fishing Association, *Tel:* 01626 834032, *Water:* A tidal water that is incorporated in the local flood defence system. Extreme care should be taken as flash tidal flooding is common. *Species:* Dace, Roach, Skimmers, Mullet and Carp to over 20lb. Stock changes with flow of higher tides.

NORTH TAWTON

North Tawton Angling Specimen Group

Contact: Mr. J.D. Mansfield, 4 Taw Vale Close, North Tawton, *Tel:* 01837 880048, *Mobile:* 07828 324566, *Water:* Fishing waters in Avon, Somerset, Devon & Cornwall. Lake, River & Sea fishing from shore only. *Species:* Any species listed in the British

Ashley Hugo
with a 20lb 4oz
Mirror from
Salmonhutch

records. *Charges:* Membership: £10 per year adult. £5 under 14 and OAPs. *Season:* June 1st - May 31st. *Methods:* Abide by regulations laid out on lake or river that the group are fishing.

Spires Lakes

Contact: Barry Ware, Riverside, Fore Street, North Tawton, *Tel:* 01837 82499, *Water:* Two lakes, 25 peg match lake and 2 acre lake. *Species:* Carp 30lb, Tench 5lb, Roach 1lb 8oz, Rudd 1lb, Bream 3.5lb, Perch 4.6lb, Orfe 6lb, Ghost Carp 1lb, Crucian Carp 2lbs 8ozs. *Permits:* On site kiosk, self service. *Charges:* £6 Day ticket, £4.50 Evening, £4.50 Juniors & O.A.P.s. *Season:* Dawn to dusk. *Methods:* Barbless hooks, no boilies, no tiger or peanuts.

OKEHAMPTON

Millaton - Wrigley Fishing Syndicate

Contact: Mr Vic Barnett (Syndicate Sec.), 5 Weir Close, Mainstone, Plymouth, *Tel:* 01752 708206, *Mobile:* 07710 552910, *Water:* 3 small ponds, each cannot be seen from the other. A very private and secluded fishery. *Species:* Carp, Tench, Golden Tench, Bream, Perch, Gudgeon, Roach, Rudd, Large Brown Goldfish (2.5lb), Gold Carp. *Permits:* To join the syndicate, costs in the first year are: £10 joining fee, £50 for year. After the first year cost is £50 p.a. 5 day tickets - price on booking (around £5 per day). More details from the above contact or phone 01837 861100, allowing for a long ring please. The above applies to 'season tickets'. *Charges:* As above. *Season:* No close season. *Methods:* Barbless hooks only. No Carp over 2lb to be retained in keepnets. Knotless nets only. No boilies. All spawning fish to be returned to the water immediately after photographing or weighing. Syndicate members may camp overnight and generally come and go as they wish.

Millaton Farm Coarse Fishery

Contact: Gareth or Jessica Charles-Jones, Millaton Farm, Bridestowe, Okehampton, *Tel:* 01837 861100, *Water:* 3 large lakes, 2 small (from 0.75 to 2 acres). *Species:* Carp - Koi 9lb, Ghost 10.5lb, Mirror 15lb, Common 14lb, Crucian 2.5lb, Leather. Tench, Bream 4lb, Perch 1lb, Roach, Rudd, American Sun Bass 2oz. *Permits:* Up to 5 day tickets allowed. You MUST RING day before to book space before setting out. *Charges:* £5 per day per rod. *Season:* Dawn to dusk all year round. *Methods:* Barbless hooks only. No boilies, hemp, peanuts. Groundbait in moderation. No keepnets, dogs, radios.

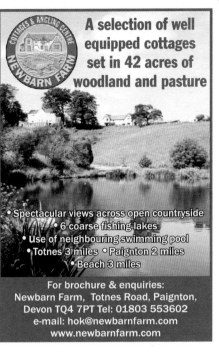

Week Farm ♿

Contact: John & Grenville Hockridge, Bridestowe, Okehampton, *Tel:* 01837 861221, *Mobile:* 07866 854121, *Water:* Two 0.5 acre lakes & one 0.25 acre lake. *Species:* Mixed Carp (Common, Mirror, Crucian), Bream in 0.25 acre, Roach, Rudd & Green Tench. *Charges:* £5 per day plus £1 extra rod, £2 evening. Children & OAP half price. *Methods:* Barbless hooks only, all nets to be dipped, night fishing by arrangement, no dogs. EA rod licence required.

PAIGNTON

New Barn Angling Centre ♿

Contact: Catherine & Richard Soley, Newbarn Farm, Totnes Road, Paignton, *Tel:* 01803 553602, *Water:* 6 ponds up to 1.25 acre suitable for juniors (parent supervision), beginners, pleasure and specimen anglers. *Species:* Carp to 28lb, Ghost Carp to 18lb, Tench to 7lb, Roach to 3lb 8oz, Bream to 9lb, Perch to 4lb 8oz, Rudd to 2lb 8oz, Eels (mirror lake only) 7lb 8oz. *Permits:* No EA rod licence required. Purchase day tickets on arrival. *Charges:* £7 up to 2 rods, additional rod £1.50 per day - Junior £5. Adults (14+) 3 day ticket £18, 5 day ticket £30, 7 day ticket £42 (n.b. days taken anytime over a year). *Season:* Open all year 7am to dusk. Night fishing available. 9 fishing shelters around main lake, first come first served. Reservations for disabled anglers. £5 advance booking fee to reserve swims. *Methods:* Barbless hooks only, no keepnets, no nuts. All baits effective: maggots, luncheon meat, sweetcorn, boilies, bread & pellets. Sensible ground baiting allowed, float fishing and ledgering (ledger rigs will be checked to ensure safety), summer time good for floating baits. No artificial baits.

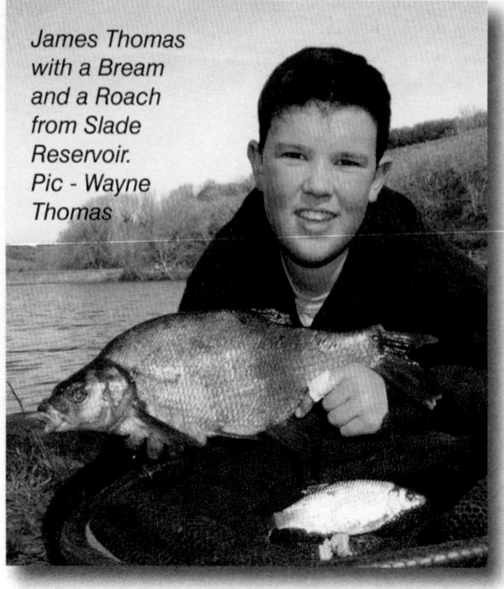
James Thomas with a Bream and a Roach from Slade Reservoir. Pic - Wayne Thomas

Town Parks Coarse Fishing Centre ♿
Contact: Mr J. Hewitt, Town Park Farm, Totnes Road, Paignton, *Tel:* 01803 523133, *Water:* Specimen Carp lake 1.5 acres (max 16 anglers at any one time). Match lake 2 acres (21 pegs) available for club/block bookings, phone for details. *Species:* Carp lake - Mirror and Common Carp to 35lbs. Match lake - Carp 10lbs, Crucian Carp 3lbs, Tench 5lbs, Chub 4lbs, Bream 4lbs, Roach 2lbs, Rudd 1lb, Perch 4lbs. *Permits:* No E.A. Rod licence required. *Charges:* Carp lake - Full day £7, Night (6pm - 9am) £10, Evening (4pm - Dusk) £5, 24 hrs £14. Match lake - Full day £6, Night (6pm - 9am) £9, Evening (4pm - Dusk) £4, 24 hrs £13. *Season:* 24hrs, 365 day a year. Night fishing available. *Methods:* A full list of rules are posted on site.

PLYMOUTH

Plymouth & District Angling Club
Contact: Bill Cox, 17 Thetford Gardens, Eggbuckland, Plymouth, *Tel:* 01752 317329, *Water:* 3 lakes at Cadover Bridge, two at St. Germans. Tench - ranging in size from 0.5 to 2 acres. *Species:* Carp to 29lb 8oz, Tench 6lb, Bream 8lb 8oz, Rudd 11lb 6oz, Roach 2lb 8oz and Crucians. *Permits:* Clive's Tackle and Bait, 182 Exeter St, Plymouth. Tel: 01752 228940. *Charges:* £52 membership fee. Juniors £10. OAP's £25. *Season:* Open all year. St Germans and Cadover 24 hours. *Methods:* Barbless hooks. No Carp in keepnets. Unhooking mats for all Carp.

Plymouth & District Angling Club (Filham Lake) ♿
Contact: Bill Cox, 17 Thetford Gardens, Eggbuckland, Plymouth, *Tel:* 01752 317329, *Water:* 2.5 - 3 acre lake (Filham Lake). *Species:* Roach, Carp, Crucian, Bream and Tench. *Permits:* Membership packs from Clives Tackle and Bait - 01752 228940. Day tickets from The Cobblers Shop in Ivybridge. *Charges:* £6.25 day ticket. *Season:* Open all year. *Methods:* Barbless Hook. Carp friendly nets to be used (nothing over 3lb in net).

Plymouth Command Angling Association (Ponds) ♿
Contact: Mr Vic Barnett Hon. Sec., 5 Weir Close, Mainstone, Plymouth, *Tel:* 01752 708206, *Mobile:* 07710 552910, *Water:*

Two lakes of 0.75 and 1.25 acres for coarse fishing within ten minutes of Plymouth. Also member access to several associated waters in the south west. *Species:* Carp, Tench, Bream, Perch, Roach, Rudd, Crucians, Goldfish, Eels, Golden Carp and some Koi. *Permits:* Membership is open to all serving members of HM Forces. Associate membership is also open to ex-serving members of HM Forces, no matter when the time was served. Day tickets available from Manadon Angling Supplies, Plymouth and Clives Tackle and Bait, £5 per person, up to 8 per day in total. *Charges:* Costs for full membership or associate membership are available on application or enquiry at the above contact. A Carp society has been formed for the specimen angler - details on application. *Season:* No close season for coarse fish. *Methods:* Barbless hooks only at the coarse fishery. Knotless keepnets to be used as per E.A. guidelines on minimum 3 metres length. All spawning fish are to be returned to the water immediately. No Carp over 2lb to be kept in keepnets.

Sunridge Fishery ♿

Contact: RM and M Hammett, Sunridge Nurseries, Worston, Yealmpton, Plymouth, *Tel:* 01752 880438, *Mobile:* 07734 557212, *Water:* Approx. half acre private lake that can be reserved for exclusive use. Established 30 years. *Species:* Mirror and Common Carp up to 27lb. *Permits:* From above at the Nurseries. *Charges:* £6.50 adult day, £4.50 child/OAP. May vary 2008. *Season:* Open all year dawn to dusk, night fishing by arrangement only. *Methods:* Barbless hooks only, no keepnets (except by prior arrangement).

Warleigh Barton Fishery

Contact: Andrew Kent, Tamerton Foliot, Plymouth, *Tel:* 01752 771458, *Mobile:* 07811 339569, *Water:* 2 acre lake plus 0.25 acre pond. *Species:* Mirror and Common - Now up to 30lbs. *Permits:* Day tickets. *Charges:* £10/day, £15 for 24 hrs. *Season:* All year. *Methods:* Barbless hooks, no keep nets.

SEATON

Horriford Fishing ♿

Contact: Mr Pady, Horriford Farm, Colyford, Colyton, *Tel:* 01297 552316, *Water:* 2 ponds - 1 with access for disabled. *Species:* Bream (5lb), Roach (1lb), Tench (6lb), Carp (15lb), Perch (2lb), Rudd (1.5lb). *Permits:* From farmhouse or on bank. *Charges:* Day ticket £5. Half day ticket £3. 6 month season tickets available £50 single, £60 familiy. *Season:* Open all year dawn to dusk. *Methods:* Barbless hooks only, no boilies.

SOUTH BRENT

Hatchlands Coarse Fishery

Contact: Malcolm Davies, Greyshoot Lane, Rattery, South Brent, *Tel:* 01364 73500, *Water:* Two 2 acre lakes. *Species:* Carp to 22lb, Tench, Roach, Bream, Rudd and Gudgeon. *Permits:* E.A. licence required. *Charges:* £5 per person per day. *Season:* Open all year. *Methods:* Barbless hooks only. No large Carp in keepnets.

Little Allers Coarse Fishery

Contact: M & J Wakeham, Little Allers Farm, Avonwick, South Brent, *Tel:* 01364 72563, *Mobile:* 07855 427510, *Water:* 2 acre lake. *Species:* Carp, Bream, Tench, Roach, Rudd. *Charges:* £5 per day adults, £3 under 16, £3.00 evening ticket after 5pm. Payments at hut in car park (correct money). *Season:* Open all year dawn to dusk. *Methods:* Barbless hooks only, no Carp in keepnets. No dogs allowed. No bait boats.

SOUTH MOLTON

Furzebray Carp Lakes

Contact: MJ and TJ Kingdon, Furzebray Farm, George Nympton Road, South Molton, *Tel:* 01769 572653, *Water:* 3 acre specimen lake. 0.5 acre Pads Lake. *Species:* Specimen Lake: Carp to over 20lb and Perch. Pads Lake: Carp, Rudd, Perch and Koi. *Permits:* Bookings only on 01769 572653. *Charges:* Specimen Lake: Day £11, concessions and under 16 £8. 24 hours £18, concessions and under 16 £14. Pads Lake: dawn to dusk £8.

Oaktree Fishery ♿

Contact: George Andrews, Bottreaux Mill, West Anstey, South Molton, *Tel:* 01398 341568, *Water:* Three 2 acre lakes. *Species:* Carp over 35lb, Tench to 8lb, Bream, Roach, Perch to over 5lb, Koi Carp, Catfish to 40lb. *Permits:* On site only from tackle and bait shop. *Charges:* Day tickets: Adults from £6, Specimen lake £7, Junior/OAP from £5, Specimen lake £6, Eve tickets: Adult £5.00, Specimen lake £6. Junior/OAP £4 Specimen lake £5. Extra rods £3. *Season:* Open all year 24hrs. *Methods:* Barbless hooks only. No nut type baits. See board at fishery.

TAVISTOCK

Milemead Fisheries ♿

Contact: Mr Harry Dickens, Mill Hill, Tavistock, *Tel:* 01822 610888, *Water:* Three Lakes of 2 acres each. Match Lake available for bookings, please phone for details. Regular Sunday open matches and Thursday evening matches in the summer. 8 Peg Canal. New specimen Carp lake now open. *Species:* Specimen lake Carp to 25lb (average 13lb). Other lakes: Carp to 18lb. Tench to 4lb, Bream to 4lb 8oz's, Roach to 2lb 6oz's, Rudd to 1.5lb, Crucians to 1lb 4oz's. *Permits:* Available from lakeside tackle and bait shop. *Charges:* Adult - Day ticket £7, Concession £6, Evening tickets available Adult £4.50, Concessions £3.50. Specimen Lake £10 day, £20 for 24hrs. *Season:* All year excluding Christmas Day and Boxing Day, 7am to Dusk. *Methods:* Barbless Hooks, No keepnets, All nets to be dipped prior to fishing, Please read the rule boards.

TIVERTON

Angling 2000 (Dart Raffe)

Contact: Westcountry Rivers Trust, 10 Exeter Street, Launceston, Cornwall. *Tel:* 0870 774 0704, *Water:* 1.5 acre lake. *Species:* Carp, Tench, Roach, Rudd, Eels. *Permits:* From the above. *Charges:* £7.50 day. *Season:* All year. *Methods:* Barbless, 3 rods max, no ground bait, nuts, beans, no keepnets. Night fishing by arrangement.

Bickleigh Mill

Contact: Mr Kim & Suzanne Sproat, Bickleigh Mill, Bickleigh, Tiverton, *Tel:* 01884 855419, *Water:* Bickleigh Mill fishing ponds. *Species:* Carp, Tench and Bream. *Permits:* Only at above. *Charges:* £4 per day. £2.50 half day. *Season:* Easter to end of September. *Methods:* Rods available.

Coombe Farm Fishponds

Contact: Mrs Curtis, Coombe Farm, Cadleigh, Tiverton, *Tel:* 01884 855337, *Mobile:* 07855 416369, *Water:* 3 lakes totalling 0.5 acre. *Species:* Carp to 20lb, Roach, Tench to 4lb, Bream to 1.5lb. *Charges:* £3 per day. *Season:* Open all year. *Methods:* No boilies.

Tiverton & District Angling Club ♿

Contact: Exe Valley Angling, 19 Westexe South, Tiverton, *Tel:* 01884 242275, *Water:* 11.5 Miles on Grand Western Canal,

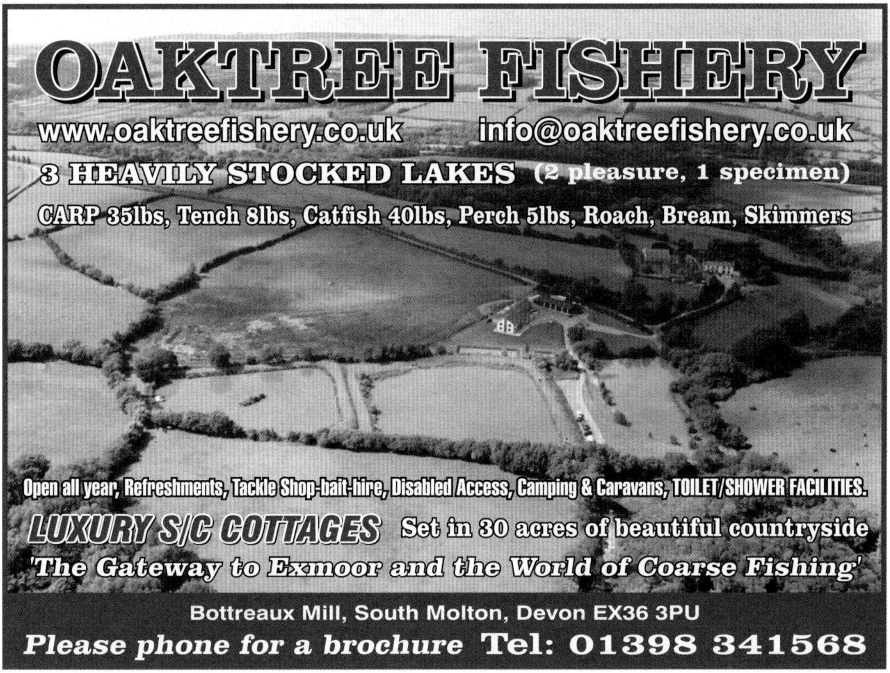

STILLWATER COARSE

1.25 acre mixed fishery lake at Exebridge. Various stretches on several rivers in Somerset. *Species:* Canal: Carp, Bream, Tench, Roach, Perch, Pike, Eels. Lakeside: Carp, Bream, Roach, Tench, Eels, Crucian Carp. *Permits:* Please ring Exe Valley for details. Also available from: Exeter Angling Centre, Enterprise Angling Taunton, Topp Tackle Taunton & Minnows Caravan Park - beside Grand Western Canal. *Charges:* Senior: Day £5, Annual £25. Conc: Junior & OAP Day £3, Annual £12. *Season:* Open all year. *Methods:* Canal Methods: Any. Restrictions: Fish from permanent pegs, no night fishing, no cars on bank, no digging of banks or excessive clearance of vegetation. Lakeside Methods: Any. Restrictions: No night fishing, no boilies, Trout pellets or nuts, one rod only, fishing from permanent pegs, no dogs, nets to be dipped. Ring Exe Valley Angling for full details.

West Pitt Farm Fishery ♿

Contact: Susanne Westgate, Whitnage, Nr. Tiverton, *Tel:* 01884 820296, *Mobile:* 07855 582374, *Water:* 3 lakes up to 2.75 acres. *Species:* Common & Mirror Carp, Bream, Tench, Roach, Rudd, Crucians, Golden Tench, Chub, Golden Orfe. *Permits:* Self service day tickets £5 per day (correct money please). *Charges:* £5/day, £3.50 evenings. *Season:* All year, no closed season. Open dawn till dusk. *Methods:* No boilies. Barbless hooks only, nets to be dipped, groundbait in moderation.

TORQUAY

Butterlake Fishing Club

Contact: John Palmer, 37 Allerbrake Road, Newton Abbot, *Water:* Freshwater Pond at Compton. *Species:* Tench, Carp, Perch, Crucian Carp. *Permits:* To apply and join the waiting list please apply in writing to John Palmer. *Charges:* Day tickets restricted to members and their families. *Season:* Open all year. *Methods:* Keepnets permitted.

TORRINGTON

Bakers Farm

Contact: Mr & Mrs Ridd, Bakers Farm, Moortown, Torrington, *Tel:* 01805 623260, *Water:* 1 acre lake. *Species:* Mirror & Common Carp, Tench, Roach & Rudd. *Charges:* £5 per rod per day. *Season:* Open all year. *Methods:* Barbless Hooks, No large Carp in keepnets.

Darracott

Contact: South West Lakes Trust Fishery Assistant, *Tel:* 01288 361262, *Water:* Reservoir 3 acres. *Species:* Roach up to 1lb. Mixed bags to 20lb plus of Roach, Rudd, Bream and Tench. Perch to 2.25lb. Carp to 15lb. *Permits:* From: Whiskers Pet Centre (01805 622859), Summerlands (01237 471291), Bideford TIC

(01237 477676), Kingfisher (01271 344919) and Barley Grove Service Station (01805 623340). *Charges:* Full day £5.25, concession £4.25, 24 hour £9.50. Season tickets available from Summerlands Tackle (01237 471291) - additional fisheries £25 each. *Season:* Open all year 24 hours a day.

Stevenstone Lakes

Contact: Alan & Rebecca Parnell, Deer Park, Stevenstone, Torrington, *Tel:* 01805 622102, *Water:* Three lakes, total of four acres in a parkland setting. *Species:* Mirror Carp 26lb, Common 13lb, Tench 6lb, Rudd 1lb, Eels 3lb. *Permits:* Only at Deer Park. *Charges:* Day tickets £10 per day per person. *Season:* Open 7am to sunset all year around. *Methods:* Barbless hooks only, no boilies, no nut type baits, no fish over 2lb in keepnets, no dogs, no litter. Unhooking mats essential.

TOTNES

East Moore Farm Fishery

Diptford, Totnes, *Mobile:* 07855 892879, *Water:* 1 lake totalling 2 acres. *Species:* Carp to 12lb, Rudd, Tench, Bream, Roach. *Charges:* On site, £7 day (2 rods per person). Under 13 half price, but must be accompanied by an adult. *Season:* Dawn to Dusk, open all year, night fishing by prior arrangement. *Methods:* No keepnets, except in matches, landing mats must be used, no boilies, barbless hooks only. Full rules at Fishery.

UMBERLEIGH

Golland Farm

Contact: Mr Nigel Tuck, Golland Farm, Burrington, Umberleigh, *Tel:* 01769 520550, *Mobile:* 07867 552157, *Water:* 2 half acre

Andy Towers at Stafford Moor's Beaties Lake with a 25lb 8oz Carp

lakes. Brook fishing for wild Brown Trout. In beautiful picture perfect surroundings. *Species:* Hundreds of Carp, average 6lb, run to 13lb+ easy pleasure fishing, Tench and Roach. Quality hard fighting fish. *Permits:* Available from Farm House. *Charges:* Day tickets. £5 per person per day or night. *Season:* Lakes open all year, brook fishing seasonal. *Methods:* Barbless hooks only, no Carp in keep nets, no spinning.

WINKLEIGH

Okehampton Coarse Fishing Club

Contact: Mr Peter O'Hora, Ferndale, 99 Station Road, Okehampton, *Tel:* 01837 55929, *Mobile:* 07973 394595, *Water:* Enclosed stillwater at Brixton Barton Farm. *Species:* Common Carp to 8lb, Roach, Rudd. *Permits:* Fishing only with a member. *Charges:* £3.50 Guest, £7.50 Adult, £5 Junior, £12.50 Family ticket for full membership. Prices may vary for 2007. *Season:* 12 months, sunrise to sunset. *Methods:* Barbless hooks. No fish over 4lb in keepnets.

Stafford Moor Fishery ♿

Contact: Andy or Debbie Seery, Dolton, Winkleigh, *Tel:* 01805 804360, *Water:* 8 acre specimen lake, 100 pegs match fishery (bookings available); 100 peg pleasure lake. 4 acre Carp bagging water (3lb to 10lb fish). 3 acre lake with Tench, Crucians and Bream. *Species:* Carp 30lb, Tench 5lb, Bream 5lb, Roach 2lb, Rudd 1.5lb, Eels 5lb. 318lb match record. *Permits:* At lodge at Stafford Moor. Specimen lake pre-booking only. *Charges:* £7 pleasure/day, £5.50 conc./OAP/Junior; £8.50 specimen/day (12 hours) £8.50 night (12 hours). *Season:* All year. *Methods:* The method is banned, barbless hooks (max. size 6), night fishing by arrangement.

YELVERTON

Coombe Fisheries ♿

Contact: Mr Stephen Horn, Yelverton, Plymouth, *Tel:* 01822 855585, *Mobile:* 07899 958493, *Water:* Two 1 acre lakes. *Species:* Coarse fish: Rudd, Roach, Various Carp (28lb). Tench (8lb) *Permits:* . *Charges:* £5 per day, £4 evening. *Season:* No close season, dawn to dusk. Night fishing by arrangement. *Methods:* Barbless hooks, no peanuts.

Stillwater Trout

ASHBURTON

Venford

Contact: South West Lakes Trust, *Tel:* 01822 855700, *Water:* Reservoir 33 acres. *Species:* Wild Brown Trout. *Charges:* Free to holders of a valid Environment Agency Licence. *Season:* 15 March - 12 October. *Methods:* Angling by spinning, fly or bait.

AXMINSTER

Lower Bruckland Fishery

Contact: David Satterley, Lower Bruckland Farm, Musbury, Axminster, *Tel:* 01297 551197, *Mobile:* 07721 429077, *Water:* 3 Large lakes. *Species:* Tringle Lake: Rainbows to 30lb & Wild Browns. *Permits:* Available at Angler's Hut by car park. *Charges:* Catch and release: £18/day, £15/half day, £10/evening. Four fish ticket £20, Two fish £15. *Season:* 1 March - 30 November. *Methods:* Catch & Release, max hook 10, Barbless - Catch & Keep, any method except Spinners.

BARNSTAPLE

Blakewell Fisheries ♿

Contact: Mr Richard & John Nickell, Blakewell Fisheries, Muddiford, Barnstaple, *Tel:* 01271 344533, *Water:* 5 acre lake. *Species:* Rainbow to 22lb 11oz. Brown to 8lb 8oz. *Permits:* On Site. *Charges:* 6 Fish £28, 5 Fish £26, 4 Fish £24, 3 Fish £22, 2 Fish £20. Price may change in 2008. *Season:* All Year. *Methods:* Fly Only.

Bratton Water

Contact: Mike or Jan, Rye Farm, Loxhore, Nr. Barnstaple, *Tel:* 01271 850642, *Water:* Five acre site. *Species:* Rainbow and Brown Trout. *Permits:* E.A. rod licence required. *Charges:* 2 fish £18. 3 fish £20. 4 fish £22. 5 fish £25. 6 fish £30. *Season:* Open all year, 9am to dusk. *Methods:* Fly only. No catch and release.

Southwood Fishery

Contact: Nigel Early, Bratton Flemming, *Tel:* 01271 343608 or 01598 710787, *Mobile:* 07767 492800, *Water:* 2.5 acre lake, max 10 rods. *Species:* Rainbow to 20lbs plus. *Permits:* Must be obtained in advance. Please phone numbers above. *Charges:* £18 for 2 fish, £20 for 3 fish, £25 for 4 fish. £30 for a 6 fish day ticket. *Season:* Open all year. *Methods:* Tickets must be pre-booked. Fly only, children under 16 must be accompanied by a fishing adult.

BEAWORTHY

Trout Lake

Contact: Mr Zyg Gregorek, Anglers Nirvana, The Gables, Winsford, Halwill, *Tel:* 01409 221559, *Water:* 3 acres. *Species:* 5 different species of Trout. *Permits:* Only at Anglers Paradise. Pre booking advisable. *Charges:* £20 per 8 hours. *Season:* All year. 8am to 9pm or dusk (which ever is earlier). *Methods:* Catch and release only, fly only. Barblesss hooks only. Landing nets must be used. Anglers Paradise rules and regulations apply.

BIDEFORD

Fosfelle Country House Hotel (Game)

Hartland, Bideford, *Tel:* 01237 441273, *Water:* Pond approx. half acre. *Species:* Rainbow & Golden Trout. *Charges:* £18

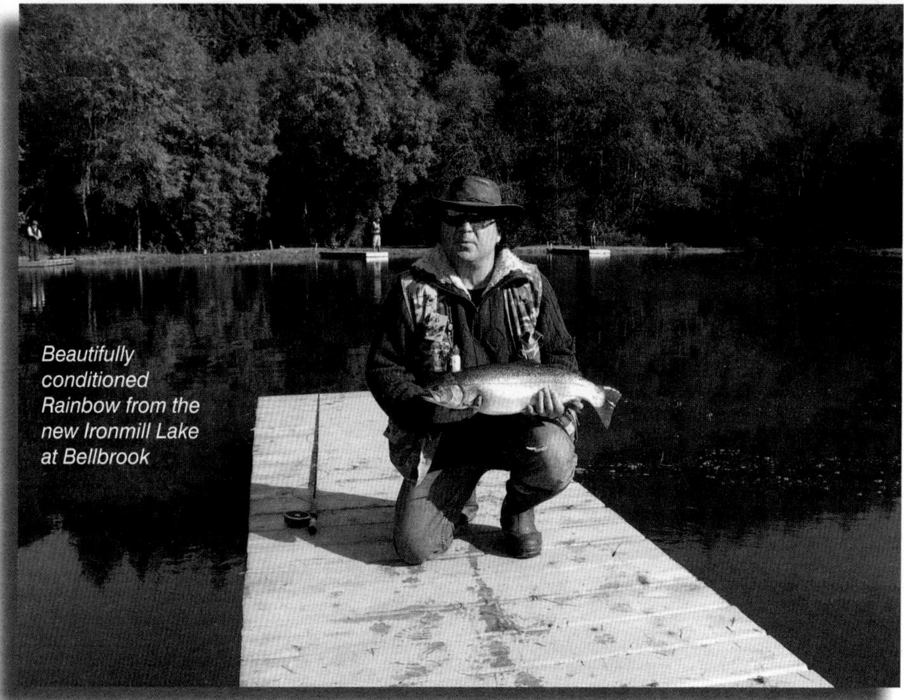
Beautifully conditioned Rainbow from the new Ironmill Lake at Bellbrook

half day - 2 Trout, full day £23 - 3 fish. *Season:* Open all year. *Methods:* Displayed on site.

Torridge Fly Fishing Club

Contact: Mr A Smith (secretary), 6 Brecon Close, Bideford, *Tel:* 01237 478614, *Mobile:* 07816 518632, *Water:* 2 x 4 acre reservoirs situated 2 miles east of Bideford. *Species:* Stocked Rainbow Trout from 1.5 to 8lb. Natural Browns to 5lb. *Permits:* 2 day tickets allowed each day. *Charges:* Day tickets: from Summerlands Fishing Tackle, Westward Ho!, Tel. 01237 471291. £15 per day (3 fish limit) Season tickets: £130 (waiting list, membership limited to 30). *Season:* 14th April - 16th December for Rainbow Trout, 14th April - 30th September for Brown Trout.

Valley View Lakes and Lodges (Trout)

Contact: Matt Pearce and Brett Bassett, Buckland Brewer, Nr Bideford, *Tel:* 01237 459049/459053, *Mobile:* 07919 102287, *Water:* Half acre lake. *Species:* Rainbow Trout. *Charges:* £5 per fish. *Season:* All year.

CHAGFORD

Fernworthy

Contact: South West Lakes Trust, *Tel:* 01647 277587, *Water:* Reservoir 78 acres. *Species:* Brown Trout. *Permits:* Self Service Kiosk on site. *Charges:* Full day £11.50, Concession £9.50. Season permits also available from Summerlands Tackle (01237 471291). *Season:* 1 April - 12 October. *Methods:* Catch & Release operates (Barbless hooks must be used).

CHUDLEIGH

Kennick ♿

Contact: South West Lakes Trust, *Tel:* 01647 277587, *Water:* Reservoir 50 acres. *Species:* Premier rainbow fishery, boats available booked in advance via the ranger. Rod average 2006: 3.08 fish per rod per day. *Permits:* Self service at Kennick hut. *Charges:* Full day £19.50, Concession £16, Evening £16, boats £12 per day. Season permits also available from Summerlands Tackle (01237 471291). *Season:* 29 March - 31 October. *Methods:* Catch and release available (barbless hooks must be used), fly fishing only.

Kennick Fly Fishers Association ♿

Contact: Mike Boston, 5 Shirburn Rd, Torquay, *Tel:* 01803 325722, *Water:* 45 acre reservoir. *Species:* Rainbow & wild Brown Trout. *Permits:* Club members able to obtain SWLT discounted tickets. *Charges:* Membership is £10 annual subscription. Under 16yrs free. *Methods:* I.A.W. SWLT byelaws.

CULLOMPTON

Goodiford Mill Fishery (Trout Lakes) ♿

Contact: David & Anne Wheeler, Goodiford Mill, Kentisbeare, Cullompton, *Tel:* 01884 266233, *Water:* One 0.5 acre Trout lake. *Species:* Rainbow - 17lb 5oz, Brown Trout - 20lb 4oz, Tiger Trout. *Permits:* Rod licence required. *Charges:* £30-5 fish, £25-4 fish, £20-3 fish, £15-2 fish. Children under 14 must be accompanied by an adult. 10% reduction on all ticket prices for over 65s. *Season:* All year. *Methods:* Max 10 longshank. Full rules on application.

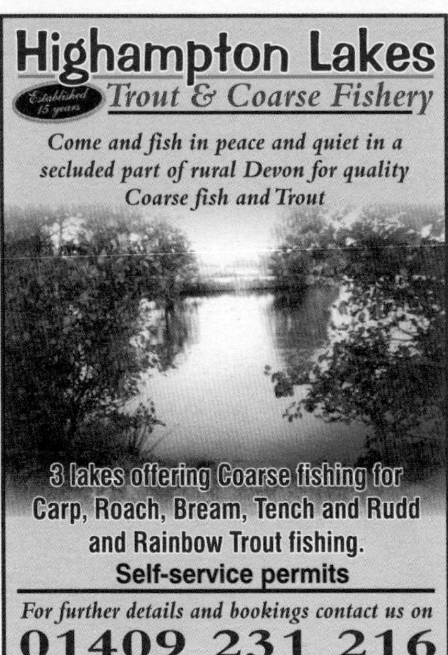

HATHERLEIGH

Highampton Trout and Coarse Lakes

Contact: Greenacre Farm, Highampton, Beaworthy, *Tel:* 01409 231216, *Water:* Re stocking for spring 2008. *Species:* Rainbow Trout. *Permits:* Day tickets available from lakes car park. *Charges:* £24 - 4 fish, £18 - 3 fish, £12 - 2 fish. Evening ticket 4.30pm onwards. *Season:* Open all Year. *Methods:* No fish to be returned to lake.

HOLSWORTHY

Mill Leat Trout Fishery

Contact: Mr Birkett, Thornbury, Holsworthy, *Tel:* 01409 261426, *Water:* Two lakes totalling 3 acres. *Species:* Rainbow Trout. *Charges:* £6 plus £4 per kg. No Limit. *Season:* 1st April - 31st October. *Methods:* Fly only.

HONITON

Hollies Trout Farm ♿

Contact: Fiona Downer, Sheldon, Honiton, *Tel:* 01404 841428 / 0845 2267714, *Water:* Stream fed lake. *Species:* Rainbow & Brown Trout. Best Rainbow 18lb 12oz (July 1993). Best Brown 11lb 14oz (May 2004). *Charges:* 2 fish - £15, 3 fish - £20, 4 fish - £25, 5 fish - £30. Concessions for O.A.P. and under 12's. *Season:* Open all year dawn to dusk.

Stillwaters Lake ♿

Contact: Michael Ford, Lower Moorhayne Farm, Yarcombe, Honiton, *Tel:* 01404 861284, *Water:* One acre lake for Brown and Rainbow fishing. Sea Trout fishing on the River Axe. *Species:* Trout up to 17lb 10oz in lake (2003) and 10lb 4oz in lake (2006). Best Sea Trout in 2006 3.5lbs. River Axe Sea Trout and a few Salmon. *Charges:* £13 per day. £15 for a morning, £15 afternoon. *Season:* March 1st - November 30th. *Methods:* Fly only. Catch and release, no keepnets.

LIFTON

Arundell Arms (Trout Lake)

Contact: Mrs Anne Voss-Bark, The Arundell Arms, Lifton, *Tel:* 01566 784666, *Water:* Three acre private lake. Also river fishing on Tamar, Lyd, Carey, Thrushel, Wolf and Ottery. *Species:* Rainbow & Brown Trout. *Permits:* Arundell Arms. *Charges:* Lake £31. *Season:* Open all year. *Methods:* Fly only on lake.

OKEHAMPTON

Meldon

Contact: South West Lakes Trust, *Tel:* 01409 211507, *Water:* Reservoir 57 acres. *Species:* Wild Brown Trout. *Charges:* Free to holders of a valid Environment Agency Licence. *Season:* 15 March - 12 October. *Methods:* Angling by spinning, fly or bait.

Roadford ♿

Contact: South West Lakes Trust, Angling & Watersports Centre, *Tel:* 01409 211507, *Water:* Reservoir 738 acres. *Species:* Brown Trout, boats available booked in advance via the centre. *Permits:* Angling & Watersports Centre at Lower Goodacre. *Charges:* Full day £11.50, Concession £9.50, Evening £9.50, boats £12 per day. Season permits also available on site or from Summerlands Tackle (01237 471291). *Season:* 29 March - 12 October. *Methods:* Fly fishing only, catch and release available. (barbless hooks must be used).

SOUTH BRENT

Avon Dam

Contact: South West Lakes Trust, *Tel:* 01822 855700, *Water:* Reservoir 50 acres. *Species:* Wild Brown Trout. *Charges:* Free to holders of a valid Environment Agency Licence. *Season:* 15 March - 12 October. *Methods:* Angling by spinning, fly or bait.

Hatchlands Trout Lakes

Contact: Malcolm Davies, Greyshoot Lane, Rattery, South Brent, *Tel:* 01364 73500, *Water:* 6 acres. *Species:* Rainbow, Brown, Golden, Blue and Brook Trout. *Permits:* E.A. Licence required. *Charges:* Prices from £10 for 2 fish. Other prices on application. Sporting ticket from £18. *Season:* Open all year. *Methods:* Barbless hooks on catch and release.

SOUTH MOLTON

Wistlandpound ♿

Contact: South West Lakes Trust, *Tel:* 01598 763719, *Water:* Reservoir 41 acres. *Species:* Intermediate Rainbow Trout. A Wheely Boat is available for disabled anglers via the Calvert Trust (01598 763221). *Permits:* Challacombe Post Office (01598 763229), The Kingfisher (01271 344919), North Devon Angling Centre, Combe Martin (01271889123), Variety Sports (01271 862039), Calvert Trust. *Charges:* Full day £14, Concession £12.50, Evening £12.50. Season permits also available from Summerlands Tackle (01237 471291). *Season:* 15 March - 31 October. *Methods:* Fly fishing only, catch and release available - barbless hooks must be used.

Wistlandpound Fly Fishing Club ♿
Contact: Nigel Bird, 9 Kingston Avenue, Combe Martin, *Tel:* 01271 883252, *Water:* Fishing regular monthly competitions at Wistlandpound and other waters. Regular social events. Juniors welcome. *Species:* Rainbow Trout 1.5 to 2lb. Brown Trout 8oz to 1lb. *Permits:* Permits to fish Wistlandpound available at a reduced rate - members only. *Charges:* Subsciptions (March to March): Adults £12, Under 16s 50p. Free tuition arranged. *Season:* Seasonal at Wistlandpound. Competitions all year round. *Methods:* Fly fishing only.

TAVISTOCK

Tavistock Trout Farm & Fishery ♿
Contact: Abigail Underhill, Parkwood Road, Tavistock, *Tel:* 01822 615441, *Mobile:* 07970 608890, *Water:* 5 lakes totalling approx. 4 acres. *Species:* Rainbow Trout (Osprey/Kingsfisher & Heron 1.5 to 14lb), Brown Trout. *Permits:* E.A Licences available. *Charges:* Full day 6 fish permit for all lakes is £40 including catch and release. 6 fish ticket £34. 5 fish £29. 4 fish (8 hours) £24. 3 firsh (5 hours or evening) £19.50. 2 fish (5 hours or evening) £14.50. *Season:* Open all year 8am - dusk. Closed Christmas Day and Boxing Day. *Methods:* Max hook size 10.

TIVERTON

Bellbrook Valley Trout Fishery
Contact: Mr Chris Atwell, Bellbrook Farm, Oakford, Tiverton, *Tel:* 01398 351292, *Water:* 6 Lakes totalling 6 acres. *Species:* Rainbow Trout (25lb 12oz), Exmoor Blue (8lb 6oz) and Wild Brown Trout (7lb 8oz). *Charges:* Half day prices: Three fish normal lakes £18, 2 fish specimen lake £22. Range of rover tickets, allowing mix of normal and specimen, from £25. Catch and release - £15 ticket, plus first fish can be taken. Full day tickets available. *Season:* Open all year 8.00am / dusk (No later than 9.00pm). *Methods:* Fly only, some catch & release available depending on weather and time of year.

STILLWATER TROUT

TOTNES

Newhouse Fishery

Contact: Paul Cook & Kirsty Cook, Newhouse Farm, Moreleigh, Totnes, *Tel:* 01548 821332, *Mobile:* 07803 128777, *Water:* 4 acre lake (also see entry under River Fishing, Avon, Devon). *Species:* Rainbow Trout, Brown Trout. *Charges:* Various tickets available. Bag limits may be made up in beginners lake. *Season:* Open all year. 8am to 1 hour after sunset. *Methods:* Fly only, barbed hooks.

YELVERTON

Burrator

Contact: Burrator & Siblyback Flyfishing & Angling Assn., *Tel:* 01579 384649, *Water:* Reservoir 150 acres - Fishery operated by Burrator & Siblyback Fly Fishing & Angling Association Tel: 07815 995585. See their entry. *Species:* Low Cost Rainbow & Brown Trout (all brown Trout must be returned). *Permits:* Yelverton Garage. *Charges:* Full Day £12 (4 fish limit). Season (contact 01579 384649) £175 adult, £30 junior. *Season:* 1st March – 31 October. *Methods:* Fly fishing only, catch and release available - barbless hooks must be used.

Burrator & Siblyback Fly Fishing & Angling Association

Contact: Brendan Sullivan (Hon Sec), 15 Trelawney Rise, Callington, Cornwall. *Tel:* 01759 384649, *Mobile:* 07815 995585, *Water:* Burrator reservoir, Yelverton, Nr Tavistock, Devon. 150 acres of flyfishing for Rainbow and Brown Trout. (All Brown Trout - catch and release) *Species:* Regular monthly competitions at various venues. Mostly at Burrator Reservoir during season. Stocking by Burrator & Siblyback Fly Fishing & Angling Association. *Permits:* Open to all. Season tickets available from - Mr J Marman. Contact No. 07712 765722 or Paul, The Fisherman, 2 King Street, Tavistock Tel: 01822 611148. *Charges:* Family membership £15, members £12. All Juniors under 18 must be accompanied by an adult. Day ticket available at Esso garage Yelverton, Devon - Price £12 (four fish limit). *Season:* Contact Brendon at the above number. 1st March - 31st October. *Methods:* Fly fishing only - no spinning

Burrator Fly Fishers

Contact: Terry Buttle (secretary), *Tel:* 01752 794687, *Water:* Burrator Fly Fishers Association is a small club running competitions during the summer and winter, with fishing trips to local stillwaters. Regular monthly meetings in the winter. *Species:* Stocked Rainbow and Brown Trout. *Permits:* Esso Garage, Yelverton. *Charges:* Club membership £10 per year, includes membership of club insurance scheme. *Season:* 1st March – 31 October. *Methods:* Fly only. Barbless hooks encouraged.

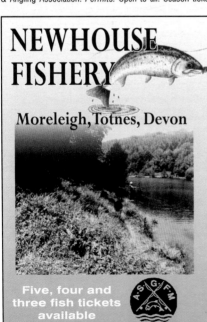

Sea Fishing

BARNSTAPLE

Combe Martin Sea Angling Club

Contact: Wayne Thomas, The Shippen, Loxhore Cott, Nr Barnstaple, *Tel:* 01271 850586, *Charges:* Family £15, Senior £10, Junior £1.

Triple Hook Club

Contact: Dennis Toleman, 32 Pilton Lawn, Barnstaple, *Tel:* 01271 378595, *Mobile:* 07815 009260, *Water:* Shore fishing, 8 boat trips, regular fly fishing & coarse fishing matches plus training sessions & tuition. *Permits:* Monthly meeting at Barnstaple & District Social Club (ex RBL) St Georges Road, Barnstaple, first Tuesday in month. New members welcome. Family orientated club, please contact Dennis on number above or come to our meetings. *Charges:* £5 membership, matches £5, Juniors £3. *Season:* All year round.

BIDEFORD

Appledore Shipbuilders Angling Club

Contact: Andrew Atkinson, 33 Western Avenue, Appledore, Bideford, *Mobile:* 07967 937906, *Water:* Shore and boat fishing. Roving monthly competitions. Annual festive competitions. Founded in 1971, 50 plus members. South West Federation member. New members welcome. *Charges:* £6 Adult. £2 Juniors. *Season:* All year round.

Bideford & District Angling Club (Sea)

Contact: Mr Graham Mountjoy, Honestone Street, Bideford, *Tel:* 01237 472916, *Water:* Bideford based club with coarse, game, boat & sea sections; Over 600 members fishing throughout South West. Competitions: First Sunday in every month. Please phone for further details. *Permits:* Membership form from club, open 7pm-11pm *Charges:* £7 per annum. £3 associates. £2 OAPs. £1 juniors.

Cheeky Monkey

Contact: Liz, Lizzies Shop, The Quay, Appledore, *Tel:* 01237 471033, *Water:* Taw and Torridge estuaries. *Species:* Bass *Charges:* £10 per person - 2 hour trip / £20 per person - 4 hour trip. *Season:* Spring to Autumn *Methods:* Trolling and bottom fishing.

Sanderling

Contact: Randall, 1 Yeo Drive, Appledore, *Tel:* 01237 479585, *Mobile:* 07779 443472, *Water:* Estuary fishing. 2 hour trips in Sanderling, fully licenced and insured for 12 anglers. £10 per person. Rod and bait supplied if required. *Species:* Bass, Plaice etc. *Charges:* Two hour trip - £10 per head, rod and bait supplied. *Season:* June to September.

BRIXHAM

Brixham Sea Anglers Club

Contact: Mr L.E. Turner (Secretary), Castor Road, Brixham, *Tel:* 01803 853930, *Water:* Licenced Club. Holders of world record for Conger eel at 133lb 4oz. Shore fishing from Exmouth to Plymouth. Boat fishing. Wednesday night competitions on the breakwater from May to September. Bingo and social events. Junior section. *Permits:* Please telephone or write for an application form. *Charges:* £15 per year adult. £3 junior plus £5 joining fee (adults only).

Seaspray III (Mackerel Fishing)

Contact: Bill Ford, Brixham, *Tel:* 01803 851328, *Mobile:* 01803 855453, *Season:* Mackerel boat from Easter to end September.

CLOVELLY

Jessica Hettie

Contact: Clive Pearson, *Tel:* 01237 431405 (eve), *Mobile:* 07774 190359, *Water:* Sea Angling trips. Lundy trips, anglers welcome. *Species:* Pollack, Mackerel, Bass. *Season:* April to October.

Ralph Atkinson Angling Charters

Contact: Ralph Atkinson, Isis, Irsha Court, Irsha Street, Appledore, *Tel:* 01237 475535, *Mobile:* 07774 164086, *Water:* Inshore and offshore reefs, wrecks and banks and deep sea in the Bristol Channel onboard 'Hooker'. *Species:* Tope, Shark, Bass, Pollack, Rays, Congers, Huss. *Permits:* 20 mile day or night licence for up to 8 people. Fully equipped with all safety gear and tackle. *Charges:* Individuals: Adults - £45 full day, £28 half day. 6 hour adult £36. 6 hour under 12 £24. 4 hour under 16 £16. To book boat: 8 hours £300, 6 hours £240, 4 hours £180. Discounts for multiple trips. *Season:* April - October. Boat leaves Clovelly. Full day leaves 9am and returns at 5pm. Half days 9am-1pm or 1pm-5pm.

CREDITON

Crediton Inn Angling Club

Contact: NFSA Head Office: 01364 644643.

DART

African Queen
Contact: Alan Hemsley, *Mobile:* 07885 246061.

DARTMOUTH

Bassillica
Contact: Tony Cooney, *Mobile:* 07866 806585.

Dartmouth Angling & Boating Association
Contact: Mervyn G Yalland (Chairman), 7 Fordworth Cottages, Hallsands, Kingsbridge, *Tel:* 01548 511195, *Mobile:* 07971 749395, *Water:* Predominantly sea fishing, some coarse fishing. *Charges:* Membership £8 individual, £15 couple, £3 Junior. (Clubhouse phone: 07977 843754).

Gemini
Contact: Dave Harrison, *Tel:* 01803 851766, *Mobile:* 07968 599245.

Saltwind of Dart
Contact: Lloyd Saunders, *Tel:* 01803 557551, *Mobile:* 07831 315477.

Samuel Irvin 3 ♿
Contact: Ian Noble, Mill Pool House, 7 Market Street, Dartmouth, *Tel:* 01803 834598, *Mobile:* 07780 970803, *Water:* Fishing inshore banks and reefs, mid channel wrecks and Channel Island trips. *Species:* Plaice, Turbot, Bass, Cod, Pollack, Ling, Conger, Whiting, Brill, Bream, Ray, Shark. *Charges:* From £30 per person per day. *Season:* Fishing all year round. *Methods:* Disabled anglers please phone for more information.

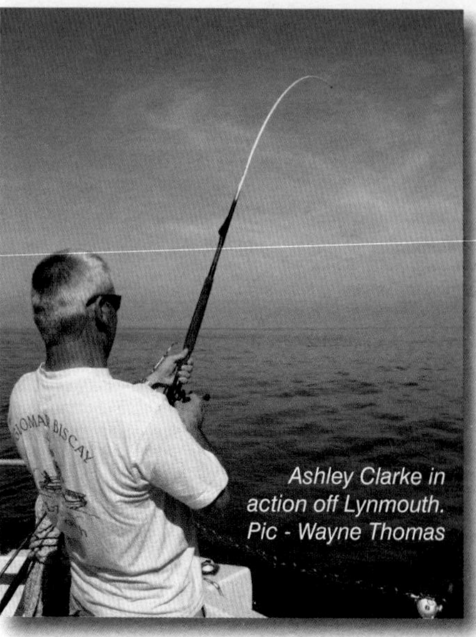

Ashley Clarke in action off Lynmouth. Pic - Wayne Thomas

EXETER

Axminster Sea Angling Club
Contact: Mark Somers, Beggars Roost, Smallridge, Axminster, *Tel:* 01297 33168, *Water:* Various locations along the Devon/ Dorset coastline from Abbotsbury down to Budleigh Salterton. *Species:* All species of sea fish excluding mini species are targeted. All competitions are run on aggregate specimen basis with no more than 2 fish of each species being brought to the scales. Where possible catch and release is also used to maximise conservation of fish stocks. *Permits:* N/A *Charges:* Seniors - £5 membership juniors/OAP's - £1. Entry to all competitions is £3.50. £1.50 is retained by the club to cover annual costs. The remaining £2 is paid back as prize money. *Season:* Club year runs 1st Jan - 31st December with 1 competition + 1 club meeting being held every month. Club meetings are always on the 1st Tuesday of the month at The Hunters Lodge Inn in Axminster starting 8pm. AGM is held on 1st Tuesday in October.

EXMOUTH

Blue Thunder
Contact: Mike Deem, Blue Waters, Exton, Exeter, *Tel:* 01392 875001, *Water:* Operating from Exmouth, Devon 33ft Lochin angling boat, Blue Thunder. *Species:* Wreck fishing for Bass, Cod and Pollack. *Charges:* £400 for boat. £40 for individual angler. *Season:* 7.00am - 5.30pm daily.

Exmouth Sea Angling Association
Contact: NFSA Head Office: 01364 644643.

Smuggler of Braye
Contact: Colin Dukes, *Tel:* 01626 890852, *Mobile:* 07974 437740, *Water:* Channel Island, mid channel wrecking.

Stuart Line Fishing
Contact: Leanne O'Donnell, *Mobile:* 07977 203099, *Water:* Lyme Bay. *Species:* Mackerel, Ling, Pollack, Whiting, Conger

Eel. *Permits:* N/A *Charges:* Mackerel £7. Deep Sea £12. Prices may vary for 2008. *Season:* Easter to end of October. *Methods:* Rods and reels, using feathers or hooks.

Tamesis

Contact: Nigel Dyke, *Tel:* 01769 580376, *Mobile:* 07970 909614.

HONITON

Honiton Sea Angling Club

Contact: Mike Spiller, 6 Charles Road, Honiton, *Tel:* 01404 43397, *Mobile:* 07779 308093, *Water:* A club for family membership. Regular competitions, junior matches, boat & casting competitions held. Casting tuition, member of England team. *Species:* Any sea fish. *Charges:* Please call for charges. All competitions are free to enter. *Season:* Club meetings are held on the third Tuesday of each month at the Honiton Motel. All welcome - old and new members.

ILFRACOMBE

Kerry Kim

Contact: Eddie Bennellick, 6 Sea View, Ilfracombe, *Tel:* 01271 864143 / 01271 864143.

Obsession Charters ♿

Contact: Andrew Bengey, The Moorings, 3 Mount View, Ilfracombe, *Tel:* 01271 866325, *Mobile:* 07971 462024, *Water:* Bristol Channel. Lundy Island. North Cornish coast. *Species:* Most British saltwater species. *Charges:* On application. *Season:* Fishing all year round. *Methods:* No restrictions.

Osprey

Contact: Paul Barbeary, 77 Hillinton, Ilfracombe, *Tel:* 01271 863010, *Mobile:* 07970 101407, *Water:* Bristol Channel, Lundy Island. *Species:* Most British water species. *Charges:* On application. *Season:* All year round. *Methods:* No restrictions.

IVYBRIDGE

Bridge Sea Angling Club

Contact: NFSA Head Office: 01364 644643.

Plymouth City Engineers Sea Angling Club

Contact: NFSA Head Office: 01364 644643.

KINGSBRIDGE

Kingsbridge & District Sea Anglers

Contact: Devon Angling Centre, *Tel:* 01548 580888, *Water:* Regular monthly boat and shore matches, strong junior section, matches with other clubs in region. New members welcome. *Permits:* From Devon Angling Centre. *Charges:* Seniors £10, juniors £5 (under 16), family £15 (2 adults, 2 children). Child protection policy in force. Prices may vary in 2008.

LYNMOUTH

Exmoor Coast Boat Cruises Ltd

Contact: Matthew Oxenham, Glenlyn Gorge, Lynmouth, *Tel:* 01598 753207, *Water:* Boat fishing in the Lynmouth area. *Species:* Mackerel, Pollack, Family trips beside the Valley of Rocks. *Charges:* £10 per person for short family Mackerel drifts. 1 hour trip. *Season:* May to August. *Methods:* Rod and Line jigging Mackerel feathers.

PAIGNTON

Our Joe-I
Contact: Simon Pedley, *Tel:* 01803 551504.
Paignton Sea Angling Association
Contact: Les Harding, Ravenswood, 26 Cliff Road, Paignton, *Tel:* 01803 553118, *Charges:* Membership Dec 07 - Nov 08 Angling £12, Junior £3 (5-16 yrs), Senior £3 (16-18 yrs).
Seafield Sea Angling Club
Contact: NFSA Head Office: 01364 644643.
Tuonela
Contact: Peter Bingle, *Tel:* 01803 666350, *Mobile:* 07715 735842.

PLYMOUTH

British Conger Club
Contact: Sec. Mrs D. Byrne, 2 Drake Court, 264 Citadel Road, Plymouth, *Tel:* 01752 223815, *Water:* National Club *Species:* Conger Eel. Minimum qualifying sizes: Shore - 25lb. Reef - 30lb. Wreck 40lb. *Charges:* Full/associate members £15 per year. Seniors £7.50. Juniors £2.
D.O.E Sea Angling Club
Contact: Mr A Parker, 9 Ashford Close, Mannamead, Plymouth, *Tel:* 01752 666706, *Water:* Sea angling from Weymouth to Bristol. *Species:* All as listed on NFSA Specimen list. *Charges:* £16 Senior , £2 junior. *Season:* All year. *Methods:* All fishing to stringent minimum sizes. Catch and release encouraged.
Dartmoor Pirates S.A.C.
Contact: NFSA Head Office: 01364 644643.
Devonport Sea Angling Club - 'The Peelers'
Contact: NFSA Head Office: 01364 644643.

Combe Martin SAC Chairman Nick Phillips with a 6.5lb grey mullet.

Ford Hotel S.A.C. (Plymouth)
Contact: NFSA Head Office: 01364 644643.
Gypsy Mariners Angling Club
Contact: NFSA Head Office: 01364 644643.
Naval Stores Sea Angling Club
Contact: NFSA Head Office: 01364 644643.
Plymouth Command Angling Association (Sea)
Contact: Mr Vic Barnett Hon. Sec., 5 Weir Close, Mainstone, Plymouth, *Tel:* 01752 708206, *Mobile:* 07710 552910, *Water:* Boat & shore fishing. *Species:* All sea fish. *Permits:* Membership is open to all serving members of HM Forces. Associate membership is also open to ex-serving members of HM Forces, no matter when the time was served. *Charges:* Costs for full membership or associate membership are available on application or enquiry at the above contact.
Plymouth Federation S.A.C.
Contact: NFSA Head Office: 01364 644643.
Plymouth Inter Boat A.F.
Contact: NFSA Head Office: 01364 644643.
Plymouth S.A.C.
Contact: NFSA Head Office: 01364 644643.
Rodbenders S.A.C.
Contact: Mr Dennis, *Tel:* 01752 338192, *Water:* Small sea angling club fishing mostly in Devon and Cornwall. Regular meetings on the last Wednesday of each month. Juniors welcome. Regular competitions. *Charges:* Seniors £8. OAP, student and junior £4. FAmily (up to 3 people) £12. Contact Mr Dennis.
Roving Rods Sea Angling Club Plymouth
Contact: The Secretary, 92 Charfield Drive, Plymouth, *Tel:* 01752 777114, *Water:* The Roving Rods Sea Angling Club has been running for more than 35 years and at present there are 38 Senior members and 10 Junior members. The current members are predominantly shore anglers however the club does have both boat and shore trophies and awards. *Season:* Our angling year runs from 1st January to 31st December. Monthly meetings are held on the 2nd Wednesday of each month at the Land Registry Sports and Social Club, Crownhill. All members are welcome.
Royal Naval & Royal Marines A.A.
Contact: NFSA Head Office: 01364 644643.

Scorpion
Contact: Dave Brett, Plymouth, *Tel:* 01752 551548, *Mobile:* 07779 427691, *Water:* Can accomodate 10 anglers wreck and reef angling.

Sea Angler II
Contact: Malcolm Jones, 50 Darwin Crescent, Laira, Plymouth, *Tel:* 01752 316289, *Mobile:* 07977 097690, *Water:* Lochin 33 Sports Fisherman.

Size Matters ♿
Contact: Graham Hannaford, Plymouth, *Tel:* 01752 500531, *Mobile:* 07890428630, *Water:* 45ft sports angling boat. *Species:* Bass, Conger, Cod, Ling, Pollack, Coalfish, Bream, Turbot, Plaice. *Charges:* Packages tailored to your requirements. Phone for details. *Season:* Fishing all year round.

Specimen Angling Group of Plymouth
Contact: NFSA Head Office: 01364 644643.

Stonehouse Creek Sea Angling Club
Contact: NFSA Head Office: 01364 644643.

SALCOMBE

Anglo Dawn II
Contact: Chris Roberts, Higher House Farm, East Prawle, Kingsbridge, *Tel:* 01548 511500, *Mobile:* 07967 387657, *Water:* Reef, banks inc Skerries, mid channel wrecking, Guernsey. *Species:* Cod, Pollack, Ling, Plaice, Rays, Bass, Conger, Whiting, Mackerel, Bream. *Charges:* Reefs or Banks £300. Up to 25 mile wrecking £380. 25 miles plus £420. Blue Shark £285. Prices are for boat for a full day, individual prices and shorter charters are available. Mackerel trips in summer £10 per person. Prices may change in 2008. *Season:* All year round.

Calypso and Serendipity
Contact: Kevin Oakman, *Tel:* 01548 843818, *Water:* Mackerel fishing and angling trips. *Charges:* Please enquire.

Phoenix
Contact: Chris Puncher, 19 St Dunstans Road, Salcombe, *Tel:* 01548 842840, *Mobile:* 07855 315770.

Tuckers Boat Hire
Tel: 01548 843444, *Season:* June to August.

Whitestrand Boat Hire
Tel: 01548 843818, *Water:* Please enquire for further details.

SEATON

Lillie May
Contact: Paul Godfrey, 8 Prince Charles Way, Beer, *Tel:* 01297 23455, *Mobile:* 07779 040491, *Water:* General Sea Fishing. *Species:* Bass, Pollack, Black Bream. Cod, Channel Whiting, Ling, Gurnard. *Charges:* 8 hours deep sea £160. One hour Mackerel trip £7, children £5. *Season:* Fishing all year round.

TEIGNMOUTH

Teignmouth Sea Angling Society
Contact: NFSA Head Office: 01364 644643.

TORQUAY

Anne Clare
Contact: Kevin Tate, Torquay, *Tel:* 01803 315125, *Mobile:* 07989 527180, *Water:* 35ft Blythe catamaran for 12 anglers. Channel Island trips. *Charges:* Individuals welcome. Also trips to Guernsey. *Season:* All year.

Torbay & Babbacombe Association of Sea Anglers
Contact: D. Stevens, Westerly, Small Lane, Broadclyst, Exeter, *Tel:* 01392 461747, *Charges:* Membership fees are as follows: £15 per senior member, £18 per couple, £20 per family membership (2 adults, max. 2 children), £3 per junior member (15yrs and under), £5 per student member (16-18 in full time education). Application forms can be obtained from secretary.

Torbay S.A.F.A.
Contact: NFSA Head Office: 01364 644643.

TOTNES

Baywater Anglers
Contact: Martyn Green (co-ordinator), 31 Collapark, Totnes, *Tel:* 01803 863279, *Mobile:* 07704 602 180, *Water:* A light tackle sea angling club offering not only shore and boat trips but also instruction in a variety of techniques including fly fishing, beachcasting, Bassing etc. Also organise game fishing trips. *Charges:* Membership: £10 senior, £3 junior, £15 family, £5 student aged 16-18.

WESTCOUNTRY

National Federation of Sea Anglers
Contact: Head Office, Level 5, Hamlyn House, Mardle Way, Buckfastleigh, *Tel:* 01364 644643, *Water:* Sea Angling. *Species:* All sea fish. *Permits:* None apply. *Charges:* Membership £26 per year. Family membership £30. Juniors free. *Season:* None applicable.

South West Federation of Sea Anglers
Contact: Andy Alcock, 45 Newstead Road, Weymouth, *Tel:* 01305 772318, *Water:* South West coastal waters.

Alf with a spectacular Koi caught on floating crust from Anglers El Dorado.

WHERE TO STAY

Wooda Lakes
Holiday Lodges
www.woodalakes.com

Secluded lodges set in 22 acres of glorious, tranquil Devon countryside teeming with wildlife, flora and fauna.

Two well managed lakes, one mixed and one Carp only.

Just 15 minutes from safe, sandy beaches

For more information and a brochure
Wooda Lakes, Pancrasweek, Holsworthy Devon EX22 7JN

Telephone 01409 241 934

South Farm
Holiday Cottages & Fishery
GREAT Fishing
GREAT Accommodation

In a beautiful rural environment - six comfortable, heated, self catering cottages with woodburners and lovely views. Four well stocked Coarse fishing lakes with Carp, Roach and Chub.

Other facilities include: Spa, Sauna, Tennis, Games Barn, Pool (summer)

Telephone 01823 681078 for a Brochure
email: info@southfarm.co.uk
Honiton, Devon www.southfarm.co.uk

Four Ponds Fishery

CARP AND COARSE FISHING
'AT IT'S DEVON BEST'

The Carp Specimen Lake at 3 acres is stocked with 85 beautiful Carp, from 15lb to 30lb with approx. 25 fish over 20lb plus some large Tench.
The Kingfisher Coarse Lake at 1.25 acres is heavily stocked with Carp & Ghosties to 14lb, Tench to 8lb, Roach, Perch & Crucians to 3lb. Also Bream to 9.5lb Rudd & Golden Rudd.
The Family/Carp Lake is stocked with 12,000 carp to 2lb and is a slightly smaller tree lined lake.

The Fishing Lodge is a fully equipped, attractive & comfortable two bedroomed cottage in the beautiful Devon countryside.

Bowdens Lane, Shillingford, Devon EX16 9BU
Tel: 01398 331169 www.fourponds.com

Fosfelle
COUNTRY HOUSE HOTEL

A 17th Century Manor House set in six acres of peaceful surroundings.

Fully Licenced - Excellent Cuisine

In the grounds of Fosfelle Country House Hotel there are two fishing lakes offering both Fly and Coarse fishing.
Fosfelle Lakes offer a tranquil location for those who need a break from a hectic lifestyle. They are generously stocked with Rudd, Tench, Roach and Carp for the coarse angler and Trout for the fly angler.

Caravan & Camping facilities available

HARTLAND, BIDEFORD, DEVON.
TEL: 01237 441273

Newhouse Farm
Cottages

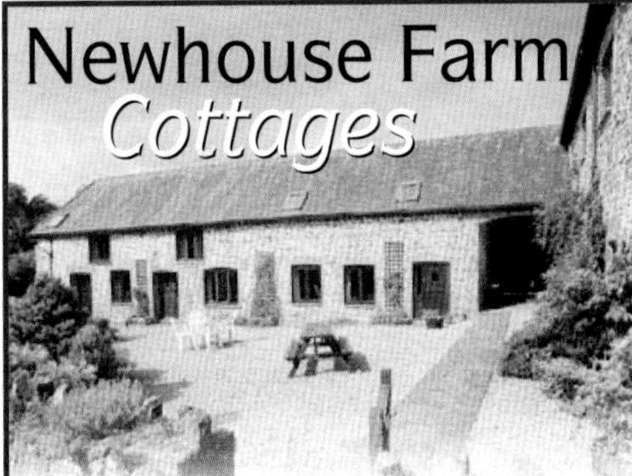

Eight beautifully appointed Grade II listed stone barns in 23 acres
sleeping from 2 to 40 from £235 to £1575

fishing lake

Heated indoor pool, games room and childrens play areas, pets welcome.

Contact Keith & Doreen Jenkins
t:01884 860266 f:01884 861590
e: info@newhousecottages.com
www.newhousecottages.com
Witheridge Tiverton Devon EX16 8QB

Superb Fishing...

100 year old 'Top Lake'
Carp to over 32lb 6oz, Bream to over 7lb, Tench to 6lb, Perch to 3lb, Rudd and Roach to 2lb.

Purpose built 'Match Lake'
Stocked with Carp, Skimmers, Roach, Rudd, Tench and Crucians - great fishing with bags to over 200lbs.

River Fishing
Just a short walk to the river Culm.

Upton Lakes
FISHING HOLIDAYS

Accommodation

Superbly equipped, spacious two and three bedroomed static homes

Situated right next to the lakes with Fully equipped kitchens, bathroom, shower, modern toilets, gas heating, hi-fi, T.V. and video. Enjoy the superb countryside views from your veranda over an evening barbecue!

DELUXE and SUPREME accommodation catering for all tastes and budgets!

Local Attractions

Shopping in Exeter, fun for the kids at Crealy Adventure Park, Diggerland or Quadworld. Walking, Riding and Golf plus Dartmoor and both north and south coasts within easy reach

FREE brochure on
07830 199690
or visit our web site...
www.upton-lakes.co.uk

Upton Lakes Fishing Holidays,
Upton Farm, Cullompton,
Devon EX15 1RA

Fishing Holidays in South Devon

Cofton Country
HOLIDAYS

On a superb award-winning park, just minutes from the sea, lie Cofton Lakes, five private well-stocked and well-featured coarse fishing waters.

Healthy carp up to 20lbs, roach, rudd, bream and tench are standard fare here. And fishing is even more of a delight in the beautiful surroundings, teaming with wildlife.

Fishing here is exclusively for holidaymakers at Cofton, open all year, so a fishing break outside the normal tourist season could really pay dividends as the pressure on the lakes decreases.

On the park pitches are available for touring caravans, motor homes and tents. There are also holiday homes, cottages and luxury apartments – many open all year.

All facilities are available in season including swimming pools and the Swan pub.

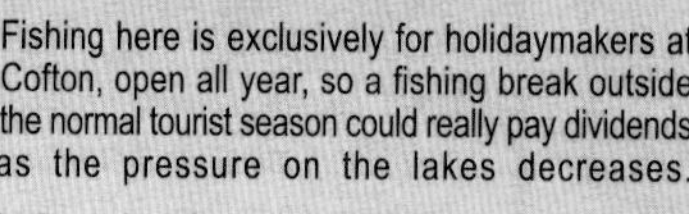

0800 085 8649 ***www.coftonholidays.co.uk***
DAWLISH • SOUTH DEVON

Book Review *by The Editor*

The River Cottage Fish Book

Hugh Fearnley Whittingstall and Nick Fisher
ISBN 978-0-7475-8869-6. Price £30.

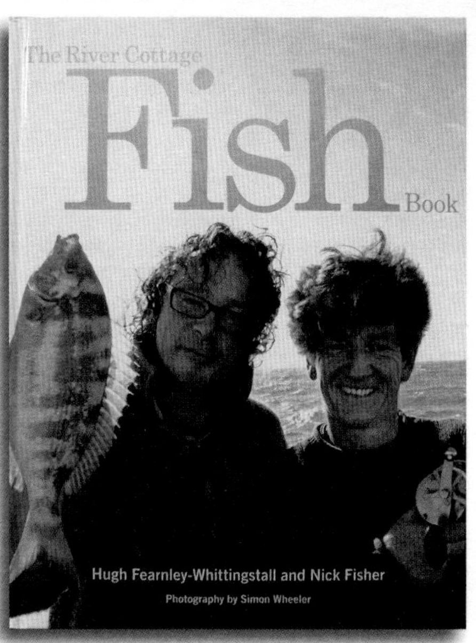

Yet another cookbook on the back of a successful TV series? Basically yes, but a book having far more empathy with its subject matter than most. There is an underlying passion throughout this publication, which has been written by two enthusiastic anglers who love their fishing and their fish. In fact there is very nearly as much space devoted to fish 'science' as there is to cooking.

The book starts with 'Understanding fish' which goes into the nutritional properties of various types of fish in some detail. Also effects of pollution on fish and the near future of fish science. This, naturally, leads into 'Sourcing fish' which covers how fish are caught or farmed and, vitally, how you can buy your fish in the most sustainable way. It is essential that we, as consumers, are made aware of the incredible amount of damage we have caused to fish populations across the globe and are educated as to what we can do to repair that damage.

The mouth watering bit follows with hundreds of beautifully photographed recipes covering all species of fish and shellfish. Smoked, poached, raw - you name it - it's in there.

The last section of the book comprises nearly 200 pages of fascinating and very detailed information on individual species; sea, game, coarse and shellfish. As an angler you will find this illuminating, awe inspiring and frequently frightening. The life cycles of individual species are covered in a very accessible way, not overly scientific, with humour and honesty. Each species is also considered for its sustainability and information is given on how they are currently fished for or farmed, the state of stocks, and what the near future may hold. This information will, I am sure, shock many readers.

Some of the information on policy concerning fish quotas, minimum size regulations and enforcement is jaw dropping in its stupidity and short sightedness. The way some species have been fished to the brink of extinction beggars belief.

Fish are amazing. Take the European eel for instance. If someone invented it's life cycle as a work of fiction it would be considered ridiculous. Quite how evolution arrived at that one I will never understand! We have no more right to be on this planet than any other species, we can't live without them and the loss of any is unacceptable.

A few freshwater species not commonly (these days) considered table fish are included. Perch, for instance, were considered a delicacy above salmon by the Victorians (when the salmon was so common to be seen as a poor mans fish). In Finland and Sweden native wild Perch are prized even more than trout and salmon. Any Perch that do reach the markets here (netted from the Lake District) are exported to Europe.

The best fish to eat is always one you have caught yourself, there is no shame in killing a fish from a healthy, sustainable population. In fact it's currently a much better option than cod and chips!

Exmoor's inspirational streams

Wayne Thomas

I had a good friend around the house recently and as always we were deep into talk of fish and all things piscatorial. Having become enthusiastic about the delights of river trout I began waxing lyrical about good books on river trout. Selecting several tomes on the subject I made some suggestions on good reading matter.

A few days later it struck me how many of these books related to fishing for the wild trout of Exmoor and how the small crimson spotted trout had inspired some of our greatest angling writers. I guess this should come as no surprise with such fantastic rivers as the Exe, Lyn and Taw having sources within its boundaries.

Books often give a fascinating insight into the times in which they were written and angling books are no exception to this rule. Portraying life from the view of the angler gives far more information on the times than many would imagine. Of course I am inclined to refer here to a time when angling literature was less technically inclined than today. These days angling writers have a tendency to focus on technicalities, techniques and tackle. In days gone by the day by stream and the delights of the waterside took precedence; as it should. One of my favourites has to be "Exmoor Streams", Notes and jottings with Practical Hints for Anglers by Clavde. F. Wade published in 1903.It tells of an Exmoor before the age of the motor car. A horse drawn carriage takes the angler to the upper reaches of the River Lyn.

Conservation was certainly not a major consideration as huge numbers of small trout were taken from the streams. "catching eighty trout in this comparatively short piece on one July day, all with the fly". Compare this to today when the vast majority of fish are returned to preserve stocks. I had imagined that in 1900 visitors would have had little impact but this is not so even in the days before the car. "There is a beautiful bit of water up from the farm at cloud, but its not so easy to catch fish in as it used to be in the old days before all the tourists came to look for John Ridd's "water slide". Trains and steamers brought rich Victorians to the area and our author is concerned at how they will impact on his beloved Exmoor.

Of course one of the fascinations in reading an old book is comparing what was then to what is now. On New Years day my wife and I took a walk at Brendon. On crossing the road bridge I looked downstream and immediately recognised the old bridge pictured in my old Exmoor Streams book virtually unchanged over a century later. Looking at other old sepia images within the pages of this book I realise that in some places little has changed.

Inevitably there are tales of big fish and it's the salmon of the Lyn that give the big fish stories in Exmoor Streams; " In the sixties a well known actor, who was very fond of salmon fishing in the Lyn, got hold of a monster in this pool said to have weighed 40lb and I believe nearly died of exhaustion. All day long messengers were going to and from Lynmouth telling the latest stages of the struggle." Note that when the author talks of the sixties he is referring to the 1860's

"Exmoor Streams", has been reprinted in a limited centenary edition by Rothwell and Dunworth. A few copies may remain in their shop in Dulverton. Failing that it may be possible to pick up an original copy from Antiquarian book dealers.

"Going fishing" Travel Adventure in Two Hemispheres, by Negley Farson is considered by many one of the all time classic angling books. The author visits the rivers Exe and Barle where he talks of an old bailiff who tells "of the flies which are inevitably killed by the oil seeping into the water from the tarred roads and motor cars". Despite this reference to fears of pollution there is always the feeling that years ago things were far more romantic and this is reinforced when the author talks of "An imperturbable scene which fills you with contentment." And " I like to watch the plover, tumbling about in the sky over the red, ploughed fields ; and Mr rat ,emerging from his hole and going about his business; the silent, ceaseless flight of the swallows over some shallow stream". Of course today's angling authors seldom wax lyrical about such things as I stated earlier.

The Carnarvon Arms at Brushford has a rich tradition of angling history. Sadly it has been converted into luxury timeshare apartments. In a book entitled "The Philandering Angler," Author Arthur Applin romances about his visits "I suppose the charm of fishing at the 'Carnarvon Arms' was an informality and friendliness that pervaded both the river and the Inn". Speaking of the Rivers Barle and Exe Mr Applin writes," You could not wander along the banks of either the Exe or the Barle without finding happiness waiting for you, whether you chose the valley where the rivers united to slide quietly through sleepy meadows, or on the moors where the Exe rushes down narrow channels." The book is illustrated by that fine writer and illustrator "BB" who also mentions his travels on Exmoor in his travel book, "The White Road Westwards".

Reading these angling writers accounts from a different age we realise how much has changed in the Britain of today. The gentry who walked the river banks undoubtedly had much leisure time in contrast to the lower classes that had to work each daylight hour. Society has changed whilst the waters that tumble down through moorland valleys remain relatively unchanged their inhabitant's descendants of the crimson spotted trout and silver salmon that delighted earlier generations who cast a line.

In more recent times Exmoor waters have proved inspiration to that fine modern day angling writer John Bailey. In his 1985 book, "Travels With A Two Piece" John describes trips to the Barle and fishes near Tarr Steps. He revisits the river again in his book "In Wild Waters", where he describes the capture of a summer grilse in his normal beguiling manner.

Exmoor's gurgling streams have inspired many anglers over many generations and I feel sure that they will continue to do so for many more generations. If you are inspired to cast a line for Exmoor's trout or salmon and cast in the shadow of some of angling greatest writers then a day with a professional guide such as Nick Hart is to be recommended.

Angling Books With Reference to Exmoor

Exmoor Streams - Notes and jottings with Practical Hints for Anglers by Claude. F. Wade. Published in 1903 by Chatto & Windus London - James G Commin, Exeter.

Philandering Angler - By Arthur Applin Published by Hurst and Blacket

Travels with a Two Piece - By John Bailey Published by The Crowood Press in 1985

"In Wild Waters "- By John Bailey Published by The Crowood Press in 1989

Reflections from the Waters Edge - By John Bailey. Published by The Crowood Press 1987

The Fishing Year - By John Parsons. Published by Collins in 1974

The Art of Trout Fishing on Rapid Streams - By H.C. Cutcliffe F.R.C.S Published by Sampson Low, Marston, Searle and Rivington in 1883

The Pursuit of Wild Trout - By Mike Weaver Published by Merlin Unwin Books in 1991

Casting for Recovery

Charlotte Fiander

Over the past year, fly-fishing has firmly established itself as a potentially life-changing activity following the launch of Casting for Recovery UK and Ireland, a non profit support and educational programme which provides fly fishing retreats specifically tailored for women who have or have had breast cancer.

Casting for Recovery was founded in America in 1996 and has since spread through Canada and arrived in the UK and Ireland at the beginning of 2006. Although the link between breast cancer recovery and fly-fishing might not be immediately apparent to the uninitiated eye, Casting for Recovery provides a unique opportunity for women whose lives have been profoundly affected by breast cancer to gather in a beautiful, natural setting and learn the skill of fly fishing, "a sport for life." Participants are offered the opportunity to meet new friends, and have fun, away from the daily pressures of life in a tranquil and relaxing environment, incorporating counselling, educational services and the sport of fly-fishing to promote mental and physical healing. Weekend retreats are provided to any woman who has suffered, or is suffering, with breast cancer, with medical clearance from their doctor, and each retreat provides full medical support alongside a psychotherapist and several fly-fishing instructors to offer a forum for women with similar experiences, learn a new skill and gain a respite from their everyday concerns. Retreats are fully funded by the Countryside Alliance and all fly fishing equipment and clothing is provided by Orvis UK, so there is no cost to participants.

The first retreat was held in September 2007 at Duncton Mill, West Sussex and was a huge success. Twelve ladies participated of all ages and the experience was wholly positive, with some catching their very first fish. Everyone learned the fundamentals of fly casting, entomology, knot-tying, equipment basics - but most importantly, participants spend time on the water practicing catch-and-release fishing.

Having successfully tested the waters, three more retreats have been planned for 2008 with the first one being held in March at the Arundell Arms in Lifton, Devon. It is wonderful that such a worthy initiative is finding a home in Devon for the weekend, and great thanks are extended to Anne Voss-Bark, owner of the Arundell Arms, who was so impressed with the initiative and its aims that she had to get involved. Devon seems like a natural backdrop for such a serene and

All the participants on the first Casting for Recovery UK and Ireland retreat at Duncton Mill, West Sussex, September 2007. Programme coordinator Sue Hunter is pictured on the far right.

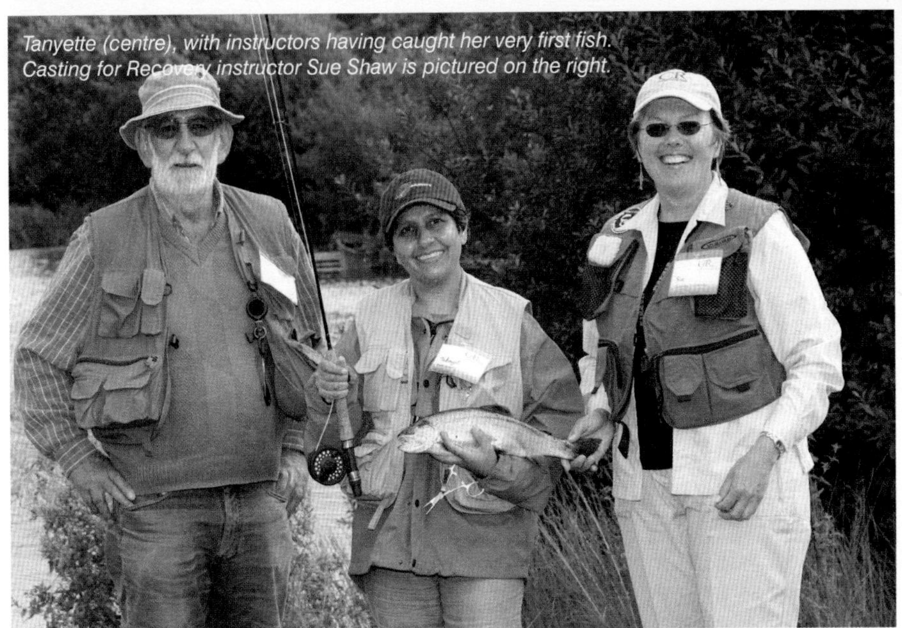

Tanyette (centre), with instructors having caught her very first fish. Casting for Recovery instructor Sue Shaw is pictured on the right.

soothing weekend, and offers ideal surroundings for participants to escape their daily concerns and relax with new friends and the waters of the South West couldn't provide a better respite for participants. The momentum of the organisation can only be strengthened in the relaxing and tranquil Devon countryside.

Indeed, Casting for Recovery will also be paying a visit to Cornwall in the spring, taking a stand at the Caerhays Castle Open Day on 11th May at Gorran near St Austell. We are delighted to be bringing Casting for Recovery to this family day, which will feature fly fishing demonstrations as well as a diverse range of activities such as face painting, maypole dancing, laser clay shooting, a toy stall and even a novelty dog show.

Further retreats are planned for Builth Wells, Powys in April and back at Duncton Mill, West Sussex in September. Although the application processes are unfortunately closed for the first two, applications for Duncton Mill will be taken until late June. It is hoped that a retreat in Ireland will be confirmed later in the year.

All of this is possible due to the hard work and determination of Sue Hunter, Programme Co-ordinator of Casting for Recovery UK and Ireland, former England Ladies Fly-fishing Captain and breast cancer survivor. Sue brought the initiative over to the UK and Ireland following her own diagnosis, after fly-fishing was suggested by a friend to aid her recovery and she quickly developed a passion for the sport that she wished to share. The therapeutic benefit from the fly-fishing technique mimics the soft tissue and joint mobility exercises recommended following breast cancer, and enjoying the tranquil surrounding offered on each retreat, alongside the expert assistance offered provides a holistic approach to recovery.

The opportunities to be involved in such an initiative are few and far between, and Casting for Recovery UK and Ireland are always looking for more volunteers. Any gesture, however small, is greatly appreciated, from a few additional flies sent to help these brave ladies experience the sport for the first time, to fly-fishing instructors, medical practitioners, and greeters to work on the retreats themselves. Every action helps each person on the retreat, and is a wonderful chance to pass on and share in the enthusiasm for the sport beyond the norm.

www.castingforrecovery.org.uk

The South West Federation of Fly Fishers

The South West Federation of Fly Fishers belongs to the Confederation of English Fly Fishers. The Confederation is, amongst other things, responsible for running National and International Fly Fishing Teams and Competitions. The grassroots of all the National and International Competitions are the Regional Eliminators run by Federations all over the Country. The South West Federation will run one eliminator at Chew Valley Lake on Sunday 27 April 2008.

Anyone can enter provided that they are over 18 years of age, and have been domiciled in ENGLAND for 3 years. Competitors can ONLY enter eliminators in ONE Region in any one year. Anyone who has previously fished at International Level for another Country is NOT eligible to fish.

If you are interested in competitive Fly Fishing, with the chance to fish for England, write to me at the address below or give me a ring.

J.A. Loud,
153/155 East Street,
Bedminster,
BRISTOL BS3 4EJ
Tel (Daytime) 0117 9872050
Tel (Evenings) 0117 9232166

The Federation of Peninsula Fly Fishers

The Federation of Peninsula Flyfishers was formed to represent flyfishers in the South West Peninsula who wish to enter the national competitions organised by the Confederation of English Flyfishers (CEFF) which can lead to you fishing for your country. Two of our members fished for England in International matches in 2007 and three have qualified for 2008. It could be you qualifying for 2009! We also run some friendly competitions and social events for members.

Please contact the persons listed below for more details and an application form.

Tight lines!

Loch Style Eliminator

Sunday 27th April 2008 at Blagdon Lake.
Please contact Andy Gooding.
01626 824771 (home) or 07976 766727 (mob)

Rivers Eliminator

Saturday 31st May 2008 on the River Teign at Fingle Bridge.
Please contact Andy Gooding.
01626 824771 (home) or 07976 766727 (mob)

Airflo Classic Bank Open

Regional eliminator at Innis Fishery, St Austell.
Please contact Dave Johns on 01726 852382.

Bet he's glad he took a flask!
Slightly inclement weather at Witherington Farm.
Pic - ©Brian Gay. www.angling-images.com

DORSET

DORSET

RIVER FISHING

STILLWATER COARSE

STILLWATER TROUT

SEA FISHING

WHERE TO STAY

Dorset Game Road Directions

108. Amherst Lodge

From the A35 Bridport to Honiton road, take the Hunter's Lodge turning at Raymonds Hill onto the B3165 towards Lyme Regis. After 1.4 miles turn right down Cathole Lane. Keep to the right into St Marys Lane and you will come to Amherst. Tel: 01297 442773.

109. Environment Agency Fishery

Wareham Royalty, Piddle Fishery. Directions are supplied with permits.

Dorset Coarse Road Directions

110. Christchurch Angling Club (Coarse & Game)

Please enquire at local Tackle Shops or Tel: 01202 480009.

111. Higher Kingcombe Lodge

From Exeter head north from A379, at Sandy Gate roundabout take second exit onto M5 to Taunton/Honiton/Barnstaple. Take exit Honiton/Exeter A3015 bear left onto the Honiton roadramp and bear left at A30. Take A35 until reach Bridport, second exit at roundabout near Westbay, onto Sea Road North. Continue across next two roundabouts to Beaminster. Right at petrol station through Beaminster. Follow B3163 road for 1 mile, taking second right turn signposted Hooke. Second left through village to Higher Kingcombe. Cross small crossroads, we are third on right. Tel: 01300 320537.

112. Little Canford Ponds

Wessex Water fisheries. Tel: 0845 600 4 600.

113. Litton Lakes

Please Tel: 01308 482574 for directions.

114. Lyons Gate Fishing Lakes

On the A352 between Dorchester (12 miles) & Sherborne (7 miles) well signposted off the road. The fishing lakes are inside the caravan & camping park. Tel: 01300 345260.

115. Mangerton Valley Coarse Fishing

From Bridport take A3066 North for approx. 2 miles. Continue straight across mini roundabout, then turn immediately right. Look out for our sign after 1 mile. Tel: 01308 458482.

116. Martin's Farm Fishery

Please Tel: 01202 823631or 07717 887357 for directions.

117. Osmington Mills

Approaching from Wareham on the A352 Dorchester road turn left at the A353 Weymouth junction. At the Osmington Mills sign opposite the Garage, turn left and follow the lane to Holiday Park. Approaching from Weymouth, follow the A353 Wareham road. Pass through Osmington and turn right at the sign for Osmington Mills. Follow lane to Holiday Park. Tel: 01305 832311 for directions.

118. Wood Farm Caravan Park

7 miles west of Bridport on A35, entrance off roundabout with A3052 (access to fishing through caravan park). Tel: 01297 560697.

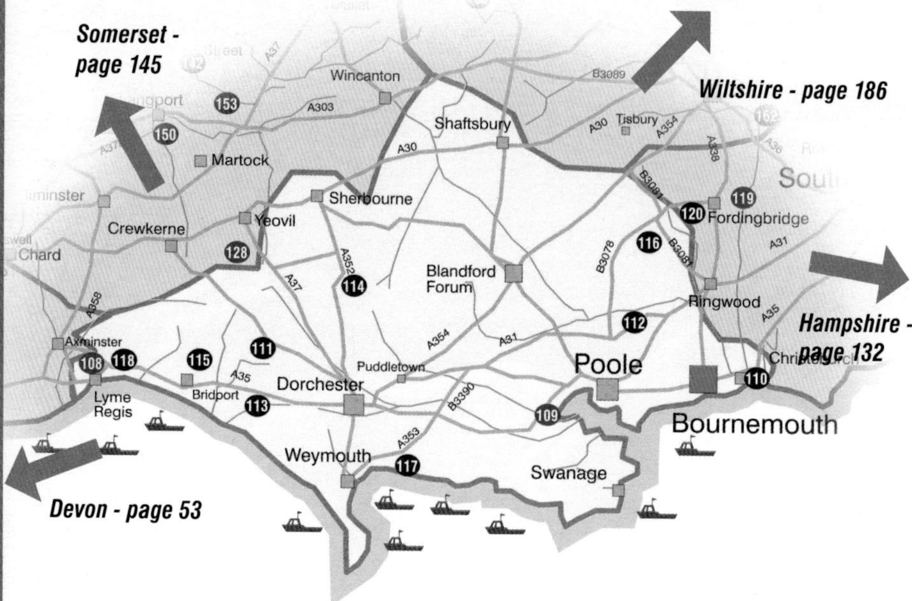

Only advertisers are located on this map.

Dorset River Fishing

ALLEN

Wimborne St Giles

Contact: Simon Cooper, Fishing Breaks, The Mill, Heathman Street, Nether Wallop, Stockbridge, Hants. *Tel:* 01264 781988, *Water:* One mile on the village water. Single rod. *Species:* Brown Trout. *Permits:* By phone or e-mail from Fishing Breaks. *Charges:* May 1 to 18 £125. May 19 to June 15 £150. June 16 to September 30 £100. *Season:* May to September. *Methods:* Dry fly & Nymph only.

THE 'HAMPSHIRE' AVON

For detailed description of the Hampshire Avon and tributaries, see under Hampshire River fishing.

RIVER AVON PEWSEY - CHRISTCHURCH

Fisheries located between Pewsey and Salisbury are predominantly managed for Brown Trout fly fishing. A mixture of Coarse, Salmon and Trout fishing is available on the main river between Salisbury and Christchurch.

Winkton Fishery

Contact: Paul Jerome, Suite 21D, Magnolia House, 19-21 Stour Road, Christchurch, *Tel:* 01202 480009, *Mobile:* 07714 449523, *Water:* Christchurch Angling Club controlled stretch of approx. one mile on the lower river near Christchurch. *Species:* Barbel 13lb, Chub 7lb 7oz, Dace 1lb, Pike 25lb, Carp 26lb, Roach 3lb, Perch 3lb. *Permits:* Available from: Davis Tackle, 71-75 Bargates, Christchurch (01202 485169) *Charges:* Day ticket £9 (2 rods per day, coarse only). *Season:* Coarse: 16th June to 14th March from one hour before sunrise to two hours after sunset. *Methods:* No spinning. Coarse fish only. No Barbel in keepnets. Any Salmon, Sea Trout or Salmon Parr caught accidentally should be returned immediately.

FROME

The Frome rises through chalk on the North Dorset Downs near Evershot, and flows south east through Dorchester, and finally Wareham, where it confluences with the River Piddle in Poole harbour.

The River Frome is well known for its excellent Salmon, Brown Trout and Grayling fishing. There are also good numbers of coarse fish in certain areas; although access is limited sport can be very rewarding. Salmon and Trout fishing is generally controlled by syndicates and local estates.

RIVER FISHING

Dorchester Fishing Club
Contact: Mr J.Grindle (Hon. Sec.), 36 Cowleaze, Martinstown, *Tel:* 01305 889682, *Mobile:* 07810 555316, *Water:* Approx. 6.5 miles of double bank on the Frome near Dorchester, Brown Trout fly fishing. *Species:* Brown Trout, Grayling. *Permits:* John Aplin, Dorchester (01305) 266500 *Charges:* Day tickets and membership available. Please telephone John Aplin for day tickets and John Grindle for membership details. *Season:* April 1st - October 14th. *Methods:* Dry fly and Nymph only. Barbless hooks are encouraged.

East Burton Estate
Cliff Cottage, Moreton, Dorchester, *Tel:* 01929 462270, *Water:* Fishing on two carriers of the River Frome near Wool. *Species:* Brown Trout and Grayling with occasional Sea Trout and Salmon. Pike in winter. *Permits:* From the above. *Charges:* On application. *Season:* Trout from 1 May to 1 October. EA byelaws apply.

Moreton Estate
Contact: Simon Cooper, Fishing Breaks, The Mill, Heathman Street, Nether Wallop, Stockbridge, Hants. *Tel:* 01264 781988, *Water:* Chalkstream fishing with good mayfly hatch. *Species:* Brown Trout. *Permits:* By phone or e-mail from Fishing Breaks. *Charges:* May 15 to 31 - £100. June £85. July to October - £65. *Season:* May to October. *Methods:* Dry fly & Nymph only.

River Frome (Town Section)
Contact: Purbeck Angling Centre / Deano or Barry, 28 South Street, Wareham, *Tel:* 01929 550770, *Water:* One mile stretch of the River Frome. *Species:* Roach, Dace, Grayling, Eels, Pike, Salmon, Trout, Sea Trout, Mullet, Bass, Flounder, Carp and Perch. *Permits:* Enquiries to Purbeck Angling Centre. *Charges:* Free fishing on public section. Enquiries to Purbeck Angling Centre. *Season:* Normal closed seasons apply. *Methods:* This stretch is run as a Coarse Fishery only. All Game and Saltwater fish are to be returned immediately.

Wareham & District Angling Society
Contact: Deano Watts, c/o Purbeck Angling Centre, 28 South Street, Wareham, *Tel:* 01929 550770, *Water:* River waters on Piddle and the Frome. 3 lakes Wareham area plus 5 near Dorchester. *Species:* Coarse. Roach 3lb+, Pike 30lb+, Dace 1lb+, Grayling record. *Permits:* Purbeck Angling Centre Tel: 01929 550770. *Charges:* Senior £45, O.A.P's £22.50, Junior £10. Membership runs from June 1st to May 31st. *Season:* Two lakes at Wareham and five at Dorchester open during Coarse closed season. *Methods:* Barbless, no litter, no cans, variations as per membership book.

Wessex Chalk Streams Ltd. (Frome)
Contact: Richard & Sally Slocock, Lawrences Farm, Southover, Tolpuddle, Dorchester, *Tel:* 01305 848460, *Water:* Wild Browns, Stocked Browns and Grayling in lower beats. *Species:* Brown Trout. Some beats with all wild fish, other beats with stocked browns to augment the wild fish. *Permits:* From the above address. *Charges:* From £45 to £95 day. Generous discounts for large bookings. *Season:* 1st April - 15th October. *Methods:* Barbless hooks, catch and release.

Wrackleford Estate Fishery ♿
Contact: Oliver Pope, Dorchester, *Tel:* 01303 267643, *Mobile:* 07980 694487, *Water:* Seven beats on four miles of Frome chalkstream. *Species:* Predominately Brown Trout. *Permits:* From the above. *Charges:* On application. *Season:* April 1 to October 15. EA Byelaws apply. *Methods:* Dry fly only. Some beats suitable for disabled access, please phone first for further details.

Wayne Killestein and daughters with a cracking Koi from Plymouth Command AA's Hemerdon Lakes near Plympton, Plymouth

PIDDLE AND WEST DORSET STREAMS

'West Dorset' streams include the River Brit, Asker, Bride and Char. These streams are relatively short, 'steep' water courses supporting populations of mainly Brown Trout and Sea Trout.

The River Piddle rises at four major springs near Alton St. Pancras, initially flowing south before turning east at Puddletown towards Poole Harbour, where it confluences with the River Frome. This small chalk stream offers excellent Brown Trout fishing, with Salmon, Sea Trout and coarse fish in the lower reaches. The Agency operates a salmon and sea trout rod fishery in this area. Other fish species can be found in the River Piddle including, Roach, Dace, Pike and Perch. Much of the fishing is controlled by local syndicates and estate waters; further information about these groups can be obtained from the aforementioned Frome, Piddle and West Dorset Fishery Association.

Environment Agency - Piddle Fishery
Contact: Fisheries Recreation & Biodiversity Officer, Environment Agency, Rivers House, Sunrise Business Pk, Higher Shaftesbury Rd, Blandford, *Tel:* 08708 506506, *Water:* 2.5km of bank fishing on the Lower Piddle. *Species:* Salmon & Sea Trout. *Permits:* 14 permits per annum. Closing date for applications 31 January *Charges:* £225 plus vat (2007 charges), subject to annual review. *Methods:* Salmon - compulsory catch and release, barbless hooks must be used and the use of worms banned.

Manor of Wareham
Contact: Guy Ryder, The Estate Office,, Manor of Wareham, Cow Lane, Wareham, *Tel:* 01929 552666, *Water:* Stretch on River Piddle single bank fishing. *Species:* Brown Trout and Sea Trout. *Charges:* Season tickets only. Price on application. *Season:* E.A. Byelaws. *Methods:* E.A. Byelaws.

Wessex Chalk Streams Ltd. (Piddle)
Contact: Richard & Sally Slocock, Lawrences Farm, Southover, Tolpuddle, Dorchester, *Tel:* 01305 848460, *Water:* Seven beats. *Species:* Brown Trout only. Wild and stocked. *Permits:* From the above address. *Charges:* From £35 to £80 day. Generous discounts for large bookings. *Season:* 1st April - 15th October. *Methods:* Catch and release. Fly only.

STOUR

The River Stour in Dorset is well known by anglers across the country for the quality of its fishing. Over the years many British record captures have been made here, for example, the current Roach record stands at 4lb 3oz, taken from the Stour near Wimborne.
The Stour rises on the Greensand at St. Peters Pump in Stourhead Gardens and flows through Gillingham. Nearby it is joined by the Shreen Water and the River Lodden. The Stour stretches out for 96 km, passing through the Blackmoor Vale down to the sea at Christchurch; the total fall over this distance is approximately 230m. Other notable tributaries along its length include the River Tarrant confluencing near Spetisbury, the River Allen at Wimborne and the Moors River coming in near Christchurch. The Stour confluences with the River Avon at the 'Clay Pool' in Christchurch, before flowing into the harbour area and ultimately out into the English Channel.

Dorchester & District Angling Society
Contact: Andy Miller, Weymouth, *Tel:* 01305 815143, *Water:* 5 miles on Dorset Stour, 1.5 miles Dorset Frome plus lakes at Kingcombe and Warmwell. R. Brue Somerset plus water sharing agreements and Federation waters on Somerset Levels. *Species:* Roach, Dace, Chub, Pike, Gudgeon, Perch, Eels, Carp, Bream, Grayling. *Permits:* 'Reels & Deals', Weymouth, Aplins Tackle Dorchester, Weymouth Angling Centre, Surplus International, Dorchester. Purbreck Angling, Weymouth. Dennings Tackle, Weymouth. *Charges:* Adult members £47. Reductions for Juniors & Spouses. Members guest tickets, no day tickets, half-year membership from December 1st. *Season:* June 16th - March 14th, Stillwater open all year. *Methods:* Various, specific to particular waters.

Gillingham & District A A (Stour)
Contact: Simon Hebditch (Hon. Secretary), 8 Maple Way, Gillingham, *Tel:* 01747 821218, *Mobile:* 07990 690613, *Water:* 7 miles Upper Stour - Gillingham to Marnhull. Also Turners Paddock lake at Stourhead. Mappowder Court 4 lakes at Mappowder. *Species:* Roach 3lb, Chub 4lb 8oz, Barbel 6lb, Pike 21lb, Dace 1lb, Bream 6lb, Gudgeon 3oz, Perch 3lb 4oz, Tench 3lb, Carp 10lb, Eels 4lb. Trout, Grayling 2lb 8oz. *Permits:* Mr P Stone (Treasurer) The Timepiece, Newbury, Gillingham, Dorset, SP8 4HZ. Tel: 01747 823339. Mr J Candy, Todber Manor Fisheries Shop, Tel: 01258 820384. *Charges:* £5 day ticket, £30 season ticket. £15 juniors and concessions. (probable charges for 2008). *Season:* June 16th to March 14th. *Methods:* Best stick float with maggot casters and bread. Large lump of bread for Chub. Sweetcorn also very productive for Chub. Feeder for Bream.

Lower Stour / Christchurch Harbour
Contact: Paul Jerome, Suite 21D, Magnolia House, 19-21 Stour Road, Christchurch, *Tel:* 01202 480009, *Mobile:* 07714 449523, *Water:* Christchurch Angling Club stretch of Dorset Stour downstream of Iford Bridge and Christchurch harbour. *Species:* Roach 2lb, Dace 1lb, Pike 20lb, Bream 7lb, Perch 3lb, Carp 30lb, Eels 5lb, Mullet 10lb. *Permits:* Available from Davis Tackle (01202 485169); Pro Tackle (01202 484518); Christchurch Angling Centre (01202 480520). *Charges:* Christchurch Harbour: Annual adult £40, junior/conc. £20. Weekly adult £20, junior/conc. £10. Day ticket adult £5, junior/conc. £3. Lower Stour: Weekly adult £20, junior/conc. £10. Day ticket adult £7.50, junior/conc. £4. *Season:* Coarse: 16th June to 14th March. *Methods:* See club rules for individual waters.

Muscliffe & Longham
Contact: Neil Cooke, 904 Wimborne Road, Moordown, Bournemouth, *Tel:* 01202 514345, *Water:* 1.5 miles river Stour at Muscliffe and 0.25 miles at Longham. *Species:* Chub, Barbel, Roach, Dace, Pike, Eels, Minnow, Gudgeon and Perch. *Permits:* Free (owned by Bournemouth Council). *Charges:* Free. E.A. licence required. *Season:* 16th June to 14th March. *Methods:* No restrictions.

Ashley Gogan with a stunning 10lb 4oz Avon Barbel

Ringwood & District A.A. (Stour)
Contact: Mr Darren Smith, Cozy Corner, 5 Hilton Road, New Milton, Hants. *Tel:* 01425 611335, *Mobile:* 07702 300384, *Water:* 11 stretches on Stour including total control of Throop fishery and various stretches upstream to Stourpaine. *Species:* Throop - Barbel to 16lb, Chub 8lb. Middle regions good general Roach, Chub, Bream, Pike, Perch, some Trout, Grayling and Carp. *Permits:* Ringwood Tackle. Tel: 01425 475155. Christchurch Angling Centre Tel: 01202 480520. *Charges:* Adult £110, Junior £45, concessions for OAP's and disabled; Throop day tickets £9.00. Concessions, O.A.P's, Disabled and Juniors available from local tackle dealers. Prices may vary in 2008. *Season:* As per coarse season. *Methods:* Details in permit or reverse of ticket.

Stalbridge Angling Association (Stour)
Contact: Bernie Ackland, *Tel:* 01935 474284, *Water:* 2.5 miles Stour, Lanshire Lake, Stalbridge. *Species:* Bream, Tench, Roach, Dace, Pike, Chub, Rudd. *Permits:* C.C. Moores Ltd (animal foods), Stalbridge, 01963 362234. Bernie Ackland, 4 Russel Ave., Milborne Port, 01935 474284. *Charges:* Senior Annual £25 no joining fee, Junior (under 17 years) £10 & Concessions (Reg. Disabled & OAPs) £14 no joining fee. Husband and wife ticket £35. Day Tickets £5 senior, £2.50 junior. *Season:* Normal river closed season.

Sturminster & Hinton A.A ♿
Contact: Mr R. Brown (membership sec.), Uplands Close, Broad Oak, Sturminster Newton, *Tel:* 01258 473178, *Water:* 14 miles mid River Stour, one small lake (Stokewake Lake) members only. Plus joint fisheries at Lodden Lakes, Gillingham. *Species:* Roach 3lb 2.5oz, Chub 6lb 3oz, Tench 7lb 3.5oz, Bream 9lb, Perch 3lb 6oz, Carp 20lb 10oz, Pike 26lb 10oz, Dace 11.5oz. *Permits:* Candy's Newsagents, The Square, Sturminster Newton. Marsh's Electrical, The Square, Sturminster Newton. Todber Manor fisheries, Todber, Nr Sturminster Newton. Membership Sec. (Full Season and Lodden Lakes). The Bull Tavern, The Bridge, Sturminster Newton. Conyers, Blandford. *Charges:* £5 day, £10 week, Junior season £6, Adult season £30, Concession £25. *Season:* March 14th - June 16th. *Methods:* No dogs, radios, no live baiting. One rod, second rod only for Pike. Barbless hooks at lakes. No night fishing. Always carry your membership permit.

Throop Fisheries
Contact: Ringwood & District Angling Club, Mr Darren Smith, Cozy Corner, 5 Hilton Road, New Milton, Hants. *Tel:* 01425 611335, *Mobile:* 07702 300384, *Water:* Northern edge of Bournemouth. 10 Miles of river bank on Dorset Stour & Stillwater Mill Pool. *Species:* Barbel to 16-02, Chub to 8-10, Carp 32lb, Roach 3lb, Tench 8lb, Perch 3lb, Dace 10oz, Pike 31lb, Bream 9lb. *Permits:* Ringwood Tackle - Tel. 01425 475155, Bournemouth Fishing Lodge - Tel. 01202 514345. Christchurch Angling Centre - Tel: 01202 480520. *Charges:* Day tickets £9, to be obtained before fishing. Prices may vary in 2008. *Season:* 16th June - 14th March inclusive. *Methods:* See reverse of tickets.

Wimborne & District Angling Club (Stour)
Contact: Mr J Burden (Game Secretary), 35 Hardy Crescent, Wimborne, *Tel:* 01202 889324, *Water:* 10 miles River Stour, 17 lakes, 1 mile River Avon *Species:* Trout & Coarse Fisheries. *Permits:* Certain waters are available on Guest Tickets £6 from Wessex Angling Centre, 321 Wimborne Rd, Oakdale, Poole, Dorset. Guest tickets to members only. *Charges:* Membership: £95, Junior £25, under 12 accompanied by an adult free. *Season:* Coarse - all year round. Sea Trout - April 16 to Oct 31. Salmon - 1 Feb to 30 Sept. 4 x Trout Lakes - 1 Mar - 31 Oct. *Methods:* Barbless hooks on Coarse Stillwaters, no floating baits.

Stillwater Coarse

BEAMINSTER

Higher Kingcombe Lodge

Contact: Mr Crocker, Higher Kingcombe, Dorchester, *Tel:* 01300 320537, *Mobile:* 07967 968846, *Water:* 7 lakes - approx. 5 acres of water in total. *Species:* Carp (Mirror, Common & Ghost), Perch, Roach, Rudd, Bream, Tench. Specimen lake - Carp to 29lb. *Permits:* Permits from local Post Office. *Charges:* Day ticket £5, Evening (after 6pm) £3, Night Fishing £10, Juniors (16 and under) £2.50 per day. *Season:* Open all year. *Methods:* Max 2 rods per person, barbless hooks only, under 14's must be accompanied by an adult.

BLANDFORD

Milton Abbas Lakes

Contact: Wayne Little, Milton Abbas, Blandford, *Tel:* 01258 880919, *Mobile:* 07780 966117, *Water:* Three acre day ticket lake. Please note lake is adjacent to 8 acre syndicate lake - no fishing permitted for day ticket anglers. *Species:* Carp 10lbs up to 18lbs, Grass Carp to 16lbs, Tench to 6lbs, Roach to 2lbs, Crucian Carp, Bream, Tench, Perch & Eels and Pike to 20lb. *Permits:* Maximum of 10 anglers per day. Tickets on the bank. *Charges:* Adult £10 per day. Juniors £5 per day (Must be under 16 and accompanied by an adult). *Season:* No close season. Fishing times 7am until Sunset. *Methods:* No keep nets or Carp sacks, 2 rods only. No peas, nuts or beans, a suitable landing net and unhooking mat if Carp fishing, no dogs, fires, swimming or bait boats.

BOURNEMOUTH

East Moors Lake

Contact: Mr. Nicolas Hoare, East Moors Farm, East Moors Lane, St. Leonards, Ferndale, Bournemouth, *Tel:* 01202 872302, *Water:* 1.5 acre lake. *Species:* Mainly Carp, Tench and Roach. *Charges:* Please telephone for details. *Methods:* Barbless hooks only, no boilies, no keepnets, no dogs. Children under 14 must be accompanied by adult.

Throop Fisheries (Coarse Lake)

Contact: Ringwood & District Angling Club, Mr Darren Smith, Cozy Corner, 5 Hilton Road, New Milton, Hants. *Tel:* 01425 611335, *Mobile:* 07702 300384, *Water:* Stillwater Mill Pool. Also 10 Miles of river bank on Dorset Stour. *Species:* Barbel, Chub, Carp, Roach, Tench, Perch, Dace, Pike. *Permits:* Christchurch Angling Centre - Tel: 01202 480520. *Charges:* Day tickets £9, to be obtained before fishing. Prices may vary in 2008. *Season:* 16th June - 14 March (Open every day between these dates). *Methods:* No night fishing.

BRIDPORT

Highway Farm

Contact: John & Pauline Bale, West Road, Bridport, *Tel:* 01308 424321, *Water:* 2 small lakes in quiet, secluded valley. *Species:* Carp, Roach, Rudd. *Permits:* From the Post Office. Bridport *Charges:* £5 day / £3 half day. From 2pm *Season:* Open all year, dawn to dusk. No night fishing. *Methods:* No boilies or keep nets. Barbless hooks only. No dogs.

Mangerton Valley Coarse Fishing Lake

Contact: Clive & Jane Greening, New House Farm, Mangerton Lane, Bradpole, Bridport, *Tel:* 01308 422884, *Water:* 1.6 acre lake. *Species:* Carp to 28lb (Common and Mirror), Roach, Tench. *Permits:* From Post Office. *Charges:* £7 day, £4 half day, £3 evening. *Methods:* Barbless hooks. No boilies or beans. No nuts, no dogs. Night fishing by arrangement. All children under 12 to be accompanied by an adult.

Washingpool Farm Fishing

West Bay Watersports, 10a West Bay, Bridport, *Tel:* 01308 421800, *Water:* 2 lakes (1 x 1.5 acre, 1 x 1.75 acre). *Species:* Carp to 30lb, Mirror, Common, Crucian, Ghost 15lb, Wild Carp, Tench, Roach, Rudd & Bream. *Charges:* Limited Day tickets in advance from West Bay Watersports. £5 per day 2 rods. £3 half day. *Season:* Open all year dawn to dusk. *Methods:* Barbless hooks only, no keepnets.

CHRISTCHURCH

Avon Tyrrell Lakes

Contact: Dave Clarke, Avon Tyrrell House, Bransgore, Christchurch, *Tel:* 01425 672347, *Water:* Two lakes totalling approx. 2.5 acres. *Species:* Carp, Tench, Roach, Bream, Perch and Rudd. *Permits:* On site from reception. *Charges:* £6 Day Tickets Adults. £3 Juniors(Under 16). Season Tickets also available, please note Night Fishing only available on a season ticket. Prices may change in 2008. *Season:* Open mid June to mid March - 08.30 to 17.00hrs on day ticket from June 2008. *Methods:* Barbless Hooks, No keepnets, No nut baits. See rules on site.

Hordle Lakes ♿

Contact: M.F. Smith, Hordle Lakes, Golden Hill, Ashley Lane, Hordle, Nr New Milton, Hants. *Tel:* 01590 672300, *Mobile:* 07778 954799, *Water:* Seven spring fed lakes set in 11 acres. *Species:* Double figure Carp. Tench, Roach, Rudd, Bream and Perch. *Permits:* From the fishery. Can also issue EA rod licences on site. *Charges:* Adults £9 per day. OAPs £7. Children £6. *Season:* Open all year 7am to dusk. Night fishing by arrangement. *Methods:* All fish to be returned immediately. No groundbaiting, loose feeding only. Barbless hooks only, no larger than size 6. No boilies, beans, nuts or Trout bait. Full rules at the fishery.

Whirlwind Lake

Contact: Mr & Mrs Pillinger, Whirlwind Rise, Dudmore Lane, Christchurch, *Tel:* 01202 475255, *Water:* Secluded lake. *Species:* Common, Crucian and Mirror Carp, Roach, Rudd, Tench, Chub etc. *Permits:* On site and local fishing tackle shops. Davis Tackle, 75 The Bargates, Christchurch: 01202 485169. Pro Angling, 248 Barrack Road, Christchurch: 01202 484518. Advanced booking advisable, limited number available. *Charges:* Adults £8.50 day ticket. £5 half day (limited places). Children (must be accompanied) £5 day. *Season:* Open all year. *Methods:* Barbless hooks only, no keepnets, no boilies.

CORFE

Arfleet Mill Lakes

Contact: Mr B Charron, Dairy Cottage, Knitson, Corfe Castle, *Tel:* 01929 427421, *Water:* 1 acre spring fed lake, 1 acre deep water lake and a young anglers pool. Situated off the B3351 near Corfe Castle. *Species:* Carp to 29lb 3oz, Roach, Rudd, Tench, Perch and Eel. *Permits:* Purbeck Angling in Wareham or Clealls Stores in Corfe Castle. *Charges:* £6.50 day - 2 rods, £3.95 1/2 day and concessions for children under 16. Night fishing by appointment. *Season:* 2008 open early April until end of October. *Methods:* No Trout pellets, no keepnets, barbless hooks only, no ground bait.

CRANBORNE

Gold Oak Fishery

Contact: Mr J Butler, Gold Oak Farm, Hare Lane, Cranborne, *Tel:* 01725 517275, *Water:* Seven small lakes. *Species:* Carp to 20lb, Green and Golden Tench to 5-6lb, Perch 2.5lb, Roach 2lb, Chub 4lb, Bream 3lb. *Charges:* £10 per day. *Season:* All year. *Methods:* No large fish in keepnets, barbless hooks, dogs on lead. Under 16s must be accompanied by an adult.

Martins Farm Fishery

Contact: Mary and Jonathan Stephens, Martins Farm, Woodlands, Verwood, *Tel:* 01202 823631, *Mobile:* 07717 887357, *Water:* 2.5 acre spring fed lake. *Species:* Carp to 26lb, Tench to 5lb, Perch, Roach, Rudd. *Permits:* Tel: 01202 823631 *Charges:* £10 Adult day ticket, £5 after 4pm. Juniors (12 and under) half price. *Methods:* No keepnets, barbless hooks, no hemp. Boilies in moderation.

Wimborne & District Angling Club (Coarse Lakes)

Contact: Mr J Burden (Game Secretary), 35 Hardy Crescent, Wimborne, *Tel:* 01202 889324, *Water:* 12 coarse lakes, 10 miles river Stour, 1 mile river Avon. 5 Trout lakes. See also entry under Stour. *Species:* Mixed Coarse. *Permits:* Certain waters are available on guest tickets. £6 from Wessex Angling, 321 Wimborne Rd, Oakdale, Poole. Guest tickets to members only. *Charges:* Membership: £95, Junior £25, under 12 accompanied by an adult free. *Season:* All year round. *Methods:* Barbless hooks on Coarse Stillwaters, no floating baits.

DORCHESTER

Dorchester & District Angling Society (Coarse Lake)
Contact: Andy Miller, Weymouth, *Tel:* 01305 815143, *Water:* See entry under Stour. Coarse lakes at Kingcombe and Warmwell. *Species:* Carp, Tench, Perch and Roach. *Season:* Lakes open all year. *Methods:* Barbless hooks only. No boilies or bivvies on lakes.

Gillingham & District A.A. (Mappowder Court)
Contact: Simon Hebditch (Hon. Secretary), 8 Maple Way, Gillingham, *Tel:* 01747 821218, *Mobile:* 07990 690613, *Water:* Mappowder Court Fishing Complex (4 lakes), Mappowder Nr Dorchester. (see also entry under river fishing Stour). *Species:* Crucian/Crucian cross 2lb, Carp 22lb, Tench 4lb, Eels 3lb, Roach 2lb, Rudd 1lb, Gudgeon, Perch 2lb, Bream 3lb, Barbel 1lb, Grass Carp 8lb. *Permits:* Mr P Stone (Treasurer) The Timepiece, Newbury, Gillingham, Dorset, SP8 4HZ. Tel: 01747 823339. Mr J Candy, Todber Manor Fisheries Shop, Tel: 01258 820384. Kings Stag Garage, Kings Stag, Nr Hazelbury Bryan. *Charges:* £5 day ticket, £30 season ticket. £15 juniors and concessions. (probable charges for 2008). *Season:* Open all year. *Methods:* Barbless hooks. Mainly pole fishing. Big baits for double figure Carp on Pheasant lake. Pole on Spring lake for mixed bags.

Litton Lakes
Contact: Andrew Romans, Charity Farm, Litton Lane, Litton Cheney, *Tel:* 01308 482574, *Water:* 1.5 acre lake. *Species:* Carp, Roach, Rudd, Bream, Tench, Perch, Trout. *Charges:* Dawn to dusk: adult £6. Under 16 years £4.50. *Season:* Open all year. 24 hour fishing. *Methods:* Barbless hooks, No Keepnets, Landing nets to be disinfected, Maximum 2 rods per person, Juniors to be accompanied by an adult, No dogs, No fires, No litter.

Luckfield Lake Fishery
Contact: John Aplin, 1 Athelstan Road, Dorchester, *Tel:* 01305 266500, *Mobile:* 07889 680464, *Water:* 1.5 acre clay pit in beautiful surroundings. *Species:* Carp to 28lb, Tench to 9lb plus, Roach to 3lb plus. *Permits:* As above. *Charges:* Day £6, Night £10, half season £50. *Season:* Open all year. *Methods:* No keepnets, barbless hooks.

Lyons Gate Fishing Lakes
Contact: Stuart Jones, Lyons Gate, Nr Cerne Abbas, Dorchester, *Tel:* 01300 345260, *Water:* Four lakes totalling approximately 3.5 acres. *Species:* Carp to 35lb, Tench to 11lb, Chub, Barbel, Bream, Golden Orfe, Roach, Rudd. *Permits:* On bankside. *Charges:* £5 p/day (2 rods), night fishing can be arranged. *Season:* Open all year dawn to dusk. *Methods:* Barbless hooks only. Full details at the fishery.

Meadow Lake
Contact: R.A. Allan Reese, Riverside Cottage, Forston, Dorchester, *Tel:* 01305 269912, *Water:* 0.1 acre lake. *Species:* Carp to 19lb, Roach, Bream. *Charges:* £3 per day. £6 overnight. £2 after 2pm. Half day is half price. *Season:* Open all year. *Methods:* Barbless hooks. No keepnets. No groundbait.

Pallington Lakes
Contact: Mr Simon or Mrs Tini Pomeroy, Pallington, Dorchester, *Tel:* 01305 849333, *Mobile:* 07887 840507, *Water:* 3 coarse fishing lakes and a stretch of the river Frome. *Species:* Lakes: Carp to 42lb 6oz, Tench to 12lb 3oz, Perch to 4lb 13oz, Grayling to 3lb 12oz, Roach 3lb, Bream 10lb, Rudd 3lb. *Permits:* Lakes are private club water - members only. Please contact us for membership details. River available for Grayling fishing. Please contact the above for details and availability. 2 acre Stonze Pool is available for day ticket and session anglers - 8 peg limit, so

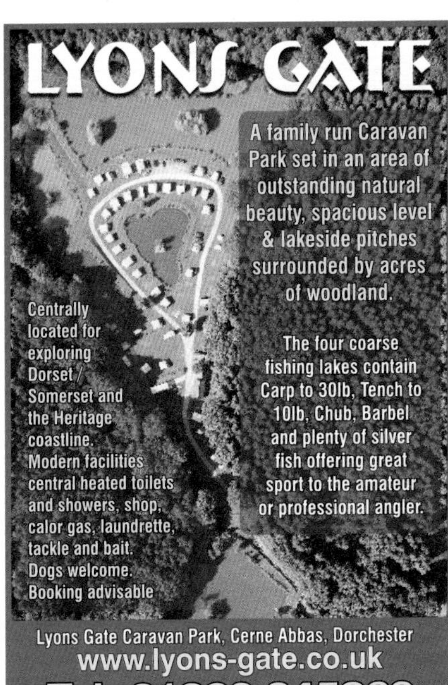

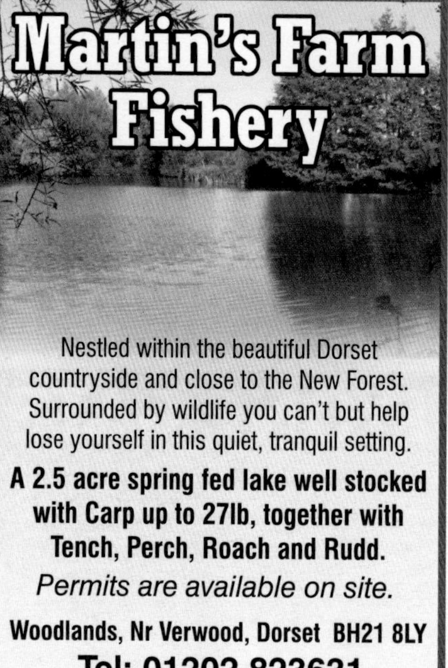

booking is essential. *Charges:* Lakes: All year round season ticket. River limited rod ticket £25 per day. Day ticket Stonze Pool £12 day, £22 for 24 hours - 2 rod limit. *Season:* All year round. Shop open daily 9 to 10am. River fishing by appointment. *Methods:* Barbless hooks, No keepnets. No nut baits. All anglers must be in possesion of a fish antiseptic. All Carp anglers must use minimum 36 inch landing net and a unhooking mat supplied free of charge for use at Pallington Lakes. All anglers must observe fishery rules.

GILLINGHAM

Culvers Farm Fishery

Contact: V.J. Pitman, Culvers Farm, Gillingham, *Tel:* 01747 822466, *Water:* One 1.5 acre lake. One 3 acre lake. *Species:* Carp, Bream, Roach, Chub and Tench. *Charges:* Day £6. Half Day £4. OAP's and under 16 £4 all day. *Season:* Open all year. No night fishing. *Methods:* Barbless hooks only. No Boilies. No keepnets allowed.

Gillingham & District A.A. (Lodden Lakes) ♿

Contact: Simon Hebditch (Hon. Secretary), 8 Maple Way, Gillingham, *Tel:* 01747 821218, *Mobile:* 07990 690613, *Water:* 2 lakes (5 acres and 3 acres). *Species:* Carp to 27lb, Pike to 25lb, Crucians to 4lb, Tench to 7lb, Eels to 7lb, Roach to 2lb, Bream to 9lb, Grass Carp to 18lb. *Permits:* As R.Stour. *Charges:* As R.Stour to join club. Guest Tickets - £4. Season Ticket - £10 day, £20 day/night. Must be a member of either Gillingham or Sturminster. *Season:* Open all year. *Methods:* Large Carp favour boilies, Pike on deadbaits, Bream on pole or feeder with worm, pellet and g/bait, Tench from margins on worm/caster.

LYME REGIS

Wood Farm Caravan Park

Contact: Jane Bremner, Axminster Road, Charmouth, *Tel:* 01297 560697, *Water:* 2 ponds totalling approx. 1 acre. *Species:* Carp, Rudd, Roach, Tench & Perch. *Permits:* Rod licences sold. *Charges:* £4 day ticket. £17 week. £40 season. *Season:* All year. *Methods:* No boilies, keepnets. Barbless hooks only.

POOLE

Bourne Valley Park

Contact: Sarah Austin, Alderney, Poole, *Tel:* 01202 261325, *Water:* Small fishing lake used as an introduction to angling for local people up to about 16 years old. *Species:* Rudd and Carp. *Charges:* Free of charge. *Season:* Open all year. *Methods:* Barbless hooks only. No boilies. No litter. Full rules on site.

RINGWOOD

Moors Valley Country Park ♿

Contact: The Rangers, Horton Road, Ashley Heath, Nr Ringwood, *Tel:* 01425 470721, *Water:* The Moors Lake covers an area of 9 acres. Maximum depth 2 meters. *Species:* Tench to 6lb, Roach to 2lb, Perch to 2lb, Rudd 2lb, Pike to 20lb. Most river species ie Dace/Gudgeon etc. *Permits:* Fishing is from the bays marked by wooden posts on the west bank and has disabled access. Permits from visitor centre. *Charges:* £3.75 Adults (17 - 65yrs), £3.20 65yrs plus, £2.70 Junior (Up to 16yrs). Car park charges vary throughout the year, pay on foot system. *Season:* Moors lake from 16th June to 14th March. *Methods:* Rod licence required for over 12yrs. Fishing from 8-30am to dusk, no keepnets, no boilies, barbless hooks, wooden bays only, float/ledger/feeder/dead bait for Pike. Max two rods per angler.

SHAFTSBURY

Coking Farm Fishery

Contact: Chris, Coking Farm, West Stour, Nr Shaftsbury, *Tel:* 01747 839879, *Mobile:* 07789 003044, *Water:* Three lakes: 4.25, 3.5 and 2.5 acres. *Species:* Tench to 8lb, Carp 32lb, Catfish 35lb, Roach 2lb, Rudd 2lb, Crucians 2lb, Bream 6lb. *Charges:* Rush Lake (mixed) £6. Meadow Lake (Carp) £6, £12 for 24 hrs. Woodlands Lake (Carp and Catfish) £8, £15 for 24 hrs. *Season:* Open all year. *Methods:* Barbless hooks only. No keepnets. No nuts. Unhooking mats and suitable quality landing net must be used.

Immaculate 22lb 14oz Carp from Todber Manor.

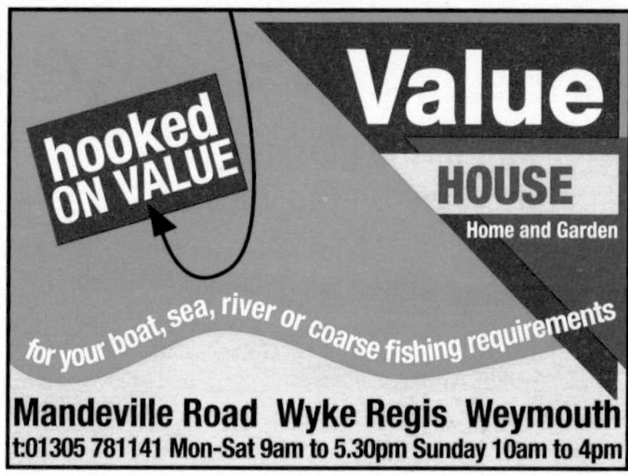

STALBRIDGE

Stalbridge Angling Association (Coarse Lake) ♿

Contact: Bernie Ackland, *Tel:* 01935 474284, *Water:* Lake at Lanshire Lane, Stalbridge. See also entry under Stour. *Species:* Carp (18lb), Perch (2lb), Chub, Roach. *Permits:* C.C. Moores Ltd (animal foods), Stalbridge, 01963 362234. Bernie Ackland, 01935 474284. *Charges:* Senior £25. Disabled/OAP £14. Junior £10. Day Ticket Senior £5, Junior £2.50. *Season:* No closed season on lake. *Methods:* No Boilies or Nuts. No fixed method feeders or fixed leads. No keepnets. Barbless hooks only to be used. Some pegs suitable for disabled. Parking within 15 metres of water.

STURMINSTER NEWTON

Gillingham & District A.A. (Whitepost Lakes)

Contact: Simon Hebditch (Hon. Secretary), 8 Maple Way, Gillingham, *Tel:* 01747 821218, *Mobile:* 07990 690613, *Water:* 2 x 1acre lakes. *Species:* Carp to 7lb, Crucians/Crucian cross to 1lb, Tench to 4lb, Roach, Rudd, Perch and Eels. *Permits:* As R.Stour. *Charges:* As R.Stour. *Season:* Open all year. *Methods:* Pole, Waggler or feeder for Carp. Sweetcorn, pellet, maggots or meat good for Carp.

Sturminster & Hinton A.A (Coarse Lakes)

Contact: Mr R. Brown (membership sec.), Uplands Close, Broad Oak, Sturminster Newton, *Tel:* 01258 473178, *Water:* One small lake (Stokewake Lake) members only plus 14 miles mid River Stour. See entry under River Fishing - Dorset - Stour.

Todber Manor Fisheries (Big Hayes) ♿

Contact: John Candy, Manor Farm, Todber, Sturminster Newton, *Tel:* 01258 820384, *Mobile:* 07974 420813, *Water:* 8.5 acre lake with 18 woodchipped swims. *Species:* Carp to 33lb 8oz. *Permits:* From on site tackle shop. *Charges:* £10 per day. £20 for 24 hours. *Season:* Open all year. *Methods:* No keepnets or sacks. Minimum 42" landing net. Unhooking mats must be used. Call the tackle shop or visit website for full details.

Todber Manor Fisheries (Paddock Lake) ♿

Contact: John Candy, Manor Farm, Todber, Sturminster Newton, *Tel:* 01258 820384, *Mobile:* 07974 420813, *Water:* 1.5 acre lake with seven well spaced, woodchipped swims. *Species:* Carp 28lb 3oz, Catfish 38lb 5oz. *Permits:* From on site tackle shop. *Charges:* £10 per day. £20 per 24 hours. Whole lake £100 for 24 hours. *Season:* Open all year. *Methods:* Common sense rules apply. Call the tackle shop for full details.

Todber Manor Fisheries (Park Lake) ♿

Contact: John Candy, Manor Farm, Todber, Sturminster Newton, *Tel:* 01258 820384, *Mobile:* 07974 420813, *Water:* 3 acre canal style lake with 38 wooden platforms. *Species:* Carp 12lb, Barbel 6lb 1oz, Tench 5lb, Roach 1lb 14oz, Bream 4lb 2oz, Hybrids 2lb plus. *Permits:* From on site tackle shop. *Charges:* £6 per day. *Season:* Open all year. *Methods:* Common sense rules apply. Call the tackle shop for full details.

Todber Manor Fisheries (Wadmill) ♿

Contact: John Candy, Manor Farm, Todber, Sturminster Newton, *Tel:* 01258 820384, *Mobile:* 07974 420813, *Water:* Four acre lake, 20 swims. *Species:* Pike 22lb, Carp 27lb 8oz, Bream 8lb, Perch 3lb, Tench 6lb. *Permits:* From on site tackle shop. *Charges:* £8 per day. £15 per 24 hours. *Season:* Open all year. *Methods:* Common sense rules apply. Call the tackle shop for full details.

Todber Manor Fisheries (Whitepost Top) ♿

Contact: John Candy, Manor Farm, Todber, Sturminster Newton, *Tel:* 01258 820384, *Mobile:* 07974 420813, *Water:* One acre lake, 14 swims with wooden platforms. *Species:* Carp to 10lb, Tench 5lb, F1s 2lb, Crucians 2lb. *Permits:* From on site tackle shop. *Charges:* £6 per day. *Season:* Open all year. *Methods:* Common sense rules apply. Call the tackle shop for full details.

WAREHAM

Silent Woman Lakes

Contact: David Sowry, Cold Harbour, Bere Road, Nr Wareham. *Tel:* 01929 554153, *Water:* One 3,5 acre lake - 10 swims. One acre lake - 4 swims. *Species:* Pike, Carp, Tench. Fish to 45lb in large lake. *Permits:* From above. *Charges:* Prices on application. Night fishing by arrangement. *Season:* Open all year, dawn to dusk. *Methods:* No boilies, no barbed hooks. Care must be taken of all fish. Full rules at fishery - must be followed at all times.

Wareham & District Angling Society (Coarse Lakes)

Contact: Deano Watts, c/o Purbeck Angling Centre, 28 South Street, Wareham, *Tel:* 01929 550770, *Water:* See entry under River Fishing, Frome. 8 lakes including Breach Pond and Pitmans Pond. *Species:* Carp 25lb+, Bream 10lb+, Crucians 3lb+ and Tench 8lb+. *Permits:* Purbeck Angling. *Season:* Some 12 months, Others normal season applies. *Methods:* As specified in club book.

WEYMOUTH

Osmington Mills Holidays

Contact: Reception, Osmington Mills, Weymouth, *Tel:* 01305 832311, *Water:* 1 acre lake. *Species:* Carp, Tench, Bream, Roach. *Permits:* Caravan Park reception, Ranch House stables reception and on the bank. *Charges:* £6 per day Adults, £3.50 under 16, £4 Evening ticket after 5pm. *Season:* May 23rd - March 15th. Times may vary in 2008. *Methods:* Barbless hooks, no keepnets, no particle bait. Maximum 2 rods. Night fishing by arrangement. No parking at lakeside. Full rules on site.

Radipole Lake ♿

Contact: Weymouth tackle shops, Weymouth, *Water:* 70 acres plus. Fishing only permitted in locations shown on licence. *Species:* Carp 30lb+, Roach and Rudd 2lb+, Pike, Mullet, Tench, Trout, Eels and Perch. *Permits:* Reels and Deals, 61b St. Thomas Street, Weymouth: 01305 787848. Weymouth Angling Centre, 24 Trinity Road, Weymouth: 01305 777771. Permits must be shown to RLAS bailiff on request. Bailiffs carry ID card. *Charges:* Per season charges. Adult £50, Junior (under 16) £25, O.A.P/Disabled £35 (must show badge or disabled rod licence). No overnight fishing on day tickets. Per week charges. All tickets £20. Per day charges. Adult £6, Junior £4, O.A.P/Disabled £6. Tickets are half price from 1st December to 14 March except day tickets. *Season:* 16th June - 14th March. Parts of the lake are shut in winter for rare birds. See permit for more details. No angler may fish for more than 72 hours in one swim. They must move if they wish to continue fishing. *Methods:* 3 rod max, no lead weights, no live baiting, barbless hooks only, bivvies and keepnets permitted, no Carp over 3lb to be kept in keepnets.

Warmwell Holiday Park

Contact: Robert Bray, Warmwell, Nr Weymouth, *Tel:* 01305 854023, *Mobile:* 07828 461059, *Water:* 3 lakes. 2 acre Carp lake (fish to 34lb+) - 20 swims pre-booking only. 2 mixed fishing lakes. *Species:* Carp to 20lb+, Perch to 4lb, Pike to 20lb, Rudd, Crucians, Eels. *Permits:* Day tickets available all year, but must be purchased in advance. Contact fishery manager on number above. *Charges:* Non residents £7.50. Specimen fishing for non residents £9 a day or £18 for 24 hours. *Season:* Open all year. *Methods:* Specimen Lakes: Barbless hooks. No nuts, beans or pulses. 2 rods max. No keepnets. No remote control boats. Unhooking mats must be used. Minimum 10lb line.

WIMBORNE

Clump Hill Farm Fishery ♿

Contact: Jim, Mannington, Wimborne, *Mobile:* 07711 013494, *Water:* One acre lake. *Species:* Carp to 30lb. Common, Crucian and Mirror. Chub 7lb. Perch 3lb. Roach and Rudd. *Permits:* On the bank. *Charges:* £7 per day for two rods. £5 OAPs and under 14s. *Season:* Open all year 7am to 7.30pm or dusk if earlier. Night fishing only by prior arrangement. *Methods:* Barbless hooks only. No keepnets. No dogs. No radios.

Crooked Willows Farm

Contact: Mr & Mrs VJ Percy, Mannington, Wimborne, *Tel:* 01202 825628, *Water:* 1.5 acres. *Species:* Carp to 20lb, Tench to 6lb, Chub 4lb, Roach, Rudd & Crucians. *Permits:* Available on bank. *Charges:* £5/day, Juniors £4. Under 15s must be accompanied by an adult. *Season:* Dawn to Dusk all year round. *Methods:* Barbless hooks only, no groundbait, no keepnets, no dogs.

Little Canford Ponds ♿

Contact: Kay Harvey, Wessex Water - Fisheries & Recreation, Cornish Way West, Galmington, Taunton, Somerset. *Tel:* 0845 6004600, *Water:* Approx. 2 acres with facilities for the Disabled including fully accessible fishing platforms. *Species:* Carp, Bream, Roach, Perch Tench, Rudd, Pike. *Charges:* Adults £44, Conc. £25, Junior £22, Night fishing additional £15, under 12 years free if accompanied by an adult permit holder - max of 2 per adult.

Riverside Lakes ♿

Contact: Tony Perkins, Riverside Farm, Slough Lane, Horton, *Tel:* 01202 821212, *Water:* 3 lakes over 6 acres. *Species:* Carp, Koi, Rudd, Tench, Perch, Roach, Bream, Orfe & Eels. *Permits:* Bailiff collects money & issues tickets on-site. *Charges:* £8 Day ticket, £5 Senior & under 14. Summer half day tickets after 4 pm £5. *Season:* All year. *Methods:* No barbs, no night fishing, no keepnets, no improper equipment, no boilies.

Whitemoor Lake

400 Colehill Lane, Colehill, Wimborne, *Tel:* 01202 884478, *Water:* 2 acre lake with 44 pegs and half acre canal with 20 pegs. Disabled toilet facilities. *Species:* Carp 31lb 2oz, Tench 9lb, Perch 4 - 9oz, Roach 2lb, Rudd, Bream 6lb - 5oz. *Permits:* Tickets on the bank. Night fishing by arrangement. *Charges:* Adults £6, Juniors £4, O.A.P's £5. Evenings £4. *Season:* No close season. *Methods:* No barbed hooks, no keepnets, no braid.

Remember a ♿ means the fishery has disabled facilities - contact them direct for further details

Fin-perfect Rainbow from Bellbrook

Stillwater Trout

BRIDPORT

Mangerton Mill

Contact: Mrs Harris, Mangerton Mill, Mangerton, Bridport, *Tel:* 01308 485224, *Water:* 1 acre lake. *Species:* Rainbow Trout. *Permits:* Post Office. *Charges:* £6 to fish. £9 up to 2 fish. £13 up to 3 fish. £17 up to 4 fish. *Season:* 1st April - 31st December. *Methods:* Max hook size 10.

CRANBORNE

Wimborne & District Angling Club (Trout Lakes)

Contact: Mr J Burden (Game Secretary), 35 Hardy Crescent, Wimborne, *Tel:* 01202 889324, *Water:* 5 Trout lakes plus Brown Trout on the river Avon. See also entry under Stour. *Charges:* Membership: £95, Junior £25, under 12 accompanied by an adult free.

DORCHESTER

Flowers Farm Fly Fishers ♿

Contact: Alan.J.Bastone, Flowers Farm, Hilfield, Dorchester, *Tel:* 01300 341351, *Water:* 5 lakes total 3.75 acres. *Species:* Rainbow & Brown Trout. Best fish in 2003 - 13lb 4oz Rainbow and 5lb 8oz Brown. *Permits:* Some 12, 25 and 50 fish tickets available. Prices on request (Tel/Fax: 01300 341351). *Charges:* £25 per day, £18 half day, £14 evening. *Season:* Open all year 5.30am to dusk. *Methods:* Single fly, max size 10, Bank fishing only.

Wessex Fly Fish. Trout Lakes

Contact: Richard & Sally Slocock, Lawrences Farm, Southover, Tolpuddle, Dorchester, *Tel:* 01305 848460, *Water:* Four lakes and pools totalling four acres. Also see entries under Frome and Piddle. *Species:* Rainbow Trout average 3lbs. *Permits:* From the above address. *Charges:* Lakes: Day ticket £24. 3 fish ticket £20, 2 fish ticket £15, Tuition is also available. 55's and over £12 for 2 fish, £5 for additional fish. *Season:* Lakes: April 1st to October 31st. Half price tickets to clear stock from 1 to 15 November only. *Methods:* Fly only. Lakes: Max 10 h/s. Rivers: Barbless or de-barbed.

LYME REGIS

Amherst Lodge

Contact: Mr B Stansfield, Amherst Lodge, St Mary's Lane, Uplyme, Lyme Regis, *Tel:* 01297 442773, *Water:* 6 stream fed Trout lakes totalling 4 acres. *Species:* Rainbow to 7lb. Brown Trout to 4lb (catch and release only). *Permits:* Go to rod room on arrival. *Charges:* From £15 for two fish bag. Catch & release £15 day or £10 up to 4 hours. *Season:* Open all year 9am to dusk. Must book if arriving before 9am. *Methods:* Small imitative patterns only. Barbless for catch & release. In season upper lakes are dry fly only.

WIMBORNE

Whitesheet Trout Lakes / Hamer Trout Lake

Contact: Paul Jerome, Suite 21D, Magnolia House, 19-21 Stour Road, Christchurch, *Tel:* 01202 480009, *Mobile:* 07714 449523, *Water:* Three lakes totalling seven acres. Also Hamer Lake. Fishing for Christchurch Angling Club members and their guests only. No day tickets for non members. *Species:* Rainbow and Brown Trout. *Permits:* Available from: Davis Tackle (01202 485169); Ringwood Tackle (01425 475155); Avon Angling (01425 461038); Pro Tackle (01202 484518); Christchurch Angling Centre (01202 480520); Bournemouth Fishing Lodge (01202 514345). *Charges:* Club member: 5 fish £16, 2 fish £8, sporting ticket £12. Guest: 5 fish £26, 2 fish £14, sporting ticket £18. *Season:* Open all year dawn to dusk. *Methods:* Single fly only. See ticket for complete rules.

Sea Fishing

BOURNEMOUTH

Bay Angling Society
Contact: NFSA Head Office: 01364 644643.

Boscombe & Southbourne S.F.C.
Contact: NFSA Head Office: 01364 644643.

Bournemouth & District S.A.A.
Contact: Paul Blens, *Tel:* 01202 249188, *Water:* Promoting boat and shore angling. *Charges:* £9 joining fee. Always looking for new members.

Dorset Police Sea Angling Club
Contact: NFSA Head Office: 01364 644643.

Pokesdown & Southbourne Ex SMC
Contact: NFSA Head Office: 01364 644643.

Post Office Angling Group (Bournemouth)
Contact: NFSA Head Office: 01364 644643.

Winton Workmens A.C.
Contact: NFSA Head Office: 01364 644643.

BRIDPORT

Channel Warrior
Contact: Chris Reeks, *Tel:* 01460 242678, *Mobile:* 07785 730504.

West Bay Sea Angling Club
Contact: c/o Westbay Watersports, 10a Westbay, Bridport, *Tel:* 01308 421272, *Mobile:* 07977 365068, *Water:* Regular competitions throughout year, many on world famous Chesil Beach. Boat and Junior sections. *Charges:* Seniors & Senior Citizens £13 p/a, Juniors £7.

CHRISTCHURCH

Christchurch & District Fishing Club
Contact: Keith Mills, *Tel:* 01202 426211, *Charges:* Adults £8. Family £16 (2 adults and dependant children). Senior £4. Junior £4.

Christchurch Royal British Legion
Contact: NFSA Head Office: 01364 644643.

Christchurch Shore Fishing Club
Contact: NFSA Head Office: 01364 644643.

Mudeford Mens Club S.A.A.
Contact: NFSA Head Office: 01364 644643.

DORCHESTER

Blandford Sea Angling Club
Contact: NFSA Head Office: 01364 644643.

LYME REGIS

Amaretto III
Contact: Steven Sweet, High Cliff House, Sidmouth Road, Lyme Regis, *Tel:* 01297 445949, *Mobile:* 07836 591084.

Beer and District S.A.A.
Contact: Dave Graham, 20 Underleys, Beer, Devon. *Tel:* 01297 20672.

Blue Turtle
Contact: Douglas Lanfear, *Tel:* 01297 34892, *Mobile:* 07970 856822.

Lyme Regis Sea Angling Club
Contact: Steve Sweet, No 1 Highcliff House, Sidmouth Road, Lyme Regis, Devon. *Tel:* 01297 445949, *Mobile:* 07836 591084, *Water:* Club restarted in 2002, new members welcome. Boat & shore fishing. Regular monthly matches. Tuition available. Contact Ron at number above. *Charges:* Membership £12, Juniors free.

Marie F and Sunbeam
Contact: Harry May, *Mobile:* 07974 753287, *Water:* Lyme Regis *Charges:* 1hr Mackerel fishing trips, children welcome - Adults £8, Children £6 (all tackle included). Daily deep sea fishing, 8.30 - 11.30, £18 (all tackle included). Prices apply to both boats. *Season:* Easter to the end of October.

Neptune and Pegasus
Contact: Peter Ward, *Tel:* 01297 443606, *Mobile:* 07768 570437.

Susie B
Contact: Ron Bailey, Marsh View, Lyme Road, Axminster, Devon. *Tel:* 01297 34244, *Mobile:* 07850 180331, *Water:* Lyme Bay. Deep Sea charter licenced for 11. MCA 60 mile approved. *Species:* Bass, Pollack, Cod, Conger Eel, Black Bream, Whiting, Wrasse, Shark, Skate. *Charges:* £350 for 8 hour charter. *Season:* Open all Year. *Methods:* Fish conservation practiced and encouraged.

POOLE

Albion Sea Angling Club
Contact: NFSA Head Office: 01364 644643.

Aries II
Contact: Duncan Purchase, *Tel:* 01425 278357, *Mobile:* 07759 736360.

Hamworthy Royal British Legion Sea Angling Club
Contact: NFSA Head Office: 01364 644643.

Lady Betty Charters
Contact: Ade Ponchaud, 36 Rowbarrow Close, Poole, *Tel:* 01202 600731, *Mobile:* 07939 531009, *Water:* Between St. Aldhelms Head and The Needles, up to 6 miles offshore. Also Poole Harbour. *Species:* Mackerel, Bream, Rays, Tope, Conger, Flatfish, Bass, Cod, Whiting. *Charges:* 4hr trip from £170, 8hr trip from £240. *Season:* All year, Daytime and evenings.

Lychett Bay Angling Club
Contact: NFSA Head Office: 01364 644643.

Mistress Linda
Contact: Phil Higgins, Poole, *Tel:* 01202 699730, *Mobile:* 07860 794183.

North Haven Yacht Club (Fishing)
Contact: NFSA Head Office: 01364 644643, *Tel:* 01202 708830.

Our Gemma
Contact: Mervyn Minns, *Tel:* 01425 274636, *Water:* Under 20 mile radius. Fast boat, can accommodate 8 anglers. *Season:* All year.

Poole & District Sea Angling Association
Contact: NFSA Head Office: 01364 644643.

Poole Bay Small Boat Angling Club
Contact: Martin Burt, c/o 32 Alton Road, Poole, *Tel:* 01202 721955, *Mobile:* 07771 748486, *Water:* Club waters are from St Catherines on the Isle of Wight to Portland Bill in the west. *Species:* NFSA Wessex Division specimen sizes adopted. *Permits:* None needed. *Season:* Fishing all year.

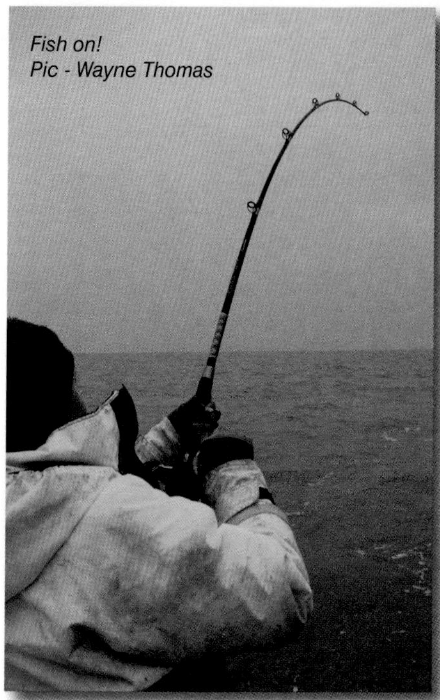
Fish on!
Pic - Wayne Thomas

Poole Charter Skippers Association
Contact: NFSA Head Office: 01364 644643.

Poole Dolphins Sea Angling Club
Contact: Eric Tripp, 9 Market Street, Poole, *Tel:* 01202 578469, *Water:* Club meetings at Broadstone Conservative Club on the second Thursday of each month at 8pm. For further information contact Nick Diffey on 01202 578469.

Random Harvest 11
Contact: Andy Adams, *Mobile:* 07802 672227, *Water:* Inshore Bass, reef fishing, wreck fishing 5 day channel island trips. *Season:* All year round. *Methods:* Can supply Abu.

True Blue
Contact: Steve Porter, 25 Verity Crescent, Poole, *Tel:* 01202 665482, *Mobile:* 07967 598669, *Water:* Fast, stable southboats 11m catamaran fishing out of Poole. *Species:* Specialising in Bass. Promoting catch and release. Also wreck and general mark fishing. Channel Islands trips. *Charges:* Varies depending on type of trip.

SWANAGE

San Gina Charter Boat
Contact: Swanage Angling Centre, 6 High Street, Swanage, *Tel:* 01929 424989, *Water:* Deep sea fishing trips. Fully licenced for 10 anglers. Experienced Skipper.

Swanage and District Angling Club
Contact: Swanage Angling Centre, *Tel:* 01929 421301, *Water:* Fishing around Swanage and Purbeck coast with good fishing on Swanage pier. *Species:* Bass, Pollack, Rays, Dogfish, Pouting, Mackerel, Plaice, Turbot, Congers, Bream, Flounder.

WEYMOUTH

Atlanta
Contact: Dave Pitman, *Tel:* 01305 781644, *Mobile:* 07721 320352.

Bonwey
Contact: Ken Leicester, *Tel:* 01305 821040, *Mobile:* 07831 506285.

Channel Chieftain V
Contact: Pat Carling, *Tel:* 01305 787155, *Mobile:* 07976 741821, *Season:* All year.

Flamer III
Contact: Colin Penny, 47 Ferndale Road, Weymouth, *Tel:* 01305 766961, *Mobile:* 07968 972736, *Water:* English Channel. *Species:* All species. 59 different species landed in 2007. *Charges:* Boat booking- £370 to £500. Individuals £40 to £55. Price dependant on type/length of trip. *Season:* Fishing all year round. *Methods:* Reef, Bank, Wreck and 3 to 5 day Westcountry trips. Species hunts and competitions.

Individuals Sea Angling Club ♿
Contact: Trevor Sutch, 67 Windmill Grove, Portchester, Fareham, Hants. *Tel:* 02392 201696, *Mobile:* 07786 962540, *Water:* Hampshire and Dorset coast line. *Species:* All sea fish. *Charges:* None *Season:* All year *Methods:* Promoter of the Southern Premier League. Please enquire for further details. Close proximity pegs available for disabled anglers.

Lady Godiva
Contact: David Gibson, 10 Portwey Close, Weymouth, *Tel:* 01305 750823, *Mobile:* 07766 145054, *Water:* English Channel and Channel Islands. *Species:* Bass, Cod, Pollack, Bream, Turbot, Plaice, Brill, Shark and others. *Charges:* From £360 to charter the boat for a day. *Season:* All year. *Methods:* Uptide, downtide, anchored and drifting over sandbanks and wrecks.

Out-Rage
Contact: Rod Thompson, *Tel:* 01305 822803, *Mobile:* 07970 437646.

Peace & Pleanty II
Contact: Chris Tett, *Tel:* 01305 775775, *Mobile:* 07885 780019, *Water:* Channel Island and Charters. *Methods:* Shimano tackle provided.

Top Cat
Contact: Mr Wellington, *Tel:* 01305 823443, *Mobile:* 07966 133979.

Valerie Ann
Contact: Ron Brown, *Mobile:* 07976 520607, *Water:* Reef bank and wreck fishing, also Jurassic coast trips. *Season:* All year round.

Weymouth Angling Society
Contact: Mr Patterson, Commercial Road, Weymouth, *Tel:* 01305 785032, *Water:* All shore line from Lyme Regis to Christchurch harbour. *Species:* Bass, Pollack, Plaice, Flounder, Cod, Sharks, Ray, Wrasse, Conger, Gurnard, Pouting, Dogfish and a variety of Sharks. *Permits:* N/A. *Charges:* Membership available at £10 single, £15 couples pa. Largest Southwest junior membership at £2 pa. *Season:* Open. *Methods:* Restrictions in competitions only.

WIMBORNE

Marden - Edwards Sea Angling Association
Contact: NFSA Head Office: 01364 644643.

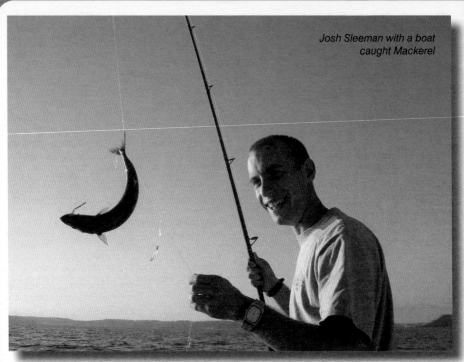

Josh Sleeman with a boat caught Mackerel

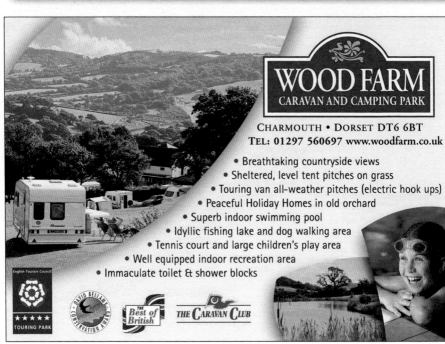

WHERE TO STAY

The British Disabled Angling Association

The British Disabled Angling Association (BDAA) was founded in 1996 by Terry Moseley to help develop opportunities for people with disabilities to access the activity of fishing in the UK. In the early days the Registered National charity had just 18 eager members on its books, so popular was the demand that in just 10 years the membership had grown to a staggering 24,500 with calls from all over the globe requesting help and advice and a staggering 3.5 million hits per year on its web site www.bdaa.co.uk for all sorts of information on how people with disabilities, regardless of how severe, can go fishing.

As of January 2008, BDAA no longer offers a membership; or charges any joining fees, however its not all bad news. The trustees have changed our outdated system to now offer a supporters registration to be known as "The Friends of BDAA"; this registration system has replaced the former online membership we offered, which was being abused and proved difficult to monitor and maintain effectively.

The new system of registration will allow us to provide regular information updates, news, projects ensuring our information & services are directed to those people who are interested in our work & wish to support our aims & objectives by signing up to "The Friends of BDAA". In order for the new system to take effect we have closed membership to BDAA and will not renew memberships as from January 2008, the board of trustees will remain as the guardians of the charity as detailed in the charities constitution June 1996.

With help and advice from its professional consultants the BDAA has now secured a respected position within angling and government to become a representative body for all disability issues within angling, the organisation is inclusive and empowers disabled people into its management structure to offer the very best in advice, support and events.

In the UK 54,000 disabled people hold a fishing licence, of whom 1,000 fish competitively and the majority for pleasure, we firmly believe that many more would fish if they realised the possibilities. BDAA want to inform people how accessible angling is becoming an activity which has no discrimination regardless of your disability, gender or age you can just visit the outdoors in a healthy environment just for enjoyment or competing up to national level or World level.

The BDAA is funded by public donations and disability project funded by Dreamstore UK (www.dreamstoreactive.org), the Environment Agency and the English Federation of Disability Sport. The charities activities include advising fisheries & local authorities on access, and producing a booklet 'Inclusive Angling'. This explains how to create accessible pathways, platforms and car parking areas, and provide the extra services that make fisheries inclusive for anglers with disabilities. The BDAA caters for disabled coarse, specimen, sea and game anglers. It has its own salmon fishing rights on the River Doon in Ayrshire Scotland, offers help for disabled people who want to try specimen angling, sea fishing aboard the adapted catamaran MV Freedom in Weymouth and fly fishing through the Wheelyboat Trust.

Fishing is especially attractive to young disabled people and their development, the BDAA offers educational visits to special schools, hospitals, residential and community centres to encourage disabled and newly disabled either to try fishing for the first time or come back into fishing after disability. Our educational introduction to fishing gives both teachers and children an insight to what fishing can offer as a therapeutic activity, we have proven that fishing increases attention spans, offers social inclusion, sense of achievement and motor skills development. By contacting the BDAA, we can arrange a visit to your centre or, if an individual, post you an introductory pack giving information on all types of fishing and what it involves. The BDAA has a comprehensive web site that has a mass of information that is constantly accessed and downloaded by people all over the world.

So in all from 5 to 95 years the BDAA can help you to go fishing, why not give it a try?

BDAA, 9 Yew Tree Road, Delves, Walsall, West Midlands WS5 4NQ Tel: 01922 860 912
Email: terry@bdaa.co.uk www.bdaa.co.uk

A Season on the Hampshire Avon

Budgie Price.
(Wessex Salmon and Rivers Trust)

Living on the Hampshire, Dorset border, I am fortunate to have an almost infinite number of choices when it comes to angling location.

Not a million miles away, the Stour winds its way through the hills of the Dorset countryside and offers excellent sport. The ever-growing need for aggregate has culminated in a large number of gravel pit fisheries, offering anglers who prefer to fish still water, the opportunity to do so on a grand scale. Finally, and not least, the Hampshire Avon; a much changed and sometimes maligned river that should satiate the needs of most anglers.

With choices come decisions and while some divide their time between all three, I chose long ago to devote my time almost entirely to the Avon. When anglers visit her banks today they do so increasingly, not in search of the huge bags of roach and dace on which her reputation was built, but in the hope that their prayers of big barbel and chub will be answered. Be it the nostalgic wish for roach or the real possibility of big barbel, the Avon, whether viewed in the throes of harsh winter or the untroubled days of midsummer, remains a jewel set perfectly into the landscape to be cherished and preserved for future generations.

Avoiding the rush

June 16th always poses a quandary for me; I should be straining at the leash that is the close season, too excited to contemplate fishing anywhere but the river. But if you consider the fish and the flurry of activity after three months of relative peace, it must seem to them, like the bombardment of Dresden. Gallons of hemp, caster and maggot are bait droppered into each likely looking swim, along with "front lead" "back lead" and bulging PVA bag. Therefore, I stay firmly welded to my tench swim, content to let the hordes do battle, while avoiding the rush for favourite swims. Within two weeks most will return to the daily grind of "nine till five", leaving us "reglers" in relative peace.

A very 'special' Chub at 8lb 1oz

First love

Barbel are my first love, probably because for years they were my nemesis and because when my duck was finally broken by a fish of 7lb 8oz pounds from the Royalty, the milestone of a double was almost as insurmountable. I used to delay my barbel fishing until August however, my impatience to bank my first fish of the season increased yearly until the procrastination lead to frustration. The carpet bombing of bait isn't as effective on the Avon as it once was and it took ages before I committed the ultimate betrayal of using boilie and pellet in the river and longer to accept the guilt for doing so.

Times change however, and the fish, having been weaned onto the high-protein offerings by other angler's, voted with their stomachs. My uncle Dick suggested one particular variety of boilie, the results proved remarkable and I was hooked. It's so important to have confidence in your bait, especially on the Avon where you might wait all day for just one bite.

Started with a bang!

My season started with a bang and a totally unexpected barbel of 14lbs 1oz. Although my mate Pete, who had decided not to fish this particular swim and was walking away as I arrived, predicted a "big un". The fish was a strikingly perfect creature that fought like a lion and presented me with a new personal best that had previously stood at exactly 13lbs. I wondered, could the season get any better? In fact, for a while I was jinxed, perhaps for daring to consider that it might. Such fish cause you to question line strength and, although it was landed safely, I wondered if I should consider replacing my line. I was offered an alternative to try and re-loaded the spools on both reels. Circumstances dictate that I fish with a mate and Trev suggested a change in hook pattern, to a purpose made barbel hook.

What followed was an advertisement for sticking with what you know and over the next few weeks, I blanked, missed bites, dropped, snapped off or pulled out of fish time and again. Eventually, I lost my cool, had the line ripped from both spools, grabbed a spool of 10lb Sensor, a packet of my favourite pattern hooks and went back to what I knew. It's as important to have confidence in your tackle, as it is in your bait. Almost an entire month had been lost, along with three doubles, plus others, it's not a mistake I shall repeat.

All but one of last seasons chosen swims were determined by their distance from the car park. The first, we called it the "sheep dip", had definitely not had any angler attention, there being not a blade of grass out of place. On close inspection, we were thrilled to spot three good barbel that we estimated to weigh approximately 9lbs, 12lbs and 13lbs. In the same swim was a big sleepy carp, well over 25lbs and several chub of varying size, one of which we referred to as a "bloody hell, bloody hell" chub. I'm sure most anglers will recognise that description, it happens during one of those double-take moments when you can't quite believe your eyes; we couldn't put a number on it, it was that huge.

Eager anticipation

Our first day on this swim was largely passed tea drinking and bird watching, our attention taken by a peregrine hunting way up in a late August sky and It was mid-afternoon before we lowered a boilie into the swim and settled back in eager anticipation. The bite came almost immediately and although we didn't see the culprit, the bend in the rod and the ferocity of the initial run, pointed to the carp. The next bait found a bream, and then, in comparison to the big fella, a small chub of 5lb 8oz and finally the smallest of the three barbel, which weighed 9lbs10oz confirming our estimations.

I would like to report the capture of the two bigger barbel and indeed the chub, but we couldn't induce them to feed, despite changes in bait and tactic. They remained tantalisingly close, skulking just beneath the surface water crowfoot. Finally, humiliated by defeat having persevered for weeks, we limped away, vowing not to return until next year. Instead, we went upstream to an old favourite swim of Trev's, where a shallow run drops into a deepening pool of some repute.

Over the next few sessions, I caught bream, a few chub and two stunning barbel of 10lbs 10oz, and 12lbs 4oz and lost another double at the net. One other swim, into which we had thrown a few baits, lay in a small meadow and was crying out for further exploration. Remarkably, it too had seen little attention and despite my being sceptical of its credibility as a barbel swim, just into darkness the net was slipped under another beauty of 11lbs 12oz. We vowed to spend more time there next season, especially as my final double, a fish of 11lbs 4oz, came from the same swim a week later.

An impromptu session, grabbed after a couple of hours of centre-pin tuition for my little brother, just about topped off my season. I hadn't fished this particular swim for several seasons and had only chosen to out of nostalgia. I decided to show it one of Dick's boilies, which, on my second cast, snared what we initially took to be a barbel and which fought like one for about 20 seconds.

Something special

However, when what could have been initially taken for a grass carp, save for its big white lips, slipped over the rim of the net, we gasped in unison. Both Trevor and I shared PB chub of 6lb 12oz and we knew that this one was something a bit special. We gave my brother a shout; there was a strong possibility that none of us would witness another of its size in our lifetimes and when, along with our nerves, my scales settled on 8lbs 1oz, I was fairly convinced that we wouldn't! She lay in the shallows at our feet, recovering with her head to the current for some seconds and we agreed that, even at over 8lb she was still outsized by the "bloody hell, bloody hell" chub we hadn't dare put a number on. The urge to return to the river next morning, was outweighed by my anxious preoccupation with verification of scale accuracy, I needn't have been concerned, the weight stood.

The Avon barbel's powerful, pugnacious, obstinate and unrivalled determination in combat would test the abilities of most anglers, all in all not a bad season. Roll on next year.

HAMPSHIRE

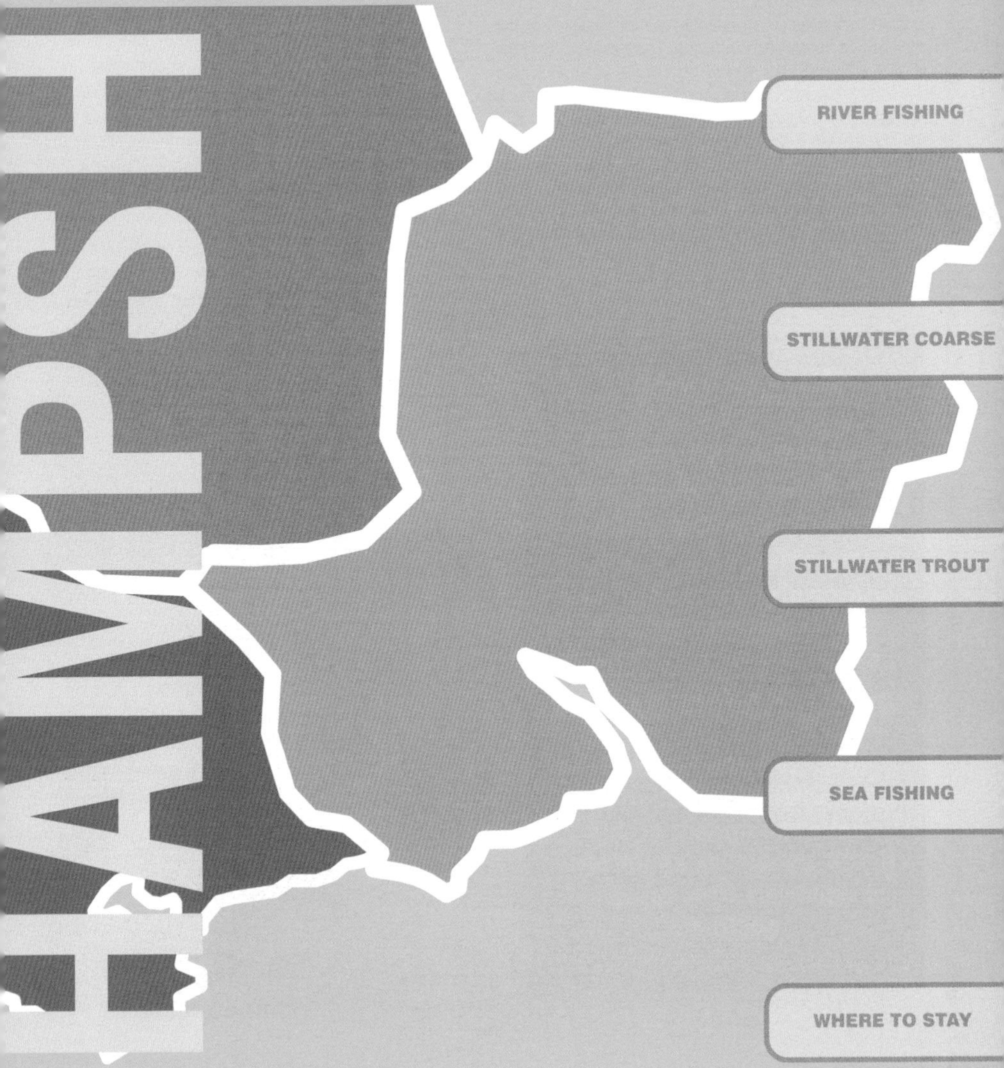

HAMPSHIRE

RIVER FISHING

STILLWATER COARSE

STILLWATER TROUT

SEA FISHING

WHERE TO STAY

Hampshire Game Road Directions

119. Christchurch Angling Club (Coarse & Game)
Please enquire at local Tackle Shops or Tel: 01202 480009.

Hampshire Coarse Road Directions

120. Lake Farm Fishery
Exit M27 at junction 1, signposted The New Forrest. Take the third exit on the roundabout (signed Fordingbridge) onto the B3079. Following the signs to Fordingbridge bearing left onto the B3078 (approx. 10 miles to Fordingbridge) On entering the town and crossing the bridge over the River Avon, turn immediately left at the mini roundabout onto the High Street. Follow signs to Sandleheath until reaching the Sandleheath crossroads (approx.1 mile) Turn left at the crossroads, signed Alderholt. Over the bridge and turn right at the mill signed Lower Daggons, Lake Farm is approx. 600 metres on the left. Tel: 01425 645106.

Please note..

All of the information on fisheries, clubs and charters in this guide is published in a fully searchable format on our web site at:

www.gethooked.co.uk

The web site includes additional information that does not appear in this guide, as well as an archive of editorials from previous editions.

Hants River Fishing

THE 'HAMPSHIRE' AVON

The River Avon is one of England's most famous rivers, and is revered by all anglers for the quality of fish that live in it. This river creates a certain mystique that captivates the attentions of fishers from all walks of life.
The River Avon rises in the Vale of Pewsey and, with its tributaries the Bourne and Wylye, drains the chalk of Salisbury Plain. The River Nadder, which is joined by the Wylye near Salisbury, drains the escarpment of the South Wiltshire Downs and the Kimmeridge clays of the Wardour Vale. The River Ebble and Ashford Water also drain the South Wiltshire Downs and join the Avon downstream of Salisbury and Fordingbridge respectively.
Below Fordingbridge, a number of streams drain the New Forest area. The Avon finally drains into Christchurch harbour, where it is joined by the Rivers Stour and Mude before discharging into the English Channel.

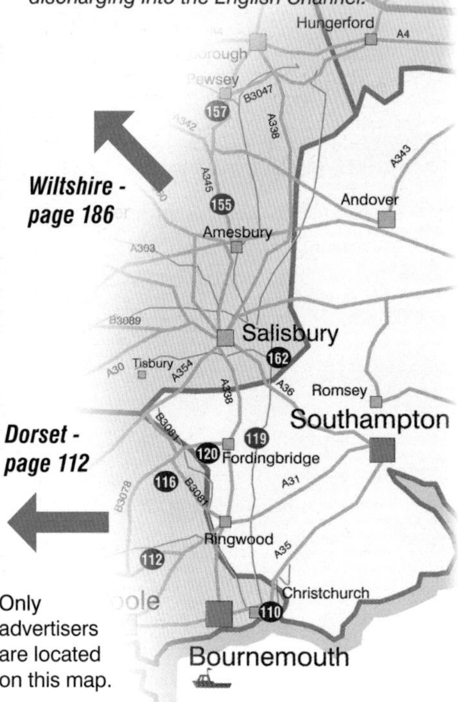

Britford (Coarse)
Contact: London Angler's Association, Izaak Walton House, 2A Hervey Park Road, London. *Tel:* 0208 5207477, *Water:* Several stretches of the Hampshire Avon. *Species:* Roach 4lb, Barbel 10lb, Chub 7lb, plus specimen Dace, Grayling, Perch & Pike. *Permits:* Day membership tickets available from Fishery Keeper on the bank - £8 Seniors per rod, maximum of 2 rods. £4 Juniors & OAPs and registered Disabled per rod, maximum of 2 rods. *Charges:* Senior: £41 - Junior: £23 - OAP/Reg. Disabled: £24 - Partners Ticket: £60 - Club affiliated membership available on request.. *Season:* Current EA byelaws apply. *Methods:* See members handbook.

Britford (Game)
Contact: London Angler's Association, Izaak Walton House, 2A Hervey Park Road, London. *Tel:* 0208 5207477, *Water:* Several stretches of the Hampshire Avon. *Species:* Trout & Salmon. *Permits:* Salmon & Sea Trout - Day membership permit available from Fishery Keeper on bank - £20 per day. Trout fishing - £10 per day (available from Fishery Keeper on bank). *Charges:* Prices may change in 2008. *Season:* Current EA byelaws apply. *Methods:* See members handbook.

Christchurch Angling Club (Salmon & Sea Trout)
Contact: Paul Jerome, Suite 21D, Magnolia House, 19-21 Stour Road, Christchurch, Dorset. *Tel:* 01202 480009, *Mobile:* 07714 449523, *Water:* Many miles of double bank fishing on the Hampshire Avon, including the Somerley Estate. Also Sea Trout on the Dorset Stour. *Species:* Salmon 25lb plus. Sea Trout 12lb plus. *Permits:* Club Membership required. *Charges:* Membership: Adult £145, Conc. £110. Junior £56. Somerley Estate Salmon membership is an additional £135. *Season:* Salmon: 1 February to 31 August. Sea Trout: 15 April to 31 October *Methods:* Salmon: Fly only from 1 February to 15 May. Spinning permitted from 15 May to 31 August. Shrimp and Prawn permitted from 16 June to 31 August.

Fordingbridge Park Day Ticket Fishing
Fordingbridge Recreation Ground, Fordingbridge, *Tel:* 07939 514346, *Water:* 500 yards of fishing on the Hampshire Avon. *Species:* Chub 6lb 2oz, Roach 3lb 6oz, Dace 1lb, Rainbow Trout 6lb, Eels 1lb, Pike 23lb, Perch 1lb, Carp 16lb. *Permits:* Day Tickets must be purchased in advance from one of the following outlets: Fordingbridge Service Station (Total Garage, 500 yds from fishery). *Charges:* £5 Adults per Day age 16-64. £2.50 per day for Juniors (15 and under) and Senior Citizens (65 plus). *Season:* Coarse Fishing June 16th, March 14th 7.30am - Darkness. Trout Fishing April to June by arrangement only - Contact 07939 514346. *Methods:* Max 2 rods per person. No fishing under power lines or in play area. Tickets must be purchased in advance.

Lifelands / Ringwood Fishery
Contact: Paul Jerome, Suite 21D, Magnolia House, 19-21 Stour Road, Christchurch, Dorset. *Tel:* 01202 480009, *Mobile:* 07714 449523, *Water:* Christchurch Angling Club controlled double bank fishing on the Hampshire Avon at Ringwood. *Species:* Barbel 14lb, Chub 7lb, Dace 1lb, Pike 30lb, Carp 20lb, Roach 2lb, Grayling 2lb. *Permits:* Available from: Ringwood Tackle (01425 475155), Avon Angling (01425 461038). *Charges:* Day ticket: Adult £9, Junior/conc. £5. *Season:* Coarse: 16th June to 14th March. *Methods:* See club rules for individual waters.

Ringwood & District A.A. (Christchurch)
Contact: Mr Darren Smith, Cozy Corner, 5 Hilton Road, New Milton, *Tel:* 01425 611335, *Mobile:* 07702 300384, *Water:* 2 miles on Hampshire / Avon river. *Species:* Barbel - 16lb 7oz, Chub - 8lb, Roach - 3lb, Pike - 30lb, Bream - 10lb, Perch - 3lb, Carp - 34lb, Dace - 10oz, Brown Trout, Sea Trout and Salmon. *Permits:* Davis Tackle - 01202 485169 Christchurch. *Charges:* Prices may vary in 2008. £10 day ticket. *Season:* June 16th - March 14th, Coarse fishing. *Methods:* Rolling meat, float fishing for Dace/ Roach. Legered pellets for Barbel.

Ringwood & District A.A. (Hampshire Avon)
Contact: Mr Darren Smith, Cozy Corner, 5 Hilton Road, New Milton, *Tel:* 01425 611335, *Mobile:* 07702 300384, *Water:* Severals fishery at Ringwood upstream of Ibsley bridge and a number of stretches around Fordingbridge. *Species:* Barbel to 15lb 5oz, Chub to 7lb 6oz, Roach 3lb plus, Pike 30lb plus, Bream 10lb plus, Perch, Carp, Dace, Salmon, Sea Trout, Brown Trout. *Permits:* Ringwood Tackle. Tel: 01425 475155 *Charges:* Adult £110, Junior £45, Concessions, O.A.P's, Disabled £70 (Joining fee-£20 adult, £5 junior (under 12's)). Prices may vary in 2008. *Season:* Slight variations to coarse season due to Salmon fishing, Current E.A. byelaws apply. *Methods:* Details in Permit.

Wessex Salmon and Rivers Trust
Contact: B.G.Marshall, 63 Forestside Gardens, Poulner, Ringwood, *Tel:* 01425 485105, *Water:* Wessex Salmon and Rivers Trust are a registered charitable trust workng to restore and conserve the ecology of the lowland southern rivers and enhance their populations of all species of fish, invertebratres and flora.

The sun shining at Lands End
Pic - ©Brian Gay. www.angling-images.com

DUN

Holbury Lane Lakes (River Dun)
Contact: Fishery Manager, Holbury Lane, Lockerley, Romsey, *Tel:* 01794 341619, *Mobile:* 07817 252441, *Water:* 1000yds of river Dun, a tributary of the river Test, plus four Trout Lakes (see Stillwater Trout, Romsey). *Species:* Brown Trout 1.5lb average. *Charges:* On application. *Season:* Pre booking essential. 1 May - 30 September. *Methods:* Single fly, max size 10, no catch and release, priest and net must be carried by anglers.

TEST

Nine Mile Water
Contact: Simon Cooper, Fishing Breaks, The Mill, Heathman Street, Nether Wallop, Stockbridge, *Tel:* 01264 781988, *Water:* 1.7 miles double bank fishing on Wallop Brook, tributary of the Test. *Species:* Brown Trout. *Permits:* By phone or e-mail from Fishing Breaks. *Charges:* April £85, May - June £95, July-September £95. *Season:* April - July *Methods:* Dry fly & Nymph only.

Timsbury Fishing (Test)
Manor Lane, Timsbury, Romsey, *Tel:* 01264 365165, *Water:* Three miles on the river Test. *Species:* Brown Trout, Grayling, Roach, Perch, Dace, Chub, Pike, Carp. *Permits:* By booking in advance. *Charges:* £75 per person game. £18 per person coarse. *Season:* Game: 1 May to 30 September. Coarse: 1 October to 14 March. 9am to 9pm. *Methods:* Upstream dry fly.

Stillwater Coarse

ANDOVER

Andover Angling Association

Contact: Tracy or Mike, c/o Challis Tackle, 60 Mylon Road, Andover, *Tel:* 01264 361103, *Water:* Rooksbury Mill Lake - 2 acres. Foxcotte Lake - 2.75 acres. Anton Park Lake - 8 acres. *Species:* Rooksbury - mixed coarse. Foxcotte - mixed coarse. Anton Park - mixed coarse, predominately Pike in winter. *Permits:* Available from Challis Tackle. *Charges:* Rooksbury - £6 one rod, £8 two rods, no concessions. Foxcotte - £5 one rod, £7 two rods, no concessions, club membership available. Anton Park - £5 one rod, £7 two rods. *Season:* All lakes open all year. *Methods:* Rooksbury - no live bait, no night fishing. Foxcotte - no live bait, night fishing by appointment only. Anton Park - no live bait, night fishing by appointment only.

CHRISTCHURCH

Orchard Lakes

Contact: Mr J Southcombe, New Lane, Bashley, New Milton, *Tel:* 01425 612404, *Mobile:* 07790 915434, *Water:* 3 small lakes, largest 2 acres. 50 peg match lake. *Species:* Carp, Tench, Bream, Roach, Rudd, Perch and Chub. *Permits:* Day tickets on the bank or on site shop. *Charges:* All lakes - £8 per day. £6 concession. *Season:* Open all year 7am to dusk. *Methods:* Barbless hooks only. No keepnets.

RINGWOOD

Hurst Pond

Contact: Ringwood Tackle, *Tel:* 01425 475155, *Water:* 1.5 acre pond at Hedlands Business Park, Blashford, Ringwood, Hants. *Species:* Carp 22lb, Tench 6.5lb, Roach 2.5lb, Rudd 2lb, Perch 3lb 12oz, Crucians 2.5lb, Eels 5lb. *Charges:* £7.50 for concessions, £10 a day, £15 for 24 hours, limited to 6 tickets a day - booking advised. *Season:* Open all year.

Ringwood & District A.A. (Coarse Lakes)

Contact: Mr Darren Smith, Cozy Corner, 5 Hilton Road, New Milton, *Tel:* 01425 611335, *Mobile:* 07702 300384, *Water:* 3 lakes at Northfield, plus 1 at Hightown on the outskirts of Ringwood. *Species:* Hightown - Mixed fishery with Carp to 38lb 14oz, Tench, Bream, Roach, Rudd, Pike, Eels. Northfield - Big Carp to 30lb, Tench to 12lb, Bream, Roach, Rudd, Pike. *Permits:* Ringwood Tackle. Tel: 01425 475155 *Charges:* Adult £110, Junior £45, concessions for OAP's and disabled. Available at Ringwood Tackle, West St., Ringwood, 01425 475155. Prices may change for 2008, please enquire. *Season:* All year fishing available. *Methods:* Details in Permit.

Somerley Lakes

Contact: Paul Jerome, Suite 21D, Magnolia House, 19-21 Stour Road, Christchurch, Dorset. *Tel:* 01202 480009, *Mobile:* 07714 449523, *Water:* Christchurch Angling Club controlled series of former gravel pits. Meadow Lake and King Vincent's Lake. *Species:* Carp 40lb, Pike 30lb, Bream 10lb, Perch 4lb, Roach, Tench and Rudd. *Permits:* Available from: Ringwood Tackle (01425 475155), Avon Angling (01425 461038). *Charges:* Day ticket: Adult £9, Junior/conc. £5. *Season:* 16th June to 14th March. Night fishing available to members only with prepaid permit from tackle shops. *Methods:* No nuts or pulses. See club rules for individual waters.

Turf Croft Farm Fishery

Contact: Keith, Stephen, Christine Duell, Forest Road, Burley, Nr Ringwood, *Tel:* 01425 403743, *Mobile:* 07850 086021, *Water:* 8 acre lake - naturally spring fed. *Species:* Ghost Carp to 28lbs, Mirror Carp to 28lbs, Tench to 6lbs, Bream to 4lbs, Perch to 2lb, Rudd, Red Rudd, Golden Tench to 5lb, Roach & Crucians to 2.5lbs. *Permits:* Day ticket only. No Night fishing. *Charges:* £10 per two rods maximum. *Season:* Open all year. Dawn to dusk in winter. *Methods:* No boilies, no nut baits, no hemp, no keepnets, natural bait.

ROMSEY

Headlands Farm Coarse Fishery

Contact: John Harris, Wellow, Romsey, *Tel:* 01794 323801, *Mobile:* 07776 202000, *Water:* Two lakes covering 5.5 acres. *Species:* Mixed Coarse in both lakes. One lake contains Pike. *Charges:* £10 day. £15 24 hours. £15 Night fishing. *Season:* Open all year. *Methods:* Strict rules regarding litter and groundbait on site. No spinning.

Longbridge Lakes (Lee)

Contact: John Dennis, Broadlands Estate, *Tel:* 01794 518885, *Mobile:* 07973 523358, *Water:* 2,5 acre lake plus 0.5 acres of canal fishing. *Species:* Tench to 8lb, Carp 30lb, Bream, Perch, Crucians, Roach and Rudd. *Permits:* From local tackle shops or on the bank. *Charges:* Day ticket (7am-9pm) £10. 24 hours (booking only) £16. Half day £5. *Season:* Open all year. *Methods:* Full rules at lake to be followed at all times. Strictly no boilies, nuts, beans or peas.

Timsbury Fishing

Manor Lane, Timsbury, Romsey, *Tel:* 01264 365165, *Water:* Two Carp lakes. 21 peg and 12 peg. *Species:* Carp. *Permits:* On the bank. *Charges:* £8 per day. £5 concessions. *Season:* 7am to dusk. *Methods:* Any method.

Whinwhistle Fisheries ♿

Contact: John Hardeley, Whinwhistle Road, East Wellow, Romsey, *Tel:* 01794 324485, *Mobile:* 07816 187648, *Water:* Three Coarse lakes. *Species:* Mixed coarse. *Permits:* From the on site tackle shop. *Charges:* On application. *Season:* Open all year. *Methods:* Pellets only if bought at the fishery. Full rules on site.

STOCKBRIDGE

Golden Pond Fishery

Contact: Jeff Hounslow, Fullerton Road, Fullerton, Stockbridge, *Mobile:* 07734 669738, *Water:* One acre lake with 16 pegs. *Species:* Mixed Coarse. *Permits:* On the bank. *Charges:* Day ticket £7. Junior, OAP, concessions £5. Night fishing £12.50. 24 hours £16. *Season:* Open all year. *Methods:* No whips. No nut baits. No boilies. Landing nets and unhooking mats to be used. Barbless hooks only.

STILLWATER COARSE

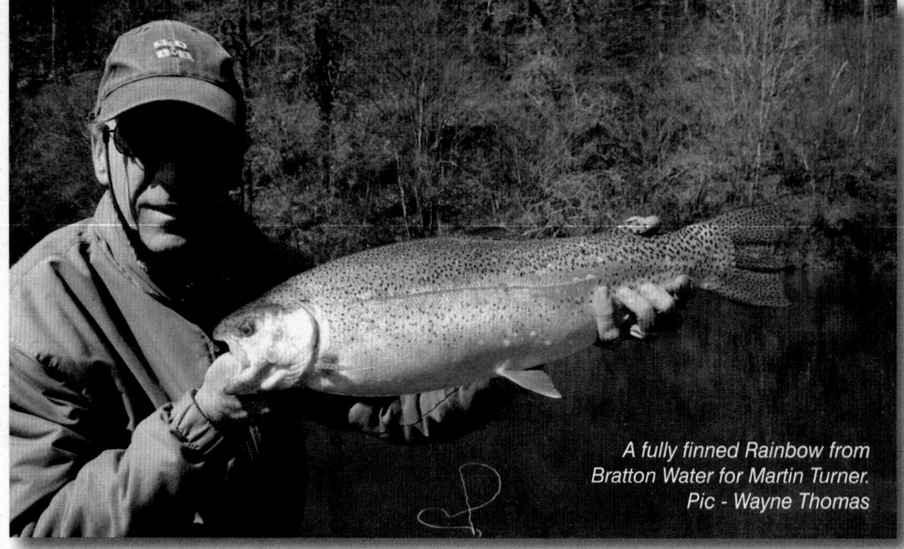
A fully finned Rainbow from Bratton Water for Martin Turner. Pic - Wayne Thomas

Stillwater Trout

FORDINGBRIDGE

Damerham Fisheries

Contact: Mike Davies, The Lake House, Damerham, Fordingbridge, *Tel:* 01725 518446, *Water:* 6 lakes. 1.5 mile Allan River. *Species:* Rainbow Trout (Sandy, Lavender, White & Electric Blue Rainbow Trout). *Permits:* Season Rods. *Charges:* Full Season Rod £1,800 (30 visits), 1/2 Season Rod £1020 (15 visits), 1/4 Season Rod £700 (10 visits). Guest Day Rods £70. Please phone to confirm prices. *Season:* Monday 3 March - Sunday 28 September 2008. *Methods:* Fly only.

Rockbourne Trout Fishery

Contact: Rockbourne Trout Fishery, Rockbourne Road, Sandleheath, Fordingbridge, *Tel:* 01725 518603, *Water:* 6 Spring fed lakes. Stream closed. *Species:* Rainbow / Brown Trout, Triploids. *Permits:* From the fishery. *Charges:* Please telephone for prices. *Season:* Open all year except Xmas. *Methods:* Fly only, max hook size 10 long shank, no droppers, tandem/double/treble hooks, no dogs.

ROMSEY

Holbury Lane Trout Lakes

Contact: Fishery Manager, Holbury Lane, Lockerley, Romsey, *Tel:* 01794 341619, *Mobile:* 07817 252441, *Water:* 4 lakes totalling 7.5 acres plus 1000yds on the river Dun (see River Dun entry). *Species:* Rainbow Trout 2lb to 5lb, Blue Trout 2lb to 5lb and Brown Trout 3lb plus. *Permits:* 10 or 25 fish ticket. *Charges:* 2 fish half day £25. 4 fish full day £37. *Season:* 8.30am to dusk. *Methods:* Single fly, max size 10, no catch and release, priest and net must be carried by anglers.

Woodington Trout Fishery

Contact: John Hardeley, Romsey Road, East Wellow, Romsey, *Tel:* 01794 324485, *Mobile:* 07816 187648, *Water:* Four lakes. *Species:* Rainbow and Brown Trout. *Permits:* From the on site tackle shop. *Charges:* On application. *Season:* Open all year. *Methods:* Fly fishing.

STOCKBRIDGE

John O ' Gaunts ♿

Contact: Mrs E Purse, 51 Mead Road, Chandlers Ford, Southampton, *Tel:* 01794 388130, *Mobile:* 02380 252268, *Water:* 2 Lakes approx. 7 acres in Test Valley. *Species:* Rainbow Trout (various sizes). *Permits:* Available from Fishery Tel: 02380 252268 or 01794 388130. *Charges:* £40 - 4 fish Full Day, £21 - 2 fish Half Day. Prices may change in 2008. *Season:* February 1st - November 30th inclusive, Wednesdays & Saturdays throughout December and January. *Methods:* Fly and Nymph only. No barbless hooks, no catch and release, no keepnets.

Sea Fishing

LYMINGTON

Challenger II

Contact: Mike Cottingham, *Tel:* 01425 619358, *Mobile:* 07884 394379.

Lymington & District Sea Fishing Club

Contact: Fishing Club HQ, Bath Road, Lymington, *Tel:* 01590 674962, *Water:* Boat and shore fishing, with strong Junior section. Fishing for trophies throughout the year. New members welcome. *Charges:* Adults - £7.00 joining fee, plus £14 p/a subs. Juniors - £2.50 joining fee, plus £5 p/a subs. O.A.P the same as juniors.

A Little Patience

Nick Fisher. Photos Paul Quagliana.

No-one has ever accused me of being mature. Quite the opposite in fact. According to my wife, the best way to describe my character after 46 years of evolution is 'infantile'. I am not a patient man. Not blessed with much composure or equanimity.

And yet, people always assume that fishermen must be very patient, self-contained, contemplative types. I am none of these. Normally, I'm a twitchy, restless, impatient cur, with all the restraint of a hungry stoat. But, just the other day, I surprised myself. I did something almost grown up. Photographer Paul Quagliana phoned me to say he was fishing at Sutton Bingham reservoir. Did I want to come along? He'd fished there twice before this season and caught limit-bags both times, fishing a floating line with nymphs and buzzers from the bank. 'It was brilliant ... stacks of fish', said Paul. 'I must have lost as many as I caught. Probably more'.

Sutton Bingham reservoir, near Yeovil in Somerset, is only ten miles from my home. I had not fished there yet that season, and it fishes famously-well in the early months. So it would've been churlish not to take Paul up on his invite.

I arrived in the middle of one of the most beautiful afternoons we had so far that year. Too beautiful. As I walked around the south bank to where Paul was fishing, I could feel hot sun on the back of my neck. It was a bright, warm, cloudless spring day; absolutely rubbish for trout fishing. Too much sun pushes the trout into deeper water and normally kills their appetite in the middle of the day. Paul had already tackled-up and was happily thrashing the reservoir with efficient determination. I'd passed several grinning anglers swaggering towards Sutton Bingham's excellent fish cleaning room, with bulging bags of rainbow trout. And I even witnessed a couple of anglers netting fish as I walked to Paul's plot.

Although I'd set my rod up at my truck, I didn't do what I'd normally do and start whipping the water before my shadow's even caught up with me. Instead, I sat down beside Paul, watched

him fish and had a good butcher's at what all the other anglers were doing. It was now 3.30pm, the sun was at its height still, and although plenty of fish had been caught in the morning, but from what I could see, the fish had stopped feeding. Takes were sporadic and timid. Anglers were gradually losing interest too.

'I had a knock almost first cast', said Paul. 'But nothing since. Not a sausage'. It was that one tiny tug on his string that got Paul all pumped-up and keen to catch. That one pull, and the hazy promise of more like it, kept Paul casting relentlessly over the next three hours. It fuelled him with expectation. But without a single repeat-performance from the fish. It was during this three hour period, that I suddenly grew up and became all mature. I could have thrashed the reservoir to frothy foam and tried every combination of fly and flyline, until I either caught a fish or went mad in the attempt. Or, I could sit still and do absolutely nothing, until the time felt right. Until the fish started to show themselves again; either breaking the surface as they fed on invertebrate fly life, or by putting a substantial bend in another man's rod.

Neither happened for hours. Ages. So I did nothing. I chatted with a couple of fishermen. I wandered a bit further around the reservoir, but mostly I sat still, watched, chewed the fat with multi-casting Paul, and waited.

Most people reading this probably think I'm a total tosser to claim that sitting still and not fishing is a virtue. But believe me, it would have been far easier to pick up the rod and do what I always do; thrash with optimism. To sit out the dog-day afternoon with a vague hope that things might begin to look up later, took guts. Not just lethargy.

After three and a bit hours, things started to happen. Most other anglers had bagged up, or buggered off, so their absence probably helped the trout move closer in, as the air cooled, the light levels dropped and flies started hatching and rising from the water's surface.

I moved to a nearby swim and started to cast. I'd been at the reservoir nearly four hours by now, and had not so much as wetted a line. The first take came within three casts. An anorexic little nibble-pluck, into which I struck and missed; the small size 12 gold head hare's ear nymph failing to find any mouth to hook into. Because I wasn't feeling too tired and emotional from an afternoon of horse flogging the water, I was able to deduce that the way the surface current and wind made the floating line bend from left to right, might mean it'd be more effective to strike the rod sideways, away from the bend, rather than upwards in a conventional strike. Next cast, I had a chance to put my theory into practise. The gentle nudge-take was transformed into a three-pound rainbow fighting for his life, purely by altering the direction of my strike.

Paul was perplexed. He'd put in the hours. He'd thrashed the lake to foam. But, unreasonably, I caught the first fish. And so it went on. For every one I caught, he lost one, or missed a take. As my bag filled, Paul's frustration increased. And Paul knows me well enough to be absolutely sure I'm no better an angler than he is. Just, I wasn't so tired and burned-out with casting.

I caught fish because by 7pm I was still fresh and able to cast consistently. Paul had submitted to all those annoying failings of tiredness; when you catch a tree on your backcast, wrap your leader round the fly line, tangle your trace, snap-off on the strike. All the things I would normally do, but didn't this time. Because I exercised a little patience and waited.

Does this mean I'm becoming mature? Or am I just an annoying prat who's carping on about the one day he caught a few trout?

Keeping the Tills Rolling

Steven Lockett

For many in the wider community, angling is nothing more than a worm at one end and a fool at the other. In actual fact, angling drives a huge economy, which is very important for our region, particularly when it comes to attracting visitors. Some of the larger fisheries cater exclusively for holiday makers. Although the lakes are not available for locals to patronise, the anglers that fish them bring trade to our tackle shops, restaurants and pubs and enable us to enjoy the better service that is offered as a result of plentiful trade.

Clawford Vineyard near Holsworthy in Devon has been recognised nationally for the quality of both the accommodation and the fishing. Similarly, smaller sites bring tourists on a regular basis to both fish and spend down here in the south west. Everything from a holiday park to a B&B to a camping site, if they have water to fish, anglers will flock to them all year round.

As a photojournalist who concentrates mainly on the match fishing side of the sport, I have seen first hand the numbers of anglers who come down our way to chase the money on offer at the region's fishing festivals. The Torbay Sea Angling Festival, held in September each year, sees over 400 anglers battling for the prizes. Something like a quarter of the field travel from all corners of the country to pit their wits against the local hot shots. This event is backed by the local council, who recognise the impact it has on the economy of the bay, and are proud to support it.

Parkdean, who own several holiday centres around the UK, host a number of large events every year at their Whiteacres complex near Newquay. For many of this country's top match anglers winning one of the spring or autumn festivals is the best way to become a name. The climax of these yearly events is the Parkdean Masters, a £25,000 winner-takes-all match fished by 24 of the very best UK match anglers in front of the Sky Sports cameras. To qualify for the match, you first have to win one of the resident's matches or win a lake during a festival week. This gives you an invite to fish the Preston Innovations Festival, held in October, along with 179 other hopefuls. Pitting your skills against the likes of former World Champion, Tommy Pickering; Fish A Mania regular (former winner and Parkdean Masters winner), Steve Ringer; Drennan Team England star and last year's Parkdean Master, Des Shipp, you may hope to finish in the top 24 at the end of five day's hard work. Saturday dawns and you can make your way to your peg on Jenny's Lake for a titanic five hour struggle against both fish and the cream of the UK's match talent. Who knows? Maybe your name is on that cheque?

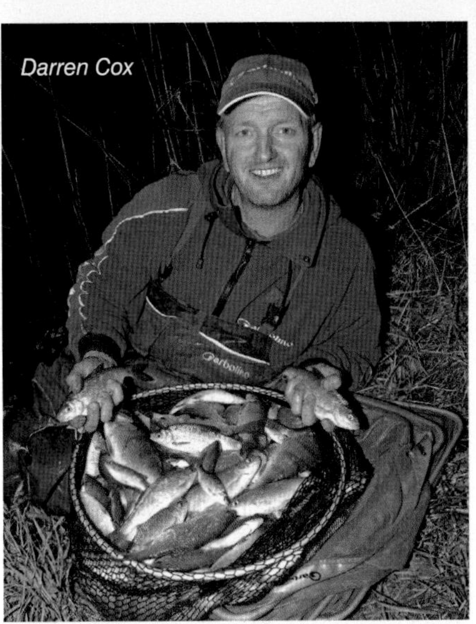
Darren Cox

These types of events have become almost a circuit, where regular faces crop up time and again. Not only is this a wonderful way to make new friends and rub shoulders with some of the best in the business, it is also testament to the quality of fishing we have on our doorstep. Clint Elliot at Whiteacres, John Candy at Todber Manor and Andy Seery at Stafford Moor, know how to make people welcome and also know what it takes to keep them returning.

In August 2006, Stafford Moor saw the first event in the 'Maniac' series that now sees two matches per year. 80 tickets are sold on a first come first served basis for £50. On the Saturday, those 80 anglers line up across the whole complex in sections of 10. The aim is to finish first or second in your section and thus qualify for the Sunday final. On the Sunday, those 16 anglers fish on Tanners Lake for a £2,000 winner-takes-all pot. It sounds simple enough, but who could have foreseen the way the fishing would go on all three of the events to date? Andy's fishery has a reputation for ton-up weights in the matches and the first Stafford Maniac final saw three tons hit the scales, with a lowest weight of 44lb. Incredible fishing, but even more incredible was winner Paul Garrett from Glastonbury pipping Midlands based visitor, Mark Saunders by a solitary ounce; 131lb 1oz to 131lb 0oz. Paul went home a happy man; Mark vowed to return...

The second event was held in August 2007 and once again had a nail biting finish, this time between the two youngest competitors in the final. Keeping the money local was Bristol's Rory Andres, who saw off Matt Parsons from Somerton by 121lb 6oz to 119lb 9oz. 18 year old Rory has not been match fishing for long, but helped by his dad, John, he has watched some of the visiting stars to help him improve and can now compete with the best.

November 2007 saw the first Silver Maniac match, fished using the same format, but with carp banned. So popular was this event that Drennan Team England Manager, Mark Downes, headed down the M5 from his Redditch home to take part. Another close fought battle ensued, with less than 5lb splitting the top four. Exiled Mancunian, Harry Billing, saw off two international stars in third placed Paul Filmore and fourth placed Des Shipp, and Mick Dagnell, the husband of Team England Lady's international Claire in second, with his 63lb 2oz net of roach and skimmers. This event is one that is sure to be a sell out every year, with plans already afoot to run it twice a year from 2009. Other Stafford Moor fixtures are spring and autumn festivals plus regular fish-ins organised from angling forums. They know when they're onto a good thing, so book their places well in advance. What a boost to the local economy in that little part of rural mid Devon.

Harry Billing used to travel to Whiteacres to fish the festivals there twice a year and, to misuse a phrase, liked it so much, he moved down here permanently. Silver fish were always one of his strong suits, so the December Silver Fish

Rory Andres and Matt Parsons

Festival at Whiteacres was a big draw. This is a week long event, but only 60 tickets are available for this one, although it may expand this year to offer 72 places. 2007 saw Andy Dare win to follow in the footsteps of Garbolino's UK boss and Drennan Team England star, Darren Cox and Fox Match backed Derek Willan from 2006 and 2005 respectively. Andy is another to settle around the Newquay area having enjoyed his trips from Nottinghamshire to compete in the festivals.

So not only do anglers from all over the country visit our region to stay, fish and soak up the unique Westcountry atmosphere, some of them become a permanent fixture. I landed in Devon in 1998 from Leicestershire (albeit with Somerset in my blood) and it doesn't take long listening to accents on any weekend match to work out the numbers of 'blow-ins' who are a part of the wider community. Brummies, Cockneys and Yorkies make up a healthy number of the coarse fishermen and women who add life to the whole Western peninsula.

It's time to stand up and be proud to be an angler. To help visitors to our region appreciate the fantastic fishing we have down here and to be an angler who supports local businesses and keeps those tills rolling.

Steve Lockett has worked supplying pictures and articles to most of the major angling publications in Europe for the last ten years. He is now in partnership with fellow photojournalist Brian Gay. Together they run V2V Angling Productions Ltd, filming high quality DVDs for the angling market.

Please see our advert and offer on page 198

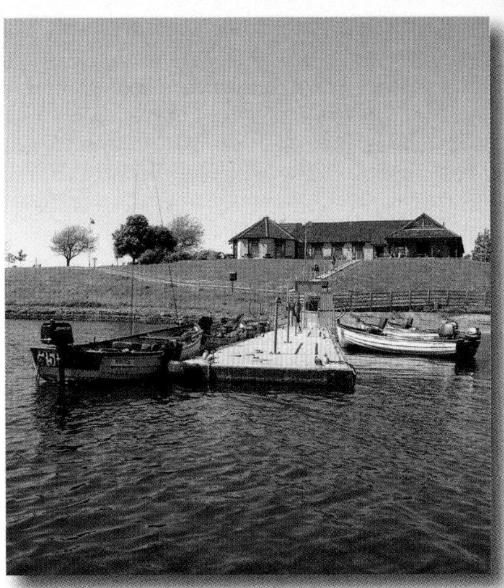

Tuition

Anyone can learn to fly fish and it's not as hard as you may think. You don't need to have any tackle or expensive equipment to start with and Bristol Water supply tutors, helpers and experts to make sure that everyone can enjoy a day at the water.

Our Chief Instructor, Mike Gleave, is STANIC* qualified and a REFFIS* guide. These nationally recognized qualifications, and his long experience both of teaching and practising the art of flyfishing, make him the ideal person to introduce newcomers to the sport. As well as running the courses listed here, Mike is available for private instruction, and we can thoroughly recommend his services.

**Salmon and Trout Association National Instructor's Certificate; Register of Experienced Fly Fishing Instructors and Schools*

Casting Tuition

We offer two-hour casting tuition sessions for beginners and near beginners most Saturday mornings from 11am to 1pm during the fishing season. Tackle is provided if needed; groups are kept small and advance booking is essential.

Fly Fishing Tuition

Once a month, normally on the last Saturday, we offer a fishing class with carefully supervised bank fishing. The four hour course also covers fly selection, entomology and safety; groups are small and advance booking is essential. Boat Fishing instruction for one or two persons can also be organised. The sessions last four hours with the date and time to be arranged by mutual agreement with the instructor.

Beginners' Days

We offer beginners a chance to try fly fishing on Saturday afternoon sessions throughout the fishing season and some weekdays during August. Here they will learn the basics of fly casting and fishing, as well as have the chance to bank fish and, if available, boat fish during the session. Tackle can be supplied. Minimum age for juniors is 12 years. Advance booking is essential as there will be limited places on each session. Apply to Woodford Lodge.

Free Tuition with John Horsey

John Horsey, our local professional guide, has fished here for many years and is well qualified to give advice and help to newcomers and regulars to the fisheries. This advice is available to anglers **Free Of Charge!** On six occasions during the season John will be available at Chew Valley to give assistance from boat or bank. You can book him for an hours free tuition. Just ring Woodford Lodge to reserve your place on one of the following dates: 7th April, 1st May, 3rd June, 1st July, 19th August, 1st September.

Competitons

Bristol Water host many competitions each season including local Club events and National & International contests. We also arrange various competitions for local anglers and teams.

There is an evening league held at Chew Valley throughout the spring & early summer. The ten event series is very popular and there are prizes in each round and for the overall champion. The best five results of each anglers are used to decide the winner of the league. after each event there is a complimentary buffet and drink. The Bristol Water Teams Challenge is for teams of six local or regular BW customers. This is a fun event taking place from the boats on Chew Valley. There are no prizes, just the honour of having your teams name on the carved wood fish trophy. The event finishes with a free buffet for all the competitors.

Lexus European Open.

2008 will again see the English Final of the Lexus Teams competition held at Chew Valley. Over six days 33 teams of six anglers will compete for places in the International Final. This year we will also see the final of the Lexus Individual contest held at Chew Valley. For details of all the above events contact us on the telephone number below.

Enquiries and Bookings.

Phone or write to Bristol Water Fisheries, Woodford Lodge, Chew Stoke, Bristol. BS40 8XH. Telephone 01275 332339 for a free brochure, for all enquiries and for bookings.

Weekly update by web or direct via email.

Visit our web site for regular updates on the fishing at: **www.bristolwater.co.uk**

If you would like the weekly fishing results and news to be emailed to you please email: woodford.lodge@bristolwater.co.uk to be added to the list.

"Angling Facts"

The sport of angling is a healthy outdoor pursuit enjoyed by a greater percentage of the population than any other sport. It makes a great contribution to the national economy but, more importantly, anglers have done more for the conservation of our natural environment than any other group - and for longer. In spite of this our wonderful sport and the environment that supports it is under constant threat. These threats take many forms and include invasion by alien species, anti-angling groups, diffuse pollution, widespread use of chemicals, soil erosion, global warming, drought, floods and over abstraction of water from our rivers etc. The list seems endless. In order to protect and effectively represent our sport to Government and other Agencies our different national bodies have got together to form the Fisheries and Angling Conservation Trust (FACT). The following national bodies are members of FACT: -

Anglers' Conservation Association **(ACA)**. Angling Trades Association **(ATA)**
Association of Stillwater Game Fishery Managers **(ASGM)**
National Association of Fisheries and Angling Consultatives **(NAFAC)**
National Federation of Anglers **(NFA)**. National Federation of Sea Anglers **(NFSA)**
Professional Coarse Fisheries Association **(PCFA)**. Atlantic Salmon Trust **(AST)**
Salmon and Trout Association **(S&TA)**. Specialist Anglers Alliance **(SAA)**

However the effective representation of our sport at a national level is very costly both in terms of money and resources. At present FACT is entirely funded by its constituent members who in turn rely upon the members for finance. If we are to continue fighting our corner it is important that all who partake in our sport support our national bodies. If you are not already a member please join at least one of them NOW. A contact list is shown below:

ACA - Fighting pollution and protecting the interests of anglers.- 01568 620447.
NAFAC - National body of local/regional fisheries & angling stakeholder groups - 0121 454 2886.
NFA - Governing body for coarse angling – 0115 981 3535.
NFSA - Governing body of sea angling – 01364 644643.
S&TA - Governing body for game fishing – 0207 283 5838.
SAA - National body for specimen anglers – 01442 398022

JOIN US NOW AND HELP PROTECT OUR SPORT

THE GET HOOKED GUIDE

SOMERSET

Incorporating Bristol, Bath and North Somerset

SOMERSET

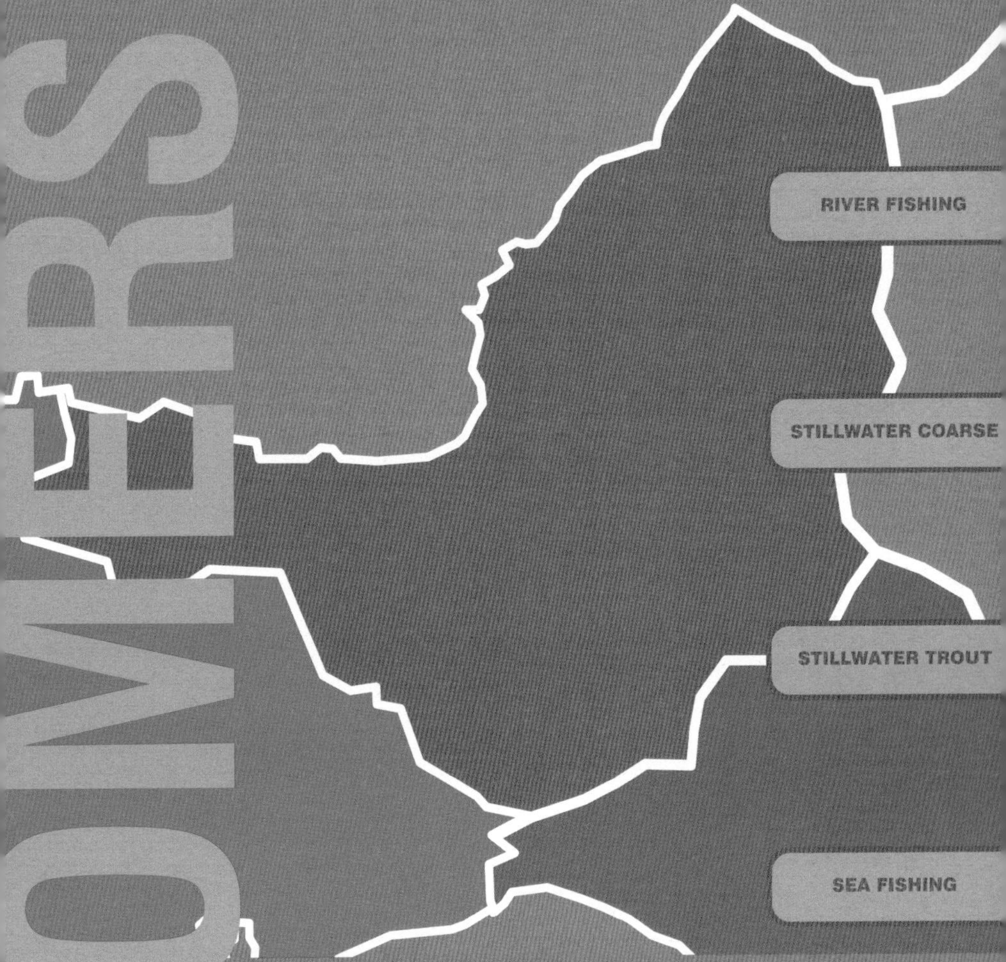

RIVER FISHING

STILLWATER COARSE

STILLWATER TROUT

SEA FISHING

WHERE TO STAY

Somerset Game Road Directions

121. Blagdon
Bristol Water fisheries are well signposted from major roads. Tel: 01275 332339.

122. Cameley Trout Lakes
Situated 10 miles between Bristol, Bath & Wells. Off A37. Tel: 01761 452423.

123. Chew Valley
Bristol Water fisheries are well signposted from major roads. Tel: 01275 332339.

124. Clatworthy
Wessex Water fisheries. Tel: 0845 600 4 600.

125. Hawkridge
Wessex Water fisheries. Tel: 0845 600 4 600.

126. Lance Nicholson River Fishing
Permits & directions available from Lance Nicholson, 9 & 11 High Street, Dulverton, Somerset. Trout & Salmon fishing on the Exe, Barle & Haddeo. Tel: 01398 323409.

127. Litton
Bristol Water fisheries are well signposted from major roads. Tel: 01275 332339.

128. Sutton Bingham
Wessex Water fisheries. Tel: 0845 600 4 600.

129. The Barrows
Bristol Water fisheries are well signposted from major roads. Tel: 01275 332339.

130. Wimbleball
Signed from the B3190, Bampton village and the A396. Tel: 01398 371372.

Somerset Coarse Road Directions

131. Alcove Angling Club
Please Tel: 0117 9658280 or 07714302031 for directions. Maps are issued with membership.

132. Amalgamated Fisheries Ltd
Please Tel: 0117 9672977.

133. Avalon Fisheries
Take the road from Shapwick to Westhay, turn right just prior to the Peatmoor Visitors Centre.Tel: 07855 825059.

134. Bridgwater Angling Association
Please contact Mr John Hill. Tel: 01278 424023 or Mr Mike Parnell. Tel: 01278 459032.

135. Bullock Farm Fishing Lakes
From Junction 20, M5 follow B3133 for Yatton. Drive through village of Kenn, turn right for Kingston Seymour. Follow signs for Bullock Farm Fishing Lakes. Tel: 01934 835020.

136. Burnham-on-Sea Holiday Village
From M25 take exit 22 turn left at first roundabout onto A38 towards Highbridge. Continue over mini roundabout, turn right onto B3139 to Burnham. After Total Garage turn left onto Marine Drive. The park is 400 yards on left. Tel: 01278 783391.

137. Cider Farm Lakes
From J22 M5 take the third exit at roundabout towards Cheddar Gorge - A38. At next roundabout take first exit towards Weston-Super-Mare A370. Keep on A370 for approx. 2 miles. Take the left turning, signposted Lympsham, after speed camera! Follow road through village, past cricket ground, continue out of village, then turn left, signposted Berrow/Brean. Follow road over railway bridge, Cider Farm Lakes on left hand side. Tel: 01278 751401.

138. Durleigh Reservoir
Wessex Water fisheries. Tel: 0845 600 4 600.

139. Edney's Fisheries
Signed off Mells to Vobster Road. Turn into Popples Lane, leading to Edney's Farm. Grid ref 72/50.5. Tel: 01373 812294 or mobile 07941 280075.

140. Emborough Ponds
Please contact Thatchers Pet & Tackle, 18 Queen Street, Wells, Somerset. Tel: 01749 673513.

141. Emerald Pool Fisheries
Off the A38 at West Huntspill, turn into Withy Road by the Crossways Inn. Take the next right Puriton Road. Travel for approx. 0.5 mile, over Huntspill River, take the next track on the left. Pool on the right at the top of the track. Please watch for new brown road signs from A38 to fishery. Tel: 01278 794707.

142. Godney Moor Ponds
Please Tel: 01458 447830 for directions.

143. Laburnum House
Please Tel: 01278 781830 for directions.

144. Lands End Farm Fishery
From M5 junction 22, turn left at first roundabout, then first left and follow road to T junction, turn left signposted Wedmore, continue through village of Mark, then into Blackford where you turn right by the school signposted Heath House. Follow road to crossroads, turn right, then second right, fishery is at bottom of lane. Tel: 07977 545882.

145. Leverets Specimen Carp Lake
Please Tel: 01749 890303 for directions.

146. Northam Farm Touring Caravan Park
Leave the M5 at junction 22. Follow signs to Burnham-on-Sea, Brean. Continue through Brean village and Northam Farm is on the right 0.5 mile past Brean Leisure Park. Tel: 01278 751244.

147. Plantation Lakes Ltd
From Bristol: Weston-Super-Mare A370. Turn towards Yatton B3133 at Congresbury traffic lights. Go right through Yatton. Turn left towards Kingston Seymour. Just after the Bridge Inn. At village take middle lane. From M5. junction 20. Clevedon. Turn left at both roundabouts onto B3133 towards Yatton, after approx. 3 miles turn right towards Kingston Seymour. At village take middle lane. Tel: 07795 104897.

148. Tan House Farm Lake

M4 exit junction 18 onto A46 Stroud to Chipping Sodbury on to B4060 Wickwar. Continue until see Rangeworthy sign, turn left into Bury Hill Lane. Alternatively M5 to junction 14 to Wickwar to Chipping Sodbury B4060 for 1.5 miles. Take 3rd road on right to Rangeworthy and Bury Hill Lane. Tel: 01454 228280.

149. The Sedges

Exit M5 at J23, continue to Puriton Hill heading for Street/ Glastonbury. When reach T junction turn right, continue for approx. 3 miles. Cross motorway bridge take 1st left through housing estate watch out for sleeping policemen! When exit Eastern Avenue take left turn, then first right into Dunwear Lane. You will see our sign. Please Tel: 01278 445221 or mobile 07980 128404 for directions.

150. Thorney Lakes

Directions from A303 to Muchelney. Turn off A303 dual carriageway signposted Martock Ash. Follow signs to Kingsbury Episcopi, at the T junction in village turn right, through the village of Thorney, over river bridge & disused railway. Lakes are on right. Thorney Lakes & Caravan Park. Tel: 01458 250811.

151. Trinity Waters

Off M5, Junction 23, take A38 to Bridgwater, take first right turning after Express Park roundabout. First right at traffic lights, over River Parrett, turn right at traffic lights to Chilton Trinity. Take second right down Straight Drove (No through road).1st gate on right for Wild Marsh & Middle Marsh Lakes, 3rd gate on right for Woodland Lake. Please Tel: 01278 450880 or 07720 542141 for directions.

152. Velocity Angling Complex

Take the B3151. Fishery situated at Blakeway Farm between Wedmore and Westhay. Tel: 07789 760213.

153. Viaduct Fishery

From Yeovil take the A37 north towards Ilchester and then the B3151 to Somerton. Turn left onto the B3153 (Signposted Somerton) and go up hill to mini roundabout. Go straight over roundabout and take first right through housing estate to T junction. Turn left and almost immediately first right onto track to fishery. Tel: 01458 274022.

154. Warren Farm Holiday Centre

Leave the M5 at junction 22 and follow the B3140 past Burnham-on-Sea to Berrow & Brean. We are situated 1.5 miles past Brean Leisure Park. Tel: 01278 751227.

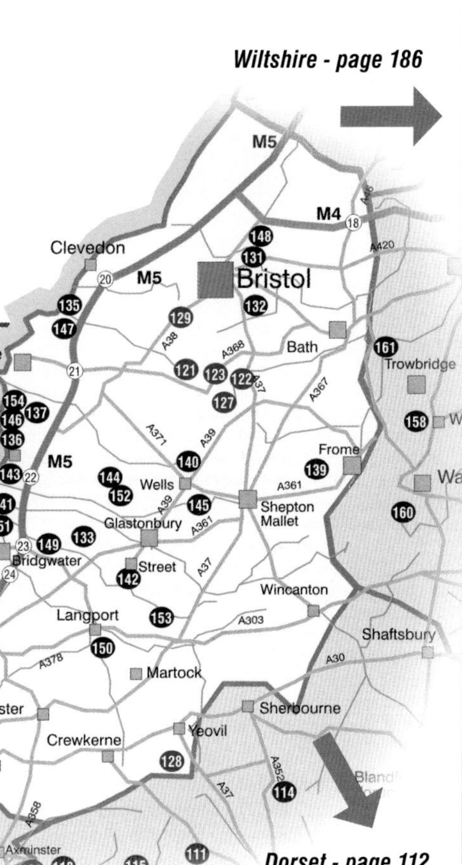

Only advertisers are located on this map.

Somerset River Fishing

AXE

The River Axe emerges from the Mendip Hills at Wookey Hole and from here to below Wookey the river is Trout water. The river deepens as it crosses low lying land at the foot of the Mendips to the sluices at Bleadon and Brean Cross, the tidal limit. Fish species in the lower reaches include Bream, Roach, Tench, Dace and Pike.

Weston-Super-Mare A.A ♿

Contact: Weston Angling Centre, 25a Locking Road, Weston-super-Mare, *Tel:* 01934 631140, *Water:* River Axe, River Brue, South Drain, North Drain. Summer Lane Pond, Locking Pond. *Species:* Bream, Tench, Roach, Carp, Gudgeon, Perch, Rudd, Chub & some Dace. *Permits:* Weston Angling Centre. *Charges:* Season £27, Week £12, Day £5. Senior £27, Junior £11, OAP's / Concession £14. *Season:* Old River Axe, Summer Lane and Locking Ponds - year round. *Methods:* No boilies, no nuts, no cat foods.

BARLE

See under Devon - Exe and tributaries.

Paddons

Contact: Mrs M. McMichael or Mr P. Jones, Northmoor Road, Dulverton, *Tel:* 01398 323514, *Water:* 400 yards single bank on River Barle. *Species:* Brown Trout & Salmon. *Permits:* Lance Nicholson Gun Shop, Gloster House, High Street, Dulverton, Somerset. Tel: 01398 323409. *Charges:* Day ticket - Adults £5, Juniors £1. *Season:* March 15th to September 30th. *Methods:* Fly fishing.

River Barle Fishing

Contact: Lance Nicolson, Beasley Mill, 9 High Street, Dulverton, *Tel:* 01398 323409, *Mobile:* 07971 699247, *Water:* 2.5 Miles of double bank fishing on the River Barle. *Species:* Brown Trout to 3.5lbs plus. Salmon - 15lbs. Rainbow Trout - 3lbs. *Permits:* Trout and Salmon licence required. Fishing permits from Lance Nicholson, 9-11 High St., Dulverton. Tel: 01398 323409. *Charges:* £12 per day for Trout and £25 per day for Salmon. *Season:* Trout: March to Sept. Salmon: 15 Feb to end Sept. *Methods:* Fly and Spinner ONLY.

BRIDGWATER AND TAUNTON CANAL

Cut in 1827 the canal provided a good commercial waterway between the two towns. The canal has been recently restored for navigation but there is only infrequent boat traffic. The canal offers excellent coarse fishing from the towpath for Roach, Bream, Tench, Rudd, Perch & Pike.

HUNTSPILL RIVER / SOUTH DRAIN / CRIPPS RIVER / NORTH DRAIN

The Huntspill River is a man made drainage channel, excavated in the 1940s and connected to the River Brue and South Drain via the Cripps River. The North Drain was dug c1770 to drain low lying moors to the north of the River Brue. The Huntspill is a notable coarse fishery and is often the venue for national and local match fishing competitions. Catches consist primarily of Bream and Roach. The North and South Drain and Cripps River contain similar species and also offer good sport for the coarse angler.

Bridgwater Angling Association ♿

Contact: Mr A Danahy, 127 The Old Basin, Somerset Bridge, Bridgwater, *Tel:* 01278 457022, *Water:* 6 miles on the Bridgwater & Taunton Canal, Fishing on the rivers Cripps, Brue, North & South Drain, King's Sedgemoor Drain, Langacre Rhine & The Huntspill. Stillwater fishing at Combwich, Walrow, Dunwear & Screech Owl and Bridgwater Docks. *Species:* All types of Coarse Fish. *Permits:* Available from Tackle outlets throughout Somerset area including Somerset Angling, 74 Bath Road, Bridgwater, Tel; 01278 431777. Megabaits Unit H Cartwright Business Park, Colley Lane, Bridgwater, Tel; 01278 424614. Watts News, Edward Street, Bridgwater, Tel; 01278 422137. Scoops, 77 St Johns Street, Bridgwater. Veals Tackle 1a Church Street, Highbridge, Tel; 01278 786934. *Charges:* Adult 1 rod £30, 2 rods £40, 3 rods £55 4 rods £70. Senior citizens 1 rod £20, 2 rods £27.50, 3 rods £40, 4 rods £50. (7-11 years) 1 rod £6. (12-17 years) 1 rod only £8 + £10 for 2 rods. Disabled 1 rod £20, 2 rods £27.50, 3 rods £40, 4 rods £50. Day ticket £6. 7 day ticket £25. Prices may change in 2008. *Season:* E.A. byelaws apply. Bridgwater and Taunton Canal open all year. *Methods:* Full rules and map with permits.

BRISTOL AVON AND TRIBUTARIES

The River Avon flows from its sources near Sherston and Tetbury to its confluence with the Severn at Avonmouth some 117 kilometers and is fed by many tributaries on its way. The headwaters of the River Avon, the Tetbury and

Sherston branches join at Malmesbury. Both are important Trout streams where fishing is strictly preserved and there is little opportunity for the visiting angler to fish these waters.

Malmesbury to Chippenham

Coarse fisheries predominate in this section, although Trout are stocked by fishing associations in some areas. Arguably one of the best fisheries in the country, this section contains a wide range of specimen fish. Local records include: Roach 3lb 2oz, Perch 3lb 3oz, Tench 8lb 5 1/2oz, Bream 8lb 8oz, Dace 1lb 2oz, Chub 7lb 10oz, Carp 20lb 8 1/4oz and Pike 33lb 3oz. Also many Barbel to 12lb have been reported.

Chippenham to Bath

Upstream from Staverton to Chippenham the Avon continues to be an important coarse fishery, both for the pleasure angler and match fisherman. The river flows through a broad flood plain and provides a pastoral setting. In the faster flowing sections chub, Roach, Dace and Barbel can be caught in good numbers.

Bath to Hanham

Between Hanham and Bath much of this length retains a rural character and is an important coarse fishery used by pleasure and match anglers. The National Angling Championships have been held here. Roach, Bream and Chub are the main catches and, in some favoured swims, Dace. Very good catches of Bream are to be had with specimen fish. 'Free' fishing is available through Bath from the towpath side between Newbridge and Pulteney Weir. Carp of 20lb have been reported caught downstream of Pulteney and Keynsham Weirs.

Hanham to Avonmouth

Between Netham Dam and Hanham Weir the river is affected by spring tides. The water has a very low saline content and this length of river provides reasonable coarse fishing. Below Netham Dam the river contains mostly estuarine species but some sea Trout and Salmon have been seen.

Amalgamated Fisheries Ltd

Contact: Jeff Parker, 16 Lansdown View, Kingswood, Bristol, *Tel:* 0117 9672977, *Water:* Approx. 80 miles Coarse Fishing on Bristol Avon & Somerset Rivers & Streams. Stillwaters at Lyneham, Calne, Malmesbury, Bath and Pawlett near Bridgwater. Trout only water on Cam Brook. Too much to list here, please contact the secretary for full details. *Species:* All coarse species. *Permits:* Full Membership available from the Secretary. Veterans over 70 years contact the secretary for details of discounted membership. Full members only may

fish at Tockenham Reservoir, Burton Hill lake at Malmesbury & Shackells Lake. Day Tickets for all waters except Burton Hill & Tockenham are available at Tackle Shops. Limited night fishing. *Charges:* Adults £45 (discount for early purchase). Adult and child £55. Concessions £15. Night fishing full members £50 per year. *Methods:* No metal cans or glass bottles in possession, no fresh water fish as livebait, maximum 2 rods per angler, full rules on application.

Really pleased with this catch at Trinity Waters

Avon Valley Country Park (River Avon)
Bath Rd, Keynsham, Bristol, *Tel:* 0117 9864929, *Water:* 1.5 miles on River Avon. *Species:* Tench & Coarse fish. *Permits:* From above. *Charges:* £6.50 Adult entrance to park (includes ticket to fish), £6 Child, £6 Senior Citizen. *Season:* Park open: Easter - 1st November 10am - 6pm. Current E.A. Byelaws apply on the river.

Bathampton Angling Association (Box Brook)
Contact: Dave Crookes, 25 Otago Terrace, Larkhall, Bath, *Tel:* 01225 427164, *Water:* 3 miles of Box brook (tributary of Avon). Split into 2 beats at Middle Hill and Shockerwick. *Species:* Brown Trout (occasional Rainbows) Grayling. *Permits:* Local fishing tackle shops. *Charges:* Adults £25, Juniors £8, O.A.P £7. Registered disabled £7, Under 12's free. Members only special day permits must be purchased before fishing. *Season:* Fishing from 1st April to 15 October inclusive. *Methods:* Traditional Fly/Nymph only.

Bathampton Angling Association (Bristol Avon Claverton)
Contact: Dave Crookes, 25 Otago Terrace, Larkhall, Bath, *Tel:* 01225 427164, *Water:* 2.5 miles Bristol Avon up and downstream from Claverton. *Species:* Bream to 6lbs, Chub to 5lbs, Roach to 2.5lbs, Pike to 25lbs, Barbel to 13lbs. *Permits:* Local fishing tackle shops. *Charges:* Adults £25, Juniors £8, O.A.P £7. Registered disabled £7, Under 12's free. Members only. *Season:* Standard river close season, night fishing on application. *Methods:* Club byelaws apply.

Bathampton Angling Association (Bristol Avon Kelston)
Contact: Dave Crookes, 25 Otago Terrace, Larkhall, Bath, *Tel:* 01225 427164, *Water:* 2 miles of Bristol Avon at Kelston. *Species:* Bream to 8lbs, Roach to 2lbs, Pike to 20lbs, Chub to 3lbs, Barbel to 8lbs. *Permits:* Local fishing tackle shops. *Charges:* Adults £25, Juniors £8, O.A.P £7. Registered disabled £7, Under 12's free. £3 day tickets available to Non-Members. Tickets must be purchased before fishing. *Season:* Standard river close season. *Methods:* Club byelaws apply.

Bathampton Angling Association (Bristol Avon Newbridge)
Contact: Dave Crookes, 25 Otago Terrace, Larkhall, Bath, *Tel:* 01225 427164, *Water:* 1.5 miles of Bristol Avon at Newbridge, downstream of Bath. *Species:* Bream to 10lbs, Chub to 4lbs, Roach to 2.5lbs, Pike to 16lbs. *Permits:* Local fishing tackle shops. *Charges:* Adults £25, Juniors £8, O.A.P £7. Registered disabled £7, Under 12's free. £3 day tickets available to Non-Members.Tickets must be purchased before fishing. *Season:* Standard river close season. *Methods:* Club byelaws apply.

Bathampton Angling Association (Bristol Avon Saltford)
Contact: Dave Crookes, 25 Otago Terrace, Larkhall, Bath, *Tel:* 01225 427164, *Water:* 1.5 miles of Bristol Avon at Saltford. *Species:* Bream to 8lbs, Roach to 2lbs, Chub to 3lbs. *Permits:* Local fishing tackle shops. *Charges:* Adults £25, Juniors £8, O.A.P £7. Registered disabled £7, Under 12's free. £3 day tickets available to Non-Members. must be purchased before fishing. *Season:* Standard river close season. *Methods:* Club byelaws apply.

Bristol & West Federation of Anglers
Contact: Hon Sec. B Lloyd, 386 Speedwell Road, Kingswood, Bristol, *Tel:* 0117 9676030, *Mobile:* 07831 311582, *Water:* Bristol and West waters are; Swineford to Keynsham, Jack Whites Cottage (Londonderry Farm) all right hand bank downstream. *Species:* Roach, Chub, Carp, Barbel, Pike. *Permits:* Open to affiliated clubs, including Bristol, Bath and Wilts Amalgamation.

Bristol City Docks Angling Club
Contact: Bob Taylor, 118 Northcote Road, Downend, Bristol, *Tel:* 01179 040261, *Mobile:* 07990 573831, *Water:* 3 miles on Bristol Avon from Chequers Weir to Netham. Feeder canal (Netham - docks), Bristol Docks system. *Species:* Skimmers, Bream, Roach, Dace, Chub, Pike, Eels, Carp, Tench and Perch. *Permits:* All Bristol tackle shops and Harbour Masters office, or from secretary above on 01454 773990 or 07790 573831. Free Fishing on Bristol Avon Chequers to Netham. *Charges:* Season: Senior & 2 Juniors under 12 £15, Seniors £12.50, Concessions, Disabled, Juniors, O.A.P's £6.50, Day tickets in advance: Seniors £2.50 + Concessions £1, Day tickets on the bank issued by Bailiff: Seniors £5, Juniors/Conc £2. Prices may change in 2008. *Season:* 1st April - March 31st inclusive, River - normal close season applies; Docks and Feeder Canal open all year. *Methods:* Docks: Pole and Feeder. Pole & Waggler on Feeder Canal. All normal river tactics on the Avon. Daily update information from Tony on 0117 9517250.

Bristol PSV Club
Contact: Mike Wilson, Bristol, *Mobile:* 07850 731137, *Water:* Well established club, fishing waters in Gloucester, Bristol, Bath & Somerset. 25 matches a year. Meeting 1st Tuesday of every month in the Midland Spinner on London road, Warnley. *Charges:* Membership £20 per year. Juniors welcome. Call in to the Midland Spinner.

Frys Match Group
Contact: Mr Merv Sivell, *Mobile:* 07811 746484, *Water:* 63 Pegs - 2 mile stretch single bank fishing. *Species:* Carp, Barbel, Bream, Roach. *Permits:* Membership available to all, please contact Merv Sivell. *Charges:* £15 season ticket or £2 day ticket. Under 16 fish for free if accompanied by adult member. *Season:* E.A. Byelaws apply. No night fishing.

Mardon Angling Club
Contact: Mr Austin, 65 Grange Avenue, Hanham, Bristol, *Tel:* 0117 9839776, *Water:* Open to all. Regular monthly meetings, full match calendar (previously Alcan Angling Club). Members can fish Bristol Avon from Jack White's to Swineford as Club is member of Bristol and West Federation of Anglers. *Species:* Most coarse species. *Charges:* Please contact above. Charges £10 per annum, children under 16 free. *Season:* All year. *Methods:* All members must observe specific rules of each fishery.

BRISTOL FROME

The Bristol Frome rises at Dodington and offers a fair standard of coarse fishing on the lower sections. The upper section contains limited stocks of Brown Trout, Roach and Perch. This tributary of the River Avon is culverted beneath Bristol and discharges into the Floating Harbour.

Frome Vale Angling Club
Contact: Nigel Vigus (Secretary), 32 Rock Lane, Stoke Gifford, Bristol, *Tel:* 01179 759710, *Water:* 1 mile river Frome; half acre lake (Winterbourne). Bristol Avon - Keynsham - Swinford approx. 3 miles. *Species:* Carp, Roach, Bream, Tench, Pike, Perch, Chub. *Permits:* As above. *Charges:* Per season: Seniors £20 - Juniors £7 - OAP's/Disabled £5. Day tickets not available. *Season:* From June 16th - March 14th. Closed season March 15th - June 15th. *Methods:* Barbless hooks on all waters. Lakes: barbless hooks, no floating baits, hooks no larger than size 10.

BOYD

The River Boyd rises just south of Dodington and joins the Bristol Avon at Bitton. In the middle and lower reaches coarse fish predominate. The upper reaches above Doynton contain Brown Trout.

BY BROOK

The Broadmead and Burton brooks together form the By Brook which flows through Castle Combe and is joined by several smaller streams before entering the River Avon at Bathford. Brown Trout predominate above the village of Box, mostly small in size but plentiful in number. At Box and below the fishery is mixed and Dace to 14oz and Roach of 2lb are not uncommon.

MARDEN

The River Marden is fed by springs rising from the downs above Cherhill and joins the river Avon upstream of Chippenham. Brown Trout occur naturally in the upper reaches. Downstream of Calne coarse fish predominate and weights of more than 30lb are regularly caught in matches. The Marden Barbel record stands at over 10lb.

SOMERSET FROME

The Somerset Frome is the main tributary of the Bristol Avon. It drains a large catchment area which is fed from the chalk around Warminster and limestone from the eastern end of the Mendips. There are numerous weirs and mills mostly disused. The tributaries above Frome provide ideal conditions for Brown Trout with fishing on the River Mells. The middle and lower reaches provide excellent coarse fishing.

Airsprung Angling Association (Frome)
Contact: Bill Turner, 124 Langford Rd, Trowbridge, Wilts. *Tel:* 01225 766219, *Water:* River Frome at Stowford Farm (near Farleigh, Hungerford). See also entry under Wiltshire, River Fishing, Kennet & Avon Canal. *Species:* Carp, Bream, Chub, Roach, Rudd, Dace, Tench, Perch, etc. *Permits:* Wiltshire Angling, 01225 763835; West Tackle, Trowbridge, 01225 755472. Trowbridge Road Post Office, Bradford-upon Avon. *Season:* Subject to normal close season. *Methods:* Details from Association.

Avon & Tributaries Angling Association
Contact: Andrew T Donaldson, 104 Berkley Road, Bishopstone, Bristol, *Tel:* 01179 442518, *Water:* Somerset Frome, Cam, Wellow, Midford Brooks. *Species:* All Coarse species and Trout. *Permits:* No day tickets, guest ticket from individual members. *Season:* In rules. *Methods:* In rules.

Edenvale Farm
Edenvale Farm, Mill Lane, Beckington, Frome, *Tel:* 01373 830371, *Water:* One mile of single bank on the Frome. *Species:* Coarse fish and some Trout. *Permits:* Permits from farmhouse. Please telephone first. *Season:* E.A. close season applies. *Methods:* No dogs or radios. No unaccompanied children.

Frome Angling Association (River)
Contact: Gary Collinson, 2 Bath Street, Frome, *Tel:* 01373 471437, *Mobile:* 07958 495283, *Water:* 12 miles River Frome - 10 acre lake. See entry under Stillwater Coarse, Frome. *Species:* River: Roach, Chub, Bream. Lake: Tench, Carp, Roach, Pike. *Permits:* Please ring Gary Collinson 01373 471437. *Charges:* £15 Senior, £7 Junior Under 16 and O.A.P's. Day tickets £3. *Season:* 16th June to March 14th, unless changes in legislation occur. *Methods:* No restrictions.

MIDFORD BROOK

The Midford Brook runs through well wooded valleys with mostly mixed fishing on the lower reaches and Trout fishing in upper reaches. The largest Brown Trout recorded weighed 5lb 6oz.

KENNET AND AVON CANAL

There are some 58 kilometres of canal within the Bristol Avon catchment area which averages one metre in depth and thirteen metres in width. The Kennet & Avon Canal joins the River Avon at Bath with the River Kennet between Reading and Newbury. The canal was opened in 1810 to link the Severn Estuary with the Thames. The canal, now much restored, provides excellent fishing with Carp to 25lb, Tench to 5lb also Roach, Bream, Perch, Rudd, Pike and Gudgeon.

Bathampton Angling Association (Kennet & Avon Canal)
Contact: Dave Crookes, 25 Otago Terrace, Larkhall, Bath, *Tel:* 01225 427164, *Water:* 6.5 miles of Kennet and Avon canal. From Bath to Limpley Stoke Hill. *Species:* Bream to 4lbs, Chub to 3.5lbs, Roach to 2lbs, Pike to 20lbs, Carp to 24lbs, Tench to 3lbs. Perch to 2.5lbs, Eels to 3lbs. *Permits:* Local fishing tackle shops. *Charges:* Adults £25, Juniors £8, O.A.P £7. Registered disabled £7, Under 12's free. £3 day tickets available to non-members must be purchased before fishing. *Season:* Open all year. *Methods:* Club bye-laws apply.

BRUE

The River Brue is a Trout fishery from its source above Bruton to Lovington. From here to Glastonbury a number of weirs provide areas of deep water and coarse fish predominate, notably Chub and Roach, together with Bream, Dace and Pike. Similar species may be found between Glastonbury and Highbridge where the river is channelled across the Somerset Levels and connected with a number of drainage channels such as the Huntspill River and North Drain.

Glaston Manor Angling Association
Contact: Adam Mitchell, NFU Office, 1 Sadler Street, Wells, *Tel:* 01749 673786, *Water:* Brue - approx. 15 miles both banks; Lydford on Fosse to Westhay. 3 miles on River Sheppey plus South Drain from Catcott Bridge back to source. Also see entry in Stillwater Coarse, Street. 1.75 miles approx. on North Drain. *Species:* Roach, Chub, Bream, Dace, Perch, Gudgeon, Pike, Tench and Carp. *Permits:* Thatchers Tackle, Wells, Tel: 01749 673513 or Street Angling Centre, High St, Street, Somerset Tel: 01458 447830. *Charges:* Day ticket £5. Junior membership £9, Senior membership £28, OAP and disabled £14, Junior Disabled £4.50. *Season:* Current E.A. byelaws apply. *Methods:* No live bait permitted, full rules on day ticket and annual permit.

Highbridge Angling Association (River)
Contact: Mr C Brewer, 8 Willow Close, East Huntspill, Near Highbridge, *Tel:* 01278 786230, *Water:* Basin Bridge, East Huntspill *Species:* Carp to 33lb, Pike to mid 20's, all other coarse species. *Permits:* Thyers Tackle, Highbridge - 01278 786934. Also available from other local tackle shops. *Charges:* Day tickets £3, 7 day ticket £10 or season ticket £20. Senior citizen £10. *Season:* March 15th - June 16th closed season. *Methods:* No live baiting, full list with ticket.

Merry Farm Fishing
Contact: Mr Peter Dearing, Merry Farm, Merry Lane, Basonbridge, *Tel:* 01278 783655, *Water:* 600 yards on the River Brue. *Species:* Pike 20lb plus, Bream 7lb, Tench 6lb, Chub 2lb, Carp 18lb, Roach 1.5lb, Gudgeon, Ruffe, Perch 4lb. *Permits:* Day tickets. *Charges:* £2 per day. *Season:* 16 June to 14 March. *Methods:* No restrictions.

Mill House Fishing
Contact: Mr & Mrs M Knight, Mill Road, Barton St. David, Nr. Somerton, *Tel:* 01458 851215, *Water:* Mill stream off river Brue - owners rights to fish. *Species:* Chub, Trout, Eels. *Permits:* Available at fishing and tackle shop in Street: Street Angling Centre, 160 High St, Street. 01458 447380. *Charges:* £4 for day pass. £10 for monthly pass. *Season:* Season starts around mid June.

Walleden Farm Fishery (Brue)
Contact: Andrew Wall, East Huntspill, Highbridge, *Tel:* 01278 786488, *Mobile:* 07886 732945, *Water:* Section of river Brue. See also entry under Stillwater Trout. *Species:* Trout. *Permits:* From the above. *Season:* Open all year. *Methods:* Any legal method.

CAM AND WELLOW BROOKS

The Cam and Wellow Brooks, rising on the north side of the Mendip Hills, flow through what was a mining area and now provide good quality Trout fishing controlled by local fishing associations.

Cameley Lakes (River Cam)
Contact: J. Harris, Hillcrest Farm, Cameley, Temple Cloud, Nr Bristol, *Tel:* 01761 452423, *Water:* Fishing on River Cam. See also entry under Stillwater Trout, Bristol. *Species:* Rainbow and Brown Trout, wild Trout. *Permits:* Details on request. *Charges:* Details on request. *Season:* Details on request. *Methods:* Details on request.

CHEW

The River Chew rises near Chewton Mendip and flows through the Bristol Waterworks Reservoirs at Litton and Chew Valley Lake. The river continues through Chew Magna, Stanton Drew, Publow, Woolard and Compton Dando to its confluence with the River Avon at Keynsham. A mixed fishery for most its length and is particularly good for Roach, Dace and Grayling below Pensford.

Bathampton Angling Association (River Chew)
Contact: Dave Crookes, 25 Otago Terrace, Larkhall, Bath, *Tel:* 01225 427164, *Water:* One mile of river Chew at Compton Dando, near Keynsham. *Species:* Roach, Chub, Grayling, Brown Trout, Rainbow Trout, Dace, Perch. *Permits:* Local fishing tackle shops. *Charges:* Adults £25, Juniors £8, O.A.P £7. Registered disabled £7, Under 12s free. Members only. *Season:* Open all year. Fly and worm for Trout from 15 March to 15 June inclusive. *Methods:* Club bye-laws apply.

Keynsham Angling Association
Contact: Keynsham Angling Association, PO Box 137, Bristol, *Tel:* 07788 981061, *Water:* Four miles on Bristol Avon (Swineford to Chequers) and 2.5 miles on the Chew (Compton Dando to Keynsham) *Species:* Most species. *Charges:* Members only fishing. Membership details from club website or Keynsham Angling Centre Tel: 01179 867507. Adult membership £15. Juniors under 16, OAP and disabled £7.50. *Season:* Current E.A. Byelaws apply. *Methods:* Details in members handbook. On rivers Chew and Avon there are no restrictions other than current E.A. Byelaws.

Knowle Angling Association (River Chew)
Contact: Keith Caddick, 41 Eastwood Crescent, Brislington, Bristol, *Tel:* 01179 857974, *Mobile:* 0794 634 7581, *Water:* 5 miles of upper and lower river Chew, 2.5 miles river Yeo. 2 lakes - Publow and Ackers lake at Pensford. Plus fishing at Chew Magna reservoir (see Stillwater Trout, Bristol). *Species:* Brown Trout 1.5 to 4lb and Rainbow Trout 1.5 to 6lb. *Permits:* From Keith Caddick. Guests of members only. *Charges:* £95 annual membership 2008. New members pay extra £5 entrance fee. Memberships of 65 and over £65 plus £5 entrance fee for new senior memberships. Juniors £27. *Season:* All rivers 1 April - 15 October. Lower Chew open all year. Trout 1st April to 15 October. Coarse Fish and Grayling 16 June to 14 March. *Methods:* Fly only on upper Chew. Any method on Lower Chew. Any method on river Yeo.

EXE & TRIBUTARIES

See description under Devon.

Beasley Mill
Contact: P. Veale, Lance Nicholson, 9 High Street, Dulverton, *Tel:* 01398 323409, *Water:* Approx. 1 mile double bank on Barle at Dulverton. *Species:* Trout and occasional Salmon. *Permits:* As above. *Charges:* £12 Trout, £25 Salmon. *Season:* 15th March - 30th September. *Methods:* Any legal method.

Broford Fishing
Contact: P. Veale, Lance Nicholson Fishing, Tackle & Guns, 9 High Street, Dulverton, *Tel:* 01398 323409, *Water:* Approx. 5 miles bank fishing on Little Exe. *Species:* Wild Brown Trout with occasional Salmon. *Permits:* As above. *Charges:* £12 per day - Trout. £25 per day - Salmon. *Season:* 15th March - 30th September. *Methods:* Fly Only for Trout. Any legal method for Salmon.

Dulverton Angling Association
Contact: P. Veale, Lance Nicholson Fishing, Tackle & Guns, 9 High Street, Dulverton, *Tel:* 01398 323409, *Water:* Approx. 5 miles bank on Exe & Haddeo. Membership open to all. *Species:* Brown Trout & Salmon. *Permits:* No charge - Members only. *Charges:* Adults £25. Junior £1 (all juniors under 16 must be accompanied by an adult). *Season:* 15th March - 30th September. *Methods:* Any legal method.

Exe Valley Fishery (River Exe)
Contact: Andrew Maund, Exebridge, Dulverton, *Tel:* 01398 323008, *Water:* Half a mile of single bank on the Exe. Three fly only lakes at Dulverton. *Species:* Salmon Trout and Grayling. *Permits:* Day Tickets from Exe Valley Fishery. *Charges:* Contact for details. *Season:* EA Byelaws apply. *Methods:* Trout and Grayling fly only. Salmon fly or spinner.

ISLE

The River Isle rises near Wadeford and soon after its source is joined by a tributary from Chard Lake. Trout are found as far as Ilminster but below the town coarse fish predominate. The profile of the river is fairly natural though a number of shallow weirs provide increased depth in places. Species caught in the lower stretches include Chub, Dace and Roach.

Chard & District Angling Club
Contact: John Barron, *Tel:* 01460 63593, *Water:* Approx. 1.5 miles on the river Isle. Also Perry Street Pond, see entry under Stillwater Coarse. *Species:* Dace, Roach, Chub, Perch, Bream, Gudgeon. *Permits:* Barrons, Holyrood St., Chard. Tel: 01460 63593. *Season:* Closed season 14th March to 16th June on river.

Ilminster & District A.A. (River Isle)
Contact: P. Lonton, Mashala, Cottage Corner, Ilton, Ilminster, *Tel:* 01460 52519, *Water:* Approx. 6 miles on the river Isle. *Species:* Roach, Chub, Perch, Bream, Dace, Pike. *Permits:* Day tickets from Ilminster Warehouse. Membership details from the secretary. Annual membership tickets from Ilminster Warehouse, Yeovil Angling Centre, Somerset Angling, Bridgwater. *Charges:* £20 annual membership. Day tickets £4. Junior £6. O.A.P's £10. *Season:* Current E.A. Byelaws apply. *Methods:* Club rules apply.

KENN AND BLIND YEO

The New Blind Yeo is an artificial drainage channel which also carries some of the diverted water of the River Kenn. Both waters contain good Roach with Bream, Rudd, Carp, Perch, Tench and Pike.

Clevedon & District F.A.C.
Contact: Mr A Law, 3 Riverside Park, Yeo Park, Clevedon, *Tel:* 01275 856107, *Water:* 6 miles - Blind Yeo / River Kenn. *Species:* Roach, Bream, Rudd, Eels, Perch, Pike & Tench. *Permits:* NSAA Permit at all local tackle shops. *Charges:* Season - Seniors: £25, Juniors/OAP: £13; Weekly - £13; Daily - £4.50. *Season:* June 16th - March 14th inc. *Methods:* Waggler/Stick, Pole, Ledger, no live baits, no coarse fish to be used as dead bait.

KENNET AND AVON CANAL

See under Bristol Avon and tributaries

THE KINGS SEDGEMOOR DRAIN

The Kings Sedgemoor Drain is an artificial drainage channel dug c1790. As well as draining a large area of moor it also carries the diverted water of the River Cary and excess flood flows from the River Parrett. The KSD is a very well known coarse fishery and is used for both local and national match fishing competitions. Fish species present include Roach, Bream, Tench, Perch and Pike.

PARRETT

The River Parrett rises in West Dorset and there is some Trout fishing as far as Creedy Bridge upstream of the A303. Below this point a number of weirs and hatches result in deeper water and slower flows. The resulting coarse fishery contains a wide variety of species including Roach, Bream, Rudd, Chub, Dace, Carp, Crucian Carp and Pike. Similar species are found in the lowest freshwater section at Langport where the Rivers Isle and Yeo join the Parrett to form a wide deep river which becomes tidal below Oath Sluice.

Langport & District Angling Association ♿
Contact: Den Barlow, Florissant, Northfield, Somerton, *Tel:* 01458 272119, *Water:* 5 miles on the river Parrett. Coombe Lake - 2.75 acres, no closed season for lake. Normal closed season applies to river *Species:* All common coarse species except Barbel. *Permits:* Fosters Newsagency, Bow Street, Langport. *Charges:* Annual £15, junior £7, disabled/OAP £6. Weekly £5. Senior day £3, Junior day £1 for river only. *Season:* Closed season on river only. Membership from 16th June to 15th June inc. Night fishing permitted on river only from Langport A.A. controlled banks. *Methods:* Lake: Barbless hooks, No boilies, No Carp in keepnets.

Somerset Levels Association of Clubs
Contact: Newton Abbot Fishing Association, Adam Bojar (Hon. Secretary), PO Box 1, Bovey Tracey, Newton Abbot, Devon. *Tel:* 01626 834032, *Water:* See entry under Newton Abbot Fishing Association Devon, Stillwater Coarse. Rights to numerous parts of the Parret, Brue, Isle and other stretches of drain in the Langport area. *Species:* All coarse species.

Stoke Sub Hamdon & District A.A. (River)
Contact: Mr Derek Goad (Secretary), (H.Q. at Stoke Working Mens Club), 2 Windsor Lane, Stoke-Sub-Hamdon, *Tel:* 01935 824337, *Water:* Upper Stretches River Parrett approx. 10km. See also entry under Stillwater Coarse, Yeovil, Bearley Lake. *Species:* Carp, Tench, Roach, Rudd, Bream, Perch, Dace, Chub, Pike, Eel, Gudgeon, Ruffe. Trout Fishing also available. *Permits:* Season permits only. Available from Post Office, Montacute and Yeovil Angling Centre, Yeovil. Also available from secretary. *Charges:* Season tickets: Senior £15, Juniors/OAPs £8 (Bearley Lake). Juniors under 14 must be accompanied by an adult. *Season:* Trout 1st April - 31st October. Lake all year. Coarse river 16th June - 14th March. *Methods:* Trout: No maggot. River Coarse: No restrictions.

Tiverton & District Angling Club (River Parret)
Contact: Exe Valley Angling, 19 Westexe South, Tiverton, Devon. *Tel:* 01884 242275, *Water:* Various stretches on several rivers in Somerset including Isle, Brue and North Drain. See also entry under Stillwater Coarse, Devon, Tiverton. *Permits:* Please ring Exe Valley for details. Also available from: Exeter Angling Centre, Enterprise Angling Taunton, Topp Tackle Taunton & Minnows Caravan Park - beside Grand Western Canal *Charges:* Senior: Day £5, Annual £25. Conc: Junior & OAP Day £3, Annual £12. *Season:* Coarse: closed 15th March to 16th June. Trout: open from 15th March to 30th September. Salmon: open 14th February to 30th September.

SOMERSET FROME

See under Bristol Avon and tributaries

TONE

The River Tone rises on the edge of Exmoor National Park and not far from its source it feeds into and out of Clatworthy reservoir. From here to Taunton there are some twenty miles of fast flowing Trout river, though Grayling, Dace and Roach appear near Taunton where weirs provide increased depth. Through the town and just below, Chub, Dace and Roach predominate but at Bathpool the river becomes wider, deeper and slower. Roach, Bream, Carp, Tench and Pike are the typical species in this stretch which continues to the tidal limit at New Bridge.

Taunton Angling Association (Tone)
Contact: Matthew Hawkins, 70 Tone Hill, Tonedale, Wellington, *Tel:* 01823 664388, *Mobile:* 07748 642004, *Water:* 6 miles on River Tone (See also entries under Taunton and Bridgwater Canal & Stillwater Coarse). *Species:* Roach 2lb, Pike 3lb, Dace 1lb, Bream 10lb, Tench 5lb, Perch 3lb, Carp 30lb, Grayling 2.5lb, Chub 6.5lb. *Charges:* Season £34. Day tickets £5 senior, £3 junior. *Season:* Closed from 14th March to 16th June. *Methods:* All fish (including Pike and Eels) to be returned alive.

Wellington Angling Association
Contact: Grahame Woodward, 1 Waterloo Rd, Wellington, *Tel:* 01823 663236, *Water:* Approx. 3 miles on River Tone. Both banks from Holywell Lake to Nynhead. *Species:* Brown Trout. *Permits:* Membership only. *Charges:* Joining fee £15, annual membership £12. *Season:* As EA season - 1 April to end October. *Methods:* No spinning.

WEST SEDGEMOOR DRAIN

This artificial channel was excavated in the 1940s on the lines of existing watercourses. Coarse fish species present include Bream, Roach, Tench and Carp.

Taunton Angling Association (W. Sedgemoor Drain) ♿
Contact: Matthew Hawkins, 70 Tone Hill, Tonedale, Wellington, *Tel:* 01823 664388, *Mobile:* 07748 642004, *Water:* 2 miles of West Sedgemoor Drain, easy access for disabled anglers (also see entries under Stillwater Coarse). *Species:* Bream 7lb, Roach 2.5lb, Eels 2lb, Tench 8lb, Pike 29lb, Perch 2lb, Rudd 2lb, Carp 26lb. *Charges:* Season £34. Day tickets £5 senior, £3 junior. *Season:* Closed from 14th March to 16th June. *Methods:* All fish (including Pike and Eels) to be returned alive.

Remember a ♿ means the fishery has disabled facilities - contact them direct for further details

YEO

The River Yeo rises near Sherborne and between here and Yeovil the river is a coarse fishery, though tributaries such as the River Wriggle have Brown Trout. Below Yeovil a number of weirs produce areas of deep water and the resulting fishery contains good Dace together with Roach, Chub, Bream and Pike.

Ilchester & District A.A.
Contact: Mr B Bushell (Chairman), 1 Friars Close, Ilchester, Yeovil, *Tel:* 01935 840767, *Water:* River Yeo above and below Ilchester. *Species:* Chub, Roach, Dace, Bream, Gudgeon, Tench, Perch and Carp. *Permits:* Tackle shops in Yeovil. Yeovil Angling Centre. Ilchester Post Office. From Club Chairman at above address. *Charges:* Season ticket £12. OAP/junior £6. Weekly ticket £5. *Season:* Open 16th June to 15th March. *Methods:* Current E.A. Byelaws apply. Club rules on ticket and fishery map.

Mudford Angling Club
Water: 3.5 miles double bank on river Yeo. *Species:* Chub, Bream, Dace, Roach. *Charges:* Club membership available from Yeovil District Angling Centre: 01935 476777.

N. Somerset Association of Anglers
Contact: Mr Newton, 64 Clevedon Rd, Tickenham, Clevedon, *Tel:* 01275 856107, *Water:* Blind Yeo, Kenn, Brue, Apex Lake, Newtown Ponds & Walrow Ponds, Tickenham Boundry Rhyne, North Drain (also see entry Stillwater, Coarse, Highbridge). *Species:* Roach, Bream, Eels, Perch, Rudd, Carp, Pike, Tench. *Permits:* NSAA Permits available at all local Tackle Shops. *Charges:* Season: Seniors £25. Juniors/OAP/ Disabled £13. Weekly: £13. Day £4.50. *Season:* June 16th - March 14th inclusive. Apex Lake & Newtown Ponds: closed March 1st - 31st inclusive. *Methods:* Apex Lake and Newtown Ponds: Barbless hooks, No live or dead baits, no floating baits, min. breaking strain line 2.5lb.

Northover Manor Water
Contact: Mark Haddigan, Ilchester, *Tel:* 01935 840447, *Water:* 50 yards single back fishing on the Yeo. *Species:* Roach, Bream and Carp. *Charges:* Please enquire at Reception. *Season:* E.A. Byelaws.

Yeovil & Sherborne Angling Association (River Club Card)
Contact: Pete Coombes, 44 Monksdale, Yeovil, *Tel:* 01935 427873, *Water:* 4 miles rivers, Discounted tickets Viaduct Fishery. Long Load Drain. Halfway House Inn Pond, 0.5 acres, Near Yeovil. *Species:* Roach, Bream, Carp, Dace Chub, Perch, Rudd, Tench. *Permits:* Membership details from above & local tackle shops. *Charges:* No day tickets. River Club card £12, £2 off cost of day ticket at Viaduct. Contact the above or local tackle shops. Sherbourne lake seperate licence needed, but will cover for all club waters. *Season:* 16 June to 14 March on non enclosed stillwaters.

Stillwater Coarse

BATH

Bath Anglers Association

Contact: Andy Smith, 68 Bloomfield Rise, Odd Down, Bath, *Tel:* 01225 834736, *Water:* Regular matches, open to all in region. Fishing amalgamation waters. *Charges:* Contact above, or Dave Bacon at Bacons Tackle - 01225 448850. Membership free, but must be member of Amalgamated Fisheries Ltd. Adults & Children welcome.

Bathampton Angling Association

Contact: Dave Crookes, 25 Otago Terrace, Larkhall, Bath, *Tel:* 01225 427164, *Water:* Small pond at Weston village in Bath. *Species:* Carp to 10lb, Roach to 1.5lb, Bream to 2lb, Hybrids to 1lb, Tench to 4lb. *Permits:* Bacons Tackle Box, 83 Lower Bristol Road, Bath. Avon Aquatics, Willsbridge Rd., Bristol. Scott Tackle, 42 Soundwell Rd., Bristol. *Charges:* Adults £25, Juniors £8, O.A.P £7. Registered disabled £7, Under 12's free. Members only special day permits must be purchased in advance at £2 p/day. *Season:* Open all year. *Methods:* Special rules apply. Available from secretary, on website, from shop.

Bathampton Angling Association (Huntstrete Ponds) ♿

Contact: Dave Crookes, 25 Otago Terrace, Larkhall, Bath, *Tel:* 01225 427164, *Water:* 3 lake complex at Hunstrete, near Pensford. Total 11 acres 120 pegs. *Species:* Bream to 8.5lbs, Chub to 2.5lbs, Roach to 2.5lbs, Pike to 22lbs, Carp to 32lbs plus, Tench to 10.5lbs, Perch to 2.5lbs, Crucians to 2lbs, Eels to 7lbs. *Permits:* Local fishing tackle shops (members only). *Charges:* Adults £25, Juniors £8, O.A.P £7. Registered disabled £7, Under 12's free. Additional special day permit at £3.00 must be obtained before fishing. *Season:* Open all year fishing times vary according to time of year. No night fishing. *Methods:* Copies of rules available from secretary and tackle shops. Also displayed on notice boards at lakeside, and on website.

Bathampton Angling Association (Newton Park Pond)

Contact: Dave Crookes, 25 Otago Terrace, Larkhall, Bath, *Tel:* 01225 427164, *Water:* 2.5 acre lake at Newton Park, near Bath. *Species:* Bream to 2.5lbs, Chub to 7lbs, Roach to 3lbs+, Pike to 24lbs, Carp to 27lbs. *Permits:* Local fishing tackle shops (members only). *Charges:* Adults £25, Juniors £8, O.A.P £7. Registered disabled £7, Under 12's free. Additional special day permit at £3 must be obtained before fishing. Members only. *Season:* Open all year fishing times vary according to time of year. No night fishing. *Methods:* Copies of rules available from secretary and tackle shops. Also displayed on notice boards at lakeside, and on website.

Farleigh Wood Fishery (Coarse)

Wood Cottage, Tellisford, Bath, *Tel:* 01373 831495, *Water:* 1 acre coarse fishing lake. *Species:* Carp to double figures. *Charges:* £5 a day. *Season:* Open all year. Car Park. *Methods:* List of rules at fishery.

BRIDGWATER

Beeches Fishery

Contact: Andrew Bradbury, *Tel:* 01278 423545, *Water:* 9 ponds set in 5 acres of designated county wildlife site. *Species:* Carp (Crucians, Common, Mirror), Roach, Rudd, Tench, Perch and Eels. *Permits:* Limited day tickets, only available in advance from Andrew Bradbury on the above telephone number. *Charges:* Valid EA rod licence required. *Season:* Close season - March to June. No night fishing.

Bridgwater Angling Association (Coarse Lakes) ♿

Contact: Mr A Danahy, 127 The Old Basin, Somerset Bridge, Bridgwater, *Tel:* 01278 457022, *Water:* See entry under Taunton and Bridgwater Canal. Various stillwaters. Stillwater fishing at Combwich, Walrow, Dunwear & Screech Owl *Species:* All types of Coarse Fish. *Permits:* Available from Tackle outlets throughout Somerset area including Somerset Angling, 74 Bath Road, Bridgwater, Tel; 01278 431777. Megabaits Unit H Cartwright Business Park, Colley Lane, Bridgwater, Tel; 01278 424614. Watts News, Edward Street, Bridgwater, Tel; 01278 422137. Scoops, 77 St Johns Street, Bridgwater. Veals Tackle 1a Church Street, Highbridge, Tel; 01278 786934. *Charges:* Adult 1 rod £30, 2 rods £40, 3 rods £55 4 rods £70. Senior citizens 1 rod £20, 2 rods £27.50, 3 rods £40, 4 rods £50. (7-11 years) 1 rod £6. (12-17 years) 1 rod only £8 + £10 for 2 rods. Disabled 1 rod £20, 2 rods £27.50, 3 rods £40, 4 rods £50. Day ticket £6. 7 day ticket £25. *Season:* Open all year except Screech Owl (traditional Coarse close season). *Methods:* Disabled access at all lakes except Screech Owl. No reserving swims.

Bridgwater Sports & Social Club

Contact: Duncan, Danny or Nick, Bath Road, Bridgwater, *Tel:* 01278 446215, *Mobile:* 07811 359677, *Water:* 3 large ponds. *Species:* Carp to 30lb, Crucian to 3lb, Bream 6-7lb, Roach to 2lb, Perch 5-6lb, Tench to 7lb. *Charges:* £30/person - private members fishing. Limited day tickets available. *Season:* No closed season. *Methods:* No night fishing.

Browns Pond
Contact: Phil Dodds, Off Taunton Rd (A38), Bridgwater, *Tel:* 01278 444145, *Water:* 2.5 acres. *Species:* Carp to 22lb, Tench to 5lb, Bream to 6lb, Perch to 2lb & Roach. *Charges:* On site. £2 per day. *Season:* Closed May, open June 1st - April 30th; dawn to dusk. *Methods:* No night fishing, barbless hooks only, no live bait, no Carp sacks.

Burton Springs Fishery (Coarse Lake)
Contact: Tony Evans, Lawson Farm, Burton, Nr Stogursey, Bridgwater, *Tel:* 01278 732135, *Mobile:* 07804 210303, *Water:* Approx. 2 acre lake. *Species:* Mirror, Common, Leather Carp, Ghost Carp to 30lb, Tench to 5 lb, Perch to 3.5lbs. *Permits:* Self Service at fishing lodge. *Charges:* £8 per day, 2 rods, £15 for 24hrs. Night fishing strictly by arrangement. *Season:* Open all year 8am - 9pm or dusk. Night fishing by arrangement. *Methods:* Barbless hooks only, no nuts.

Durleigh Reservoir
Contact: Wessex Water, *Tel:* 0845 600 4600, *Water:* 80 acre reservoir *Species:* Carp, Roach, Bream, Perch, Tench and Pike *Permits:* Contact Ranger Paul Martin on 01278 424786 *Charges:* Day Ticket £6, Day Concession £4, Evening Ticket £4, Book of Tickets £45 for 10 *Season:* Open all year except Christmas day, Boxing day, New Years Eve and day.

Plum Lane Fishery
Contact: Mrs J. Goodland, Plum Lane, Dunwear, Bridgwater, *Tel:* 01278 421625, *Water:* 1 acre pond. *Species:* Predominately Carp to 10lb plus Tench. Roach and Skimmers. *Permits:* On site. *Charges:* £5 per adult (1 rod). *Season:* Open all year. *Methods:* Barbless hooks only. No keepnets. No Braid. Advice available on site.

Summerhayes Fishery ♿
Contact: Peter Wakelin, Somerset Bridge, Huntworth, *Tel:* 01278 451043, *Mobile:* 07866 557896, *Water:* Several lakes - totalling 6 acres. *Species:* Carp to 22lb, Bream, Tench, Roach, Rudd, Perch, Ghost Carp to 16lb. *Charges:* On bank £6 day, £4.50 Concessions. Disabled access. *Season:* Open all year dawn to dusk. *Methods:* Barbless hooks, no nuts. Maximum 2 rods.

Taunton Road Ponds
Contact: Phil Dodds, Off Taunton Rd (A38), Bridgwater, *Tel:* 01278 444145, *Mobile:* TA6 4QE, *Water:* 3.5 acres. *Species:* Large Carp to 32lb, Tench to 6lb, Bream to 13lb 6oz, Perch to 3lb, Rudd to 2lb, Skimmer Bream to 12oz & Roach to 8oz. *Charges:* On site, £2 per day. *Season:* Closed May, open June 1st - April 30th. Dawn to dusk. *Methods:* No night fishing, barbless hooks only, no live bait, no Carp in keepnets, no Carp sacks.

The Sedges ♿
Contact: Jamie & Denise Cook, River Lane, Dunwear, Bridgwater, *Tel:* 01278 445221, *Mobile:* 07980 128404, *Water:* 3 lakes totalling 6.5 acres. *Species:* Perch, Tench, Rudd, Roach, Bream, Carp to 20lb. *Charges:* On bank: £6 adult day, children accompanied by adult £6. OAPs/Disabled £6. *Season:* Open all year dawn to dusk. No entry before 6am. *Methods:* No Carp sacks, barbless hooks only, unhooking mats to be used. Strictly no nuts or boilies.

Trinity Waters ♿
Contact: John and Sue Herring, Trinity Waters, Straight Drove, Chilton Trinity, Bridgwater, *Tel:* 01278 450880, *Mobile:* 07720 542141, *Water:* Currently 5 lakes: 6.5 acres, 3 acres, 2 acre and 1acre. *Species:* Rudd to 2lb. Roach to 2lb. Perch to 3lb. Tench to 8lb. Golden Tench to 5lb. Bream to 11lb. Mirror, Common to 20lb and Grass Carp to 23lb. Mirror and Common to 30lb

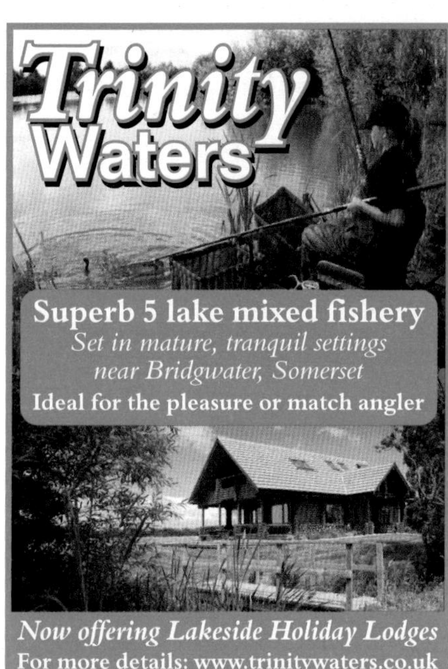

in specimen lake. Plus Chub, Barbel and F1's now introduced. *Permits:* On site only. *Charges:* £5 per day, £7.50 for two rods. £3 juniors and concessions. Match rates on request. Specimen Lake £15 day, £25 for 24 hour, £30 for 48 hour. Wildmarsh lake 6.5 acres - £20 for 24hrs, £30 for 48hrs. *Season:* Open all year dawn to dusk. *Methods:* Barbless hooks. No keepnets. No fixed rigs. Nets can be hired for £1 a day.

BRISTOL

Alcove Angling Club ♿

Contact: Ian Chapple, 255 Forest Road, Fishponds, Bristol, *Tel:* 01179 658280, *Mobile:* 07714 302031, *Water:* 4 lakes in Bristol & South Glos. One has pegs suitable for disabled, however gated access to car park. Please telephone for further information. *Species:* Carp 28lb, Bream 8lb, Roach, Tench 8lb, Rudd, Pike over 20lb, Perch. *Permits:* As above. *Charges:* Annual memberships: Adult £47. Partners of members £11, Children under 12 free, Junior 12 to 16 £16. OAP £28. Disabled £28 (helper £11). Children under 14 must be accompanied by an adult at all times. *Season:* No close season. *Methods:* As specified in membership card, Night fishing at Alcove Lido only. Barbless hooks or Micro Barb only.

Amalgamated Fisheries Ltd (Lakes)

Contact: Jeff Parker, 16 Lansdown View, Kingswood, Bristol, *Tel:* 0117 9672977, *Water:* See entry under Bristol Avon - Various stillwaters, too much to list here, please contact the secretary for full details; Stillwaters at Lyneham, Calne, Malmesbury, Bath and Pawlett near Bridgwater. *Species:* All coarse species. *Methods:* Maximum 2 rods, no metal cans or glass allowed on banks, no freshwater fish to be used as livebait. Full rules and maps available.

Bagwood Lake

Contact: Woodland Golf Club - David Knipe, Trench Lane, Almondsbury, Bristol, *Tel:* 01454 619319, *Water:* One coarse lake. *Species:* Carp. *Permits:* On site, pay in shop. *Charges:* £9-12 hour ticket. £15-24 hour ticket. Junior £7-12 hour, £10-24 hour. Tickets valid from 7am to 7pm *Season:* Please phone prior to travelling.

Boyd Valley Lake

Contact: Avon Aquatics, Jarrets Garden Centre, The Park, Bath Road, Willsbridge, Bristol, *Tel:* 01179 327659, *Water:* 1.5 acre lake. *Species:* Carp to 15lb, Tench, Roach and Bream. *Permits:* Day tickets from Jarrets Garden Centre. *Charges:* £6 per day. *Season:* Open all year. *Methods:* Barbless hooks to be used.

Carps Angling Club

Contact: John Bennett, 30a Church Road, Hanham, Bristol, *Tel:* 01179 601597, *Water:* Match orientated club (50 Sunday matches and 48 Wednesday matches for 2008). Sunday matches open to all. Matches in Carp and silver fish lakes in the region. *Species:* Scoop matches - Big money matches up to £1500 paid out. Pairs league matches, opens, Carp matches, silver matches, all these are big money makers. You need to be a member. *Charges:* Contact John at number above. Annual membership fees: Seniors £12.50, OAP's £10, Disabled £7.50, Juniors £7.50, Ladies £7.50. No match peg fees for juniors and ladies. New members joining fee £10. *Season:* Draws at 9am. 6 hour matches. *Methods:* All matches under Carps A.C. and fishery rules.

Cross Hands Angling Club

Contact: Phillip Bond - Secretary, 25 North Street, Down End, Bristol, *Tel:* 01179 754218, *Water:* The Crest lake - 30 pegs.

Hunters lake at Clutton - 20 pegs. Ashleigh Farm, Horton, Chipping Sodbury - 35 pegs. Section of River Frome. *Species:* Carp to 16lb. Tench, Bream, Roach. *Permits:* Members only - Limited membership available from above, junior section, O.A.P Section. Total adult member - 150 max. O.A.P and Junior - unlimited. *Charges:* Junior £20 p/year, OAP £20 p/year, Seniors £55 p/year. *Season:* Open all year. Hunters Lake - closed March 14th to June 16th. *Methods:* No boilies, No groundbait, barbless hooks.

Duchess Pond

Contact: Wayne Tooker (Leaseholder), 11 Cedar Way, Pucklechurch, Bristol, *Tel:* 0117 9372001, *Mobile:* 07980 091286, *Water:* 2 acre pond. *Species:* Mixed fishery plus Carp to 30lb. *Permits:* Direct from Wayne on bank. *Charges:* £5 Adults, £3 under 16. £100 season ticket. £15 for 24hrs. *Season:* Open all year Dawn to Dusk. Night Fishing available. *Methods:* Full rules displayed at Fishery.

Eastville Park Lake

Contact: Bristol Parks, 33 Colston Avenue, Bristol, *Tel:* 01179 223719, *Species:* Recently restocked with coarse fish. *Permits:* Free fishing for responsible anglers. *Season:* Open all year. *Methods:* Fishing permitted on south side of lake only. Please respect nature reserve on opposite bank.

Ham Green Fisheries

Contact: Mr Hunt, Ham Green, Chapel Lane, Pill, *Tel:* 01275 849885, *Mobile:* 07818 640227, *Water:* Two lakes. 1 acre 25 peg. 2 acre open bank. *Species:* 1 acre lake stocked with Carp, Roach, Rudd, Perch, Pike, Bream, Skimmers, Chub, Golden Tench and Golden Orfe. 2 acre lake all the above with Carp to 35lb. *Permits:* Mr Hunt, 21 Station Rd, Portishead, Bristol; also on lake side from Baliff. Veals Tackle Shop, 61 Old Market St, Bristol. *Charges:* £5 on bank for small lake. All night fishing £15. £10 on bank for big lake. *Season:* No closed season. 7am to 8pm from 16 June to 13 October. 8am to 5pm from 1 November to 30 April. Night fishing strictly by arrangement, booking essential by telephone to Mr Hunt. *Methods:* No live bait, barbless hooks preferred, no keepnets for fish over 1lb, Carp sacks allowed. Children must be accompanied by an adult. Hooking mats to be used.

Jacklands Fishery

Contact: Mrs L P Waygood, Jacklands Bridge, Clevedon Road, Nailsea, Bristol, *Tel:* 01275 810694, *Water:* 1 acre lake. *Species:* Mixed coarse fish. *Permits:* On Site. *Charges:* £6 per day. Prices may change in 2008. *Season:* Open all year. *Methods:* No boilies, no nuts.

King William IV Angling Association ♿

Contact: Jerry Pocock, 86 Tower Road South, Warmley, Bristol, *Tel:* 01179 492974, *Mobile:* 07761 799876, *Charges:* £3 joining fee. Juniors free of charge. Further details from Jerry. *Season:* Open to all in the area. Regular meetings and matches.

Kingswood Disabled Angling Club + Over 55's ♿

Contact: Chris Goodland, 58 Hawthorne Close, Patchway, Bristol, *Tel:* 01179 754789, *Water:* Bristol based Coarse fishing club meeting monthly. New members welcome. Must be registered disabled at local Social Services Office. Regular fishing trips and matches organised. Please phone for further information. *Charges:* £7.50 adults annual membership.

Paulton Lakes

Contact: John Wiles, Ruthin Villa, High Street, High Littleton, Bristol, *Tel:* 01761 472338, *Mobile:* 07709 471414, *Water:* Two lakes located off Bristol Road, Paulton. Approx. 2.5 acres. with a total of 25 swims. *Species:* Island Lake: Carp 30lb, Roach 3lb,

Chub 10lb, Tench 6lb, Eels 6lb. King Lake: Carp 12lb, Grass Carp, Crucian Carp, Tench 8lb, Chub 8lb, Roach 3lb, Rudd. *Permits:* Day tickets available from A.M. Hobbs, The Island, Midsomer Norton. Tel: (01761) 413961 and from Central Garage, High Street, Paulton. Tickets MUST be purchased in advance - not available on the bank. *Charges:* £7 per day ticket. Concessions for juniors/seniors. Season tickets available. *Season:* Closed Easter Monday to June 16th. Fishing from dawn to one hour after dusk. Night fishing by syndicate members only. *Methods:* Full details on ticket. Barbless hooks, no Carp in keepnets, unhooking mats must be used, no pre-baiting or ground baiting.

Royal British Legion Kingswood

Contact: Mr Lloyd, 386 Speedwell Road, Kingswood, Bristol, *Tel:* 0117 9676030, *Mobile:* 07831 311582, *Water:* Fishing on rivers and stillwaters. Open to all anglers - especially Royal British Legion members, regular matches.

Saint Georges Park Lake

Contact: Bristol Parks, 33 Colston Avenue, Bristol, *Tel:* 01179 223719, *Water:* Small lake. *Species:* Stocked with coarse fish. *Permits:* Free fishing for responsible anglers. *Season:* Open all year. *Methods:* Fishing permitted on south side of lake only. Please respect nature reserve on opposite bank.

Tan House Farm Lake

Contact: Mr & Mrs James, Tan House Farm, Yate, Bristol, *Tel:* 01454 228280, *Water:* Quarter mile lake. *Species:* Roach, Perch, Carp, Bream, Tench, Rudd. *Permits:* Day tickets from Farm House. *Charges:* Adult £5 per rod plus £1 for extra rods, Children & O.A.Ps £4. *Season:* Closed April 13th - May 23rd 2008. *Methods:* No Ground bait, dog & cat food, boilies, barbless hooks only. No Trout pellets.

Westcountry Disabled Angling Association ♿

Contact: Richard Day, *Tel:* 01179 832 632, *Water:* Open to all adult disabled anglers and children (must be accompanied by an adult). Fishing different venues throughout the south west region and taking part in national competitions. Alternative contact Ian Darke on 01225 336371. *Charges:* £5 p/a membership, plus peg fees.

Westcountry Waterpark

Contact: Mike Thompson, The Lake, Trench lake, Winterbourne, Bristol, *Tel:* 01454 773599, *Mobile:* 07811 108587, *Water:* 12 acre lake. *Species:* Carp. *Permits:* National. *Charges:* £10 per day (£5 smaller lakes). *Season:* Tel for details as each day varies. *Methods:* Barbless hooks, no keepnets.

BURNHAM-ON-SEA

Burnham-on-Sea Holiday Village

Burnham-on-Sea Holiday Village, Marine Drive, Burnham-on-Sea, *Tel:* 01278 783391, *Water:* Two lakes. First lake about 2.5 acres. Second around 4 acres. *Species:* Both lakes hold Carp up to 30lb, Bream 10lb 2oz, Tench 7lb 6oz, Eels 6lb 9oz, Roach 1lb, Rudd 1lb, Pike 20lb 3oz and Perch to 1lb. *Permits:* Essentials shop on site (Tel 01278 783156). *Charges:* £5.00 per day or £14 for 3 days. *Season:* Open all year. *Methods:* Barbless hooks only, No Carp over 10lb in keepnets, Night fishing by bookings only, Noise kept to a minimum.

Highbridge Angling Association (Apex Lake)

Contact: Mr C Brewer, 8 Willow Close, East Huntspill, Near Highbridge, *Tel:* 01278 786230, *Water:* Apex lake, Marine drive, Burnham-on-sea. *Species:* Mixed coarse fish. Carp to 20lb, Bream to 8lb, Roach to 3lb and Chub to 5lb. *Permits:* From local tackle dealers. *Charges:* Day tickets £3, 7 day ticket £10 or season ticket £20. Senior citizen £10. *Methods:* No night fishing.

CHARD

Chard & District Angling Club (Coarse Lakes)

Contact: John Barron, *Tel:* 01460 63593, *Water:* Perry Street Pond - 1.5 acres. Chard Reservoir - 48 acres. Sadborough Pond near Thorncombe. Also 1.5 miles on Isle see entry under River Fishing. *Species:* Roach, Bream, Carp, Tench, Perch, Eels, Rudd. *Permits:* Perry Street Ponds - members only, Membership details from Barrons, Holyrood St., Chard. Tel: 01460 63593 *Charges:* Chard reservoir £8 per day on the bank (£6 club members). Perry Street ponds free to members only. *Season:* Open all year. *Methods:* Full list of rules from fishery notice board and membership book.

Monster 'Cat' from Todber

Chard Reservoir
Contact: John Barron, *Water:* 48 acre reservoir. *Species:* Coarse fish. *Permits:* On the bank. *Charges:* 24 hour ticket - £8 non members. £6 members of Chard and District A.C. contact: Barrons, Holyrood Street, Chard. Tel: 01460 63593

CHEDDAR
Cheddar Angling Club
Contact: Cheddar Angling Club, P.O. Box 1183, Cheddar, *Tel:* 01934 743959, *Water:* 200 acre Cheddar reservoir. *Species:* Pike, Perch, Tench, Roach, Eels, Carp. *Permits:* Permits are NOT available at the reservoir. Only from: Broadway House Caravan Park, Axbridge Road, Cheddar, Somerset. Bristol Angling Centre, 12-16 Doncaster Road, Southmead, Bristol. Thatchers Pet and Tackle, 18 Queen St, Wells. Veals Fishing Tackle, 61 Old Market St., Bristol. Thyers Fishing Tackle, Church St., Highbridge. *Charges:* Seniors season permit £45, Juniors season permit £20, Seniors day permit £6, Juniors day permit £3. *Season:* No closed season. *Methods:* No live baiting, Moderate ground baiting, No dead baiting 16th June - 30th September. No night fishing. Dawn to dusk only. Unhooking mats recommended. Rod limits: seniors maximum 3 rods, juniors one rod only.

COLEFORD
Breach Valley Fishing
Contact: Lower Vobster, Coleford, Radstock, *Tel:* 01373 812352, *Mobile:* 07950 771219, *Water:* 2 ponds totalling 1.5 acres approx. *Species:* Carp to 28lb, Roach, Tench, Perch and Bream. *Charges:* Day tickets on bank £7. *Season:* Open June 14th to end of March, dawn to dusk. *Methods:* No keepnets, no boilies, barbless hooks.

CONGRESBURY
Silver Springs Fish Farm ♿
Contact: Liz Patch, Silver Street Lane, Congresbury, *Tel:* 01934 877073, *Mobile:* 07837 809005, *Water:* General coarse lake: 4.5 acres. Specimen Carp lake: 2.5 acres. *Species:* General: Carp to mid twenties, Rudd, Roach to 3lbs, Tench, Chub, Bream, Perch and Gudgeon. Specimen: Mirrors and commons to high 20's/low 30's. *Permits:* General & specimen: On site. *Charges:* General: £5 / £3.50 conc. Specimen: £8 & £5 full and concessionary respectively. *Season:* General: All year dawn till half hour before dusk. Specimen: All year *Methods:* General: Barbless hooks. Specimen: No poles, no keepnets, no nuts, barbless hooks only.

CORFE
Taunton Angling Association (Wych Lodge Lake)
Contact: Matthew Hawkins, 70 Tone Hill, Tonedale, Wellington, *Tel:* 01823 664388, *Mobile:* 07748 642004, *Water:* Wych Lodge Lake, 3 acre large Carp lake (also see entries under River & Canal Fishing). *Species:* Large Carp up to 12lb, Grass Carp 12lb, Roach, Tench 2lb, Rudd and Perch all to 2lb. *Permits:* Only from Topp Tackle, Taunton (restricted to 10 pegs). Please bring season ticket as proof of membership when purchasing day permit. Separate day ticket available for non season ticket holders. *Charges:* £3 per day. £6 for non season ticket holders. *Season:* Closed until November 2008 then open all year. *Methods:* Barbless hooks, no Carp in keepnets, no lighting of fires, no litter.

CREWKERNE
Highlands Dairy Lake ♿
Contact: J.Wyatt, Highlands Dairy Farm, Hewish, Crewkerne, *Tel:* 01460 74180, *Water:* Two 1 acre lakes and one 0.5 acre lake. *Species:* Carp, Tench, Rudd, Roach, Perch. *Permits:* At house. *Charges:* £4 per day. £5 to include night fishing. *Season:* Open all year. *Methods:* No keepnets for Carp. Barbless hooks only.
Water Meadow Fishery
Contact: Mr. Pike, Trindlewell Cottage, North Perrott, Crewkerne, *Tel:* 01460 74673, *Water:* 2 coarse lakes totalling approx. 1.75 acres. *Species:* 16 different varieties of coarse fish. *Charges:* On site - £5 day. *Season:* Open all year - dawn to dusk. *Methods:* No boilies or keepnets, barbless hooks only, ground baiting in moderation.

FROME

Barrow Farm Pond

Contact: John Nicholls, Barrow Farm, Witham Friary, Frome, *Tel:* 01749 850313, *Mobile:* 07734 978988, *Water:* Half acre lake. Re-stocked in 2006. *Species:* Carp, Perch and Tench. *Charges:* £5 adult. £3.50 children and OAPs. *Season:* February to September. Phone for details. *Methods:* No restrictions.

Edneys Fisheries ♿

Contact: Richard Candy, Edneys Farm, Mells, Frome, *Tel:* 01373 812294, *Mobile:* 07941 280075, *Water:* 3 lakes. Hard standing and parking at all lakes. *Species:* Carp to 30lb, Tench to 9lb, Roach, Rudd, Golden Rudd, Perch, Common, Mirror, Linear, Leather and Ghost Carp. Golden Orf and Blue Orf to 6lb in lake 2. In lake 2 and 3 there are Chub. *Permits:* Yearly tickets £85 Adults, £65 Under 14. *Charges:* Adults £6, Under 14 yrs £4. Night tickets available at £5 for all. Prices may change in 2008. *Season:* 24hrs a day, 365 days a year. *Methods:* Barbless hooks, no nuts, no feeding of boilies, no fish over 2lb in keepnets.

Frome Angling Association (Coarse Lake)

Contact: Gary Collinson, 2 Bath Street, Frome, *Tel:* 01373 471437, *Mobile:* 07958495283, *Water:* 10 acre lake. 12 miles river Frome - see entry under River Fishing Somerset. *Permits:* Please ring Gary Collinson 01373 471437.

Witham Friary Lakes

Contact: Mr. Miles, Witham Hall Farm, Witham Friary, Nr Frome, *Tel:* 01373 836239, *Water:* Two lakes totalling approx. 2 acres. *Species:* Carp, Roach, Tench, Perch, Gudgeon. *Permits:* On site. *Charges:* £5 a day - £7 night ticket (dusk - 8 am). *Season:* All year. *Methods:* Barbless hooks only.

GLASTONBURY

Glaston Manor Angling Association (Moorland Fishery)

Contact: Adam Mitchell, NFU Office, 1 Sadler Street, Wells, *Tel:* 01749 673786, *Water:* Moorland Fishery (stillwater), Meare and Burtle Ponds, Burtle (3 ponds in about 12 acres). See also entry under River Fishing, Brue. *Species:* Tench, Carp, Bream, Roach, Rudd, Perch, Crucian. *Permits:* Thatchers Tackle, Wells, Tel: 01749 673513 or Street Angling Centre, High St, Street, Somerset Tel: 01458 447830. *Charges:* No day tickets on stillwaters, Junior membership £9, Senior membership £28, OAP and disabled £14, Junior Disabled £4.50. *Season:* Current E.A. byelaws apply. *Methods:* Full rules on permit.

HIGHBRIDGE

Emerald Pool Fishery ♿

Contact: Mr Alan Wilkinson, Emerald Pool Fishery, Puriton Road, West Huntspill, Highbridge, *Tel:* 01278 794707, *Mobile:* 07974 862503, *Water:* 4 lakes in total. 1.5 acre lake, plus 'Sapphire Lake' - 20 peg disabled angler friendly pool for adults and juniors. Jade 30 pegs, Ruby 21 pegs, 108 pegs now on site. *Species:* Bream, Golden Orfe, Roach, Rudd, Tench, Perch, Barbel 5lb. Emerald Lake - Small Carp to 11lb. Jade 30 pegs, Carp, Barbel, Bream and Tench. Sapphire Lake Carp 10lb, Tench 5lb. Ruby Lake 1 to 5lb Carp. *Permits:* Enviroment Agency rod licence required on this water. *Charges:* £6 one rod. £1 for additional rods per person. *Season:* All year. *Methods:* Barbless hooks only, no Carp sacks, no fixed rigs, no tiger nuts. Please do not leave rods unattended. Groundbait allowed in moderation. See owners regarding keepnets.

Highbridge Angling Association (Coarse Lakes)

Contact: Mr C Brewer, 8 Willow Close, East Huntspill, Near Highbridge, *Tel:* 01278 786230, *Water:* 3 Lakes at Walrow. *Species:* Carp to mid 30's, Pike to mid 20's, Bream to 12lb, Tench to double figures and all other coarse species. *Permits:* Thyers Tackle, Highbridge - 01278 786934. Also available from other local tackle shops. *Charges:* Day tickets £3, 7 day ticket £10 or season ticket £20. Senior citizen £10. Night fishing £5. Day tickets from, Thyers Tackle, Highbridge, 01278 786934 *Season:* Open all year.

N. Somerset Association of Anglers (Coarse Lakes)

Contact: Mr Newton, 64 Clevedon Rd, Tickenham, Clevedon, *Tel:* 01275 856107, *Water:* See also entry under Yeo. Apex lake: 6 acre lake, Newtown: 3 acre lake, Walrow ponds: 2 acre lake, 3 acre lake and 6 acre lake. *Species:* Apex: Carp to 18lbs, Bream to 7lb, Pike to 15lb, Roach, Rudd. Newtown: Carp to

Emerald Pool Fishery

Quality fishing on four varied and well managed lakes

Emerald - *1.5 acre lake stocked with Carp to 22lb, Sturgeon to 4' long, Tench, Perch, Bream, Golden Orfe, Barbel to 5lb, Roach and Rudd*

Sapphire - *20 peg pool, stocked with the same fish as Emerald, with the exception of Barbel*

Jade - *30 pegs - stocked with large Carp, Barbel, Bream and Tench*

Ruby - *24 pegs - heavily stocked with Common, and Mirror Carp*

Excellent Disabled Facilities

Two Self Catering Holiday Cottages beside the lake.

PLUS FOUR NEW COTTAGES COMING IN 2008

 **Disabled Friendly** 

For further details contact

Mr Alan Wilkinson, Emerald Pool Fishery, Puriton Rd, West Huntspill, Highbridge, Somerset.

Just follow the brown Emerald Pool signs from the main A38

Tel: 01278 794707 or 0797 486 2503

108 PEGS ON SITE!

www.emeraldpool.co.uk

24lb, Pike to 27lb, Bream 7lb, Roach, Rudd, Perch. Walrow: Carp to 26lb, Bream 11lb, Tench 10lb, Pike 24lb, Roach, Rudd, Perch. *Permits:* Local tackle shops, purchased in advance of fishing. *Charges:* £4.50 day, £13 week, £25 season, junior/OAP/disabled £13. *Season:* Apex & Newtown Lakes - closed March 1st - 31st inclusive. Walrow Pond - open all year. *Methods:* Apex & Newtown Lakes: Barbless hooks, min. 2.5lb BS line, no live or dead bait, no floating bait.

ILMINSTER

Ilminster & District A.A. (Coarse Lake)

Contact: P. Lonton, Mashala, Cottage Corner, Ilton, Ilminster, *Tel:* 01460 52519, *Water:* Dillington Estate Pond. 200 yards on canal at Ilminster Recreation Grounds. *Species:* Carp, Roach, Chub, Perch, Bream, Tench, Crucians. *Permits:* Ilminster Warehouse, Yeovil Angling Centre. Membership details from the Secretary. *Charges:* Day tickets £4. £20 annual membership. £10 Oap/disabled. Junior £6. *Season:* Open all year. *Methods:* Club rules apply.

KEYNSHAM

Avon Valley Country Park (Coarse Pond)

Bath Rd, Keynsham, Bristol, *Tel:* 0117 9864929, *Water:* Small Coarse pond. *Species:* Carp to 12lb. *Permits:* From above. *Charges:* £6.50 Adult entrance to park (includes ticket to fish), £6 Child, £6 Senior Citizen. *Season:* Park open: Easter - 1st November 10am-6pm. *Methods:* Barbless hooks only, no keepnets.

Keynsham Angling Association (Coarse Lake)

Contact: Keynsham Angling Association, PO Box 137, Bristol, *Tel:* 07788 981061, *Water:* Century Ponds two lakes 0.6 acres each, see also entry under river Chew. *Species:* Mixed fishery with Carp to over 20lb, Tench, Crucians, Bream, Roach, Gudgeaon etc. *Charges:* Day ticket for club members £3.50. Available from Keynsham Angling Centre Tel: 01179 867507. *Season:* Open all year dawn to dusk. Closed alternate Sunday mornings until 1pm. See website for further details. *Methods:* Barbless hooks. No Carp in keepnets. Two rods maximum per angler.

KINGSTON SEYMOUR

Bullock Farm Fishing Lakes ♿

Contact: Philip & Jude Simmons, Bullock Farm, Back Lane, Kingston Seymour, *Tel:* 01934 835020, *Water:* 5 Lakes totalling 6.25 acres, including specialist Carp lake. *Species:* Carp - Common, Mirror, Ghost, Crucian, Grass, Purple and Koi. Tench, Roach, Rudd, Chub, Bream, Skimmer Bream, Golden Orfe, Golden Tench. *Permits:* Only at lakeside. *Charges:* £6 day ticket, £4 O.A.P's / Under 14s / Disabled. Season tickets & Match rates available. *Season:* Open all year round Dawn - Dusk. *Methods:* No boilies, Barbless hooks, Fish friendly keepnets only, No dogs, under 14's to be accompanied by an adult. Common sense!

Plantations Lake ♿

Contact: Mr James Travis, Middle Lane Farm, Middle Lane, Kingston Seymour,, Clevedon, *Tel:* 01934 832325, *Mobile:* 07795 104897, *Water:* 0.75 acre Carp lake, 2.5 acre coarse lake, 1.75 acre match lake open. *Species:* 12 Species of coarse fish incl. Barbel, Crucian Carp. 3 Species of Carp in Carp lake. *Charges:* £7 Adult (£1 extra rod), £5 Juniors/O.A.P's/Disabled. Half days (from 2pm) available: adult £5, juniors/OAPs £4. Please enquire for membership details. *Season:* All year. *Methods:* Barbless hooks.

LANGPORT

Langport & District Angling Association (Coarse Lake) ♿

Water: Coombe Lake - 2.75 acres. See entry under Parrett. *Species:* A few, very difficult to catch, Carp. Tench 6.5lb, Roach 1.5lb, Perch 2lb plus, Bream 7lb, Chub 4lb. *Permits:* Season ticket holders only - no day tickets. *Charges:* See entry under Parrett. *Season:* No closed season. No night fishing. *Methods:* Barbless hooks, no boilies, no Carp in keepnets.

Thorney Lakes

Contact: Richard or Ann England, Thorney Lakes, Muchelney, Langport, *Tel:* 01458 250811, *Water:* 4 acres of water. *Species:* A selection of coarse fish including large Carp. *Permits:* On the bank. *Charges:* £6 per day, £4 per half day after 4 p.m, £4 for O.A.Ps & Children under 16. *Season:* 16th March - 31st January. *Methods:* Barbless hooks, no boilies, nuts or pulses, all nets to be dipped on site, no night fishing.

Remember a ♿ means the fishery has disabled facilities - contact them direct for further details

LYMPSHAM

Cider Farm Lakes ♿

Contact: Mark Gibson, Dobunni Farm, Brean Road, Lympsham, *Tel:* 01278 751401, *Water:* Six Lake complex. Two match lakes with 85 pegs, three day ticket lakes. Regular open matches. Disabled friendly. *Species:* Carp to 20lbs, Tench, Bream, Chub, Golden Rudd, Roach. *Charges:* £6 one rod. £5 concessions. *Season:* Summer 7am - 6.45pm / Winter 8am - 5pm/Dusk. NO NIGHT FISHING. *Methods:* Tickets from farm shop, unhooking mats compulsory, nets/mats must be dipped, barbless hooks only, no fixed rigs, no braid, no dogs.

MARTOCK

Ash Ponds

Contact: Pat Rodford, Ash Ponds, Burrough Street, Ash, Martock, *Tel:* 01935 823459, *Water:* Three 1 acre ponds. *Species:* Carp to 30lb, Tench to 6lb and Bream. *Permits:* On the bank. *Charges:* £5 for 12 hours. *Season:* No closed season. *Methods:* Barbless hooks

SHEPTON MONTAGUE

Higher Farm Fishery ♿

Contact: Robert and Christina Dimond, Higher Farm, Shepton Montague, Wincanton, *Tel:* 01749 812373, *Water:* Three lakes. 2.5 acres in total. *Species:* Common, Mirror and Ghost Carp to 20lb. Green and Golden Tench, Bream, Rudd and Roach. *Permits:* All day tickets are sold on the bank. *Charges:* £5 adults. £3 under 14. Night fishing £7. *Season:* Open all year. *Methods:* No nuts, barbless hooks only. Full rules at the fishery.

SOMERTON

Viaduct Fishery ♿

Contact: Mr Steve Long, Viaduct Fishery, Cary Valley, Somerton, *Tel:* 01458 274022, *Water:* Six coarse lakes including one specimen lake. *Species:* Mirror Carp 27lb, Crucian Carp, Common Carp 23lb, Perch 4lb, Roach 1.5lb, Bream 6lb, Tench 8lb and Golden Tench, Rudd, Ruffe. *Permits:* Permits available from on site tackle shop. *Charges:* Day ticket £7, Under 16 £5, Summer Evening ticket £4.50, Winter Half day ticket £4.50. £2 charge for second rod; Match bookings taken. *Season:* All year. *Methods:* All nets to be dipped, no nuts or boilies, barbless hooks size 8 max, no fixed rigs, no braid, fishing from pegs only.

STREET

Godney Moor Ponds

Contact: Jamie Lock or Nick Hughes, Street Angling Centre, 160 High Street, Street, *Tel:* 01458 447830, *Water:* Approx. 4 acre Carp lake. 2 acre Bream/Tench lake. *Species:* Coarse fish including Carp. *Permits:* Only from Street Angling Centre. *Charges:* £7 per day (all genders). Minors are allowed if accompanied by an adult, cost negotiable. *Season:* April to February inclusive. Sunrise to sunset only. *Methods:* No nuts, 3 rods max. Carp fishing in large pond only. Barbless hooks only. Fisherman allowed in one pond at a time only.

Taunton Angling Association (Walton Ponds)

Contact: Matthew Hawkins, 70 Tone Hill, Tonedale, Wellington, *Tel:* 01823 664388, *Mobile:* 07748 642004, *Water:* Walton Ponds, 1 pond (also see entries under River & Canal Fishing). *Species:* Carp 25lb, Tench 3lb, Roach 1lb, Rudd 1lb, Pike 22.5lb. *Charges:* Season £34. Day tickets £5 senior, £3 junior. *Season:* Open all year. *Methods:* Barbless hooks, no Carp in keepnets.

TAUNTON

Follyfoot Farm

Contact: Rupert Preston, Follyfoot Farm, North Pertherton, *Tel:* 01278 662979, *Mobile:* 07748 400904, *Water:* Three acre Carp lake. *Species:* Mirror, Koi and Common to 30lb. *Permits:* Tickets to be acquired at shop or if closed ring Rupert on 07748 400904. *Charges:* £8 per day. £15 for 24 hours. *Season:* Open all year dawn to dusk. Night fishing by prior arrangement only. *Methods:* No keepnets, barbless hooks only, no dogs or radios. Full rules at the fishery. Only unhooking mats and landing nets supplied by the fishery to be used.

HBS Fishery

Contact: Mr Richard Bult, HBS Fishery, Adsborough, Near Taunton, *Tel:* 01823 412389, *Water:* Two lakes of 2.5 acres and half an acre. *Species:* Match Lake: Roach, Rudd, Carp, Tench, Bream (Carp to 15lb). Specimen Lake: 45 Carp between 10lb and 31lb. *Permits:* Syndicate membership only. *Charges:* Please enquire for details. *Season:* Open all year except a 1 month close season to allow fish to spawn. *Methods:* No nuts. Barbless hooks etc. Full rules at fishery.

Ridge Farm Fisheries

Contact: Janet and Ivan Sharland, Marshes Farm, Chipstable, Taunton, *Tel:* 01984 623319, *Water:* One 0.25 acre lake. One 0.5 acre lake. One 0.75 acre lake. *Species:* Carp 10lb and over, Ghost Common and Mirror, Bream 2lb, Golden Tench. *Charges:* £5 per day. *Methods:* No keepnets and barbless hooks only.

Taunton Angling Association (Bridgwater & Taunton Canal)

Contact: Matthew Hawkins, 70 Tone Hill, Tonedale, Wellington, *Tel:* 01823 664388, *Mobile:* 07748 642004, *Water:* Approx. 1 acre stillwater coarse (See also entries under Taunton and Bridgwater Canal & Stillwater Coarse). *Species:* Carp-15-16lb, Roach and Rudd-2lb and Perch-1.5lb. *Permits:* Available in all local tackle shops. *Charges:* Season £34. Day tickets £5 senior, Junior £3. *Season:* No closed season. *Methods:* All gates must be closed, no dogs, all juniors (under 12's) must be acccompanied by an adult, barbless hooks must be used.

Taunton Angling Association (Maunsel Ponds)

Contact: Matthew Hawkins, 70 Tone Hill, Tonedale, Wellington, *Tel:* 01823 664388, *Mobile:* 07748 642004, *Water:* Maunsel Ponds (two ponds). See also entries under River & Canal Fishing. *Species:* Carp 25lb, Tench 5lb, Roach 1lb, Bream 8lb, Crucians 1.5lb and Perch 2lb. *Charges:* Season £34. Day tickets £5 senior, £3 junior. *Season:* Open all year. *Methods:* Barbless hooks, no Carp in keepnets.

WEDMORE

Lands End Farm Fishery ♿

Contact: Michael Duckett, Heath House, Wedmore, *Tel:* 07977 545882, *Water:* Tealham - 2.25 acre 24 peg match lake. Johns Walter - 2 acre, 30 peg match lake. Tadham - specimen lake 1.75 acres 16 peg. Sidney's - match lake, 2 acres 24 peg open to general public in 2008. *Species:* Carp to 27lb (Common, Mirror, Ghost, Crucian) Grass Carp to 18.5lb, Bream to 8lb, Tench to 7lb 4oz and Roach 2lb, Rudd, Chub, Ide, Perch, Barbel, Golden Orfe to 4lb. *Permits:* From offfice on site. *Charges:* £6/day. After 3pm summer nights £5. £4 Concessions / OAPs / Juniors / Disabled. *Season:* Open all year. 7am to dusk in the summer. *Methods:* Barbless hooks only, no keepnets, no dog biscuits, boilies or nuts. Boilies allowed only on specimen lake.

Velocity Angling Complex ♿

Contact: Shane Alway, No. 2 Bullmead Close, Street, *Mobile:* 07789 760213, *Water:* Over 23 acres. *Species:* Large head of Roach and Rudd, Bream, Pike, Carp to 45lb. *Permits:* Environment Agency Permit. *Charges:* Prices to be confirmed for 2008 *Methods:* No live bait.

WELLINGTON

Langford Lakes (coarse lakes)

Contact: Mr. Hendy, Middle Hill Farm, Langford Budville, Wellington, *Tel:* 01823 400476, *Water:* 4 lakes. *Species:* Carp, Roach, Perch, Tench, Bream. *Charges:* Prices on application. *Season:* Open all year 8am to dusk. *Methods:* No keepnets allowed, children under 16 must be accompanied by fishing adult.

Jake Mitchell's 8.5lb common carp caught at Edneys using a pole

WELLS

Emborough Ponds

Contact: Thatchers Tackle, 18 Queen Street, Wells, *Tel:* 01749 673513, *Water:* 3.5 acre lake. *Species:* Carp to 25lb, Tench 8lb, small Roach. *Charges:* Limited membership, please enquire at Thatchers Tackle. *Season:* 1st March - 31st December.

WESTHAY

Avalon Fisheries

Contact: Vic Bush or Lee Nutland, *Mobile:* 07855 825059, *Water:* Moors Match Lake: 6 acres, 48 pegs. Heath Lake: 22 pegs of which 10 are available for night fishing. *Species:* Carp to mid 20's, Tench 8.5lb, Bream 9lb 2oz, Perch 3lb, Roach, Rudd. *Permits:* Site office and on the bank. Mobile Phone 07855 825059. *Charges:* Moors Match Lake: Adult 1 rod £7. 2 rods £9. Evening ticket (after 4.30) 1 rod £4. 2 rods £6. Junior, OAP, concessions: 1 rod £4. 2 rods £6. Evening: 1 rod £3. 2 rods £5. Heath Specimen Lake: Adult day 2 rods £10. Night 7pm-7am £15. 24 hour ticket £20. *Season:* No closed season - Open dawn to dusk. *Methods:* Moors Lake: No cat or dog meat. No boilies, bloodworm or joker. Coarse feed pellets only allowed. Heath Lake: Boilies are allowed. Trout and Halibut pellets as hookbait only. Please check rules before fishing.

WINTERBOURNE

Frome Vale Angling Club (Coarse Lake)

Contact: Nigel Vigus (Secretary), 32 Rock Lane, Stoke Gifford, Bristol, *Tel:* 01179 759710, *Water:* Half acre lake at Winterbourne. See entry under Bristol Frome. *Methods:* No cereal groundbaits. No Keepnets.

A good net full at Avalon.

YEOVIL

Stoke Sub Hamdon & District AA (Coarse Lake)

Contact: Mr Derek Goad (Secretary), (H.Q. at Stoke Working Mens Club), 2 Windsor Lane, Stoke-Sub-Hamdon, *Tel:* 01935 824337, *Water:* Bearley Lake, see also entry under River Parrett. *Permits:* Season permits only. Available from Post Office, Montacute and Yeovil Angling Centre, Yeovil. Also available from secretary. *Charges:* Season tickets: Senior £15, Juniors/OAPs £8 (Bearley Lake). Juniors under 14 must be accompanied by an adult. *Season:* Lake open all year. *Methods:* Lake: no nut baits (lake rules apply). No night fishing.

The Old Mill Fishery

Contact: Mike Maxwell, Tucking Mill Farm, Stoford, Yeovil, *Tel:* 01935 414771, *Water:* Four 1.5 acre lakes plus fishing on a tributary of the river Yeo and a canal. *Species:* 21 different species of coarse fish. River contains Roach, Dace, Chub and Barbel. Well stocked lakes with Carp to 25lb, Perch 3lb, Barbel 8lb, Bream 4lb. *Permits:* On the bank. *Charges:* Permit for lakes and river £6/day (£4 under 16yrs and OAP). £3 evening ticket 4pm onwards in summer. Club bookings taken. *Season:* Open all year 7am to dusk. *Methods:* Barbless hooks only. Keepnets allowed, but no Carp to be retained in keepnets.

Yeovil & Sherborne Angling Association (Sherborne Lake)

Contact: Pete Coombes, 44 Monksdale, Yeovil, *Tel:* 01935 427873, *Water:* Sherborne Castle Lake and all other association waters. Discounted tickets Viaduct Fishery. Also see River Club Card entry. *Species:* Roach, Bream, Carp, Perch, Rudd, Tench. *Permits:* Membership details from above & local tackle shops. *Charges:* No day tickets. Lake Section licence £36 per year, covers all waters. £2 off day ticket at Viaduct. *Season:* Open all year.

Stillwater Trout

BRIDGWATER

Burton Springs Fishery (Trout Lake)

Contact: Tony Evans, Lawson Farm, Burton, Nr Stogursey, Bridgwater, *Tel:* 01278 732135, *Mobile:* 07804 210303, *Water:* Approx. 2 acre lake. *Species:* Brown, Rainbow, Tiger & Blue Trout. *Permits:* Self service at fishing lodge. *Charges:* 4-fish ticket £26, 2-fish/ 6hr £20, sporting ticket £15 (catch & release permitted after limit). Please read rules in Lodge. *Season:* Open all year 8am - 9pm or dusk. *Methods:* Fly only. Barbless hooks only, only Rainbow Trout may be taken.

Hawkridge Reservoir

Contact: Wessex Water, *Tel:* 0845 600 4 600, *Water:* 32 acre reservoir. *Species:* Brown and Rainbow Trout. *Permits:* Gary Howe (Ranger) Tel: 01278 671840. *Charges:* Day Ticket £17 (5 fish limit); Concession Day £14 (5 fish limit); Evening ticket £10 (2 fish limit, no concessions); Days, book of 6 tickets £85; Concessions book of six tickets £73; Season Ticket £370 (4 fish limit) only 4 visit per week allowed; Boats £15 day, £8 evening. *Season:* Open 19 March - 12 October.

BRISTOL

Avon Fly Fishers Club

Contact: Bill Pugh, Bill Pugh Pets & Fishing, 410 Wells Road, Red Lion Hill, Knowle, *Tel:* 0117 9770280, *Water:* Fishing competitions, video and social evenings, plus members public liability insurance.

Blagdon Lake ♿

Contact: Bristol Water Fisheries, Woodford Lodge, Chew Stoke, Nr Bristol, *Tel:* 01275 332339, *Water:* 440 acre lake at Blagdon near Bristol. 20 rowing boats available for hire. *Species:* Rainbow Trout to 16lb. Brown Trout to 10lb. Total catch last season over 18,000. Average weight 2lb 8oz. *Permits:* Woodford Lodge, Chew Valley Lake and Blagdon Lodge, Blagdon Lake. *Charges:* Day bank: £17, OAP £15, Junior free with adult. Evening Bank: £13. Day boat £25, OAP £23, Junior £17, Afternoon boat £21, Evening £17.50, Season: £605, OAP £400 (Valid at Chew and Barrows also). *Season:* 20 March - 30 November. *Methods:* Fly fishing only.

Bristol Reservoir Flyfishers Association ♿

Contact: Martin Cottis (Sec.), 67 Four Acre Road, Downend, Bristol, *Tel:* 0117 9140157, *Mobile:* 07747 843548, *Water:* Fishing on Bristol Waterworks reservoirs. Blagdon, Chew Valley and Barrows. Competitions organised from bank and boat. Tuition offered. Full winter programme of activities including: tackle auctions, fly tying sessions, beginners and improvers casting sessions, guest speakers and quiz nights. *Species:* Rainbow and Brown Trout, fly fishing for Pike. *Permits:* Day tickets direct from Bristol Water. Club does not sell day tickets. *Charges:* £5 joining fee. Annual membership £10 full members, £5 pensioners and registered disabled, joining fee £1 juniors - annual membership fee juniors free. *Season:* End March to end of November (extension of season on banks and at Barron Tanks). *Methods:* Fly fishing only.

Cameley Lakes

Contact: J. Harris, Hillcrest Farm, Cameley, Temple Cloud, *Tel:* 01761 452423, *Water:* One 2.5 acre lake and three 1 acre lakes plus fishing on the river River Cam. *Species:* Rainbow Trout,

Brown Trout 1 - 5lb. *Permits:* Car park. *Charges:* £25 incl VAT Day ticket 4 fish. £20 incl VAT Half Day ticket 2 fish. *Season:* Open all year - 8.00 till sundown. *Methods:* Fly fishing only. Hooks no larger than 1 inch.

Chew Valley Lake ♿

Contact: Bristol Water Fisheries, Woodford Lodge, Chew Stoke, Nr. Bristol, *Tel:* 01275 332339, *Water:* 1,200 Acre lake. 32 motor boats for hire. *Species:* Rainbow Trout to 14lb, Brown Trout to 16lb. Pike to over 38lb 6oz. Total catch last season over 21,000. Average weight 2lb 8oz. *Permits:* Woodford Lodge, Chew Lake. *Charges:* Day bank: £15, OAP £13, Junior free with adult. Evening bank: £12. Day motor boat: £31, OAP £28.50, Junior £22, Afternoon £25.50, Evening £19.50. Special boat available for disabled anglers. Season £500, OAP £340 (Valid at Barrows also). *Season:* 13 March - 30 November. *Methods:* Fly fishing only. Pike trials in February, October and November.

Jacklands Trout Fishery

Contact: Mrs L P Waygood, Jacklands Bridge, Clevedon Road, Nailsea, Bristol, *Tel:* 01275 810697, *Water:* One acre lake. *Species:* Rainbow Trout from 1.5 - 12lbs. *Permits:* On site. *Charges:* Fish at £2 per lb. *Season:* Open all year dawn to dusk. *Methods:* Fly only, no catch & release.

Knowle Angling Association (Trout Lakes)

Contact: Keith Caddick, 41 Eastwood Crescent, Brislington, Bristol, *Tel:* 01179 857974, *Mobile:* 0794 634 7581, *Water:* 2 lakes - Publow and Ackers lake at Pensford. Plus fishing at Chew Magna reservoir, (also see entry in River Fishing, Chew). *Species:* Rainbow and Brown Trout up to 8lb. *Permits:* For guests of members only from Keith Caddick. *Charges:* £95 annual membership 2008. New members pay extra £5 entrance fee. £65 annual membership for senior members over 65, extra £5 entrance fee for new senior members. *Season:* Chew Magna Reservoir open all year for Rainbows. Brown Trout from 1 April to 15 October. Lakes open all year. *Methods:* Fly only on lakes and upper Chew.

Litton Lakes

Contact: Bristol Water Fisheries, Woodford Lodge, Chew Stoke, Nr. Bristol, *Tel:* 01275 332339, *Water:* 7 acre and 11 acre lakes at Coley, Nr Chewton Mendip. 1 rowing boat on each lake. *Species:* Brown & Rainbow Trout. Total catch last season over 1,400. Average weight 2lb 10oz. *Permits:* Woodford Lodge, Chew Valley Lake. *Charges:* £110 for two persons exclusive use of both lakes. Bag limit 5 fish per person. Corporate packages and tuition available. *Season:* Open all year. *Methods:* Fly fishing only.

The Barrows

Contact: Bristol Water Fisheries, Woodford Lodge, Chew Stoke, Nr Bristol, *Tel:* 01275 332339, *Water:* Three lakes of 25 acres (No. 1) 40 acres (No. 2) 60 acres (No.3) at Barrow Gurney, Nr. Bristol. *Species:* Rainbow Trout (10lb) Brown Trout (9lb). Total catch last season over 6,000. Average weight 1lb 11oz. *Permits:* Self service kiosk at the fishery car park. *Charges:* Day bank: £12.50. OAP £11. Junior free with adult. Evening bank: £10, Season: £385 O.A.P. £265. *Season:* 13 March - 30 November. *Methods:* Fly fishing only.

DULVERTON

Exe Valley Fishery

Contact: Andrew Maund, Exebridge, Dulverton, *Tel:* 01398 323008, *Water:* 3 Lakes fly only (2 + 1 + 0.75 acre lakes), 1 small lake half acre plus 0.5 miles river Exe. *Species:* Rainbow Trout. *Permits:* Day Tickets. *Charges:* Day ticket £6 for 5 fish limit, plus £3.50 per kilo, rod hire £10. *Season:* All year. *Methods:* See above.

Wimbleball ♿

Contact: South West Lakes Trust, Angling & Watersports Centre, *Tel:* 01398 371460, *Water:* Reservoir 374 acres. *Species:* Premier rainbow fishery, boats available booked in advance via the centre. Rod average 2006: 3.41 fish per rod per day. *Permits:* Self service at Hill Barn Farm, Wimbleball. *Charges:* Full day £19.50, Concession £16, Evening £16, boats £12 per day. Season permits also available on site or from Summerlands Tackle (01237 471291). *Season:* 29 March - 31 October. *Methods:* Catch and release available (barbless hooks must be used), fly fishing only.

Wimbleball Fly Fishing Club

Contact: Gareth Hodgson, *Mobile:* 07800 944283, *Water:* Regular fishing days, bank and boat. Fishing Wimbleball and other stillwaters. Strong junior section, tuition can be arranged for juniors. *Permits:* All details available from Wimbleball Fishing Lodge.

FROME

St. Algars Farm Lake

Contact: Angus Mackintosh, St. Algar's Farm, West Woodlands, Nr Frome, *Tel:* 01985 844233, *Water:* Two acre lake. *Species:* Rainbow Trout. *Permits:* From above. *Charges:* £15 - 4 fish limit. £10 - 2 fish limit all season. *Season:* 1st April - 31 October. *Methods:* Normal rules for fly fishing.

HIGHBRIDGE

Walleden Farm Fishery ♿

Contact: Andrew Wall, East Huntspill, Highbridge, *Tel:* 01278 786488, *Mobile:* 07886 732945, *Water:* Half acre Trout lake. Also section of river Brue. See entry under River Fishing. *Species:* Trout. *Permits:* From the above. *Season:* Open all year. *Methods:* Any legal method.

TAUNTON

Hawkridge Fly Fishing Club

Contact: Philip Frapple, The Dairy, Jakes, Preston Bower, Milverton, *Tel:* 01823 401098, *Mobile:* 01984 618685, *Water:* Primarily fishing on Hawkridge Reservoir. Club meetings 8pm second Monday of the month at The Volunteer Arms, Bridgwater. Visiting speakers & monthly competitions in season. Club trips, fly tying and social evenings. *Species:* Rainbow and Brown Trout. *Permits:* From the fishing lodge at Hawkridge Reservoir. *Season:* New fly fishermen welcome, old and new. *Methods:* Fly fishing only. Boats available.

WIVELISCOMBE

Clatworthy Fly Fishing Club ♿

Contact: Dave Pursey, *Tel:* 01984 624658, *Water:* 130 acre Clatworthy reservoir on Exmoor. *Species:* Rainbow and Brown Trout. *Permits:* On site from Lodge. More information about the club can be found on the fishing lodge notice board at Clatworthy Reservoir. *Charges:* Membership £5, Concessions/Junior £3, plus Clatworthy day ticket. *Season:* Open 21st March -14th October. *Methods:* Fly fishing only.

Clatworthy Reservoir ♿

Contact: Wessex Water, *Tel:* 0845 600 4 600, *Water:* 130 acre reservoir. *Species:* Rainbow and Brown Trout. *Permits:* Contact ranger Dave Pursey on 01984 624658. *Charges:* Day Ticket £17 (5 fish limit); Concession Day £14 (5 fish limit); Evening ticket £10 (2 fish limit, no concessions); Days, book of 6 tickets £85; Concessions book of six tickets £73; Season Ticket £370 (4 fish limit) only 4 visit per week allowed; Boats £15 day, £8 evening. *Season:* Open 19 March - 12 October.

YEOVIL

Sutton Bingham Fly Fishers Association

Contact: Terry Williams (sec), 72 Willow Road, Yeovil, *Tel:* 01935 471329, *Water:* Hold regular competitions throughout the season. For members only. Tuition available. Fly tying classes held during the close season. *Species:* Brown Trout to 16lb, Rainbows to 18lb. *Permits:* Day tickets on site. *Charges:* New members always welcome. Adult and junior £3 per year. Charges may change in 2008. *Season:* Mid March to end September.

Sutton Bingham Reservoir ♿

Contact: Wessex Water, *Tel:* 0845 600 4 600, *Water:* 142 acre reservoir. *Species:* Rainbow and Brown Trout. *Permits:* Contact ranger Ivan Tinsley on 01935 872389. Advisable to book boats in advance. *Charges:* Day Ticket £17 (5 fish limit); Concession Day £14 (5 fish limit); Evening ticket £10 (2 fish limit, no concessions); Days, book of 6 tickets £85; Concessions book of six tickets £73; Season Ticket £370 (4 fish limit) only 4 visit per week allowed; Boats £15 day, £8 evening. *Season:* Open 19 March - 12 October.

Sea Fishing

BATH

Gannet Sea Angling Club
Contact: NFSA Head Office: 01364 644643.

BRIDGWATER

Three B's Sea Angling Association
Contact: John Rowlands, 9 Ashton Road, Bridgwater, *Tel:* 01278 458599, *Water:* Beach and boat angling. Regular club shore matches. Open competitions and boat trips. New members welcome. Monthly meetings from 8pm on 3rd Monday of month at the Ritz Social Club, Victoria St, Burnham-on-Sea TA8 1AN. *Charges:* Annual subscription: Seniors £8. Juniors £4.

BRISTOL

Bath & Bristol Civil Service Sea Angling Club
Contact: NFSA Head Office: 01364 644643.

Bristol Channel Federation of Sea Anglers
Contact: Keith Reed, 27 St Michaels Avenue, Clevedon, *Tel:* 01275 872101, *Water:* Bristol Channel, Hartland Point. North Devon to St Davids Head, Dyfed (all tidal waters eastwards). *Species:* All sea fish, both boat and shore records, yearly update. 52 different species recorded in major (over 1lb) rec.list, 16 different species in minor (under 1lb) rec.list. Conservation awards in place, for fish caught and returned alive. *Charges:* £50 per CLUB per year inclusive of shore activities insurance. *Season:* All year round activities, shore and boat contests, small boat section with inter-club activities. *Methods:* Fishing to specimen sizes, all specimen fish awarded certificate, best of specie annually, plus fish of the month. Team & Individual annual awards. Charter Boat contests only - touch Trace rules. All fish returned alive. Shore contests, catch and release, all fish returned alive, points in place of weight.

Clevedon Breakaways Sea Angling Club
Contact: J. Aspinall, 6 Lydford Walk, Bedminster, Bristol, *Tel:* 0117 9669869, *Mobile:* 07977 393367, *Water:* Boat, Shore and Competitions in the Bristol Channel and South West. Affiliated to B.C.F.S.A. and N.F.S.A. *Species:* All species. *Charges:* Adult £20 plus £2 joining fee. Juniors £6. OAP £6 per year.

BURNHAM-ON-SEA

Burnham-on-Sea Boat Owners S.A.A.
Contact: Mr Simon Stroud, 4 Ham Lane, Burnham-on-Sea, *Tel:* 01278 794573, *Water:* Up tide fishing. *Species:* Conger, Skate, Dogfish, Flounder Cod, Bass. *Permits:* Jetty permits, annual charge £12. Available from Sedgemoor District Council and Burnham on Sea Tourist Information Centre. Tel: 01278 787 852. *Charges:* Car and trailer parking £6 for 12 hours. *Season:* All year.

Kelly's Hero
Contact: Dave Saunders, *Tel:* 01278 785000, *Mobile:* 07970 642354, *Water:* Bristol Channel and Bridgwater Bay. *Species:* Thornbacks, Conger, Bass, Whiting, Cod, Dogfish, Flounder. *Charges:* 9 hour trip £220. 12 hour trip £280. 4 hour trip £120. *Season:* All sailings dependant on weather and local tide times. *Methods:* Uptiding: best method of fishing the shallow banks of Bridgwater Bay.

Three B's Sea Angling Society
Contact: NFSA Head Office: 01364 644643.

CLEVEDON

Clevedon Pier S.A.C.
Contact: Ken Bovington, *Tel:* 01275 794059, *Water:* Shore fishing from Portishead to Kingston Seymour. *Species:* Regular meetings, matches twice monthly at weekends plus one Wednesday match per month. New members, adult and junior welcome. Please contact Ken on the number above.

DULVERTON

Dulverton & District Sea Angling Society
Contact: D.Felix, 9 Nicholas Close, Brushford, Dulverton, *Tel:* 01398 324335, *Water:* 40 members, junior and senior's welcome. Boat and shore fishing competitions once a month. Fishing both coasts, beginners welcome. Always looking for new members. *Charges:* £6 Senior / £3 Junior.

MINEHEAD

Alykat Charters and Images
Contact: Dave Roberts, 102 Periton Lane, Minehead, *Tel:* 01643 703892, *Mobile:* 07764 150648, *Water:* Bristol Channel.

Brunel S.A.C.
Contact: Keith Reed, 27 St Michaels Avenue, Clevedon, *Tel:* 01275 872101, *Water:* General deep sea angling. Plus wreck fishing. Bristol Channel, English Channel. *Charges:* £15 annual subscription. *Season:* Meetings at village hall in Coalpit Heath.

Fulmar
Contact: Steve Pilbrow, 34 Pondsford Road, Minehead, *Tel:* 01643 706627, *Mobile:* 07836 350741, *Water:* 28ft vessel, licensed for 9 people. Charter, beginners welcome. Tackle available. *Species:* Deep sea fishing on reefs and wrecks. Conger, Cod, Whiting, Tope, Bull Huss, Pollack, Mackerel, Dogfish and many more. Seasonal fish. *Charges:* Boat charters and individuals. *Season:* All year round from Minehead harbour.

Minehead & District Sea Angling Club
Contact: Steve Pilbrow, 25 Marley Close, Minehead, *Tel:* 01643 706627, *Mobile:* 07836 350741, *Water:* Established 1950. Membership open to all adults and juniors. Monthly boat fishing competitions and some shore fishing. Tuition given, beginners and infirm welcome. *Species:* Conger, Dogfish, Tope, Cod, Whiting, Huss, Rays, Whiting, Smooth Hound and many more. *Charges:* Joining fee: £15 Adults and £10 OAP's/Juniors. *Season:* All year round.

Tor Sea Angling Club
Contact: Colin Whitcombe, East Close, Station Road, Burtle, Bridgwater, *Tel:* 01278 722769, *Water:* Boat / shore fishing. *Species:* Bass, Conger, Dogfish, Tope, Pollack, Pouting, Rays, Cod, Mackerel. *Charges:* £18 p.a. Adults. Junior / Seniors £9 p.a. *Season:* Meet 3rd Monday each month, 8pm at Globe Inn, Summerton.

West Coast Tackle
Contact: Steve, The Quay, Minehead, *Tel:* 01643 705745, *Water:* Choice of 9 charters. Trips arranged for individual or parties.

Remember a ♿ means the fishery has disabled facilities - contact them direct for further details

WATCHET

Scooby Doo Too ♿

Contact: Stephen Yeandle, 3 The Courtyard, Esplanade Lane, Watchet, *Tel:* 01984 631310, *Mobile:* 07778 750939, *Water:* 07778 750939 (boat) *Species:* Skate, Ling, Cad, Bass, Gurnard, Tope, Smoothhound, Whiting. UK record holder for Bull Huss. *Charges:* £25 per person including tackle and bait (4 hours). *Season:* Fishing all year round.

Seafire

72 West Street, Watchet, *Tel:* 01984 634507, *Mobile:* 07711 215695, *Water:* Bristol Channel. *Species:* Cod, Ling, Conger, Skate, Bass, Tope, Whiting, Dogfish, Smooth Hound, Spur Dogs etc. *Season:* Fishing all year round.

WELLINGTON

Blackdown Sea Angling Club

Contact: Liz Bowran, *Tel:* 01823 666739, *Water:* Monthly meetings 1st Tuesday of the month, at the Dolphin Inn, Wellington - 8pm onwards. *Species:* Fishing from shore and boat (mainly Bristol Channel). Monthly competitions, plus open competitions. *Permits:* New members welcome, please contact Liz or come to our meetings. *Charges:* £10 p/a membership, £5 juniors and OAP's. *Season:* All year round for monthly competitions (club), open competitions end of September - end of March.

WELLS

Wells & District Sea Angling Club

Contact: NFSA Head Office: 01364 644643.

WESTON-SUPER-MARE

Weston Outcasts S.A.C.

Contact: Richard Allwood, *Tel:* 07811 325709, *Water:* Meeting monthly at the Prince of Orange, Yatton, 1st Thursday of the month - 8pm. Primarily shore angling, with regular competitions and two open matches fishing Bristol channel. *Permits:* Adults and juniors welcome, please contact Richard or come to our meetings. *Charges:* £10 membership, £15 smock.

Weston-Super-Mare Sea Angling Association

Contact: NFSA Head Office: 01364 644643.

YEOVIL

Royal British Legion (Yeovil) Sea Angling Club

Contact: NFSA Head Office: 01364 644643,

Three Counties Sea Angling Association

Contact: Colin Dowden (Secretary), 3 Tintagel Road, Yeovil, *Tel:* 01935 479985, *Water:* Association offering regular shore competitions (monthly) and boat trips from Minehead, Weymouth and Exmouth (approx. two a month). *Species:* All sea species. Trophies presented for most at presentation evening. *Charges:* Membership: Senior £10, Couple £12, Junior £3, Senior Citizen £3. Family Membership (2 adults and any juniors under 16) £12. Further details from Colin Dowden. *Season:* Events throughout the year.

Yeovil & District Sea Angling Club

Contact: NFSA Head Office: 01364 644643.

Remember a ♿ means the fishery has disabled facilities - contact them direct for further details

SEA FISHING / WHERE TO STAY

Angling and the Environment

By Mark Lloyd, Executive Director of the Anglers' Conservation Association (ACA)

Anglers have always been the first to notice when rivers and stillwaters are suffering from pollution or over abstraction. Their keen eyes and ears are needed more than ever.

As with most fieldsports, angling is dependent on a healthy environment. The abundance, size and condition of fish are indicators of the quality and quantity of water and the health of aquatic habitats. These ingredients all need to be in place to make going fishing worthwhile and therefore Britain's 3 million anglers are more concerned about the state of our rivers, lakes, canals and ponds than most.

Of course, clean, plentiful and wild waters are of benefit to everyone. They provide water for the home, industry and agriculture, habitats where many food chains begin and unique places for quiet reflection. They are also places which have been convenient dumping grounds for sewage, noxious chemicals and rubbish. Many rivers have dried up completely from too much water being taken out to fill swimming pools, wash cars, drip from unfixed taps and to water crops. Many others have been dredged and encased in concrete to try and stop them flooding or drain fields. All these things cause fish numbers to decline.

The way we look after water affects not just fish, but also our families' health and well-being, the whole economy and the risk of homes being flooded. Angling is a very obvious direct example: it generates about £3.5 billion for the UK economy each year and employs tens of thousands of people. It provides a healthy, outdoor activity in city, town and country which can be practiced by anyone between the ages of 3 and 103. It instils in youngsters a great understanding of the natural world and the mysteries of life beneath the water, without them having to go to a coral reef.

An angler is someone who fishes with a hook. Over the past 10,000 years, a huge number of ways of using hooks to catch fish have been developed and this is apparent from the daunting array of equipment in fishing tackle shops, which is the best place to go for anyone wanting to get started. The good news is, you don't have to buy everything in the shop and for less than £50 you could get enough kit to go fishing for either coarse, game (trout & salmon) or sea fish. Anyone over 12 years old also needs an Environment Agency licence to fish. Daily, weekly and annual licences are available online and from most Post Offices.

THE GET HOOKED GUIDE

Apart from tackle and a licence, anglers need clean, plentiful, wild water with fish in them. The ACA has been fighting for this right for nearly 60 years, by using the law to make polluters pay for the damage they do to our members' waters. Our in house lawyers represent our 1,000 member angling clubs and river owners completely free of charge. We have won more than 2,000 legal cases and have secured millions of pounds in compensation which has been used by our members to restore their damaged fisheries. In 60 years, we have lost only 3 cases. Our reputation means that many thousands of pollution incidents have been avoided as water companies, farmers and industrial plants have thought twice before using rivers as dumping grounds.

Thankfully, much of worst pollution has now been stopped and many of our rivers are seeing fish populations on the increase. When people imagine pollution, they think of big pipes spewing out poisons and sewage. In fact, this type of damage is now much rarer, but still happens sometimes. However, new problems have arisen which are impacting seriously on the angling economy and society as a whole. Pesticides like cypermethrin sheep dip wipe out insect life, the main food of most fish, in rivers. Endocrine disruptors washed out of sewage works make male fish become female. Silt pollution from construction and agriculture increases flood risk, puts up the cost of treating water for public supply, smothers gravels where fish breed and insects live and makes it necessary to dredge estuaries and ports much more often, which is both expensive and damaging to these sensitive habitats. What looks like a bit of harmless mud causes millions of pounds of damage to river systems.

The average person's water consumption has increased by 30% since 1970. If we continue to waste water in this way, the construction of millions of new homes in already water-stressed areas will put great strain on the ability of natural water systems to support fish, other wildlife and other uses of water. Similarly, all this new development will mean a lot more hard, impermeable surfaces like roads, driveways and roofs. Instead of soaking into the ground, rain landing on these surfaces rushes towards the nearest drain to be carried efficiently to the nearest watercourse. Unless these new developments are designed sensibly, with sustainable drainage systems and the latest water efficiency technology, Britain is on a collision course for widespread water shortages and hugely damaging flooding. We got a taste of both these future scenarios in the last two years, with drought in 2006 and floods in 2007.

To make a difference, all anglers should join one or more of the bodies which represents their interests. The Fisheries and Angling Conservation Trust (FACT) has a list of all the angling organisations on its web site at www.factuk.co.uk. Membership of the ACA is just £22 a year for individuals, £6 for juniors and more for angling clubs and riparian owners who benefit from our unique legal protection service. More information at www.a-c-a.org or from 01568 620447.

Fixing the Frome

Nick Fisher
Photos Paul Quagliana.

Thirty years ago, heavy diggers were driven to the edge of the River Frome, just downstream of Dorchester, to excavate the banks and scoop out the riverbed, in order to make the river deeper and straighter. Now, the diggers have once returned to the exact same stretch of the Frome. to fill it all back in again.

Standing on the bank of the Frome, among the recent scars and troughs of heavy plant machinery, John Aplin, river keeper and restorer, explains why his club, the Dorchester Fishing Club, is undoing all the hard work that went on three decades ago.

'It was all done in the name of flood relief,' explains John. 'The river below Dorchester was canalised; dug into a uniform U-profile for a few miles, so that more water could flow and so reduce the risk of the river backing-up to flood the town.'

You might be forgiven for assuming that in these days of global warming and scary flash flood warnings, this kind of flood relief is more necessary than ever. But, as John explained, water and flood management is still in its infancy and still very much a case of trial, error and experimentation. The error that engineers made in the 1970s was to see flood relief as a function of just the river itself, rather than in conjunction with the huge network of water meadows that spread for miles on either side of the river corridor.

Farming practices changed in the 60s and 70s; the water meadow sluice gates and hatches were allowed to fall into disrepair; the tradition of flooding meadows, to warm the soil in preparation for a second crop each year, was abandoned. As the meadows were used less, the water – rather than being leached-out to feed the network of meadows and channels – remained within the river course itself. Not surprisingly, the river couldn't cope with such a massive increase in volume being forced between its banks. And so 'canalising' rivers became the accepted method of dealing with extra flow. By taking out all the interesting kinks and bends and shallows in the river, engineers encouraged more water to pass through.

'Of course, it was hopeless for fish,' says John. 'It was just one big uniform glide with nowhere for young fish to hide and absolutely no shallow gravel redds for fish to spawn into.'

With financial help from English Nature and the Environment Agency, survey help from the Dorset Wildlife Trust and practical expertise from fisheries specialists Kingcombe Aquacare, John ordered 200 tons of local gravel to be delivered and dumped into the river.

The three sites they chose to deposit the gravel are destined to become active redds on which trout, salmon and sea trout will spawn, as early as next month. The huge gravel deposits create shallow sections of river, where it flows quicker over the stones. This extra flow increases oxygen levels and helps to wash away any silt deposit which might otherwise suffocate fish eggs. Adding these three gravel sites has more than doubled the amount of potential spawning sites downstream of Dorchester.

But John's labours don't just increase spawning redds. 'We want riffles, glides, pools and back eddies,' he says. 'We want it all. We want to create variation and improve habitat, not just in the water but on the bankside too. We've customised steep banks to encourage the local water vole population; we've made new habitat for kingfishers and other birds. And all of this has happened because we love our fishing and love this river. Really, without fishermen, none of this would ever get done.'

Since the whole of the Frome valley was declared a Special Site of Scientific Interest, much has been done to improve the river. Many water meadows have been reopened and repaired, which now means many function as intended and help regulate flow and any potential flood. It hasn't all been easy though. 'Many of the old school river owners, the retired colonels and majors, were up in arms at the thought of all these university graduates and boffins getting their hands on the river,' explains John, whose job it was to mediate between the two camps.

The range of improvements that were needed were many and varied, from putting in groynes, or upstream deflectors, to increase flow at strategic positions, to paying local farmers not to grow maize alongside the river. This is done to reduce the amount of top soil run-off that occurs in the autumn, after the maize harvest. A badly situated maize field can cause a vast amount of silt and dissolved mud entering the river and clogging the spawning. John is the first to admit that, much of the time, river restoration is guesswork. 'We're all of us on a steep learning curve,' he explains. 'We've made mistakes and hopefully we've learned from them. But at the end of the day, Nature always knows best, and it's a wise man who listens.'

A river is a living thing, with a mind and a will of its own. Many people who work in restoration have discovered that you can only manhandle and manipulate Nature so far. 'It sounds weird, I know,' says John, 'but a river responds to your respect, and even your love. Of course, you can force it to do something. We have the technology. Or, you can see what the river wants to do. The sites we've picked to locate the gravel redds were really dictated by the river. It's like it knows where these would work best. All we had to do was listen.'

For John Aplin, the work he's overseeing on the Frome is payback for all the pleasure the river has given him over the years. He moved to Dorchester aged 5 and soon started fishing the Frome. By the time he left school, he knew he wanted to be a river keeper, and has done it with great enthusiasm for the last 22 years. 'To be working on the bit of river I grew up on and loved so much, makes me a very happy man,' he said. 'One of the things that makes me most happy is to see the enjoyment that our work brings to the quality of our members' fishing.'

Brown trout sits at the top of the food chain in a river like the Frome. If you can keep brown trout healthy and growing well in a river system, then you know that the other end of the food chain is working properly. 'Look after the bottom end of the food chain,' says John, 'the invertebrates, shrimps and insect life. Keep them happy and the trout will take care of themselves.'

To find out more about river restoration, contact the Dorchester Fishing Club (www.grhe.co.uk) or Casterbridge Fisheries Management on 07889 680464 (www.riverworks.co.uk) or Kingcombe Aquacare on 01460 279200.

KEY
Name
Contact details
Qualifications
Area covered
Equipment available
Specialities
Game
Coarse
Sea

Gary & Annie Champion

Tel 01872 863551. Mobile 07968 380716
Email: champsflyfish@btopenworld.com
Gary - A.A.P.G.A.I. and FFF Masters
Annie - A.A.P.G.A.I.
Devon & Cornwall
Rods, Reels, Flys etc.

For tuition in all aspects of fly fishing. Single and double handed casting. Fresh and salt water. Fly dressing, traditional and modern. Helping you enjoy your sport more by improving your techniques.

David Pilkington / Tim Smith

Arundell Arms, Lifton, Devon PL16 0AA
Tel: 01566 784666 / Fax: 01566 784494
Email: reservations@arundellarms.com
www.arundellarms.com
Full members AAPGAI. STANIC qualified instructors.
Lifton area of Devon. Based at The Arundell Arms Hotel.
Rods, Reels Flies etc.

Individual tuition and beginners and refresher courses, including Spey casting. All aspects of fly fishing.

Colin Pape

8 Lumley Close, Kenton, Exeter, Devon, EX6 8HT
Tel: 01626 891897 / Mob: 07816 060979
Email: info@colinpapeflyfishing.co.uk
www.colinpapeflyfishing.co.uk
GAIA Level 2 Certificate in Coaching Angling (Game).
Rivers Teign, Taw, Culm & Yeo + Kennick Reservoir.
All game angling tackle provided for stillwater or river.

One to one courses tailored to the individual. Guiding on the Counties' rivers for trout, sea trout and salmon.

Mike Maslin

Moorfishing, Buckfastleigh, Devon
Tel: 01364 643701 Mobile: 07841 448747
email: mikemaslin@hotmail.com
www.moorfishing.co.uk
Level 2 CCA. GAIA
South Devon and Dartmoor.
All tackle and EA licence can be supplied.

Specialist tuition for beginners and improvers at Kennick. 2 hours to a whole day, duration to suit the needs of the client. Tackle advice given. River guiding service available.

To ensure that you get the highest quality and best value instruction, book with a qualified instructor from these pages or contact one the following organisations for more information.

Contact Information

Coarse Angling

National Federation of Anglers
The National Federation of Anglers is the governing body for freshwater angling in England.
www.nfadirect.com Tel: 01159 813535

Sea Angling

National Federation of Sea Anglers
www.nfsa.org.uk Tel: 01364 644643

Game Angling

www.fishcoach.org
Salmon & Trout Association
www.salmon-trout.org
Tel: 020 7283 5838

Instructor/Coaching Organisations:

AAPGAI:

Association of Advanced Professional Game Angling Instructors
www.aapgai.co.uk Tel: 01654 781365

REFFIS:

The Register of Experienced Fly Fishing Instructors, Schools and Guides
www.reffis.co.uk Tel: 01305 848460

GAIA:

The Professional Body for game angling instructors in the UK.
www.gameanglinginstructors.co.uk
Tel: 01490 412731

Professional Anglers Association:

(all angling styles) www.paauk.com
Tel: 02476 414999

The first fish.
You never forget it!
Pic - Margaret Livingstone

TUITION
It's never too early to start or too late to learn!

Ian Brooke
6 Ash Walk, Brentry, Bristol BS10 6RW
Tel: 07511 737210
Email: ian@anglingcoach.com
www.anglingcoach.com
Level 2 certificate in coaching angling, safeguarding and protecting children. CRB check. First aid course.

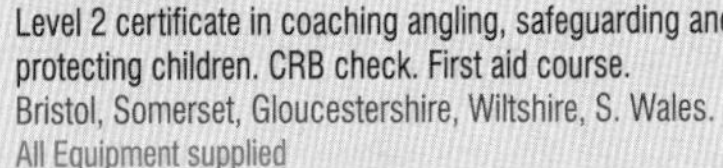

Bristol, Somerset, Gloucestershire, Wiltshire, S. Wales.
All Equipment supplied

Specialising in Pike, Carp, Barbel and Chub.

Mike Gleave
Dresden, 7 Dundry Lane, Dundry, N. Somerset BS40 8JH
Tel: 01275 472403
mike.gleave@btinternet.com
STANIC & REFFIS
Bristol & the South West, Bristol Water Fisheries.
All Tackle except clothing.

Stillwater techniques. Fly Tying.
Guiding from boat and bank at Blagdon and Chew.

Robert Jones
Valley Barn, Hawkerland, Colaton Raleigh,
Sidmouth, Devon EX10 0JA.
Tel: 07020 902090 Mobile: 0797 0797 770
Email: robertjones@eclipse.co.uk
FRICS
The West Country centred on East Devon and rivers Otter, Axe, Teign, Exe and Camel.
Transport and equipment by arrangement.

Rivers. Sea Trout by fly at night. Guiding. Bass.
For age 10 and over.

Sally Pizii
Tumbleweed Cottage, Curry Mallet, Nr Taunton
Somerset TA3 6SR
Tel: 01823 480710
Email: pizii@supanet.com
Level 2 C.C.A./STANIC/REFFIS/ADB Licenced
Westcountry
All fly fishing tackle available

Fly fishing and casting on rivers or stillwaters.
Beginners, improvers. Adults families and children.

John H Dawson
29 Bourchier Close, Bampton, Tiverton, Devon EX16 9AG.
Tel: 01398 331498 Mobile: 07816 453474
Email:info@johndawson.co.uk www.johndawson.co.uk
STANIC - Salmon, Trout and Fly Dressing
Certificate in Coaching Angling
Devon and Somerset.
Fishing tackle can be provided.

Fly fishing and casting tuition on rivers, stillwaters and sea. Guiding service. Fly dressing tuition. Fly fishing and fly dressing classes at East Devon College. Overseas fishing holidays.

Sorenson Flycasting
Ian Sorenson. Stonelea, 1 Park Cottages,
Burlescombe, Devon, EX16 7JW
Tel: 01823 672734 Mobile: 07969 413572
Email: sorenson01flycasting@hotmail.co.uk
Level 2 coaching certificate angling game.
GAIA instructor, member of Salmon & Trout association.
West Somerset, East, North and Mid Devon.
Rods, Reels, Lines and accessories available.

Learn to flyfish on lakes, rivers and beaches with a qualified instructor. Full day, half day or evenings.

Sally Pizii Coaching

Malcolm Hanson

31 Priorsfield, Marlborough, Wiltshire SN8 4AQ
Tel: 01672 511628 Mobile: 07917 792966
Email: malcolm.hanson@btinternet.com
Level 2 Game Angling, Stanic,
Level 3 National Angling Guide
Wiltshire, Gloucestershire, Avon, Dorset, Somerset, West Berkshire and Hampshire.
All tackle can be supplied.

General game angling tuition for all ages.
Guiding by appointment.

Lechlade & Bushyleaze Trout Fisheries (Tim Small)

Lechlade, Gloucestershire GL7 3QQ
Tel: 01367 253266
Email: trout@star.co.uk
www.lechladetrout.co.uk
Team of three Instructors
On site at the fishery
Rods, reels, lines etc.
Stalking and beginners a speciality.
Please telephone to book.

Tony King

Wessex Flyfishing School, Lawrences Farm, Tolpuddle DT2 7HF
Tel: 01305 789560 Mobile: 07855 196332
Email: tonykingfishing@googlemail.co.uk www.tkfishing.com
AAPGAI/STANIC/SGAIC/REFFIS.
Dorset, Wiltshire, Hampshire. Trips for Salmon/Seatrout - Scotland/Norway. Warm water salt fly fishing - Bahamas.
All tackle can be provided.

Fly casting - All disciplines. Chalk Stream - Introductions, Intermediate and Advanced Frome/Piddle/Allen. Still Water - Introductions, Intermediate and Advanced For Trout and Carp. Salt Water Sea fly fishing on Dorset coast.

The Total Fly Fishing Company Ltd

David Griffiths, James Mills & John Hotchkiss
Tel 01747 871856
Email: info@totalflyfishing.co.uk www.totalflyfishing.co.uk
AAPGAI/STANIC Trout, Salmon, Sea Trout.
The Total Experience for:
Expert Casting Tuition (AAPGAI/GAIA)
Guided chalk stream fishing.
Salmon and Sea Trout fishing in: U.K., and abroad.
Overseas saltwater fly fishing.
Bespoke Corporate days

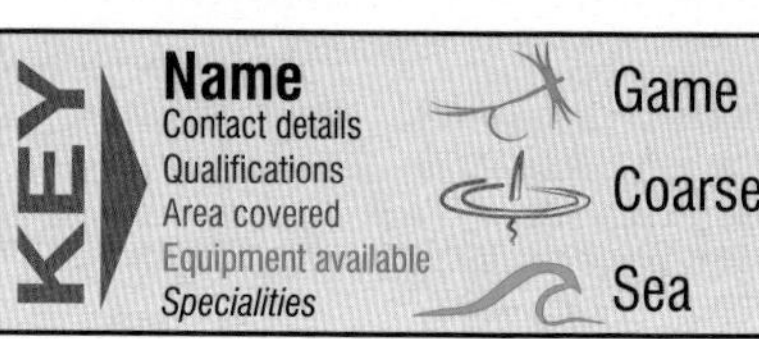

KEY
Name
Contact details
Qualifications
Area covered
Equipment available
Specialities
Game
Coarse
Sea

time to buy your rod licence

Rod licences expire on 31 March

All money raised helps to provide better fishing

Anyone aged 12 years or over who fishes for salmon, trout, freshwater fish or eels in England or Wales must have an Environment Agency rod licence. Children under 12 years of age do not require a licence.

Licence type	Licence Category	1 April 2008 to 31 March 2009
Non-migratory trout, char, freshwater fish (coarse fish) and eels	Full annual Concessionary annual Junior annual 8-day temporary 1-day temporary	£25.00 £16.75 £5.00 £9.00 £3.50
Salmon, migratory trout (sea trout), non-migratory trout, char, freshwater fish (coarse fish) and eels	Full annual Concessionary annual Junior annual 8-day temporary 1-day temporary	£68.00 £45.00 £5.00 £22.00 £7.50

You can buy your rod licence in four easy ways:

- At every Post Office in England and Wales
- By Direct Debit 08708 506 506
- Online at www.environment-agency.gov.uk/rodlicence
- Environment Agency Telephone Sales 0870 166 2662
  Lines open 8am-8pm, 7 days a week except Bank Holidays.
  Calls charged at standard rate. A small additional charge will be made.

Concessionary licences apply if:
You are aged 16 or under
You are aged 65 or over
You have a Blue Badge parking concession, or are in receipt of Disability Living Allowance.
Please contact your local Social Services Department for more information on how to get a Blue Badge.

Failure to produce a valid Environment Agency rod licence could result in prosecution and a maximum fine of £2,500

THE GET HOOKED GUIDE

The Light Fantastic

Dominic Garnett

You wouldn't use a sledgehammer to crack a nut or a flamethrower to cook a steak. So why do anglers of all disciplines use such heavy tackle to land relatively small fish? It's time to put the fun back into fishing and join the light tackle revolution says Dominic Garnett.

One of my favourite scenes from Monty Python's Flying Circus was a sketch where machine guns and rocket launchers are used to kill a mosquito. It was about the daftest case of overkill conceivable. But how far off this scenario are some of today's anglers? From specimen carp set ups on half acre ponds to the power-house rods used to tame undersized sea fish, where will it all end?

Naturally, tackle choice is a highly personal issue. The golden rule is to use "balanced" tackle, fit for the job. But somewhere into the equation must come sporting consideration, since we are all here to enjoy our fishing, aren't we? Most fish will put a pleasing bend in our carbon, given the chance; but set up too heavy and playing all but the biggest specimens becomes a chore rather than a thrill.

Something to carp about...

Brilliant though they are, carp have changed the entire mentality of coarse fishing towards big fish tactics. But whilst a trio of 3lb test curve rods may be ideal for a gravel pit, the same set up is now being found throughout the land at day ticket carp fisheries. Whilst the tackle companies cash in, anglers are missing out on a lot of fun, hauling in carp as if they were bream.

It is not just for the sake of fun that I would advocate a change of approach in these circumstances however; replace the tackle mountain with a lighter set up and you will often find a far more effective method. A light float rig will earn more bites and spook far fewer fish than casting around with heavy leads. It needn't be a small carp method either and it's interesting to note that carping pioneers such as "B.B" and Dick Walker often used 5-8 lb line where conditions permitted. My other half consistently beats the bivvy crew with a waggler or free lined bait on our local ponds; to the point where they sometimes get sick of watching her catching and pack up.

Simplicity itself: Jo Burgess took this double figure carp on a free lined mixer to 8lb line.

All well and good, you might say, but what happens when you hook a double figure carp? Not a problem with today's high standard of tackle; just take your time, set your drag carefully and play fish sensibly but firmly. In fact, even some of the specimen boys are now stepping down their tackle in search of better enjoyment and more bites. Running rigs and lighter lines are clearly the way to go when action slows on conventional tackle.

Or otherwise, next time you fish for summer carp, I dare you to take a single rod and reel and free line a mixer or piece of crust. If you find a more straightforward or exciting method, let me know.

Sea the difference?

With specimen sized fish in short supply around our coast, sea anglers too are beginning to see the sporting benefit of light tackle. And although a beach caster may be essential for distance work, there are plenty of places where big lumps of lead are totally unnecessary. Rocks, piers, estuaries and harbours are all ideal for light tackle, if you can be bothered to experiment.

The hard-fighting mackerel is probably the best example of a species undervalued because of crude conventional tackle. If you don't rate the mackerel as a fighter, try swapping the feathers and beach caster combo for a spinning rod and 8lb line. Any metal lure will also work, but to my mind there is hardly a finer sight in shore fishing than a float surging off as a mackerel takes the bait, followed by that serious looking curve in the rod. Equally, with worm or live prawn baits, the float is a thrilling way to take wrasse, pollack and even bass.

Just remember to keep tackle balanced and avoid crude rods, oversized hooks and those gruesome floats that could almost be used as buoyancy aids. That carp rod could also come in handy...

Flying Away

Bring game fishing tackle into the picture and the light approach becomes even more thrilling. Today's anglers realise that fly fishing is about far more than catching trout and can offer unbeatable fun and excitement for carp, bass, pike, pollack... you name it, the chances are it can be taken on the fly.

Once again though, provided the tackle is balanced and appropriate, stepping down our approach can be the key to a healthier fighting arc. The small stream fisherman, for example, might find using his 7-8ft wand terrific fun for still water rainbow trout. Your river tool might take on a dangerous looking curve, but in actual fact is ideal for presenting small dries and a light blank is the ideal shock absorber to protect light tippets. Fighting a two pound rainbow will never be the same again!

Seeing the light

In these size obsessed times it is all too easy to fall into the trap of gearing up too heavy. Fun becomes a secondary consideration and we forget the fighting qualities of many of the fish we catch. Yet the technical excellence of specimen tackle shouldn't dictate our fishing, which is at its most fun when we keep it simple. More often than not you'll find that straightforward, balanced tackle is perfectly capable of landing bigger fish, and scaling down a little will earn you more bites into the bargain. Clearly the final choice is yours. But for the sake of enjoyment alone, why not lighten up a little?

A 3/4 weight fly rod turns an average rainbow trout into a prize fighter.

Game Fishing Contacts For the Salmon & Trout Association

CORNWALL

S&TA Cornwall Branch
Mr A G Hawken
Tel: 01208 75513
Email: alan@aghawken.freeserve.co.uk

DEVON

S&TA North Devon Branch
Lt Col J D V Michie
Tel: 01837 871156
Email: duncmcnen@aol.com

S&TA South & East Devon and Tamar Branch
Mr C Hall
Tel: 01837 840420
Email: hall@skaigh.freeserve.co.uk

SOMERSET

S&TA Somerset Branch
Mrs S Pizii
Tel: 01823 480 719
Email: pizii@supanet.com

DORSET

S&TA Bristol & West Branch
Mr R Buckland
Tel: 01225 760465
Email: roy@buckland-1.wanadoo.co.uk

HAMPSHIRE

S&TA Hampshire Branch
Mr E P Morgan
Tel: 01730 263843
Email: ellis@ellismorgan.co.uk

S&TA West Sussex Branch
Mr K Johnston
Tel: 01903 725353
Email: Kevin_johnston@yahoo.com

S&TA Wessex Branch
Mr D Searle
Tel: 01258 840681
Email: Lesley@searle999.fsnet.co.uk

S&TA has the influence to change Government policy, legislation, and management practices to protect and improve the water environment. Stay informed and take action. Join today and make your voice heard where it matters.

Join the fight for the future of game angling and the environment.

For further S&TA information
Tel: 0207 283 5838
Email: hq@salmon-trout.org
Website:
www.salmon-trout.org

National Fishing Week 2008 Dates Announced

'All encompassing' is the theme behind this year's National Fishing Week. That's the clear message from the organisers as the dates for the festival of fishing were confirmed as 19th – 27th July 2008.

"We want to embrace all disciplines of the sport, and to this end it was crucial that we secured the help of the Angling Development Board to achieve this", said Sean O'Driscoll, Chairman of the Angling Trades Association, one of the main sponsors of the event.

"I am pleased to confirm that the Environment Agency has also shown its willingness to get heavily involved once again, and following on from the great work by Neill Sellers over the past four years I am delighted to welcome the Get Hooked on Fishing team to project manage this years event," continued Sean.

Now in its 15th year, National Fishing Week has introduced tens of thousands of newcomers to the sport, and is recognised as critical to the sport's development and future.

For further details please contact:
Sean O'Driscoll 0778 8922976

WILTSHIRE

WILTSHIRE

and Gloucestershire

RIVER FISHING
STILLWATER COARSE
STILLWATER TROUT
SEA FISHING
WHERE TO STAY

Wiltshire Game Road Directions

155. Avon Springs Fishing Lakes
Please Tel: 01980 653557 or 07774 801401 for directions.

156. Lechlade & Bushyleaze Trout Fisheries
GLOUCESTERSHIRE - Lechlade and Bushyleaze Trout Fisheries lie near the headwaters of the River Thames, 0.5 miles east of the town of Lechlade. They are clearly signposted on the A361 Swindon to Burford Road. Within easy travelling distance of Oxford, Birmingham and Bristol, and only 90 minutes from London, the fisheries are a short drive from either the M4 or the M40. Tel: 01367 253266.

157. Manningford Trout Fishery
The Fishery is 2 miles north of Upavon on the A345. Tel: 07917 646073 for more details.

Wiltshire Coarse Road Directions

158. Cuckoos Rest Fishery
Please Tel: 01373 826792 or 07850 431472 for directions.

159. Lakeside Rendezvous
Easily accessed off the A342 & is approximately a 20 minute drive. From Chippenham exit the M4 motorway. We are 90 minutes from London. Nearest train station is Chippenham with direct links to Bristol & London. Tel: 01380 725447.

160. Longleat & Shearwater
From Warminster take 362 towards Frome, follow signs to Longleat. Further information from the bailiff, Nick Robbins on 01985 844496 or 07889 625999.

161. Tucking Mill
Wessex Water fisheries. Tel: 0845 600 4 600.

162. Waldens Farm Fishery
Off the A36 Salisbury to Southampton Road near Whaddon. For further details Tel: 01722 710480 or 07766 451173.

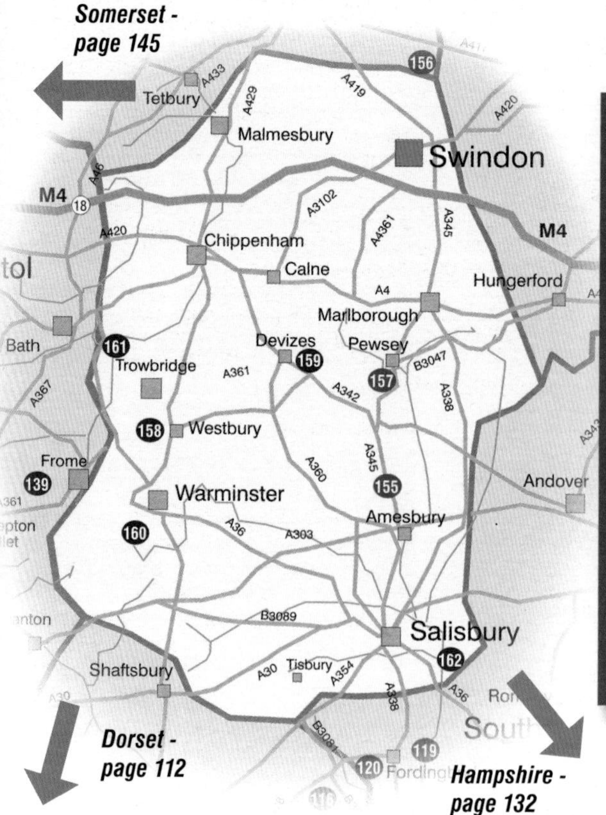

Only advertisers are located on this map.

Please note..

All of the information on fisheries, clubs and charters in this guide is published in a fully searchable format on our web site at...

gethooked.co.uk

The web site includes additional information that does not appear in this guide.

Wiltshire River Fishing

AVON HAMPSHIRE

For detailed description of the Avon, see under Hampshire river fishing.

Calne Angling Association
Contact: Miss J M Knowler, 123a London Road, Calne, *Tel:* 01249 812003, *Water:* River Avon, River Marden. *Species:* Barbel to 8lb, Pike to 8lb, Carp to 10lb, Bream to 6lb, Rudd to 8oz, Roach to 2.5lb. *Permits:* T.K.Tackle. *Charges:* Please enquire at T.K.Tackle. *Season:* River: June - March. *Methods:* No restrictions.

Salisbury & District Angling Club
Contact: Rick Polden - Secretary, The Cartshed, New Bottom Road, Stratford-Sub-Castle, Salisbury, *Tel:* 01722 321164, *Water:* Several Stretches on River Avon at Little Durnford (premium Trout fishery & Grayling), Amesbury, Ratfyn Farm & Countess Water. Also fishing on Dorset Stour (mixed fishery), River Wylye (premium Trout & Grayling), Nadder (Trout & Coarse), Bourne & Ratfyn Lake at Amesbury. Premier stocked chalkstream fishing. *Species:* All species Coarse and Game. Roach to 3lbs, Chub to 6lbs plus, Barbel to 10lbs plus, Pike to 20lbs plus. Wild Trout, Grayling plus migratory Trout and Salmon. *Permits:* Enquire via Secretary at secretary@salisburydistrictac.co.uk or club address. Day ticket available for certain waters. At Eadies Sports and Fishing Tackle, Shop Catherine Street, Salisbury. *Charges:* Membership £71. Game membership £148, prices due to rise slightly in 2008. Coarse membership open. More details from the secretary. New members £20 registration on joining. Membership for game section subject to a waiting list. *Season:* Lakes: 1st June - 31st March. Rivers: 16th June - 14th March - Coarse. 1st April - 15th October - Trout. 1st February - 31st August - Salmon. *Methods:* As per rules for each fishery.

Services Dry Fly Fishing Association
Contact: Major (Retd) CD Taylor - Hon Secretary, c/o G2 Sy,HQ 43 (Wessex) Brigade, Picton Barracks, Bulford Camp, Salisbury, *Tel:* 01980 672161, *Mobile:* 07850 790066, *Water:* 7 miles on River Avon from Bulford upstream to Fifield. *Species:* Brown Trout & Grayling. *Permits:* Fishing Restricted to Serving & Retired members of the Armed Forces and MOD civilians. For membership details apply to Secretary. *Charges:* On application. *Season:* 24 April - 14 October. Grayling until 31st December. *Methods:* Only upstream fishing permitted, dry fly exclusively during May & dry fly/nymph thereafter.

Wroughton Angling Club
Contact: Phil Sloan, 35 Maunsell Way, Wroughton, Swindon, *Tel:* 01793 813980, *Mobile:* 07747 641632, *Water:* 1.25 miles Rivers Avon and Marden at Chippenham, Reservoir at Wroughton. *Species:* Roach, Perch, Bream, Pike, Barbel, Chub, Carp, Tench. *Permits:* Contact Phil Sloan on details above. *Charges:* £25 per year. £6.50 juniors and OAPs. Prices may change in 2008. Day tickets available through Andrew Sloan. *Season:* Closed mid March. Re-opens 1 May. *Methods:* No night fishing. No peanuts, particle baits, dog biscuits or nuts of any description.

AVON WILTSHIRE

See under BRISTOL AVON

Avon Springs Fishing Lake (River)
Contact: BJ Bawden, Recreation Road, Durrington, Salisbury, *Tel:* 01980 653557, *Mobile:* 07774 801401, *Water:* 1 mile Wiltshire Avon at Durrington. Two Trout lakes, see entry under Stillwater Trout, Salisbury *Species:* Brown Trout and Grayling. *Charges:* £50 day ticket. River and Lake ticket £60. *Methods:* Fly only.

Upavon Farm
Contact: Peter C Prince, No 3, The Old Tractor Yard, Rushall, Near Pewsey, *Tel:* 01980 630008, *Mobile:* 07770 922544, *Water:* 0.75 miles on Hampshire Avon in Wiltshire. *Species:* Brown Trout, both stocked and Wild, up to 3lb avarage 1.5lb. Wild Grayling to 2lb average 1lb. *Permits:* Day, Season Permits. *Charges:* Day ticket £70, Grayling day rate £25. £500 for a season. *Season:* Brown Trout commences 15th April, ends 30th September. Grayling fishing thereafter. *Methods:* Catch and release, barbless hooks excepting annual season ticket holders.

Wiltshire Fishery Association
Contact: Richard Archer (Hon Sec.), Lanes End, Hindon Road, Dinton, Salisbury, *Tel:* 01722 717990, *Water:* An association of riparian owners and fishing club representatives. The association covers the River Avon catchment above Salisbury and it's tributaries.

BRISTOL AVON

Malmesbury to Chippenham

Coarse fisheries predominate in this section, although Trout are stocked by fishing associations in some areas. Arguably one of the best fisheries in the country, this section contains a wide range of specimen fish. Local records include: Roach 3lb 2oz, Perch 3lb 3oz, Tench 8lb 5 1/2oz, Bream 8lb 8oz, Dace 1lb 2oz, Chub 7lb 10oz, Carp 20lb 8 1/4oz and Pike 33lb 3oz. Also many Barbel to 12lb have been reported.

Remember a ♿ means the fishery has disabled facilities - contact them direct for further details

Superb 3lb 13oz Perch landed by Ashley from Ringwood Tackle

Airsprung Angling Association (Bristol Avon)
Contact: Bill Turner, 124 Langford Rd, Trowbridge, *Tel:* 01225 766219, *Water:* See also entry under Kennet & Avon Canal. Bristol Avon at Bradford on Avon, Pondfields. *Species:* Carp, Pike, Bream, Chub, Roach, Rudd, Dace, Tench, Perch, etc. *Permits:* Wiltshire Angling, 01225 763835; West Tackle, Trowbridge, 01225 755472. Trowbridge Road Post Office, Bradford-upon Avon. *Charges:* On application. *Season:* Subject to normal close season. *Methods:* Details from Association.

Avon Angling Club (Bristol Avon)
Contact: R.P. Edwards, 56 Addison Road, Melksham, *Tel:* 01225 705036, *Water:* 4 miles of Bristol Avon. See also entry under Kennet and Avon Canal. *Species:* Roach, Bream, Tench, Chub, Barbel, Perch, Pike, Eels. *Permits:* Wiltshire Angling, Trowbridge. Premier Angling, Chippenham or call 01225 705036. *Charges:* Day ticket £4. Full Licence £15. Junior/OAP Licence £5. *Season:* Current EA Byelaws apply. *Methods:* No blood worm or joker to be used.

Chippenham Angling Club
Contact: Simon Wade, *Mobile:* 07776 172649, *Water:* 3 miles on River Avon. Carp lakes at Corsham. *Species:* Barbel 15.5lb, Chub 5lb, Roach 2.5lb, Bream 10lb, Perch 4lb, Pike 33lb, Tench 9lb, Carp 20lb (all weights approximate). *Permits:* Premier Angling, Chippenham: 01249 659210. *Charges:* Please telephone for prices. *Season:* June 16th - March 14th.

Haydon Street Angling Society (Bristol Avon)
Contact: Mike Cottle, Silver Greys, 43 Dayhouse Lane, Badbury Wick, Chiseldon, *Tel:* 01793 740255, *Mobile:* 01793 531831, *Water:* Bristol Avon at Dauntsey, Dodford Farm. *Species:* Mixed including Chub, Barbel and Roach, Tench. *Permits:* Members only. No day tickets. *Charges:* Full membership £25. Annual renewal £25. *Season:* Subject to statutory close season on rivers.

Swindon Isis Angling Club (Bristol Avon)
Contact: Peter Gilbert, 31 Havelock St, Swindon, *Tel:* 01793 535396, *Water:* Two miles of the Bristol Avon at Sutton Benger above Chippenham. *Species:* Bream 9lb 9oz, Perch 4lb, Tench 9lb, Barbel 15lb, Pike 28lb, Roach 2lb 7oz, Eels to 5lbs and usual species. *Permits:* Tackle shops in Swindon, Chippenham, Cirencester and Calne. *Charges:* As per lake entry. *Season:* From 16th June to 14th March. *Methods:* No bans.

KENNET AND AVON CANAL

There are some 58 kilometres of canal within the Bristol Avon catchment area which averages one metre in depth and thirteen metres in width. The Kennet & Avon Canal joins the River Avon at Bath with the River Kennet between Reading and Newbury. The canal was opened in 1810 to link the Severn Estuary with the Thames. The canal, now much restored, provides excellent fishing with Carp to 25lb, Tench to 5lb also Roach, Bream, Perch, Rudd, Pike and Gudgeon.

Airsprung Angling Association (Kennet & Avon)
Contact: Bill Turner, 124 Langford Rd, Trowbridge, *Tel:* 01225 766219, *Water:* Two kilometres on Kennet and Avon Canal from Beehive Pub to Avoncliffe aquaduct at Bradford-on-Avon. Kings Arms Hilperton Road Bridge to Crossguns, Avoncliff. *Species:* Carp, Bream, Chub, Roach, Rudd, Dace, Tench, Perch, etc. *Permits:* Wiltshire Angling, 01225 763835; West Tackle, Trowbridge, 01225 755472. Trowbridge Road Post Office, Bradford-upon Avon. *Charges:* Day ticket £3. Full licence £23.

Season: Open all year. *Methods:* No night fishing, No fishing on match days in pegged areas. No radios etc. No fishing within 25 metres of locks etc. No bloodworm or joker; be aware of overhead cables!

Avon Angling Club (Kennet and Avon)

Contact: R.P. Edwards, 56 Addison Road, Melksham, *Tel:* 01225 705036, *Water:* 2.5 miles of Kennet and Avon Canal. See also entry under Bristol Avon. *Species:* Bream, Tench, Roach, Carp. *Permits:* Wiltshire Angling, Trowbridge. Premier Angling, Chippenham or call 01225 705036. *Charges:* Day ticket £4. Full licence £15. Junior/OAP licence £5. *Season:* All year.

Devizes A.A. (Kennet & Avon Canal)

Contact: T.W. Fell, 21 Cornwall Crescent, Devizes, *Tel:* 01380 725189, *Water:* 15 miles from Semington to Pewsey, also 6.5 acre lake. *Species:* Carp 15 - 23lb, Roach, Tench, Pike to 26lb, Bream. *Permits:* Bernies Bait, Snuff St., Devizes, Wiltshire. Tel: 01380 730712. Local tackle shops in Devizes, Melksham, Trowbridge, Chippenham, Calne, Swindon. Wiltshire Angling: 01225 763835. *Charges:* Adult £30 per season. Senior citizen £13. Junior (8-12) £9 or (12-16) £13. Day tickets £3.50 (not sold on the bank). 14 day ticket £9. *Season:* E.A. byelaws apply. *Methods:* Anglers must be in possession of current Environment Agency rod licence.

Marlborough & District A.A

Contact: Mr.M.Ellis, Failte, Elcot Close, Marlborough, *Tel:* 01672 512922, *Water:* Kennet & Avon Canal (12 miles approx.). Also 1 lake. *Species:* Roach, Perch, Pike, Tench, Bream, Carp. *Permits:* Mr M Ellis, 'Failte', Elcot Close, Marlborough, Wilts, SN8 2BB. *Charges:* Full membership £35 plus £5 joining fee, Junior up to 16 £10, Ladies £10, O.A.P's £10. *Season:* Open all year. Membership from 1st Jan - 31st Dec. *Methods:* No live baiting, no bloodworm or joker. Barbless hooks only on lake.

Pewsey & District Angling Association

Contact: Jim Broomham, 85 Broad Fields, Pewsey, *Tel:* 01672 563690, *Water:* 4 Miles Kennet & Avon canal. Milkhouse Bridge (East) to Lady's Bridge (West). *Species:* Roach, Tench, Carp, Bream, Perch, Pike, Rudd and Chub. *Permits:* The Wharf, Pewsey (Day tickets only). Season tickets from Woottons, 5 North St, Pewsey. *Charges:* Day tickets Senior £3 / Junior/OAP £2. £5 on bank. *Season:* No closed season. *Methods:* Rod and line.

NADDER

The River Nadder rises near Tisbury draining the escarpment of the South Wiltshire Downs and Kimmeridge Clay of the Wardour Vale. The River Wylye joins the Nadder near Wilton before entering the main River Avon at Salisbury.

The Nadder is well known as a mixed fishery of exceptional quality; there is a diverse array of resident species including Chub, Roach, Dace, Bream, Pike, Perch, Brown Trout and Salmon. Much of the fishing is controlled by estates and syndicates although two angling clubs offer some access to the river.

Remember a ♿ means the fishery has disabled facilities - contact them direct for further details

Compton Chamberlayne

Contact: Simon Cooper, Fishing Breaks, The Mill, Heathman Street, Nether Wallop, Stockbridge, Hants. *Tel:* 01264 781988, *Water:* Seven beats on part of the Compton Chamberlayne Estate. *Species:* Brown Trout. *Permits:* By phone or e-mail from Fishing Breaks. *Charges:* May 1-16 £125. May 17-June 15 £165. June 16-July 31 £125. August 1-September 30 £100. *Season:* May to September. *Methods:* Dry fly & Nymph only.

Tisbury Angling Club

Contact: Mr E.J.Stevens, Knapp Cottage, Fovant, Salisbury, *Tel:* 01722 714245, *Water:* 3 miles on River Nadder. 3.5 acre lake and 2.5 acre lake. *Species:* Roach, Chub, Dace, Pike, Bream, Perch, Carp, Brown Trout. *Permits:* £5 per day Guest tickets. *Charges:* £30 per season. Juniors £7.50 per season. OAPs £12.50 per season. Seniors £5 per day (dawn to dusk) Juniors £3 per day (dawn to dusk). New members welcome. *Season:* 16th June to 14th March on river and Wardour Lake. Dinton Lake open all year. *Methods:* General.

SEMINGTON BROOK

The Semington Brook is spring fed from Salisbury Plain and flows through a flat area to its confluence with the River Avon downstream of Melksham. In the upper reaches and in some of its tributaries Brown Trout predominate. Downstream of Bulkington coarse fish prevail with sizeable Bream, Chub, Roach, Dace and Perch.

STOUR

See description under Dorset, river fishing.

Stourhead (Western) Estate

Contact: Sally Monkhouse, Estate Office Gasper Mill, Stourton, Warminster, *Tel:* (01747) 840643, *Water:* 10 ponds and lakes, largest 10 acres, on the headwaters of the Stour. *Species:* Wild Brown Trout. *Permits:* Weekly permit £30. *Charges:* Season permit for fly fishing £100, no day tickets. *Season:* April to October - no time restrictions.

THAMES

Haydon Street Angling Society (Hannington)

Contact: Mike Cottle, Silver Greys, 43 Dayhouse Lane, Badbury Wick, Chiseldon, *Tel:* 01793 740255/531831, *Water:* Hannington: a prime stretch of the upper Thames. Also a small mixed coarse lake at Dauntsey, Wilts. *Species:* Mixed including Chub to 6lb and Barbel to 12lb. *Permits:* Members only. No day tickets. *Charges:* Full membership £25. Annual renewal £25. *Season:* Subject to statutory close season on rivers.

Haydon Street Angling Society (Ingelsham)

Contact: Mike Cottle, Silver Greys, 43 Dayhouse Lane, Badbury Wick, Chiseldon, *Tel:* 01793 531831, *Water:* Ingelsham: a prime stretch of the upper Thames. *Species:* Mixed including Chub, Bream and Roach. *Permits:* Members only. No day tickets. *Charges:* Full membership £25. Annual renewal £25. *Season:* Subject to statutory close season on rivers.

WYLYE

The River Wylye rises near Kingston Deverill and flows off chalk, draining the western reaches of Salisbury Plain. The river confluences with the River Nadder at Wilton near Salisbury, then joins the main River Avon which flows south to Christchurch.
This river is best described as a 'classic' chalk stream supporting predominantly Brown Trout; hence most fisheries here are managed for fly fishermen. The fishing is predominantly controlled by local syndicates and estates.

Boreham Mill
Contact: Simon Cooper, Fishing Breaks, The Mill, Heathman Street, Nether Wallop, Stockbridge, Hants. *Tel:* 01264 781988, *Water:* Single bank fishing for one or two rods. *Species:* Brown Trout. *Permits:* By phone or e-mail from Fishing Breaks. *Charges:* April 8-May 9 £75. May 10-June 15 £100. June 16-September 30 £75. *Season:* May to September. *Methods:* Dry fly & Nymph only.
Langford Lakes (River Wylye)
Contact: Wiltshire Wildlife Trust, Duck Street, Steeple Langford, Salisbury, *Tel:* 01722 792011, *Water:* Wylye - half mile. *Species:* Brown Trout, Grayling. *Charges:* £30 Trout, £20 Grayling per rod. *Season:* April 15th - Oct 14th Trout season. Oct 15th - March 14th Grayling season. *Methods:* Full details at Fishery.
Wilton Fly Fishing Club
Contact: Mr A Simmons or Hon Sec, Keepers Cottage, Manor Farm Lane, Great Wishford, *Tel:* 01722 790231, *Mobile:* 07866 343593, *Water:* Over 6 miles of chalkstream on the river Wylye (including carriers). *Species:* Wild Brown Trout, fish of 2-3lb caught every season. Past record 7lb 2oz. Large head of Grayling to over 2lb 12oz. *Permits:* Season membership only via Secretary: Roger Cullum-Kenyon, Rockvale Cottage, Redlap, Dartmouth, Devon, TQ6 0JR. *Charges:* Prices on application to secretary. *Season:* Trout 16th April to 15th October. Grayling 16th June to 14th March. *Methods:* Trout: Dry fly and upstream nymph only. Grayling: Dry fly and upstream nymph only in Trout season. Trotting also allowed from 15th October to 14th March. Barbless hooks preferred.

Stillwater Coarse

BRADFORD ON AVON

Rushy Lane Fishery
Contact: Mike or Val, South Wraxall, Bradford-on-Avon, *Tel:* 01249 714558, *Mobile:* 07780 635333, *Water:* 5 lakes to 1.25 acres - 2 with specimen Carp to 38lb, plus mixed coarse lakes. *Species:* Carp to 38lb, Tench 3.5lb and Roach 1lb. *Permits:* By telephone only. *Charges:* On application. *Season:* Open all year. *Methods:* Dawn to dusk, no night fishing, no nets on specimen ponds, no boilies, no nuts, barbless hooks only.

CALNE

Blackland Lakes
Contact: J.or B. Walden, Blackland Lakes Holiday & Leisure Centre, Stockley Lane, Calne, *Tel:* 01249 813672, *Mobile:* 07974 135825, *Water:* 1 acre and 0.75 acre. *Species:* Carp to 33lb, Tench to 5lb, Roach to 4lb, Bream to 8lb, Perch to 4lb. *Permits:* Day tickets. *Charges:* 1 rod £9, extra rods £1, junior £5, 14 - 18yrs £6, extra rod £1. Night fishing 7pm - 9am £15 adult, £10 others. Juniors must be accompanied by an adult. If camping: 1 to 5 days - £5, juniors £4. 5 days or more £4, juniors £3. Night fishing for campers £5. *Season:* Open all year. *Methods:* Barbless hooks, no ground bait, no large fish or Bream and Carp in keepnets.
Bowood Lake
Contact: Estate Office, Bowood, Calne, *Tel:* 01249 812102, *Water:* 35 acre lake. *Species:* Coarse. *Permits:* Available from the estate office. Season permits only - waiting list. *Charges:* Season only. £162 + VAT. Junior members £81 + VAT (under 16yrs) *Season:* June to March. Dawn to dusk.

CHIPPENHAM

Chippenham Angling Club (Coarse Lake)
Contact: Simon Wade, *Mobile:* 07776 172649, *Water:* See entry under Avon. Carp Lake at Corsham. *Permits:* Members only, no day tickets
Ivy House Lakes & Fisheries
Contact: Jo, Ivyhouse Lakes, Grittenham, Chippenham, *Tel:* 01666 510368, *Mobile:* 07748 144788, *Water:* 1 Acre & 6 Acre lakes. 2 Canal type sections *Species:* Carp, Bream, Roach, Tench, Chub, Perch, Crucians, Grass Carp *Permits:* On the bank day tickets, no night fishing. *Charges:* Day tickets £5 per day (1 rod). £3 Ladies O.A.Ps etc. Match booking £5. Prices may change for 2008. *Season:* All year. Gates open 6am - closed 1 hour after dusk. *Methods:* Boilies & tiger nuts banned and all meats, ground bait in moderation. No fixed feeders.
Sevington Lakes ♿
Contact: Fiona and Andrew Butler, Sevington Farm, Sevington, Chippenham, *Tel:* 01249 783723, *Water:* Natural spring fed lakes approx. 2 acres. *Species:* Mirror, Common and Crucian Carp to 27lbs plus Perch, Roach, Tench and Rudd. *Charges:* Day ticket £7 (2 rods) £3 extra rod (3 rods max.). Night fishing £14 (24hrs) All under 16's must be accompanied by responsible adult when night fishing. *Season:* Open all year, night fising by arrangement only. *Methods:* Barbless hooks. No keepnets. No bait boats.

Nice Ghostie in this bag of Carp from Avalon

Silverlands Lake
Contact: Mr & Mrs King, Wick Farm, Lacock, Chippenham, *Tel:* 01249 730244, *Mobile:* 07720 509377, *Water:* One spring fed 2.5 acre lake. *Species:* Carp, Tench, Bream, Pike. *Permits:* Only from the fishery. *Charges:* Day or night ticket £8, £2 per extra rod. 24 hour ticket £24, £2 per extra rod. Season tickets available. *Season:* Open all year. *Methods:* No nuts, dogs to be kept on a lead at all times.

Wyatts Lake
Contact: L. Beale, Wyatts Lake Farm, Westbrook, Bromham, Nr Chippenham, *Tel:* 01380 859651, *Mobile:* 07976 260180, *Water:* 2 acre lake approx. *Species:* Mirror and Common Carp to 20lb. *Permits:* On site. *Charges:* £5 per person (unlimited rods). *Season:* Open all year 24 hours a day. Night fishing available. *Methods:* Good fishing practices required and expected.

DEVIZES

Devizes A.A. (Coarse Lake)
Contact: T.W. Fell, 21 Cornwall Crescent, Devizes, *Tel:* 01380 725189, *Water:* 6.5 acre Crookwood Lake, well stocked. *Permits:* Bernies Bait, Snuff St., Devizes, Wiltshire. Tel: 01380 730712. Local tackle shops in Devizes, Melksham, Trowbridge, Chippenham, Calne, Swindon. Wiltshire Angling: 01225 763835. *Charges:* Please phone for details. *Methods:* Anglers must be in possession of current Environment Agency rod licence.

Lakeside Rendezvous
Contact: Phil & Sarah Gleed, Devizes Road, Rowde, Nr. Devizes, *Tel:* 01380 725447, *Water:* 2 acre lake. *Species:* Carp - 29lb 4oz, Bream, Roach, Perch, Rudd, Tench. *Charges:* Day tickets not available individually. Hire of whole lake is possible and by prior arrangement, can fit up to 20 anglers - £90 per day. *Season:* No closed season. *Methods:* Barbless hooks, no nuts. Keepnets permitted in competition only. All nets etc. must be dipped.

MELKSHAM

Airsprung Angling Association (Burbrooks Reservoir)
Contact: Bill Turner, 124 Langford Rd, Trowbridge, *Tel:* 01225 766219, *Water:* 15 Peg lake, 1 acre, at Bromham between Devizes and Melksham *Species:* Mixed stillwater coarse. *Permits:* Day tickets from local tackle shops; Devizes, Trowbridge, Chippenham and Cost Cutters in Bromham. *Charges:* £5 a day adult, £3 concessions. *Season:* All year. *Methods:* No boilies or nuts, no night fishing.

Burbrooks Lake
Contact: Mr Bill Turner, 124 Langford Road, Trowbridge, *Tel:* 01225 766219, *Water:* 0.75 acre Lake between Melksham & Calne, and Devizes and Chippenham in the village of Bromham (New Road). *Species:* Mirror, Common & Crucian Carp, Bream, Tench, Roach, Perch, Gudgeon, Chub. *Permits:* Please contact The Cost Cutter in Bromham Village: 01380 850337. Calne TK Tackle: 01249 812003. Premier Tackle, Chippenham: 01249 659210. Wilts Angling, Trowbridge: 01225 763835. West Tackle, Trowbridge: 01225 755472. *Charges:* £5 Adults. £3 Juniors and OAPs. *Season:* Open all year dawn to dusk. *Methods:* No night fishing, only one rod per person, no hooks above size 8.

Leech Pool Lake
Contact: Rodney Mortimer, Leech Pool Farm, Norrington, Melksham, *Tel:* 01225 703615, *Mobile:* 07813 947170, *Water:* 1.25 acres lake. *Species:* Mirror and Common Carp up to 22lb. Tench 1lb to 2lb, Bream 1lb to 4.5lb. *Charges:* £5 per rod day fishing. £10 per rod night fishing. *Season:* Open all year dawn to dusk. *Methods:* Night fishing by arrangement only. No keepnets. Barbless hooks preferred.

MERE

Gillingham & District A A (Turners Paddock)
Contact: Simon Hebditch (Hon. Secretary), 8 Maple Way, Gillingham, Dorset. *Tel:* 01747 821218, *Mobile:* 07990 690613, *Water:* Turners Paddock at Stourhead Nr Mere (see also entry under River Fishing Stour). *Species:* Tench 6lb, Bream 7lb, Carp 15lb, Roach 2lb, Rudd 2lb, Hybrids, Perch, Eels 7lb 8oz. *Permits:* Mr P Stone (Treasurer) The Timepiece, Newbury, Gillingham, Dorset, SP8 4HZ. Tel: 01747 823339. Mr J Candy, Todber Manor Fisheries Shop, Tel: 01258 820384. Mere Post Office, High Street, Mere, Wiltshire. *Charges:* £5 day ticket, £30 season ticket. £15 juniors and concessions. (probable charges for 2008). *Season:* June 16th to March 14th. *Methods:* No fish in keepnets for more than 6 hours. Leave no litter. Feeder best for Bream & Tench. Waggler in shallower water. Pole off the dam wall. No balling of groundbait. Groundbait only to be introduced via a feeder or pole cup.

WALDENS FARM FISHERY
Five lakes offering a variety of quality Coarse Fishing. Stocked with Pike, Perch, Golden Rudd, Carp, Roach, Barbel, Bream, Orfe, Crucians, Tench & Golden Tench
Plus purpose built Match Lake for Private and Club Hire
Contact: David & Jackie Wateridge
Telephone: 01722 710480
Mobile: 07766 451173
THE nfc Walden GROUP
Walden Estate, West Grimstead, Salisbury, Wiltshire SP5 3RJ

SALISBURY

Langford Lakes (Brockbank Lake) ♿

Contact: Wiltshire Wildlife Trust Fishery, Duck Street, Steeple Langford, Salisbury, *Tel:* 01722 792011, *Water:* Brockbank lake 10 acres. *Species:* Roach, Bream, Tench, Common Carp, Perch and Pike. *Permits:* Club membership, on application in advance. *Charges:* Full details on application. *Season:* Closed season 16th March - 15th June. *Methods:* No night fishing.

Longhouse Fishery

Teffont, Salisbury, *Water:* 4 lakes - Wood lake approx. 1 acre plus 3 smaller lakes. *Species:* Common, Mirror, Ghost, Koi, Crucian Carp (to double figures), Roach, Rudd (2.6lb), Perch (3.9lb), Tench (3lb), Bream (3lb). *Permits:* Lakeside only. *Season:* All year, only 10 days closed for pheasant shoot (October - January). *Methods:* Only bans are no particles (pulses) other than hemp or corn. No night fishing, no boilies, barbless hooks only. No large Carp in keepnets. Children under 16, must be accompanied by an adult.

Salisbury & District Angling Club (Coarse Lakes)

Contact: Rick Polden - Secretary, The Cart Shed, New Bottom Road, Stratford-Sub-Castle, Salisbury, *Tel:* 01722 321164, *Water:* Peters Finger Lakes and Steeple Langford. See entry under Avon Hampshire. East Wellow Lakes. *Species:* Carp to 30lbs plus, Tench to 6lbs, Roach, Bream, Perch and Pike. *Charges:* £71 per season. Concessions for Senior Citizens £55, Juniors £27. Prices due to rise in 2008. *Season:* 1st June - 31st March.

Tisbury Angling Club (Coarse Lakes)

Contact: Mr E.J.Stevens, Knapp Cottage, Fovant, Nr. Salisbury, *Tel:* 01722 714245, *Water:* See also entry under Nadder (3 mile stretch). Old Wardour Lake (3.5 acre), 2 miles south of Tisbury and Dinton Lake (2.5 acre), 2 miles north of Tisbury. *Species:* Roach, Chub, Dace, Bream, Perch, Crucian Carp, Carp. *Permits:* £5 p/day guest tickets. *Charges:* Adult £30 p/season, OAP £12.50, Juniors £7.50. *Season:* 16th June to 14th March on river and Wardour Lake. Dinton Lake open all year.

Waldens Farm Fishery ♿

Contact: David & Jackie Wateridge, Waldens Farm, Walden Estate, West Grimstead, Salisbury, *Tel:* 01722 710480, *Mobile:* 07766 451173, *Water:* 5 lakes covering approx. 7.5 acres. *Species:* All coarse fish. Specimen Pike Lake. Specimen Carp Lake. 27 peg Match Lake for club or private hire. *Permits:* From the bank. *Charges:* Day (dawn to dusk) tickets Adult £6, Junior - O.A.P. £4, Evenings 5 p.m. onwards £4. Match peg fees £4.50. Night fishing by appointment only. Season ticket £75, Junior/O.A.P season £45. *Season:* Open full 12 months. *Methods:* Barbless hooks, net dips to be used, limited groundbait, no boilies, nuts or cereals. Keepnets allowed.

Watergate Farm

Contact: Charlie Rowland, *Mobile:* 07768 515332, *Water:* One acre lake. *Species:* Carp, Tench and Roach. *Permits:* On the bank. *Charges:* £6 per day. *Season:* Open all year. *Methods:* Full rules at fishery.

Witherington Farm Fishing ♿

New Cottage, Witherington Farm, Downton, Salisbury, *Tel:* 01722 710088, *Water:* 3 Well stocked lakes. Plus 93 peg match lake. Toilet facilities for disabled. Most swims accessible to wheelchairs. *Species:* Carp - 27lb, Tench - 7lb, Roach - 2.5lb, Bream - 6lb, Rudd - 0.5lb, Chub - 3lb, Perch - 3lb. *Permits:* From on-site Tackle shop. *Charges:* Full day £6, Half day £4, Full day Junior under 16 / Disabled / O.A.P. £4. *Season:* All year 6.30am - Dusk. *Methods:* No boilies, barbless hooks, all nets to be dipped, no night fishing, keepnets only permitted on Match lake. No cat meat, braided hook lengths, fixed rigs.

SWINDON

Coate Water Country Park

Contact: Mark Jennings, c/o Rangers Centre, Marlborough Road, Swindon, *Tel:* 01793 490150, *Water:* 56 acre reservoir, 4 metres deep. *Species:* Carp over 40lb, Pike 30lb, Bream, Perch, Roach. *Permits:* On the bank or from Ranger team. *Charges:* With 'Swindon Card' £5.20, conc - £1.70. Without £6.70, conc - £3.40. *Season:* 16 June to 14 March. *Methods:* No live baiting. No barbed hooks.

Mouldon Hill Angling Club ♿

Contact: Kevin Maddison (sec), 33 Castleview Road, Chiseldon, Swindon, *Mobile:* 07776 090255, *Water:* 4.5 acre lake, 3 islands, 30ft from river Ray. *Species:* Tench 8lb, Roach to 2lb, Perch to 4lb, Crucian Carp to 1lb, Bream 6lb, Rudd to 2lb, Chub to 6lb, Dace and Gudgeon. *Permits:* Day tickets: Junior £1, Concessionary/OAP £2, Senior £4. Available from House of Angling, Commercial Road, Swindon. Cotswold Angling Centre Kemray Street Ind Est, Swindon. Spar Shop, Marigold Close, Woodhall Park, Swindon. *Charges:* Full membership: Adult (new) £20, (renewal) £15. Junior (u16) £5. April to April. *Season:* Dawn to dusk, all year, no night fishing and no close season. *Methods:* Barbless hooks only. Carp mesh keepnets to be used. Full membership required for gate access to on site parking. Disabled access can be arranged, please phone.

Alf with a really pretty 17lb Mirror on a crust.

TROWBRIDGE

Rood Ashton Lake

Contact: Marlene Pike, Home Farm, Rood Ashton, Trowbridge, *Tel:* 01380 870272, *Water:* 7 acre lake available for matches - please enquire for details. *Species:* Carp, Tench, Roach. *Permits:* Home Farm and Lake View. *Charges:* 6am - 6pm £6, O.A.P's / Juniors £4. 6pm - 11am £5, O.A.P's / Juniors £3. Please enquire for match bookings. Prices may vary in 2008. *Season:* Open all year. *Methods:* No keepnets (only competitions). No tin cans or boilies, Barbless hooks only. No nuts. No night fishing.

Tucking Mill ♿

Contact: Wessex Water, *Tel:* 0845 600 4 600, *Water:* Free coarse fishing for disabled anglers from 16th June 2008 - 14th March 2009. *Species:* Roach, Chub, Tench and Large Carp. *Permits:* The site is regularly used by disabled angling clubs including Kingswood Disabled Angling Club and The Westcountry Disabled Angling Association. Further information about the clubs and matches can be found on the notice board at Tucking mill. *Charges:* Each disabled angler may bring along an able bodied assistant, who may also fish, but has to use the same pitch. *Season:* 8am to sunset throughout the year except in the close season. *Methods:* No keepnets, barbless hooks.

WARMINSTER

Lavington Angling Club

Contact: Tony Allen (sec.), 8a Yarnbrook, Nr Trowbridge, *Tel:* 01225 752541, *Water:* Great Cheverell Lake complex. Two 3 acre lakes. One half acre lake. Also river fishing both Trout and Coarse. *Species:* Carp to 30lb, Tench 4lb, Crucian 1lb, Tench 1.5lb, Bream 3lb. *Permits:* From the membership secretary: Mr Graham Pearce, 4a Holmfield, West Lavington, Devizes. *Charges:* £30. Access to locked car park via security number known only to members. *Season:* Two lakes open all year dawn to dusk. *Methods:* Barbless hooks only. No pellets. Max 1kg groundbait. From June 16 to September 31 no keepnets between 11am and 2pm.

Longleat Lakes & Shearwater

Contact: Nick Robbins, Longleat Estate Office, Longleat, Warminster, *Tel:* 01985 844496, *Mobile:* 07889 625999, *Water:* Longleat 3 Lakes, Top lake Carp up to 32lb, Shearwater 37 acres, Carp up to 25lb. Longleat, 20 Carp over 20lb. *Species:* Carp, Roach, Bream, Tench, Perch, Rudd. *Permits:* From bailiff on the bank. *Charges:* See our website or contact Nick Robbins. *Season:* Between April to Sept 7am - 7pm. *Methods:* No keepnets or Carp sacks, no boilies except Longleat. No nuts, peas, beans on all lakes, no bolt rigs. Barbless hooks only.

Warminster & District Angling Club

Contact: c/o Steves Tackle, 35 George Street, Warminster, *Tel:* 01985 847634, *Water:* Berkley Lake - 6 acres and Southleigh Lake at Crockerton - 2 acres. *Species:* Well stocked with all coarse fish. *Permits:* Club membership only. Details from Steves Tackle. *Season:* No closed season. *Methods:* Full rules at both lakes.

WESTBURY

Brokerswood Country Park

Contact: Mrs S.H.Capon, Brokerswood, Westbury, *Tel:* 01373 822238, *Water:* 5 acre lake within 80 acre country park. *Species:* Carp, Roach, Tench, Perch, Dace. *Charges:* Adults £5, Children and Senior Citizens £4. *Season:* Closed Season 1st - 31st May. Day Visitors - From 10am to Dusk and Residents on site - 8am to Dusk. *Methods:* Barbless hooks, no boilies, no keepnets.

Clivey Fishery

Contact: Chris Haines, Clivey Fishery, Dilton Marsh, Westbury, *Tel:* 01373 858311, *Mobile:* 07815 937816, *Water:* 1 acre lake - 16 pegs, 1/3 acre lake - 8pegs. *Species:* Roach, Rudd, Bream to 2lb, Perch, Carp to 19lb, Crucians, Tench to 3lb and Gudgeon. *Permits:* On site Tackle Shop. *Charges:* £4 Day Ticket. Juniors OAPs etc. £2.50. *Season:* All year. *Methods:* Barbless Hooks only.

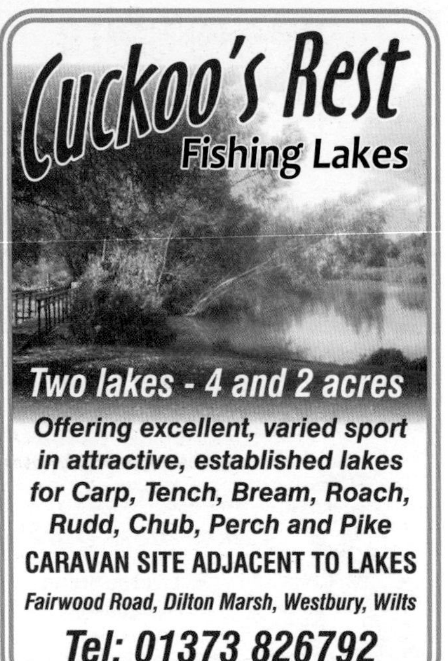

Cuckoo's Rest Fishing Lakes
Contact: Barry & Eileen Flack, Fairwood Road, Dilton Marsh, Westbury, *Tel:* 01373 826792, *Water:* One 4 acre lake and one 2 acre lake. *Species:* Carp 32lbs, Perch 2lbs 14oz, Rudd 2lbs, Bream 8lbs, Tench 6lbs, Roach 3lbs, Chub 3lbs, Pike 18lb. *Charges:* £5 p/day, £4 Juniors / OAP / Disabled. *Season:* All year 7am to Dusk. *Methods:* Barbless hooks.

Eden Vale A.A.
Contact: Steve Southall, Secretary, 18 Boulton Close, Westbury, *Tel:* 01373 302982, *Mobile:* 07979 462320, *Water:* 5.25 acre lake. *Species:* Carp (Common to 15lb, Mirror to 10lb), Bream to 3lb, Roach to 1.5lb, Perch to 1lb, Rudd to 0.75lb, possible Pike to 15lb. *Permits:* Day Tickets from Haines Angling, Dilton Marsh (01373 858311) Wiltshire Angling, Trowbridge - 01225 763835. *Charges:* Day: £5 adult - £4 junior. Members (restricted to 15 mile radius of Westbury) at present £25. New Members £10 joining fee. Applications to Sec. with S.A.E., must be sponsored by two existing members. *Season:* Open all year. *Methods:* No fixed rigs, no keepnets before June 16th, no Carp or Tench in keepnets.

Stillwater Trout

CALNE

Calstone Fishery
Contact: Estate Office, Bowood, Calne, *Tel:* 01249 812102, *Water:* 0.75 acre reservoir. *Species:* Trout (Brown & Rainbow). *Permits:* Available from the estate office. Season permits only - waiting list. *Charges:* Season only, £205 + VAT per rod. *Season:* April - October, Dawn to Dusk. *Methods:* Weekly bag limits - 2 brace. All Browns to be returned. No catch & return of Rainbow after 15th September. First 2 Rainbow must be taken on each visit.

CHIPPENHAM

Pheasant Fly Fishers
Contact: Iain MacKay, 2 Bath Road, Chippenham, *Tel:* 01225 858149, *Water:* None - A fly fishing club where members fish local waters and go on organised trips further afield. *Permits:* Please contact us on the number above or phone Alan Tonge on 01249 460401 for more details. Anglers are welcome to attend one of our regular meetings at the Pheasant Inn, Bath Road, Chippenham at 8pm on the first Tuesday of each month. Fly fishing beginners welcome. *Charges:* Club membership fees £25. May vary in 2008. *Season:* Fly fishing trips are organised throughout the year.

DEVIZES

Mill Farm Trout Lakes ♿
Contact: Bill Coleman, Mill Farm Trout Lakes, Worton, Devizes, *Tel:* 01380 813138, *Mobile:* 07761 181369, *Water:* 2 Waters of 3.5 acres each. *Species:* Rainbow Trout. All triploids from 2lb to double figures. *Permits:* Great Cheverell Post Office. One mile from fishery and open on Sunday mornings. *Charges:* 5 Fish £30, 4 Fish £25, 3 Fish £20, 2 Fish £15, 1 Fish (2hrs before dusk only) £8. *Season:* All year, 7.30am to dusk. December and January 8am to dusk. Closed every Monday except Bank Holidays. *Methods:* Fly fishing only.

PEWSEY

Manningford Trout Farm & Fishery
Contact: Aaron Hopkins, Manningford Bohune, By Pewsey, *Tel:* 07917 646073, *Water:* One 4.5 acre and one 1.5 acre, fed by the Hampshire Avon. *Species:* Rainbow Trout to 26lb 8oz. Brown Trout to 19lb 14oz. *Permits:* From the fishery. *Charges:* Details from the fishery. 4 fish £35, 2 fish £20, 2 fish ticket junior £10. Midweek O.A.P/concessions 4 fish £25, 2 fish £15. Prices may change in 2008. *Season:* Open all year from 8am to dusk. *Methods:* Fly fishing only.

SALISBURY

Avon Springs Fishing Lake (Stillwater)
Contact: BJ Bawden, Recreation Road, Durrington, Salisbury, *Tel:* 01980 653557, *Mobile:* 07774 801401, *Water:* One 4 acre lake, one 3 acre lake. One mile of upper Avon chalk stream left hand bank, see Wiltshire, River Fishing. *Species:* Brown Trout 17lb 9oz, Rainbow Trout 15lb 4oz (2002). *Permits:* EA fishing licences available on site. *Charges:* £42 per day, £26 junior. Half

day £33, junior £24, Eve £22. Pensioners day ticket £37 (Monday only). River and Lake ticket on application. *Season:* Open all year 8.30am to 8pm. *Methods:* Fly only no lures.

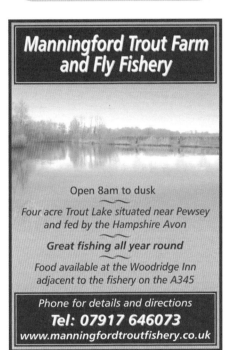

Chalke Valley Fly Fishery ♿

Contact: Norman Barter, Vella House, Bishopstone, Salisbury, *Tel:* 01722 780471, *Mobile:* 07778 769223, *Water:* 2 lakes. 'Home' lake 1 acre and 'Marsh' lake 0.6 acres. Both spring fed. Maximum 4 anglers on each lake. *Species:* All Brown Trout Triploids, "Catch and Release". *Permits:* Day permits available on request. *Charges:* Booking requested. Wheelchair access for fishing. 8am - 12 noon £20, 12 - 4pm £15, 4pm - Dusk £25. Corporate days catered for. *Season:* Open 15th April until 16th October - 8am till Dusk. *Methods:* Dry fly with barbless hooks.

Gloucestershire River Fishing

LITTLE AVON

Berkeley Estate Fishing Syndicate

Contact: T. Staniforth, 68 Firgrove, Chipping Sodbury, *Tel:* 01454 881719, *Water:* 6.5 miles of Coarse and Game fishing Little Avon from Berkeley Castle to Damery-Tortworth. *Species:* Chub, Dace, Roach, Bream, Perch, Brown Trout, Rainbow Trout and Grayling. *Permits:* From above. *Charges:* Annual membership £35. Guests may accompany members at £5 per day. Fly Fishing instruction, hourly rates advised. *Season:* Statutory. *Methods:* Trout season fly only. From June 16 any method. No spinning.

Charfield Angling Association

Contact: Mr Mark Lewis, Langford Mill House, Charfield Road, Kingswood, Wotton-Under-Edge, *Tel:* 01453 843130, *Mobile:* 07787 573468, *Water:* Approx. 3 miles of Little Avon and Ozleworth Brook. *Species:* Brown Trout, Rainbow Trout, Roach, Grayling and Chub. *Permits:* As above. *Charges:* £30 per season seniors. £15 OAPs, £7.50 juniors. *Season:* Severn Trent byelaws apply. *Methods:* Severn Trent byelaws apply.

THAMES

South Cerney Angling (Duxford Farm)

Contact: Craig Hunt, Fisherman's Rest, Broadway Lane, South Cerney, *Mobile:* 07989973217, *Water:* River Thames (Duxford Farm). A stretch of the River Thames. *Species:* Stocked with Roach, Chub, Barbel, Gudgeon, Perch, Dace and Pike. *Permits:* Permits available from our licenced clubhouse, South Cerney Post Office, and local tackle shops. Day tickets available. *Charges:* Season Permit- £50-Adults, £25-Junior/OAP/Disabled. £25-week licence.

South Cerney Angling (River Ray)

Contact: Craig Hunt, Fisherman's Rest, Broadway Lane, South Cerney, *Mobile:* 07989973217, *Water:* River Ray, Thames tributary (Cricklade) Off the A419 between Blunsden and Cirencester *Species:* Stocked with Roach, Chub, Barbel, Gudgeon, Perch, Dace and Pike. *Permits:* Permits available from our licenced clubhouse, South Cerney Post Office, and local tackle shops. Day tickets available. *Charges:* Season Permit- £50-Adults, £25-Junior/OAP/Disabled. £25-week licence.

South Cerney Angling (Thames Eysey)

Contact: Craig Hunt, Fisherman's Rest, Broadway Lane, South Cerney, *Mobile:* 07989973217, *Water:* River Thames (Eysey). A stretch of the upper River Thames. *Species:* Stocked with Roach, Chub, Barbel, Gudgeon, Perch, Dace and Pike. *Permits:* Permits available from our licenced clubhouse, South Cerney Post Office, and local tackle shops. Day tickets available. *Charges:* Season Permit- £50-Adults, £25-Junior/OAP/Disabled. £25-week licence.

South Cerney Angling (Thames Kelmscott)

Contact: Craig Hunt, Fisherman's Rest, Broadway Lane, South Cerney, *Mobile:* 07989973217, *Water:* River Thames (Kelmscott). A stretch of the River Thames *Species:* Stocked with Roach, Chub, Barbel, Gudgeon, Perch, Dace and Pike. *Permits:* Permits available from our licenced clubhouse, South

Cerney Post Office, and local tackle shops. Day tickets available. *Charges:* Season Permit- £50-Adults, £25-Junior/OAP/Disabled. £25-week licence.

WYE

Rotherwas Fishery

Contact: John Tipper - Frank Morris, 14 Thoresby Ave, Tuffley, Gloucester, *Tel:* 01452 505313, *Water:* 1 mile on the river Wye. Barbel 7lb plus, Pike to 27lb, Grayling 1lb plus. Good Dace and Roach. Also 2 x 4 acre lakes. See entry under Stillwater Coarse, Gloucester. *Species:* Carp: to 30lb. Coarse: Carp to 20lb, Bream 4lb, Perch 3lb, Tench 5lb, Roach/Rudd 2.75lb. *Permits:* Only from above. From local fishing tackle shops at Hereford. *Charges:* Day ticket £3.50. Junior £2. Season £20. Salmon Day £15. *Season:* 16th June - 30th April. *Methods:* Common sense please. Take all litter home, shut all gates and park sensibly. Please check other anglers permits. Two bailiffs patrol this beat.

Stillwater Coarse

BRISTOL

Bitterwell Lake

Contact: Mr C.W. Reid, The Chalet, Bitterwell Lake,, Ram Hill, Coalpit Heath,, Bristol,, *Tel:* 01454 778960, *Water:* 2.5 Acres. *Species:* Common, Mirror, Crucian Carp, Roach, Bream, Rudd, Perch. *Charges:* £6 -1 rod. £3 second rod, O.A.P.'s etc, Reg. disabled and arrivals after 4 pm. *Season:* Closed for spawning 4 - 6 weeks May - June. *Methods:* Barbless hooks size 8 max, no bolt rigs, no boilies, no nuts, hemp or groundbait.

CHIPPING SODBURY

Bathampton Angling Association (Coarse Lakes)

Contact: Dave Crookes, 25 Otago Terrace, Larkhall, Bath, Somerset. *Tel:* 01225 427164, *Water:* Two lakes at Lydes Farm / Players Golf Club, Codrington. *Species:* Roach to 2.5lbs, Rudd to 2lb, Tench to 6.5lbs. Carp to 20lb plus, Crucian Carp, Bream to 7.5lb. *Permits:* Local fishing tackle shops (members only). *Charges:* Adults £25, juniors £8, O.A.P £7. Registered disabled £7, Under 12's free. Additional special day permit at £2 must be obtained before fishing. *Season:* Open from 8am all year round. Closing times vary according to time of year. *Methods:* Special rules apply - available from secretary and printed on permit.

CIRENCESTER

South Cerney Angling (Dab-Chick Lake)

Contact: Craig Hunt, Fisherman's Rest, Broadway Lane, South Cerney, *Mobile:* 07989973217, *Water:* Dab-Chick Lake - 8 acre gravel pit (lake 63 - Members only) Spine Road GL7 6DF *Species:* Stocked with Carp, Tench, Roach, Rudd and Perch. *Permits:* Permits available from our licenced clubhouse, South Cerney Post Office, and local tackle shops. *Charges:* Season Permit- £50-Adults, £25-Junior/OAP/Disabled. £25-week licence. *Season:* No close season *Methods:* Night fishing permitted.

South Cerney Angling (Gillman's Lake)

Contact: Craig Hunt, Fisherman's Rest, Broadway Lane, South Cerney, *Mobile:* 07989973217, *Water:* Gillman's Lake - small, heavily stocked lake (Lake 23a - for Members and Day Tickets) Access at Wickwater lane South Cerney. *Species:* Stocked with Carp, Tench, Roach, Rudd, Perch and Bream. *Permits:* Permits available from our licenced clubhouse, South Cerney Post Office, and local tackle shops. *Charges:* Season Permit- £50-Adults, £25-Junior/OAP/Disabled. £25-week licence. Day Tickets available. *Season:* No close season *Methods:* No night fishing. Toilets on site

South Cerney Angling (Ham Pool)

Contact: Craig Hunt, Fisherman's Rest, Broadway Lane, South Cerney, *Mobile:* 07989973217, *Water:* Ham Pool - 12 acre gravel pit (Lake 18 members only). Access at Broadway Lane, South Cerney, Glos, GL7 5UH. *Species:* Carp-38lb, Tench-11lb, Roach-31/2lb, Rudd-2lb, Crucian-4lb, Pike-30lb+, Perch-2lb, Bream-10lb. *Permits:* Permits available from our licenced clubhouse, South Cerney Post Office, and local tackle shops. *Charges:* Season Permit- £50-Adults, £25-Junior/OAP/Disabled. £25-week licence. *Season:* No close season *Methods:* Night fishing permitted. Shower and toilets on site. No loose feeding boilies.

South Cerney Angling (Hills)

Contact: Craig Hunt, Fisherman's Rest, Broadway Lane, South Cerney, *Mobile:* 07989973217, *Water:* Hills - 80 acre gravel pit (Lake 17 - members only) Access at Broadway Lane, South Cerney, Glos, GL7 5UH *Species:* Stocked with Carp, Tench, Roach, Rudd, Perch and Pike. *Permits:* Permits available from our licenced clubhouse, South Cerney Post Office, and local tackle shops. *Charges:* Season Permit- £50-Adults, £25-Junior/OAP/ Disabled. £25-week licence. *Season:* No close season *Methods:* Night fishing permitted.

South Cerney Angling (Stait's Lake)

Contact: Craig Hunt, Fisherman's Rest, Broadway Lane, South Cerney, *Mobile:* 07989973217, *Water:* Stait's Lake - small commercial type lake (lake 23a - Members and day tickets) Access at Friday Ham Lane, South Cerney. *Species:* Stocked with mainly Carp and Roach and Bream. *Permits:* Permits available from our licenced clubhouse, South Cerney Post Office, and local tackle shops. *Charges:* Season Permit- £50-Adults, £25-Junior/ OAP/Disabled. £25-week licence. Day Tickets available. *Season:* No close season *Methods:* No night fishing. Toilets on site

South Cerney Angling (Whitefriars)

Contact: Craig Hunt, Fisherman's Rest, Broadway Lane, South Cerney, *Mobile:* 07989973217, *Water:* Whitefriars - 100 acre gravel pit (Lake 26 - Members only) Ashton Keynes, Wiltshire, SN6 6QR. *Species:* Stocked with Bream, Carp, Tench, Roach, Perch and Pike. *Permits:* Permits available from our licenced clubhouse, South Cerney Post Office, and local tackle shops. *Charges:* Season Permit- £50-Adults, £25-Junior/OAP/Disabled. £25-week licence. *Season:* No close season *Methods:* Night fishing permitted.

South Cerney Angling (Wick Main Lake)

Contact: Craig Hunt, Fisherman's Rest, Broadway Lane, South Cerney, *Mobile:* 07989973217, *Water:* Wick Main Lake - 22 acre gravel pit (Lake 23 - Members only) Access at Wickwater Lane, South Cerney and at Fridays Ham Lane. *Species:* Stocked with Carp, Tench, Roach, Rudd, Perch and Pike. *Permits:* Permits available from our licenced clubhouse, South Cerney Post Office, and local tackle shops. *Charges:* Season Permit- £50-Adults, £25-Junior/OAP/Disabled. £25-week licence. *Season:* No close season *Methods:* Night fishing permitted. Toilets on site

Swindon Isis Angling Club Lake No1 ♿

Contact: Peter Gilbert, 31 Havelock St, Swindon, Wilts. *Tel:* 01793 535396, *Water:* 6 acre mature gravel pit at Cotswold Water Park (Water Park Lake 19), South Cerney, Cirencester. *Species:* Tench over 10lb, Carp to 35lb, Rudd to 2lb12oz, Crucian Carp to 3lb 8oz, Bream to 10lb 3oz, usual Roach, Perch & good Pike. *Permits:* Tackle shops in Swindon, Cirencester, Chippenham and Calne. *Charges:* Club Permits: Senior £34.50. OAP and disabled £15. Juniors £15. The club permit contains two free day tickets and more day tickets can be obtained for £5 each. Year starts 1 April. Half year membership from 1 November senior £17 and junior £8. *Season:* Open all year round. Club cards start 1st April. *Methods:* No bans.

CORSE

Stone End Farm

Contact: Richard Spry, Stone End Farm, Church Lane, Corse, *Tel:* 01452 700254, *Water:* Two lakes. Front lake, 1 acre - 20 pegs. House Pond. 0.75 acre - 12 pegs. *Species:* Common and Mirror Carp to 27lb. Tench to 5lb, Bream to 7.5lb. *Permits:* On site. *Charges:* Day tickets £6. Disabled and children £4. *Season:* Open all year. *Methods:* Barbless hooks only, no groundbait. No boilies, nuts, floating baits, cat or dog meats. No keepnets. Unhooking mats must be used.

GLOUCESTER

Huntley Carp Pools

Contact: John Tipper - Frank Morris, 14 Thoresby Ave, Tuffley, Gloucester, *Tel:* 01452 505313, *Water:* 2 x 4 acre lakes. 1 with Carp to 30lb. 1 with general fish, Carp, Tench, Perch, Bream, Roach, Rudd, Crucian. Also 1 mile stretch of river Wye. See entry under Glouctershire river fishing. *Species:* Carp: to 30lb. Coarse: Carp to 20lb, Bream 4lb, Perch 3lb, Tench 5lb, Roach/Rudd 2.75lb. *Permits:* Only from above. *Charges:* To be advised. *Season:* 16th June - 30th April. *Methods:* No keepnets, barbless hooks.

Lemington Lakes

Contact: Debbie, Todenham Road, Moreton-in-Marsh, *Tel:* 01608 650872, *Water:* 4.5 acre lake, 2.5 acre lake, 2 acre lake, 1.25 acre lake, 0.75 acre lake. 5 ponds varying sizes all with coarse fish. *Species:* Each lake caters for different types of fishing with fish up to specimen sizes. *Permits:* As above. *Charges:* £7 Max two rods (£10 on Westminster Lake) - £4 Children up to 14th Birthday. Night fishing must be booked. *Season:* 7am - Dark (all year), match bookings taken. *Methods:* Barbless hooks only. Keep nets allowed on certain lakes.

TEWKESBURY

Hillview Lakes ♿

Contact: Keith Hill, Cherry Orchard Lane, Twyning, Tewkesbury, *Tel:* 01684 296719, *Water:* 6 lakes covering 4 acres. *Species:* Carp to 22lb. Tench, Bream and Orfe to 4lb+. Perch to 3.5lb. *Charges:* One rod £7. Concessions £6. *Season:* Open all year dawn to dusk. *Methods:* Keepnets only in matches. Barbless hooks only. No groundbait. Pellets can be loose fed but must be supplied by Hillview Lakes.

WOTTON-UNDER-EDGE

Lower Killcott Farm Fishing

Contact: Mr E Thompson, Lower Kilcott Farm, Nr Hillesley, Wotton-Under-Edge, *Tel:* 01454 238276, *Mobile:* 078161 48038, *Water:* 1 acre lake. *Species:* Carp to 20lb, Roach, Rudd *Charges:* £5 day, plus £1 for extra rod. *Season:* Open all year. *Methods:* Barbless hooks only, no keepnets or boilies.

Stillwater Trout

DURSLEY

Great Burrows Trout Fishery

Contact: Vernon Baxter (Manager), Nibley Green, North Nibley, Nr Dursley, *Tel:* 01453 542343, *Mobile:* 07754 502134, *Water:* Two acre lake. *Species:* Rainbow Trout (triploid) stocked from 2lb to 5lb. *Permits:* From V. Baxter on site. *Charges:* Day tickets: 2 fish £16. 3 fish £20. 4 fish £24. 5 fish £28. 6 fish £32. *Season:* Open all year except Christmas day. Fishing from 8am to one hour after sunset. *Methods:* Fly only. No lures. Barbless hooks only. Max hook size 12 longshank. No static fishing. No catch and release. No wading, fishing from platforms. Knotless landing nets only. E.A. Licence required. Tuition and equipment available.

GLOUCESTER

The Cotswolds Fishery

Contact: Mrs Celia Hicks-Beach, Witcombe Farm, Great Witcombe, *Tel:* 01452 864413, *Mobile:* 01452 863591, *Water:* 3 reservoirs - 15 acres, 5 acres and 2 plus acres. *Species:* Rainbow Trout max weight 8lbs. *Permits:* Witcombe Farm Estate *Charges:* Seasonal permits available, various prices on application. Day visitor tickets - Full day £35 (6 fish), Half day (6 hrs) £20 (3 fish), Evening £15 (2 fish). Boats £10 Full day, £5 Half day, £3 Evening. Novice 6hrs (max 3 visits) £20 (bag limit - 3 fish), pay £6 per fish taken. Prices may change during 2008. *Season:* 7 March - 30 October, from 8am to Dusk. *Methods:* Normal Game fishing for Trout, knotless nets. No catch and release.

LECHLADE

Lechlade & Bushyleaze Trout Fisheries ♿

Contact: Tim Small, Lechlade & Bushyleaze Trout Fisheries, Lechlade, *Tel:* 01367 253266, *Water:* Lechlade - 8 acres. Bushyleaze - 20 acres. *Species:* Lechlade - Rainbows to 27lb, Browns to 27lb. Bushyleaze - Rainbows to 17lb, Browns to 17lb. *Charges:* Lechlade: £50 full day, 4 fish. £35 half day, 2 fish. £25 evening, 1 fish. Bushyleaze: £35 full day, 6 fish. £30 full day, 4 fish. £27.50 half day, 3 fish. £22 evening, 2 fish. Season tickets available for both lakes. Discounted day tickets for juniors. *Season:* Open all year. *Methods:* Fly only. Boat hire and float tube hire.

Remember a ♿ means the fishery has disabled facilities - contact them direct for further details

Sea Fishing

CHELTENHAM
Bass Anglers Sportfishing Society
Contact: NFSA Head Office: 01364 644643.

STROUD
South & South West S.A.
Contact: NFSA Head Office: 01364 644643.

TEWKESBURY
Inlanders S.A.C.
Contact: Mike Ellard, 24 Grayston Close, Tewkesbury, *Tel:* 01684 292860, *Mobile:* 07952 071947, *Water:* Fishing from boat/shore, covering the westcountry with trips to Whitby and other areas. New members, adult and juniors, welcome. Affiliated to N.F.S.A. and British Conger Club.

WITHINGTON
Royal Air Force Sea Angling Association
Contact: NFSA Head Office: 01364 644643.

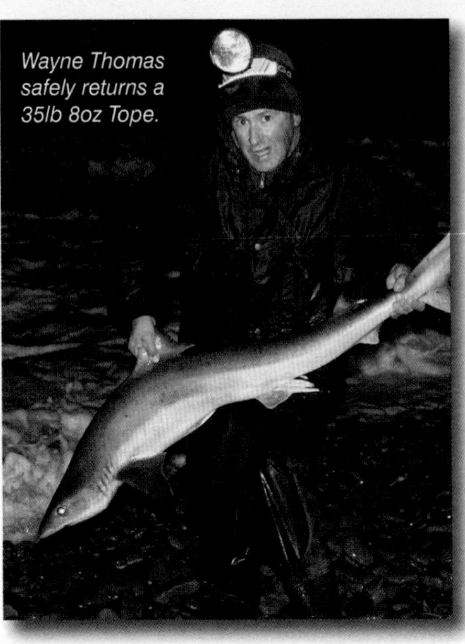
Wayne Thomas safely returns a 35lb 8oz Tope.

TRADE SUPPLIES & SERVICES

The Wheelyboat Trust

The specially designed Wheelyboat provides disabled people with hassle-free and independent access to inland waters large and small all over the UK.

Whether it's for the scenery or wildlife, sport or recreation, reservoirs, lakes, ponds and rivers are a magnet to millions of visitors throughout the year. However, by their very nature, access on and around them for wheelchair users and others with limited mobility is very much restricted.

Wheelyboats overcome all the difficulties – they are simplicity itself to board, make the entire water accessible and the level deck provides access throughout thus giving the users the dignity of their own independence. The Wheelyboat's design is very straightforward. Its principal feature is a hinged bow which, when lowered, forms a ramp making the boat very easy to board. Its shallow draught means it can be driven ashore for boarding and disembarking directly from the bank or a slipway. The flat deck ensures its disabled users can reach all corners of the boat and gives them the opportunity of using the boat independently without relying on help from others.

The Wheelyboat Trust is a registered charity dedicated to providing disabled people, young and old, with the opportunity and freedom to enjoy waters large and small. Since the Trust began in 1985 it has supplied 120 specially designed Wheelyboats to fisheries, water parks and other aquatic venues, opening up many thousands of acres of water to disabled visitors that would otherwise have remained out of bounds. The Trust's vision is straightforward—open access for disabled people on waters everywhere via a range of Wheelyboat models to meet everybody's needs.

The standard Wheelyboat accommodates up to five people but the 'stretch' Mk II on Roadford Lake can take up to ten. In 2006 the Trust designed the next generation of Wheelyboats, the Mk III model, and the Tweed Wheelyboat for accompanied use on rivers like the Tweed. The new Mk III is the flagship of the Wheelyboat Trust. Its design gives it a much wider remit than either of its predecessors and will provide even more disabled people with access to waterborne activities across a greater variety of waters all over the UK. In 2008 the Trust launches its purpose-built stillwater angling boat based on Jim Coulam's 16' GRP reservoir boat. This boat, which made its debut at the London Boat Show in January, is a larger version of the Tweed Wheelyboat.

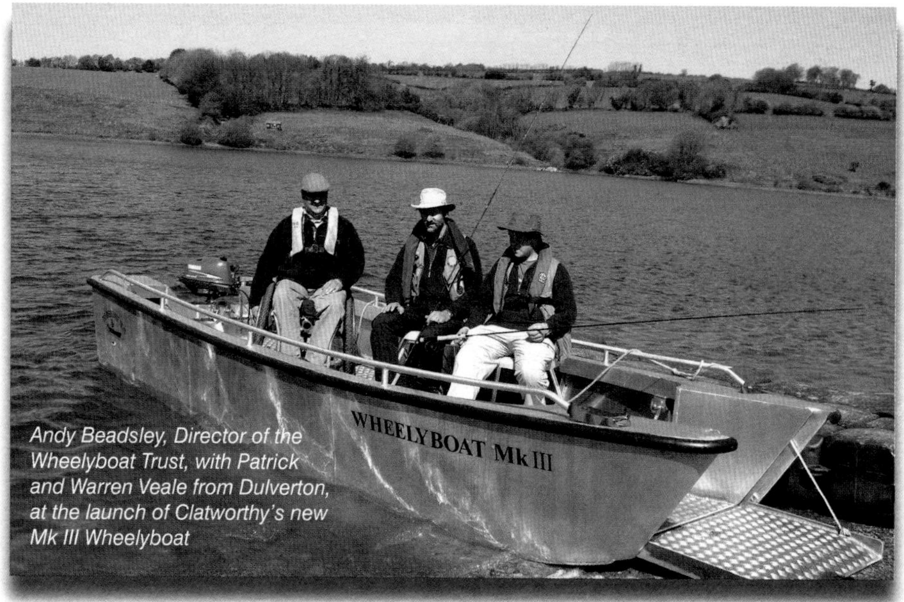

Andy Beadsley, Director of the Wheelyboat Trust, with Patrick and Warren Veale from Dulverton, at the launch of Clatworthy's new Mk III Wheelyboat

The first Mk III in the UK was launched in October 2006 on Chew Valley Lake near Bristol. In 2007, Mk IIIs were launched at Wessex Water's Sutton Bingham and Clatworthy Reservoirs and South West Lakes Trust's Siblyback Lake. The Clatworthy boat is available exclusively for trout fishing while the Sutton Bingham and Siblyback boats have multi-purpose roles, including fishing. The Wheelyboat Trust works closely with the Environment Agency, South West Lakes Trust, Wessex Water and Bristol Water to improve angling and boating opportunities for disabled people in the region. There are a number of Wheelyboat projects in hand in the South West including proposals to site Mk IIIs at Stithians Reservoir and on the Fowey and Fal estuaries.

As well as supplying Wheelyboats, the Trust presents its annual Alan Faulkner Memorial Award to the game fishery that provides disabled anglers with the most outstanding service, facilities, opportunities and access. As well as being a fitting memorial to the Trust's Founder President who conceived the idea of the 'Wheelyboat', the award also highlights the needs of disabled anglers and promotes the cause of disability angling. It has been sponsored by Suzuki for the past three years and the prize to the winning fishery is one of their super reliable four horsepower 4-stroke outboards.

For more information about the work of the Trust and the Wheelyboat (including a full UK locations list), visit the website or contact the Director. The Wheelyboat Trust is a registered charity and relies upon the generosity of charitable organisations, companies and individuals to enable it to continue providing this important service on behalf of disabled people. Donations can be made via the Trust's website:
www.wheelyboats.org.

Wheelyboats are hired like any other angling boat except that venues tend to prefer at least 24 hours notice for a booking.

THE WHEELYBOAT TRUST

Reg charity 292216
Andy Beadsley, Director
North Lodge, Burton Park, Petworth,
West Sussex, GU28 0JT,
Tel/fax: 01798 342222,
e-mail wheelyboattrust@btconnect.com
www.wheelyboats.org

Rex Harpham, SW Regional Coordinator
22 Chollacott Close, Whitchurch Road,
Tavistock, PL19 9BW
Tel: 01822 615953

Wheelyboat venues in the region...

Avon

Blagdon Lake, Blagdon 01275 332339	Trout fishing	www.bristol-water.co.uk
Chew Valley Lake, Chew Magna 01275 332339	Trout fishing	www.bristol-water.co.uk

Cornwall

Siblyback Reservoir, Liskeard 01209 860301	Trout fishing, nature watching	www.swlakestrust.org.uk

Devon

Roadford Lake, Okehampton 01409 211514	Trout fishing, nature watching	www.swlakestrust.org.uk
Wistlandpound Reservoir, Barnstaple 01598 763221	Trout fishing, nature watching	www.swlakestrust.org.uk

Dorset

River Frome, Wareham 01929 550688	Coarse fishing, pleasure boating	www.warehamboathire.co.uk

Gloucs

Bushyleaze Trout Fishery, Lechlade 01367 253266	Trout fishing	www.lechladetrout.co.uk

Somerset

Clatworthy, Taunton 01984 624658	Trout fishing	www.wessexwater.co.uk
Sutton Bingham, Yeovil 01935 872389	Trout fishing, nature watching	www.wessexwater.co.uk
Wimbleball, Brompton Regis 01398 371372	Trout fishing, nature watching	www.swlakestrust.org.uk

DSD Buildings Ltd

SUPPLIERS OF LUXURY LOG CABINS AND QUALITY STEEL BUILDINGS

Fishing Lodges
Luxurious Log Cabins
Tackle / Bait Shops
Coffee Shop / Restaurant
Office / Clubhouse
Storage
Workshop

LOG CABINS

DSD Buildings offer solid wood log cabins to meet a range of domestic and commercial requirements such as summer houses, guest rooms, home offices, garages, luxurious log homes and amenity halls.
All cabins are constructed from selected, kiln dried Nordic pine, the wood of choice because of its superior stability, limited shrinkage, light weight and beautiful grain. A comprehensive inspection process ensures that every new cabin is built from the highest quality and most environmentally sensitive materials available. The timber comes from sustainable sources with established replanting policies.
Wood is a natural insulation material, so our log cabins are extremely energy efficient. The thousands of tiny air pockets trapped in every square inch of the wood's structure slow the transfer of heat though the log, keeping the cabins warm in winter and cool in summer. All the doors are made of solid wood and the windows, whatever the style, come with thermal insulating glass.

All buildings are designed with your individual specification and needs in mind so to ensure that your building is everything you ever dreamt it could be !

All buildings can be supplied in kit form or fully erected by one of our professional erection teams– the choice is yours!

DSD Buildings Ltd, Kings Acre, Shearston, North Petherton, Bridgwater, Somerset TA6 6PL

Tel: 01278 663829 Fax: 01278 588084

www.dsdbuildings.co.uk Email: sales@dsdbuildings.co.uk

River Game

River Coarse

Stillwater Trout

Stillwater Coarse

Sea

ADVERTISERS INDEX

Tackle

Trade Supplies & Services

Hotels

Self Catering

Camping

Caravans

Bed & Breakfast

Tuition